THE CARVING OF
MOUNT RUSHMORE

THE

MOUNT

"I had seen the photographs and the drawings of
this great work. And yet, until about ten
minutes ago I had no conception of its magnitude,
its permanent beauty and its importance."

—Franklin Delano Roosevelt,
upon first viewing Mount Rushmore,
August 30, 1936

CARVING OF RUSHMORE

by Rex Alan Smith

ABBEVILLE PRESS
Publishers · New York

Editor: WALTON RAWLS

Designer: PHILIP GRUSHKIN

Library of Congress Cataloging in Publication Data
Smith, Rex Alan.
 The Carving of Mount Rushmore
 Bibliography: p.
 Includes index.
 1. Borglum, Gutzon, 1867–1941.
2. Mount Rushmore, National Memorial (S. D.)   I. Title.
NB237.B6A68 1985   730'.92'4   84-12316
ISBN 0-89659-417-3
ISBN 0-89659-533-1 (deluxe ed.)

CONTENTS

THE CARVING OF
MOUNT RUSHMORE

Foreword

High on a pine-clad mountain in South Dakota's Black Hills are carved the faces of four presidents of the United States—George Washington, Thomas Jefferson, Abraham Lincoln, and Theodore Roosevelt—each chosen for such commemoration because of his unique contribution to the building and shaping of his country.

Created as a monument not only to those men but also to the aspirations and ideals of the nation they did so much to mold, the four faces together constitute the world's most gigantic piece of sculpture. Eight hundred million pounds of stone were removed in its carving, and so huge are the faces that from brow to chin each is as tall as the entire Great Sphinx of Egypt. Ordinary men of the same proportions would stand shoulder-even with a forty-story building and could wade the Mississippi River without dampening their knees. Yet, so skillfully are the faces carved that to an observer viewing them from across the canyon they do not appear massive or coarse or even heavy. On the contrary, they look as graceful and lifelike as the finest busts sculpted in a studio. Carved upon a cliff that has changed but little since mankind first appeared on earth and has worn down less than the thickness of a child's finger since Moses led the Israelites out of Egypt, the faces will still be there, looking much as they do now, long after man has gone. All things considered, Mount Rushmore National Memorial is not only America's greatest and most enduring monument, it is all of mankind's as well.

Today the memorial is visited by well over two million people a year. When these visitors ask, as most do, "Who created it?" they are answered almost invariably with, "The sculptor, Gutzon Borglum."

In a limited sense that answer is true, but only in a limited sense. Certainly it is true that without Borglum's genius and stubborn dedication the monument might never have been carved, and the Rushmore cliff might look little different now than it did a million years ago. But that is only part of the story.

The Rushmore monument also came from the dreams of a gentle, aging scholar named Doane Robinson, and from the levelheaded judgment and legislative skill of United States Senator Peter Norbeck. Equally important was the down-to-earth business sense of John Boland, a dealer in farm implements, and the integrity and legislative ability of William Williamson, a United States congressman and attorney. Just as Borglum brought to the work talents these men did not possess, they brought to it talents Borglum did not possess. All together these men are to the Rushmore work as legs are to a table. It rests upon them all. Lacking any one of them it would have fallen, yet no single one of them could claim credit for the fact that it did not fall.

And there is more to the story, for the Rushmore memorial to a substantial extent is also the product of a United States president who learned how to fish, and to a very great extent that of a bunch of hard-working, hard-playing drill-dusty miners who did the actual work of the carving. They came not even qualified to learn the art of mountain-carving, but learn they did, and the monument stands as everlasting evidence that they learned it well.

Beyond what it owes to these men, the memorial is a creation of two brief consecutive moments in our national history—the booming 1920s and the depressed 1930s. Only because these were the kind of times they were and occurred in the sequence they did was it possible for the Rushmore project to have been conceived, approved, executed, and paid for. Even so, the challenges were so enormous and the difficulties so nearly insurmountable that it almost failed. Most people who view the monument today do realize there were great challenges to be met in its construction. They know also, since the monument does exist, that those challenges were not impossible to overcome. The creators, however, were denied the comfort of such knowledge. Attempting to do that which never had been done before, they were never sure it could be done. When obstacles arose or money ran out, as both were always doing, time and again the machinery was covered, the work was abandoned, and the mountain was returned to silence. And each time this happened there was ample reason to believe the project could not be revived again . . . ever.

Eventually, the time did come when the work had to be permanently shut down and the carving left uncompleted according to its original design, and it happened for a reason that the builders could neither have avoided nor foreseen. Although the first World War was supposed to have made the world "safe for democracy" it had not done so. By the end of the 1930s, the free nations of Europe again were fighting for their very survival, and the United States was attempting both to supply them with the arms they needed and to rearm itself as well. Continued building of the monument that had come to be called "The Shrine of Democracy" was forced to give way to the building of what President Franklin Roosevelt called "The Arsenal of Democracy"; the nation could not afford to invest in both.

All together, then, the story of Mount Rushmore Memorial is not a simple story of a sculptor and a mountain. Rather, it is a complex story of men and their times—of unusual men and unusual times combined in a sometimes caustic but always creative chemistry that ultimately produced something far different from what had been originally intended. For, in the beginning presidents had not been the intended subject, Borglum had not been the intended sculptor, and Rushmore had not been the intended mountain.

To understand how it all actually happened, the story must be told from its beginning—twelve hundred miles from Mount Rushmore, in Georgia in the fall of 1923.

1. Doane Robinson's Dream

A few miles east of the city of Atlanta, the soft-rolling Georgia countryside is abruptly interrupted by a towering dome of gray granite known as Stone Mountain. When the long sweep of forests and fields in which it lies is autumn-brushed, the mountain resembles a great blob of cold, bowl-molded porridge smoothly turned out upon a green and gold platter. That was how it looked in the fall of 1923, with one addition. At that time, high on the mountain's north wall was a web of scaffolding through which could be seen the outlines of a gigantic human head. On the scaffolding, creeping about like so many flies in the autumn sun, could be seen the tiny figures of the crew of Gutzon Borglum, a sculptor busily engaged in carving on the mountain a huge monument to the memory of the Southern Confederacy.

Calling his project ambitious would have been a feeble understatement. It was unprecedented and, according to many, even impossible. Borglum was attempting to deal with Stone Mountain as if it were a block of granite in his studio. On its sheer stone face he was planning to smooth off an area four hundred feet high and a quarter-mile long, and on these twelve vertical acres of granite he would carve bas-relief figures of hundreds of Confederate infantry, cavalry, and artillery all sweeping down to converge upon huge central figures of Robert E. Lee, Stonewall Jackson, Jefferson Davis, and four other Southern heroes not yet chosen. This Confederate memorial was intended to be far and away the world's largest and showiest artistic work. A work, therefore, exactly suited to the nature of its times and of its sculptor, Gutzon Borglum.

As for the nature of Gutzon Borglum—it was one of superlatives. In his speech, actions, and ambitions there were few half-measures. In his emotions and personality there were none at all. Which was why no matter how much those who became associated with him might be impressed by his artistic talent, they soon became even more impressed by his capacity for affection, wrath, generosity, stinginess, nobility, pettiness, charm, and sheer obnoxiousness. Of modesty and humility, it was true, Borglum had but a meager supply. Of pure, mulish stubbornness, on the other hand, he had an abundance. But most of all, Borglum thought big and dreamed big and talked big, and he was not afraid to tackle any undertaking. This, combined with his talent, made him ideally suited to the times and to the carving of mountains.

What kind of times were they? Well, in 1923 America was feeling its oats. The United States was bustling and prosperous, and the national mood was cocky and optimistic. It was a time of creative ferment—a time when inventions and creative accomplishments were occurring so rapidly that yesterday's marvel was today's commonplace, yesterday's luxury was today's necessity, and records set on one day were broken on the next. The economy was beginning to boom and the standard of living was rising like a thermometer in the sun. Every day more of even the most modest homes were being equipped with indoor plumbing, and with electricity and such attendant gadgets as electric iceboxes and irons and fans and washing machines. There was one automobile for every five people in the United States in 1923, and in that year alone Henry Ford would produce two million Model-T "Tin Lizzies" and sell them for $265 apiece. The first commercial radio broadcast had been made only two years earlier, and already more than two million homes had acquired "radio music boxes" and thousands more were being purchased daily.

The nature of the times was due to many causes, but the largest was the World War that had ended in 1918. That had been "the war to end all wars," the experts were saying, and it had made the world "safe for democracy." Americans believed this happy result had been accomplished only because of American money, American might, and the fighting spirit of the American "Doughboy." Europeans disagreed. Having borne the bloody brunt of that conflict, they figured it was *they* who had won it, and in so doing had done their American cousins an enormous favor.

The truth was, of course, that the war had neither ended war nor made the world safe for democracy. In Bavaria an unknown itinerant artist, street-demonstrator, and rabble-rouser named Adolph Hitler was fomenting a revolution that, when it came, would impose upon Germany a government more deadly and less democratic than the one it replaced. And in Russia a war-spawned revolution had already saddled that unhappy land with a dictatorship far more steely and a reign of terror more thorough than any it had known under the czars.

However, Americans paid little attention to these things. What they did pay attention to was that the United States had become the world's strongest, richest, and most productive nation. They believed that its people could do anything, build anything, be anything, and that it was only a matter of time until the United States would become the world's first Utopia.

Not all Americans felt that way, of course. Europeans, in the pride of their older civilization, were inclined to view the United States as a brawny but uncultured country relative—handy to have around in a fight or to borrow money from, but too uncouth to associate with otherwise—and in the American artistic and literary community there were many who agreed. Among them was a group of writers who were as pessimistic as they were gifted, and whom Gertrude Stein had dubbed "the Lost Generation." From a self-constructed Olympus (portable, but usually in Paris), these writers occupied themselves by taking potshots at America's sacred cows and at what H. L. Mencken called "the American Booboisie."

The national mood, however, was one of self-confidence rather than self-criticism, and of focusing on the stars rather than on the mud. Thus, even while praising Lost Generation writers for their cleverness, and while being titteringly shocked by their irreverencies, Americans of the 1920s more often found their own philosophies reflected in the homespun observations of a gum-chewing, wisecracking ex-cowboy named Will Rogers. Rogers, too, was a social critic, but in his criticism there was humor and hope and courage, an effervescent love of his fellow man, and no scorn at all. Although the Lost Generation writers were the gifted gadflies of their age and produced some of its finest literature, they did not really speak for it. The breezy, gregarious Rogers did, and he was probably the most representative American spokesman of his time.

All-in-all, it was an ebullient, upbeat time when every crossroads hamlet dreamed of becoming a new Chicago or Baltimore and expected that through the efforts of its ever-present Booster Club it actually might do so. It was a time of dreaming big and talking big, a time when a community might boast of possessing the biggest skyscraper or the biggest bullfrog, and take as much pride in the one as in the other. Building a better mousetrap might bring the world to your door, but building a bigger mousetrap was sure to.

To such a time and national mood, the spirit of Gutzon Borglum was perfectly matched. Americans believed they were the world's best people, and made no secret of it. Borglum believed he was the world's best sculptor, and made no secret of that. Americans believed in the superiority of American products, and Borglum believed in the superiority of American art. Unlike

many American artists of that time, moreover, Borglum was an ardent patriot. Hence, when Lost Generation writers hurled stones of scorn at the art
and culture of their homeland, Borglum enthusiastically hurled them right
back. Just before going to Stone Mountain, for instance, he wrote:

> Art in America should be American, drawn from American sources,
> memorializing American achievement. . . .

> We see incoming ships loaded with the second-hand or counterfeit
> art of the old world . . . we see our city buildings, our state and
> national buildings, marked and counterfeited by the symbols of a
> people a thousand years dead. . . . Against this, all that is honest, all
> that is sincere, revolts. . . .

> Those of us who can afford it steal and beg and borrow the arms,
> the dress, the emotions of Greece and Rome . . . we hang their rot-
> ting trophies on our walls, ignorant of their origin, unacquainted
> with their meaning, not even sympathetic with the emotions that
> produced them.

> We have not begun to realize that the things we desired honestly—
> liberty of conscience, freedom from European governments and
> from the stain of slavery were things to be proud of; that they are
> ours and that these things alone make us immortal; make us the envy
> of the world. If we have art of any kind . . . it should write them in
> bold lines across the pages of our history.

Borglum also believed that artistic records of the American people and
their achievements should be " . . . built into, cut into, the crust of this earth
so that those records would have to melt or by wind be worn to dust before
the record . . . could, as Lincoln said, 'perish from the earth.'"

In keeping with the mood of his times, Borglum thought American art
should be massive. He spoke of "Colossal art . . . human and soul-stirring
. . . in a scale with the people whose life it expresses," and he said: "Volume,
great mass, has a greater emotional effect upon the observer than quality of

1. Gutzon Borglum, about 1929.

form. Quality of form affects the mind; volume shocks the nerve or soul centers and is emotional in its effect. . . . The heavy pipes in an organ will, rightly played . . . make everything else on earth seem unimportant."

"Our age will some day be called 'the Colossal Age,'" declared Borglum, "yet there is not a monument in this country as big as a snuff box"; and years later he would say, "My big mission in life is to get people to look at art in a big way and to get away from this petty stuff."

Now, at Stone Mountain Borglum was creating a monument entirely in keeping with his own sentiments and those of the times—"colossal" . . . "totally American in its meaning" . . . imperishably "cut into the crust of the earth." At Stone Mountain Borglum was indeed inspiring some people to look at art "in a big way," and because one of those so inspired was Doane Robinson, State Historian for South Dakota, the shape of Borglum's life was about to be forever changed.

While reading about the work at Stone Mountain, Robinson had begun to dream about having some similar great monument carved in the mountains of South Dakota—had begun to dream about that which ultimately was to become Mount Rushmore National Memorial. But, as often happens with dreams, the final result was to be far different from Robinson's original dream, which did not include the faces of presidents nor a mountain called Rushmore. In fact, neither Robinson nor anyone other than a few people who lived near it had ever heard of Mount Rushmore. Nor, fortunately, did his dream contain any hint of the long years of struggles and quarrels and politics and discouragement that would be involved in its fulfillment. If it had, the peace-loving Robinson most likely would have strangled it at its birth.

Robinson was born in 1856, in Sparta, Wisconsin, and was christened Jonah LeRoy. "Jonah," however, is not a word that comes easily to the tongue of a toddler, and so his sister, Sadie, began calling him "Donuh." Soon his family did the same, then "Donuh" became "Doane," and Doane he remained, officially as well as unofficially, for the rest of his life.

Upon reaching manhood, Robinson took up a homestead in Minnesota. But while his hands were on plowhandles his mind was on books, and he found that sowing and reaping and building fences was not his cup of tea.

2. Doane Robinson, father of the Mount Rushmore Memorial.

Next, he studied law and set up a practice in what was then Dakota Territory. There, Robinson found he would rather write stories than briefs and would rather address audiences than juries. Soon he moved from law into literature, particularly history, and eventually into the position of South Dakota's official historian.

There are two different stories of how Doane Robinson first hit upon the idea that was to produce the Mount Rushmore memorial. The account in his private papers is true. The version he later wrote for the public is not true, which seems strange on the face of it, but there is a good probable explanation.

In his public account, Robinson said the idea had come as an "illuminating flash" while he was making a speech in a cigar-fogged room in Huron, South Dakota, on the afternoon of January 22, 1924. That was in the days when highways were known by name rather than number, when the main road across South Dakota was an alternately dirt and gravel affair undeservedly dignified by the title "The Black Hills and Yellowstone Highway." Marked by black-and-yellow banded posts, it was popularly known as "The Black and Yellow Trail." And it was while speaking to a tourist promotion group called The Black and Yellow Trail Association, claimed Robinson, that he had had his inspiration and: "While upon my feet, delivering that address, it occurred to me that a colossal monument might be carved in the granite of the Black Hills and forthwith, without consideration, I projected it upon my audience." Then, according to this account, he asked Gutzon Borglum to consider the creation of such a monument.

It is true that during that speech Robinson did suggest the carving of a monument in the Black Hills. In other respects, that is not how it happened, and we can only speculate on why he told it as if it were. Considering Robinson's inoffensive nature and Borglum's delicate ego, however, it appears likely that he did it to spare Borglum from knowing he had not been Robinson's first choice for the job.

Whatever the case, Robinson's private papers reveal that for some time past he had been trying to think up new ways of luring tourists to South Dakota. Featuring some of the nation's finest natural scenery, The Black Hills, despite the wretched roads, were already attracting large numbers of visitors. In Robinson's opinion, however, they were not attracting nearly enough, and he believed this was because, "Tourists soon get fed up on scenery unless it has something of special interest connected with it to make it impressive." While ruminating on that, he began reading newspaper stories about the tourists flocking to see the gigantic reliefs being carved into a Georgia mountain by a sculptor named Borglum. Then Robinson remembered the Needles, an area of great freestanding fingers of granite in the Black Hills, and his inspiration came.

Acting accordingly, he wrote the following letter to a man whom many at that time regarded as America's leading sculptor:

December 28, 1923

Mr. Lorado Taft
6016 Ellis Avenue
Chicago, Illinois

My Dear Mr. Taft:

South Dakota has developed a wonderful state park in the Black Hills. I enclose a brochure illustrating some features of it. On the front cover you will observe some pinnacles—we call them needles—situated high upon the flank of Harney Peak. The tops of those shown are more than 6300 feet above sea level. These needles are of granite.

Having in mind your "Big Injun," it has occurred to me that some of these pinnacles would lend themselves to massive sculpture, and I write to ask if in your judgment human figures might be carved from some of them as they stand. I am thinking of some notable Sioux such as Red Cloud, who lived and died in the shadow of those peaks. If one was found practicable, perhaps others would ultimately follow.

Pinnacles could be found immediately above the highway shown, that stand fully one hundred feet in the clear, above pedestals hundreds of feet in height, as seen from other points of vantage.

This granite is of rather coarse texture, but it is durable. There are also in the vicinity great blank walls upon which groups in relief could be executed advantageously.

The needles shown are only suggestive of the field, many others are trimmer—only a few feet in diameter—and exceedingly showy.

I shall be very pleased to hear from you, and if it appears practicable we can, perhaps, induce you to come and look us over.

Faithfully,
Doane Robinson

In going through his mail after returning from the Black and Yellow Trail meeting three weeks later, Robinson found Taft's reply. He was suffering from poor health, the sculptor said, and therefore it was "unlikely" that he could consider the proposal. Still, he had not flatly rejected it, so Robinson promptly replied with a letter he hoped would keep the matter alive. And

since his dream meanwhile had considerably expanded, he also told Taft:
"Near the summit is a little park through which the highway passes. . . . It is
studded with column after column of these pinnacles and in my imagination I
can see all the heroes of the old west peering out from them; Lewis and Clark,
Fremont, Jed Smith, Bridger, Sa-kaka-wea, Red Cloud, and in an equestrian
statue [Buffalo Bill] Cody and the overland mail."

At the same time, Robinson was finding that in his remarks to the Black
and Yellow Trail Association and subsequently to the press, he had sown the
wind and now was reaping the whirlwind. The environmentalists of 1924
were not known by that name but they existed nonetheless, and they were
having fits. In barbed editorials and steaming personal letters, Robinson's
suggestion was being condemned, and often Robinson was being condemned with it. He was promoting, they said, a commercial rape of the Black
Hills. "Why desecrate a noble work of nature with a puny work of man?"
asked one. "Statuary among the Needles would be as ridiculous as keeping a
cow in the Capitol rotunda," wrote another; and "leave the Hills alone!" was
a common cry. As the environmentalist clamor mounted, so did Robinson's
determination. "No!" he responded. He did *not* intend to desecrate the Hills.
He intended only to use a little corner of the Needles for a carved display that
would commemorate the heroes of the Old West and at the same time bring a
flood of tourist dollars to Dakota and the Black Hills. He said that if his critics had thought they could get five cents worth of gold out of each ton of the
granite, "they would unanimously subscribe to a machine to grind up the
Needles and wipe them off the face of the earth," whereas his own proposal
"will not grind up its material and pass away, but for a thousand years will
continue to bring its annual harvest of gold."

Naturally, not all of the response was unfavorable. Many editors liked the
idea and so informed their readers. Many individuals felt the same way, and
so informed Robinson. And as could have been expected, most commercial
clubs (forerunners of chambers of commerce) thought it a grand idea indeed.
More or less typical was the response of J. B. Greene, secretary of the Rapid
City Commercial Club. He wrote telling Robinson that he did not think the
carving was a practical proposition, but as far as he was concerned that did
not matter much. What did matter, he declared, was "the great amount of free
publicity with which the proposition has been attended." That, said Greene,
had been "very gratifying," and "I expect to break into one of the large metropolitan Sunday papers with appropriate photographs." However, he added:
"I will tell you in strictest confidence . . . the 'Needles' are not soft and easily
worked. . . . One old timer here remarked that 'if any sculper tried to stick his

beak in one of them needles he'd bust it off short.' That for what it's worth, but we needn't advertise it."

As the debate continued to grow, so also did Robinson's dream. By early spring he was envisioning: "Custer and his gold-discovering cavalcade winding its way through the Needles, with Red Cloud and a band of Sioux scouts, resentful and suspicious, spying on it through rifts in the pinnacles of the opposite wall, while above, a great mountain buck, wary but unafraid, inspects the pageant with curiosity."

Throughout early 1924, Robinson continued to speak of Lorado Taft as the potential sculptor. But as time passed and Taft showed no signs of changing his mind, Robinson began to mention Daniel Chester French, who had done the seated figure in the Lincoln Memorial in Washington, D.C., and also to mention that fellow who was getting so much publicity down in Georgia, Gutzon Borglum. Whether Robinson contacted French seems not to be known. However, nine months after first approaching Taft, he did write to Borglum:

August 20, 1924

Mr. Gutzon Borglum
Stone Mountain, Georgia

Dear Mr. Borglum:
    In the vicinity of Harney Peak in the Black Hills of South Dakota are opportunities for heroic sculpture of unusual character. Would it be possible for you to design and supervise a massive sculpture there? The proposal has not passed beyond mere suggestion, but if it would be possible for you to undertake the matter I feel quite sure we could arrange to finance such an enterprise. I should be glad to hear from you at your convenience.

Faithfully,
Doane Robinson, Supt.

Borglum being absent at the time, Robinson's letter was received by Borglum's assistant, Major J. G. Tucker. Tucker read it, delightedly scribbled, "Here it is, Borglum! Let's go!" across it, and forwarded it to the sculptor at his home in Connecticut. Without knowing it, Robinson had approached exactly the right man at exactly the right time.

During the previous year at Stone Mountain, Borglum had met and mastered a number of seemingly impossible challenges and had thereby convinced himself that he could indeed carve mountains. Moreover, he had received an immense amount of personal publicity from the project, and to the attention-loving Borglum—who had long chafed at the relative obscurity in which sculptors in general and he in particular labored—this was music for the soul. Thus, he had already decided that if carving one mountain was good, carving two would be better, and was pondering ways of bringing that to pass. In addition, a serious controversy was now festering between himself and the Stone Mountain Confederate Memorial Association. It had not yet come to a head, but it was threatening enough for Borglum to see the wisdom of having another job lined up—preferably another mountain-carving —just in case. Accordingly, when he received Robinson's forwarded letter he so promptly wired an answer that at two o'clock on that same afternoon it was in the historian's hands:

STAMFORD CONN 129P AUG 28 1924

YOUR LETTER FORWARDED TO ME FROM STONE MOUNTAIN. VERY
MUCH INTERESTED IN YOUR PROPOSAL. GREAT SCHEME YOU HAVE.
HOLD TO IT. THE NORTH WILL WELCOME IT. AM TWO YEARS AHEAD
IN MY SOUTHERN WORK. CAN GET TO THE BLACK HILLS DURING
SEPTEMBER.   GUTZON BORGLUM

A few hours later, a Western Union boy appeared at Borglum's door with the following reply:

TELEGRAM RECEIVED. DELIGHTED YOU CAN VISIT THE HILLS.
WHEN AND UPON WHAT CONDITIONS CAN YOU COME.
                          DOANE ROBINSON

Now the two men began exchanging messages so rapidly that within a week they had established that: Robinson was "mighty glad" Borglum was interested and would visit the Hills. . . . Borglum was "mighty glad" about it also. . . . Robinson thought the Black Hills offered a splendid opportunity for "a mighty work of sculpture," and did Borglum play golf? . . . Borglum, too, thought the Hills offered a splendid opportunity for sculpture, but neglected to say whether he played golf. . . . Robinson would arrange to meet Borglum at Rapid City and take him from there to tour the Needles, and he would arrange for Governor McMaster and Senator Peter Norbeck to be in the party. . . . Borglum thought that would be a splendid arrangement, but said there must be no publicity about his visit "until after I have seen the mountain." . . . Robinson would see that the visit was kept quiet. . . . Borglum could come "between September 19 and October 10—early date most convenient to me."

After receiving Borglum's first three wires, totalling 107 words, Robinson was sold. "Not only is Borglum acknowledged to be the world's greatest sculptor," he declared in a letter to Governor McMaster, "but he is also a wonderful fellow in every direction." In reply, the governor told Robinson that the state would reimburse Borglum for "any personal expenses" incurred in connection with his Black Hills visit. Robinson then passed the governor's message on to Borglum, only to be told that Borglum was not concerned about the expenses and intended to pay them himself.

Finally, on September 22, Borglum wired from the LaSalle Hotel in Chicago:

AM LEAVING TONIGHT ON NORTHWESTERN TRAIN NUMBER FIVE
HUNDRED THREE BOOKED FOR RAPID CITY. . . .

GUTZON BORGLUM

2. "American History Shall March Along That Skyline!"

A
t dawn on September 24, Chicago and Northwestern No. 503 was thirty-three hours out of Chicago and was hooting and clattering at forty miles an hour along the Bad River bottoms toward Rapid City seventy miles to the west. Aboard the train the early rising Borglum was already up and preparing for the day. Outside, the thrashing limbs of cottonwoods by the little river pronounced the day to be windy, but it was a refreshing morning, nonetheless, and a blessed relief from the gritty, prairie-baking heat of the day before. It was the newspaper-reading time of day, and copies of the *Rapid City Journal*, dropped off at Pierre by the evening eastbound and later picked up by the westbound No. 503, were aboard. As Borglum had requested, the paper made no mention of his trip. It did say that the Elks Theater was showing *Boy of Flanders*, starring Jackie Coogan; on a full page devoted to the problems of modern women were stories headlined, "Is Modern Woman A Rebel?" "Women Forced To Rebel," and "Women's Rebellion Good For Society"; and it announced that under South Dakota's new speed laws, "When a person is driving in excess of 25 mph and is in an accident, that person is presumed to be a careless driver and a violator of the law."

Such items as these were of little interest to Borglum. The movies he attended were almost invariably Westerns; his wife, Mary, held a doctor's degree from the University of Berlin, had studied and taught at some of Europe's leading schools, and had never shown any need nor inclination to rebel; and because he believed that speed laws were meant to control only those persons whose time was less valuable than his own, he never paid any attention to them anyhow. The *Journal's* front page story, however, was another matter:

GLOBE AIRMEN AT SANTA MONICA
FLIGHT TO END AT SEATTLE

Clover Field, California, Sept. 23—The first airplanes to encircle the earth flew home today when Lieut. Lowell H. Smith led three air-cruisers back to Santa Monica where they were built. . . . 10,000 persons greeted the fliers. . . .

History's first round-the-world flight—that was something Borglum could get excited about. He was an aviation enthusiast. He had watched early flights by the Wright Brothers and witnessed experiments by aviation pioneer Samuel Langley, and in 1917 had, himself, designed an airplane fuselage so advanced that fifteen years later aircraft manufacturers would begin giving their airplanes a similar profile. Moreover, during the World War he briefly had held a presidential appointment to investigate inefficiencies in the manufacture of warplanes. The story of that investigation is hazy, and its accomplishments are hazier still. It seems to have yielded no earthshaking results, but Borglum was always to believe it had, and it was a thing about which he loved to reminisce—but now was not the time, for, having no dining car, the train was now slowing for a breakfast stop at the little Cheyenne River town of Wasta.

Doane Robinson also was on No. 503, having boarded at Pierre on the previous evening. Now, as he detrained at Wasta he saw standing together on the platform a solemn, big-eyed boy of eleven; a man whose militarily straight back and magnificent bay window gave him the profile of an upended half-potato; and a stocky, keen-eyed, dark-moustached man who so radiated energy as to appear in motion even when standing still. Robinson had not yet met Borglum, but he knew the third man in that trio just had to be him. Hurrying up to the group, Robinson introduced himself and in turn was introduced by Borglum to Borglum's young son, Lincoln, and to his assistant, Major J. G. Tucker.

During breakfast and the remaining forty miles to Rapid City, Robinson explained to the sculptor that, unfortunately, he had not been able to get either the governor or Senator Norbeck to join them. Borglum replied that he did not mind about that, and then went on to tell the historian what he had not told him during their correspondence: he was opposed to carving Western characters in the Black Hills. They were too local. This should be a grand *national* monument commemorating America's founders and builders. On a pocket pad Borglum quickly sketched a heroic figure of George Washington standing in lonely majesty above surrounding mountains (fig. no. 3). *That*, said the sculptor, was the kind of thing they should be thinking about.

With a rasping of brakeshoes and a jangle of couplings running down its iron spine, Northwestern No. 503 rumbled to a stop beside the Rapid City depot, gave a last, weary compressed-air sigh, and was still. On the platform, a crowd of men holding their hats (and women their dresses) against the gusting of the now-hot wind revealed that, despite Borglum's request, his arrival had been kept no more secret than a confidence whispered at a bridge party. Those in the crowd did not know why Borglum had come, but they knew he *had* come and that he was famous, and they were there to greet him accordingly. Therefore, after Borglum had alighted from the train and had been greeted by all the proper dignitaries saying all the proper things, he and his party were taken by businessman Paul Bellamy on a short bus tour of the town. Meanwhile, the women of the welcoming delegation retired to Yeoman Hall where they prepared a lunch, sponsored by the Rotary Club, of prairie chickens shot especially for this occasion.

Doane Robinson at first was dismayed by all the fanfare and hoopla with which the sculptor was being greeted. He had promised to get him into town quietly, and now here Borglum was, being fussed over as if he were the Prince of Wales. It did not take long, however, for Robinson to learn that his concern was groundless, for, as he later dryly observed, "Borglum was delighted!"

Naturally, the luncheon called for speechmaking, and Borglum made a good one. He described his work at Stone Mountain, and his spellbound audience, the *Journal* reported later, "sat as figures of stone, drinking in the account."

Joined now by Dr. C. C. O'Hara, the geologist-president of the South Dakota School of Mines at Rapid City, and by mineralogist Dr. J. P. Connolly from that same institution, the inspection party, full of good will and prairie chicken, set out to look over the high country surrounding Harney Peak. After a brief inspection tour that afternoon they retired to the Game Lodge— a luxurious little resort hotel in Custer State Park—and continued their investigation the next day.

Gazing from the top of Harney Peak out across the Needles, Borglum exclaimed, "There's the place to carve a great national memorial!"

"Wait 'til we show you something a bit farther on," Robinson replied.

Soon, from another high ridge Robinson showed him a great line of domes and pinnacles flanking the south side of the peak. There was a moment of silence. Then Borglum, ever the dramatist, cried out, "Here is the place! American history shall march along that skyline!" And for the moment at least, that settled it.

The party then began the return drive to Rapid City, and Borglum, now in the first flush of a creative fever that was to remain with him until his death eighteen years later, kept looking back at the jagged silhouette of his chosen escarpment. "Look!" he said, "It's still watching us!"

In Rapid City the lionizing of the sculptor was continuing, and as the inspection party pulled up in front of the Harney Hotel they could hear from the streets the chant of newsboys crying, "Rap'd Citee Jurrnall—Gutz'n Borglum visits Hills—Fay-muss Sculptor Here—Ree Dall about it!" And on their papers was the screamer headline, "GUTZON BORGLUM VISITS RAPID CITY AND HILLS!" and a subhead:

Sculptor of World Fame Guest Here

and, beneath that, twenty inches of copy telling about Borglum and Stone Mountain but making no mention of his purpose in visiting the Black Hills. That, however, was remedied that evening at a banquet at the A&F Cafe.

At the banquet, Robinson outlined his idea for a mighty monument to be carved in the Black Hills, and then introduced Borglum, who told his audience that he was entranced by the beauty of the Hills area and the friendliness of its people; that he had long dreamed of carving "in or near the Rocky Mountains" a gigantic memorial to the spirit and meaning of America; that since beginning his Stone Mountain work he had been approached by many persons and organizations who wanted his services for some similar project, but none of their propositions had appealed to him.

But *now*, declared Borglum, he had found "a veritable garden of the gods." "I know of no grouping of rock formations," he said, "that equals those found in the Black Hills . . . nor any that is so suitable to sculpture." His listeners might wonder if the proposed Black Hills carving could be financed, he added, but they should put aside their concern. Money was no problem, he asserted, because "I come here at the earnest request of men interested in the history of the country and its founders." Furthermore, said Borglum, he was himself so enthusiastic about the proposed work that he intended to pay from his own pocket the expenses he had incurred in making this visit.

In conclusion the sculptor glowingly described the financial benefits of creating such a monument. It would engender a tourist trade so profitable as to far overshadow the cost of creating it. Moreover, the sooner the job was started the sooner this golden harvest could be reaped. Therefore, if the state would give him $10,000 to cover the cost of making geological surveys and preliminary models of the monument itself, he would go to work on it immediately.

Despite Borglum's persuasiveness, the audience's reaction was mixed. Like all such audiences, it was made up of several types. There were, for instance, a number of those Eager Enthusiasts who love Great Projects and endorse them to the last dollar and ounce of other people's money and effort, but who mysteriously fade away when called upon for money and effort of their own; their response was prompt, positive, and noisy. At the other extreme there were the Automatic Opposers, who immediately dismissed the proposition as being the most half-baked scheme they had ever heard. And occupying the two sides of the middle ground were those Stern Challengers whose support may be won only by providing overly foolproof answers to their overly blunt questions, and the Quietly Thoughtful who listen noncommitally but with open minds.

The foremost Stern Challenger—perhaps because he, too, was a dreamer-upper of grandiose schemes, many of which actually worked out—was Borglum's erstwhile sightseeing host, Paul Bellamy. And as Bellamy probed, Robinson squirmed. Thoroughly bedazzled both by the proposed monument and by Borglum, the historian wanted desperately to avoid any jarring notes. And, as he later complained to Norbeck, he felt that "Bellamy did not get the size of Borglum," with the result that "Borglum was not pleased." Again, however, Robinson need not have worried, for it was he who had not yet gotten "the size of Borglum." The fact was, Robinson's dream had now become Borglum's dream, and instead of South Dakota trying to sell it to the sculptor, it was the sculptor who was now trying to sell it to South Dakota.

Most prominent among the Quietly Thoughtful was Rapid City's mayor, businessman John Boland. In Boland's matter-of-fact mind Robinson came across as being more poetic than practical, and this Borglum seemed to be a kind of arm-waving spellbinder whose speech had been nothing more than a sales pitch. Still, being a salesman himself, Boland saw nothing wrong in that so long as what the man was selling was good for the customer, and Boland was inclined to think this carving idea was. Accordingly, upon returning to his home that evening Boland said to his wife Ethel, "I heard a pretty attractive proposition tonight. If we can pull it off it might be a great thing for the Hills."

In sizing it up afterwards, Borglum and Robinson thought the A&F Cafe meeting had produced a very positive response, and they were much encouraged thereby. But that was because they did not know—yet—that much of that response had been a reluctant flower that the sunshine of Borglum's oratory had coaxed into bloom, but for only a moment.

After the meeting, Borglum returned to Stamford and Robinson to Pierre. First, however, they agreed that Borglum would draw up preliminary sketches of the monument and a written proposal for its construction. Robinson, meanwhile, would take steps toward getting Congress to approve the use of National Forest land for the memorial, and also would attempt to get the state legislature to part with the $10,000 Borglum said he needed for preliminary surveys and models.

Now Robinson needed powerful political help, and for that he turned to Senator Peter Norbeck. Politically, Senator Norbeck, a Republican, was without question the strongest man in South Dakota, and as a personal friend of President Coolidge he had much influence in Washington as well. Moreover, he was vitally interested in the development of recreational and scenic areas, as well as parks. Knowing this, Robinson, from the very beginning of his monument dream, had kept the Senator posted on developments connected with it; and from the beginning Norbeck's response had been quietly favorable. When, for example, he learned that Robinson had written to sculptor Laredo Taft about the matter, Norbeck wrote to Robinson: "It is a new suggestion entirely. . . . But I do believe that there would be some wonderful opportunities to work out among the Black Hills Needles the very thing you suggest."

So far, however, giving such encouragement was the extent to which Norbeck had been willing to involve himself in the affair. Now, needing Norbeck's political muscle, Robinson set out to change that. Upon returning to Pierre from the A&F Cafe meeting, he wrote to Norbeck:

> Borglum has come and gone. I count it one of the great experiences of my life to have spent two days with a man of his genius and high character. . . . He paid his own expenses for the trip and talked like a man who was sure of his ground. . . . He said nothing of his plans for financing except that he came at the request of men deeply interested in a national memorial. . . . I can hardly believe this wonderful thing is to be handed to us. . . . Since the location is on the Forest Reserve . . . federal legislation would be required and I told him you would look after all that is necessary in that direction.

In late October, Borglum sent Robinson a written report and a sketch of the standing figures of Washington and Lincoln. He would carve them, he said, on a scale of men two hundred feet tall, and they should be accompanied by a figure of Theodore Roosevelt together with "large bas-reliefs of Custer and others." He estimated the job would take no more than six years and "saw no reason" why it should cost more than $1,200,000. To get it started "there should be appropriated . . . ten thousand dollars . . . which would serve as a retainer and cover all preliminary expenses." Finally, Borglum declared, "Financing of the main work offers no real difficulties. I will explain to you methods . . . that will give you ample for your plan."

But for the sculptor's announcing again that financing would be no problem, Robinson would have been shocked by his estimate of the project's cost. As it was, however, he was delighted by Borglum's report and sent copies to Norbeck and others. And he did have one suggestion for Borglum: "I feel that the Washington and Lincoln busts should form the complete preliminary scheme. . . . There will be a dignity and grandeur about these two figures standing on top of the world which, it seems to me, would be minimized by an extension."

Borglum, who seldom sent a letter when he could send a telegram, responded with a 230 word wire that began:

YOU ARE THINKING ABOUT THIS JUST AS I AM. . . . LET US HOLD TO
THAT UNBEATABLE THOUGHT OF THOSE TWO LONE GIANTS
STANDING ON TOP OF AMERICA. . . . THAT PLAN IS UNBEATABLE
AND WILL AROUSE THE NATION.

3. Borglum's original concept of what was to become the Mount Rushmore Memorial. Submitted with a written report to Doane Robinson in late October, 1924, the proposal envisioned separate figures of Washington and Lincoln, carved in the round on natural stone spires in the Needles area of the Black Hills. They were to have been on the scale of a man 200 feet tall — about half the scale of the figures at Rushmore.

And further on it contained a real shocker:

I SUGGEST . . . YOU BEGIN WITH AN ANNUAL APPROPRIATION OF
SAY TWO HUNDRED THOUSAND A YEAR FOR SAY THREE YEARS. . . .

Robinson was dumfounded. Even with Borglum's past assurances that, because he knew where to get it, money was no problem, Robinson had been having a hard time selling the monument to the Dakotans. And now this! If news were to get out that Borglum now wanted the State to appropriate $600,000, and only as a beginning at that, the whole enterprise would immediately become as dead as Caesar's horse. Still, Robinson did want the monument and he did not want to upset Borglum. Therefore, he responded by mildly observing that at some later time the legislature might be persuaded to approve such a request, but presently it was too early to propose it. And there he dropped the matter. Neither to Borglum nor anyone else did he ever mention it again.

And Robinson *was* having trouble in developing either political or public support for the monument proposal. Most state legislators he talked to were cool to it, and the incoming governor, Carl Gunderson, was actually hostile to it. As for the public: Borglum's September visit to the Hills had reawakened the environmentalists, and they, in turn, had revived the "desecration" controversy. Like a man fighting bees with his hat, Robinson tried to meet and beat down every attack and objection. These were so numerous that he developed a number of stock answers to them, such as: "God only makes a Michael Angelo or a Gutzon Borglum once every thousand years. He has proposed a work of art for South Dakota surpassing any ever before created by man." And, "God did not quite complete His job in the Harney district, but left it for man to come and create Sylvan Lake, the very jewel of that section. God always leaves it to man to . . . [develop] the seed of beauty which God has planted."

The proposal had many supporters also, of course, particularly among the press. The influential Sioux Falls *Argus Leader* supported it from the start, as did the *Aberdeen American*. And even though in later and stormier years Borglum was to remember it otherwise, the *Rapid City Journal* soon moved from cautious neutrality to strong endorsement. But probably the most exuberant exponent was the Pierre *Daily Dakotan*, which enthused: "There will probably be a Mayflower in living stone, a Plymouth Rock and landing Pilgrims—Washington with the Continental soldiers, and so on down to the men in "tin hats" and gas masks of the World War. . . . Someday gigantic statues will flank Harney Peak which will tell the story of American history and become the wonder place of the nation."

Among the monument's opponents the most waspish, both in editorials and personal letters, was Cora Johnson, a writer for the Hot Springs *Star*. So vitriolic were her attacks that Borglum would refer to her only as "that Hot Springs person," describing her as "an agent of evil." And Robinson was moved to write to her:

December 7, 1924

My Mrs. Johnson:

I long ago learned not to argue with a lady. I only ask just how you hope to justify yourself to posterity? The greatest artist in the world has proposed to bring you the most majestic monument in the world, *and ye would not.*

Faithfully,
Doane Robinson

(When Robinson sent a copy of this letter to Norbeck, the Senator responded, "I think you handled the matter just splendid.")

Fall faded and winter came on, and still the debate continued. Meanwhile, the notion of carving a great monument in the Black Hills remained just that—a notion. With little organization or direction, and promoted mainly by Borglum and Robinson, it continued to be all talk and nothing more. To keep it alive and moving, the pro-carving forces needed more and heavier artillery, and Senator Norbeck was just the man to provide that artillery if only he could be persuaded to do so. Until now the senator had done no more than give quiet encouragement to the proposal. The reason seemed to be that he thought the memorial would be a fine thing if practical to build, and in his down-to-earth way of thinking that "if" was enormous. That being the case, in early December Borglum set out for Washington to get the senator to climb wholeheartedly aboard the memorial bandwagon.

In 1920, following two terms as South Dakota's governor, Norbeck had been elected to the Senate. Hence, when Borglum went to see him he was beginning only his fourth congressional session. Although still a senatorial freshman, Norbeck by now had pretty well gotten the hang of both the senator business and Washington itself. He had found that he did like being a senator but did not like Washington and never would. After arriving there in 1921 he had written to the home folks the following impression of the place:

Nearly everybody in Washington spends from one hundred to one hundred and ten percent of what they can earn. . . . This is the first place I have ever struck where nearly everybody believes he has some particular standard to be maintained. . . . Some people feel it is much beneath their dignity to drive a car that costs less than twenty-five hundred; another group puts the limit at fifteen hundred, and a person is not rated very high here if he drives a Ford. I never realized there could be so much that is artificial about our lives. . . . There is less independence of thought and action here than any place I have ever been.

Now, three years later, he was still of the same opinion, which was why he was moving himself and his family into yet another in the long succession of rented houses they were to occupy during his senatorial years. Norbeck had noted early, and with disgust, that, after a term or two in office, many congressmen began to put down Washington roots and to forget their heritage and to think of themselves as Washingtonians first and natives of their home states only second, if at all.

Determined to see that this never happened to the Norbecks, the senator reasoned that never owning a Washington home nor even living there for long in one place might serve as a preventative. And whether or not this was the reason, throughout his long senatorial tenure Norbeck and his family were to remain undilutedly Dakotan.

At age fifty-three, Norbeck was a sturdy, 225 pound block of a man, thick of neck and ankle; a warm, twinkling-eyed man whose size, nature, and air of quiet invincibility put one in mind of a benevolent buffalo.

Upon first arriving in Washington, Norbeck had felt inwardly a good deal less self-assurance than he projected outwardly. Born to Norwegian immigrant parents in the poverty of a Dakota homestead dugout, he had become a prosperous well-driller, then governor of his state, and then a senator. Despite his Alger-like success, however, he fretted privately over his lack of advanced education—which, since he had had some college, was more imaginary than real. He fretted, too, over his lack of social graces—and, because he was possessed of a natural easy charm and gentlemanly manner, this, too, was more imaginary than real. But most of all, Norbeck was embarrassed by his tendency, especially when under pressure, to say "yoost" for "just," "vee" for "we," and "ay tank" for "I think," and to remedy that he was now taking diction lessons. But because taking them embarrassed him almost as much as the condition they were intended to correct, this was done in utmost secrecy.

Because of his fancied shortcomings, early in his senatorial career Norbeck had confided to South Dakota's Congressman William Williamson, "I have no business here." By 1924, however, it had become quite evident to others, if not to the modest Norbeck himself, that he was a remarkably competent legislator who did indeed "have business here." For the happy fact was that Norbeck, like Borglum and some of the other founding fathers of the Rushmore memorial, was a man whose total was substantially greater than the sum of his parts. And, as Congressman Williamson put it, Norbeck was, "in the field of conservation of forests, of wildlife, and the creation, development and protection of national parks and monuments . . . without a peer in the Senate."

Now, on December 6, 1924, Borglum was striving to get Norbeck enthusiastically involved in the creation of one particular monument—one which he and others were referring to as the "Mount Harney Memorial" and which was to be carved in the Black Hills. And to a substantial extent Borglum was succeeding. In this first meeting between the two men Norbeck was coming to the opinion that the sculptor was less scatterbrained than he had previously feared and was possibly as splendid an artist as Borglum, himself, thought he was. In fact, Norbeck decided, the man just might be able to pull off this carving stunt successfully. Accordingly, Norbeck decided to give his support to Borglum for at least long enough to find out if he actually could get the Mount Harney project off the ground, and as soon as the sculptor had gone the senator wired Carl Gunderson, who was then but three weeks away from inauguration as South Dakota's next governor:

> . . . I THINK THIS MIGHT BE AN OPPORTUNITY TO SECURE ONE OF
> THE NATIONAL ATTRACTIONS IN THIS COUNTRY OF THE HIGHEST
> ARTISTIC QUALITY   STOP   I SUGGEST THE STATE APPROPRIATE TEN
> THOUSAND DOLLARS TO BE MADE AVAILABLE FOR INVESTIGATION
> AND SURVEYS ONLY   STOP   IT IS AN OPPORTUNITY WE SHOULD
> NOT MISS   PETER NORBECK

Even so, Norbeck still had reservations about getting the thing financed. He thought Borglum's assurances on that point had been just a bit too rosy. In this first meeting Borglum had not impressed him as being the fabulous fund raiser that Borglum, himself, seemed to think he was. The sculptor had used Stone Mountain as an example and had said that, because of his own efforts and unique fund-raising ideas, that project had been financed easily and amply. But Norbeck, whose keen ear had already caught the first muted and unpublicized rumblings of the storm now gathering over Stone Mountain, had his doubts. Accordingly, as a warning to the more easily influenced Robinson, the senator now wrote:

> I don't want to dampen your ardor, but I feel that—notwithstanding all that is claimed [by Borglum] for it—the Stone Mountain work will come to a standstill on account of finances. . . . I do not have the feeling that any of these matters need change our plans as far as the work in South Dakota is concerned, but I do feel that in the end South Dakota will be called upon to make up a substantial part of the cost. . . . I do hope we get the ten thousand dollars.

Gunderson, however, had his own ideas about that ten thousand dollars. He responded to Norbeck's wire by saying he was "interested" in the idea of the memorial but was positively opposed to the state's making *any* appropriation for it. And more than anything else it probably was Gunderson's attitude that pushed Norbeck firmly and finally into the pro-monument camp. Norbeck told Robinson what Gunderson had said, and Robinson promptly went to see the governor-elect in an attempt to change his mind. Politely but firmly, Gunderson brushed him off. Robinson was furious. He sent Norbeck a wire so hotly ridiculing and condemning Gunderson that Norbeck first whooped at such unexpected feistiness from the age-mellowed scholar and then, for Robinson's protection, burned the message. Nonetheless, Norbeck's temper was now up also. Because of past political feuding he had no use for Gunderson anyhow, and now he was not going to let this . . . this . . . stick-in-the-mud blindly obstruct what Norbeck had suddenly decided was "the biggest single thing to come to Dakota since the first settlers arrived." Having already been pretty well won over by Robinson and Borglum, and now being challenged by a man whom he considered an over-conservative political upstart, Norbeck was ready to get into this memorial proposition with both feet. And as his first step he set out to secure the active participation of Congressman Williamson, who, like himself, had been favorable to the memorial all along but so far had avoided becoming involved in it.

William Williamson was forty-eight years old in the fall of 1924 and was beginning his second term as representative from South Dakota's third congressional district. Tall, lean, introverted, he was a man of austere habits and ironclad principles. He had little use for nightlife and no use at all for alcohol. His usual expression was wide-eyed and sober; he wore thick round spectacles; and these things, together with the way he combed his hair, gave him somewhat the appearance of a startled owl. And in a career remarkably parallel to Norbeck's, he had come up in the world the hard way.

Like Norbeck, Williamson was the son of Norwegian immigrant homesteaders. His father, Vilium, had come to Dakota Territory in 1882 and had found it—or so he wrote to his family—a *fin og deilig* (fine and charming) land. He had then filed a claim on 160 acres of it, built a fourteen-by-sixteen foot shanty with a sleeping loft, sent for his wife and five children, and moved in. But though the land may have been *deilig*, the passage of time proved it to be something less than *fin*. As a result, Williamson wrote in his autobiography: "One winter we had nothing to eat but corn meal ground at a local mill; salt pork sparingly used; no milk, and only salted lard for butter. We children got so tired of corn mush every night that we begged to go to bed without supper."

Despite these hardships, or because of them, Williamson determined early to make something of himself, and when he was only ten he discovered what that something was. While visiting the county seat one blistering summer day he took refuge in the cool shadows of the high-ceilinged courthouse, and there in a courtroom he saw: "A tall, long-haired, striking looking man . . . in a long-tailed coat and striped pants . . . majestically pacing up and down . . . ever and anon tossing his locks out of his eyes by a backward thrust of his massive head. "Then and there," Williamson later recalled, "I decided to become a lawyer."

By working successively as a farmhand, hod carrier, sheep herder, book salesman, and country schoolmaster Williamson managed to earn the education that allowed him, at age twenty-seven, to be admitted to the South Dakota bar. Not long after that he found himself acting as prosecuting attorney in a case that was to launch his public career. The case was that of one "Buffalo" George, whose business was the rustling of horses and cattle—which he had conducted so skillfully as theretofore to have been almost uncatchable and, when caught, entirely unconvictable. But now, to the happy astonishment of the public and the dismayed astonishment of "Buffalo," the methodical Williamson constructed a case so tight that the rustler wound up with a ten-year penitentiary sentence. This convinced Williamson's delighted fellow citizens that he surely must have been intended for greater things. This, in turn, ultimately led to his election in 1920 to the United States Congress.

Upon beginning his first congressional term, Williamson, again like Norbeck, was dismayed by what he found. After his first day in Congress he wrote in his diary: "I could not keep track of what was going on in the

House. The sessions seemed to me to be a bedlam of noise and confusion."
Neither was he pleased by the great number of dinner invitations he found
himself receiving. "I knew they were not wining and dining a congressman
out of the goodness of their hearts," he wrote, "but expected some return for
their lavish hospitality." Besides, "I did not like to be out at night very much."
Consequently, "I declined all such invitations." Then the favor-seekers began
showing up at his office, and this aggravated him even more because there he
was trying to cope with a flood of mail that, " . . . related to applications for
postoffice jobs; mail carriers; public lands; patents; Indian Affairs; claims of
all sorts against the government; pensions; War Risk insurance; land office
contests; requests for information and bulletins. . . ." Regarding this, he
complained, "Trying to be a statesman, which I really wanted to be, instead
of merely a messenger boy and clerk, now began to look like a forlorn hope."

Now, however, at the beginning of his third year in Congress, Williamson
had learned to make sense of the House proceedings, had learned to manage
his mail, and was able to find time to act as a legislator. Also, he had bought a
home in Washington. This was not because he liked the place—his opinion of
it was no better than Norbeck's—but was, rather, to give him something to
tinker with in his off hours. At heart, Williamson was more than anything else
a handyman and craftsman who found his greatest joy in fixing things and
building things. During the past summer, for instance, alongside a rushing
trout stream in a Black Hills canyon he had begun, unassisted, to construct a
five-room, story-and-a-half log summer home with a stone fireplace and full
basement. And his diary of his Washington years reveals him hurrying home
after a day in Congress to repair a porch or build a piece of furniture. He had
said he wanted to be a statesman, but his diary reveals him as a man who
would have found more pleasure in building a cabinet than in serving in one.
Even so, and despite his austere nature and withdrawn ways, Williamson was
to gain congressional influence much greater than one might have expected
from a man representing a sparsely settled district in an obscure state. And,
like Norbeck, he was to become a good friend of two presidents.

The first task that Norbeck and Williamson now took up in aid of the
monument was the essential one of securing from the proper authorities the
permission for its carving, and this was a complicated thing. The area Borglum was interested in lay both in a national forest and a state park. Hence,
any carving there had to be approved both by Congress and by the South
Dakota legislature, and Williamson, whose tidy legal mind was ideally suited
to such work, drafted bills to be introduced in each. The national bill he drew
up would simply grant permission for the work. His state bill would grant

similar permission and also authorize spending $10,000 of state money on Borglum's preliminary plans and surveys.

The bills were introduced in January, and the national bill was passed without opposition and on March 23, 1925, became law. The state bill, however, was another matter. There was little opposition to the carving itself— even Governor Gunderson said he would not oppose that—but there was powerful opposition to spending any state money on it. Even so, it was beginning to look as if the bill had a fair chance of being passed. As it happened, however, that chance was killed when, on February 22, the storm that had been gathering over Stone Mountain suddenly broke.

To understand the nature and effect of that tempest it is necessary to understand the nature of its principal figure and probable creator, Gutzon Borglum.

3. Gutzon Borglum—
"I Do Everything"

B eing by nature a dramatist and a romantic, Gutzon Borglum was inclined to view his life story as a novel that he, as author, was free to
revise, edit, and embellish whenever and however the spirit moved
him. This, in turn, may explain why his writings show him to have been born
in two different years, in two different places, and to two different mothers.

Throughout his life, Borglum almost always said he had been born in
Idaho. Occasionally, however, he claimed to be a California native, and on at
least one occasion answered a biographical inquiry by saying, "I am a Pacific
Coaster. I was born and bred out there."

Until his later years, Borglum gave his date of birth as March 25, 1867.
Then he changed it to March 25, 1871. He seems never to have explained why,
but his reason is not hard to guess. He made the change early in 1932 when,
according to the earlier date, he was approaching sixty-five. At that time,
however, Borglum did not look sixty-five and did not act sixty-five, and it may
be presumed that he did not want to *be* sixty-five. Accordingly, he simply
turned back the clock and became sixty-one instead. From that time forward
the latter date was the one he gave to *Who's Who In America* and is the one
shown in most encyclopedias today.

As for his mother, until 1916 Borglum listed her as Ida Michelson [sic]
Borglum when giving biographical data. From 1916 to 1923 he supplied the
name of Christina Michelson [sic] Borglum, who actually was Ida's younger
sister. Finally, from 1923 until his death he listed Ida again. On its face, this
switching back and forth seems strange indeed. However (and as will be
shown a little farther on), it probably can be explained by divided loyalties
arising from events that occurred when Borglum was still an infant.

Fortunately for the historian, records exist that establish beyond question
that John Gutzon de la Mothe Borglum was, in fact, born on March 25, 1867,

in Ovid, Idaho, and that his parents were Jens Møller Haugaard Borglum and Christina Mikkelsen Borglum.

The Borglums were Danes and fiercely proud of it, and were of the opinion that they were descended from a noble and distinguished European family. Gutzon, after he had become a successful and prosperous sculptor, financed a visit to Denmark by his father, during which the elder Borglum set out to trace the Borglum ancestry and to find out just how noble and distinguished it might have been. It was a somewhat risky undertaking, of course, for upon close inspection family trees often turn out to be a good deal shadier than expected. In the Borglums' case, however, this proved not to be true; their family tree did indeed have a noble taproot.

The Borglums were descendants of the family de la Mothe, and that family, Borglum's father discovered, had originated in the year 1190 with a medieval knight known as Conrad Reinhardt. In that year Reinhardt set out with the German emperor, Frederick Barbarossa, on a crusade to the Holy Land. Enroute, Reinhardt delivered the emperor from an attack by an animal, which was according to one account a wild boar and to another an indignant billygoat. Whichever the case, the benefit to Frederick was only temporary. Almost immediately thereafter he died of drowning, but not before he had conferred upon Reinhardt the honorary and hereditary title of De La Mothe —"the one of courage."

During the centuries that followed, some of Conrad de la Mothe's numerous descendants settled in the extreme north of Denmark. There, some twenty-five generations after the affair of the boar or goat, Borglum's father was born in 1839 and was christened Jens Møller Haugaard Borglum. As a youth Jens Borglum was trained to become a woodcarver, and also as a youth he came into contact with Mormon missionaries from America. He became converted, and at the age of twenty-five he joined a number of other Danish converts on a journey to the United States and the "New Zion" that the Mormons were creating beside Utah's Great Salt Lake. One of his fellow pilgrims was Ida Mikkelsen, the daughter of a Copenhagen furrier, and while enroute to America Jens and Ida were married.

From New York, the immigrants traveled to the Missouri River town of Nebraska City, where they joined a westbound Mormon wagon train. Jens and Ida, however, had no money for oxen and a wagon; they bought a two-wheeled pushcart instead. Then, like thousands of other "pushcart Mormons" they accomplished the almost unbelievable task of pushing and pulling their belongings in a hand-drawn cart across nine hundred rugged miles of wilderness.

The young Borglums had been in Utah scarcely a year when Ida's younger sister, eighteen-year-old Christina, arrived from Denmark to join them. Shortly thereafter, Jens, in keeping with the Mormon custom of plural marriage, married Christina also. Next, the three of them traveled north to the shores of Idaho's Great Bear Lake. There they built a primitive cabin and settled; and there, on March 25, 1867, Christina bore a son whom they christened John Gutzon de la Mothe. Shortly after Gutzon's birth, the Borglums moved back to Utah and settled in Ogden where, on December 22, 1868, Christina bore a second son named Solon Hannibal de la Mothe. Six months later Ida also bore a son, whom they named Arnold.

By this time the Borglum family was having problems, and the problems were growing. In a frontier community preoccupied with the necessities for survival, the opportunities for a woodcarver were slim indeed. Jens had five people besides himself to feed, and, at the rate the Borglums were reproducing, even five appeared to be only a temporary figure. Their situation was becoming critical. Also, Ida and Christina were constantly quarreling. And finally, their plural marriage was suffering increasing pressure from the outside. Although still sanctioned by the Mormon Church, such marriages had been contrary to United States law since 1862. As long as the Utah Mormons had remained isolated this had not mattered too much, but with the completion in 1869 of the transcontinental railroad it suddenly began to matter a great deal. Not only did the railroad pass through the heart of Mormon country, but the town of Ogden became one of its major stopping points. There, travelers actually were able to see and be delightfully horrified by this Mormon iniquity of which they had only read. As a consequence, the desks of Congress soon were piled high with letters of virtuous thunder demanding that this Mormon wickedness be stamped out forthwith. This, in turn, led Congress to set about making those Mormons with plural marriages as uncomfortable as possible.

Troubled, harassed, and sometimes even hungry, the Borglums decided in a family conference that Jens needed a more productive occupation and fewer wives. As a solution to both problems, late in 1869 they all boarded the train and headed east. At Omaha, Christina withdrew from the marriage, joined her parents (who now were living there), and later remarried. Taking the three boys, Jens and Ida then proceeded on to St. Louis where Jens set about preparing for a new career.

During the westward expansion there was an enormous demand for physicians in the new towns being established almost daily along the newly built railroads. To fill the demand, all across the West hundreds of small, quick-course medical schools had sprung up. And at one of these, the Missouri Medical College, Jens entered into the study of homeopathic medicine. In 1874 he was graduated, Anglicized his name, and, as Dr. James Miller Borglum, set up practice in Fremont, Nebraska.

Fremont was at that time a frontier town, a horse and cow town, a cowboy and Indian town. And from its raw and rowdy pioneer vitality, Gutzon (now turning seven) and Solon (just past five) began soaking up the influences that were to affect so profoundly the artistic works of both, and were to implant in both a lifelong love of the American West.

In later life Borglum was to write many accounts of incidents in his Fremont boyhood. One of these accounts gives a striking insight into his own character. Because he wrote it as if he had been a toddler at the time, when in fact he must have been seven or more years old, it bears the unmistakable mark of Borglum's tendency to embroider his own history. Even so, it provides so major a key to the understanding of this complex man that, apocryphal or factual, it belongs in every Borglum biography.

Once when he was a little boy, Borglum wrote, he went with his father on an evening house call to an outlying farm. While Doctor Borglum saw to his patient inside the house, Gutzon remained outside. He watched a golden full moon sliding up from behind the dark horizon to hang low and glowing in the evening sky, and he wanted that moon. He wanted to grasp it, to keep it, to hold it in his clutches. With outstretched arms he ran toward it, but as he ran the moon kept retreating. Finally, puffing and exhausted, he realized that he could not have his moon, and, as he wrote, "I stood weeping my heart out." When telling that story in later years, Borglum would go on to say that for more than a half-century that moon had remained hanging on his horizon, "[and] I have never reached it."

Borglum was nearing fifteen when, in 1882, his father enrolled him at St. Mary's Academy in Kansas City. It was a short-lived experience. He entered the academy in January, according to academy records, left in the following June, and never returned. Next, he seems to have worked for a time as an apprentice in an Omaha machine shop. Later, in fact, he was to use this episode as a basis for telling Senator Norbeck that he was "a master machinist in the American Federation of Labor." On the other hand, in none of his many biographies in *Who's Who* did he ever mention it. In any case, that experience—whatever it was—has to have been short-lived also, for in 1883 we find Borglum in California. There, he became apprenticed to a lithographer, and at the same time began to fulfill his longstanding dream of studying art in general and painting in particular.

As aspiring young artists usually must do, during the next several years Borglum studied and painted and struggled and studied some more, trying to sharpen his skills and, he hoped, to gain some recognition. Then, in 1888 he won an assignment to paint a portrait of the noted explorer and mapmaker of the American West, General John Charles Frémont. Completed shortly before the general's death, the painting was a success. More important, it won for Borglum the friendship and support of Jessie Benton Frémont, the general's wife. This was the first big break for Borglum, and a turning point in his life. Mrs. Frémont was, to put it mildly, a socially aggressive woman who had managed to gain considerable influence among the rich and powerful, and for years to come she was to use that aggressiveness and influence on Borglum's behalf whenever she thought it might help him.

It was in the late 1880s, also, that Borglum began taking painting lessons from Elizabeth "Liza" Jaynes Putnam, a highly educated artist from a prominent Massachusetts family who had achieved substantial recognition in the artistic community of California. In 1889—when Gutzon was twenty-two and Liza was forty—they were married, and it appears that at this point she took charge of his career. She counseled him, coached him, corrected him, and polished away the rough edges of his frontier upbringing. Meanwhile, she was busily proclaiming to one and all that Gutzon Borglum was "a true universal genius," and was using her social and professional connections for his advancement. Also, it seems to have been Liza who, in 1890, decided that Borglum's unfolding talents now should be sharpened in the schools of Paris.

So, the Borglums went to France, where Borglum studied painting and where, in addition, the first signs of Borglum the sculptor began to emerge. Shortly after his arrival, in fact, he tried his hand at a Western sculpture and so skillfully executed one of a horse standing over its dead Indian rider that it won him a membership in the Société Nationale des Beaux Arts. Moreover, while in Paris he became a student and friend of the great French sculptor Auguste Rodin.

For Gutzon Borglum these Paris years were good years; they were learning, developing years—and, also, Liza liked living in Europe. Nonetheless, in 1893 they returned to California, where Gutzon continued to paint and to dabble in sculpture as well. Then, in 1896 they went again to Europe, this time to London, where Borglum opened a studio. He was so successful there that he was asked to display his paintings for Her Majesty Queen Victoria, and a short time later he was elected to membership in the Royal Society of British Artists. Despite his success, however, after three years in London Borglum became moody and restless and filled with a dark discontent. Finally, in 1901, the Borglum family moved on again—this time back to Paris.

Solon Borglum, meanwhile, had also been developing into an artist, and considering his later start had been doing so more rapidly than Gutzon. During most of Gutzon's years of study in California, Solon remained in Nebraska working on his father's ranch. There, he dabbled in painting and took a few lessons, but he did not become serious about it until 1890, when, on their way to Paris, Gutzon and Liza stopped to visit at the ranch. Upon examining Solon's paintings, Gutzon exclaimed, "Solon! You should be a professional artist!"

Thus encouraged, Solon began to study in earnest—first in Omaha, then in California, then at the Cincinnati Art Academy, where he studied painting and sculpture both. Finally, as Gutzon had done, Solon made his way to Paris. He was there when Gutzon and Liza returned in 1901, and by his presence caused Gutzon's life to be radically and forever changed.

At that time Gutzon was again depressed and was seething with inner and yet uncrystallized conflicts. Much of his problem was Liza. To the headstrong and fiercely independent Gutzon, her constant management and manipulation of his career had become galling. Moreover, she was now fifty-two to his thirty-four, and as he later said of their marriage, "Ever since I was married at twenty-two I have tried to live an older age and have foregone my youth." Whereas Liza was happily settled into Paris life and into the luxurious apartment on which they had just signed a three-year lease, Gutzon was homesick for America. At the same time, he had also become discontented professionally. He had gained some solid recognition as a painter—which was pleasing to Liza, since she regarded his success as actually her success—but it had left him unfulfilled. In retrospect, the reason seems to have been that inside Gutzon Borglum the painter Gutzon Borglum the sculptor was now struggling to break free. Solon's presence was also serving to further intensify Gutzon's inner struggle, for Solon already *was* a sculptor. Moreover, Solon had established with his sculpture a reputation in Paris fully as great as (and in the United States much greater than) Gutzon had achieved with his painting. As a brother, Gutzon was pleased by Solon's success. As an artist, however, he was not—at least, not by so *much* success. It simply was not in Gutzon's nature to take second place to anyone ever, brother or no. He saw in Solon's greater prominence an irksome challenge to be overcome, and to be overcome as quickly as possible.

To Liza, Solon's success was more than irksome; it was disgusting. She had never liked him very much anyhow, and after he entered seriously into art she had liked him even less. Now she was fearful that the success of *that*

Borglum might somehow eclipse the glow of *her* Borglum, and she was smoldering with resentment.

In October of 1901, Solon left Paris for New York, where he planned to open a studio. Shortly after he had gone, Gutzon and Liza were at a gathering where someone referred to a piece of Solon's work as "great art." And Liza exploded. "But what does Solon know about art!," she cried. "He is not an artist!"

At that moment, or so it has been reported, something happened to Gutzon. Resentment of Liza, homesickness, the desire to become a sculptor, the challenge of Solon's success, all crystallized into a sudden decision. He would go home to America—and go alone. And he would become a sculptor. Less than a month later he had left Liza in Paris and, on a ship he had boarded in Cherbourg, was homeward bound. And by his unplanned selection of that particular ship he changed the shape of his future accidentally as much as his decision to go home had changed it deliberately. For aboard it he met Mary Montgomery, a tiny, bright-eyed, swift-witted young Wellesley graduate who was returning home from earning a doctoral degree at the University of Berlin.

Upon arriving in New York, Borglum set up a studio in the rear of 166 East 38th Street. He had scarcely gotten it established and begun to work when, in the summer of 1902, he was stricken almost simultaneously by a nervous breakdown and a near-fatal case of typhoid fever. Hearing of his illness, Liza returned from Paris to take care of him, but when she arrived she found Mary Montgomery already present on the same mission. Whether it was because of that, or because of the deep-seated differences between them, or both, Liza and Gutzon soon parted for the last time. Liza first went back to Paris, and from there returned to California where she established permanent residence.

Never a man who could stay down for long, Borglum was back on his feet and back at work by the beginning of 1903. Straightaway he began turning out sculptures as skillfully and prolifically as if he had been doing it always. This, together with Solon's already having made the name of Borglum well-known and respected in sculptural circles, gained him instant recognition. In fact, before the year was out he had been elected (with Solon's sponsorship) as a member of the exclusive National Sculpture Society.

Now, the Gutzon Borglum the world would come to know began to make his appearance—the impetuous, rambunctious, flamboyant, often abrasive Borglum who seemed always to be traveling in the eye of a self-generated hurricane. Perhaps he had always been this way, although there seems to be no record of it. Whatever the case, after his separation from Liza, his nervous breakdown, and his entry into the field of sculpture, his tempestuous nature swept full-blown into public view. And because of it, his membership in the National Sculpture Society may have been the shortest in the history of that organization. Less than a month after his election to membership, a headline in the *New York Tribune* announced:

GUTZON BORGLUM CALLS
NATIONAL SCULPTURE SOCIETY
EXHIBIT A DISGRACE

Then, almost before the ink of that story was dry, Borglum and the society (for reasons which vary according to the teller) were engaged in an even hotter conflict. According to Borglum, it arose from an attempt by him and some others to force a liberalization in the society's constitution. According to a witness to the affair, it centered around society criticism of Borglum's ethical conduct when competing with other sculptors for commissions. According to the society's official version, it had come about when Borglum accused John Quincy Adams Ward, a distinguished elderly sculptor and president of the society, of "insult and slander," and several other members of "brutality." Whatever its cause, this squabble led the society, in April of 1904, to rescind Borglum's membership, and it led Borglum to resign before notice of the society's action could be served upon him. Then, in the kind of parting shot that was to become one of his trademarks, he told the press that in matters of art, the National Sculpture Society might as well be called "The National Biscuit Company."

In the summer of 1904, several of Borglum's works were exhibited at the St. Louis World's Fair, where one of them won a gold medal. The question of which piece it was, however, is strangely confused. Borglum always claimed it was *Mares of Diomedes*, a dramatic group of stampeding horses, and it has been so listed in every Borglum biography to date. Nonetheless, the fair's records show the winner to have been *The Boer*, a piece Borglum had done while in England and which, according to a notation in his journal, had subsequently been lost. In either case, he did win a World's Fair gold medal, and from the springboard of that achievement went on to commissions of greater and greater importance.

One of these was a contract to do carved figures for New York's Cathedral of St. John the Divine—a fat contract calling for twenty-five full size statues and seventy-five lesser ones. Then, in 1907, he scored his first great coup. A large equestrian statue of General Philip Sheridan was to be erected in Washington, D.C., and in bidding for it Borglum was in competition with J. Q. A. Ward, who was perhaps the most influential American sculptor of his time and also the one with whom Borglum had had his National Sculpture Society fight. Borglum won the contract, and when the statue was unveiled in 1908 it was an immediate success. At that point, as one author later remarked, "as a sculptor Gutzon Borglum was no longer a rumor, he was a fact."

The early years of the twentieth century in New York, where he was seeking to gain recognition and make a reputation, were Borglum's whirlwind years—the most hyperactive years in his hyperactive life. With the boundless energy and inquisitiveness of a puppy, he was perpetually in motion, into everything, and constantly involved in controversy. He said, "I do everything, boxing, fencing, wrestling, horseback riding. . . ." "A man should do everything," Borglum declared, and he certainly tried to. He served on the New York Boxing Commission, joined the Aeronautical Club of America, the Architectural League, the American Numismatic Society, and was elected to membership in the exclusive Players Club. He joined the Association of American Sculptors and Painters and was elected its vice president; then he damned the association to the press by saying that in its exhibitions "only the miserable works of favorites are surreptitiously shown," and resigned. Borglum also courted the acquaintance of those who were rich or famous or both. In this he had the wholehearted assistance of Jessie Benton Frémont, and due in a large measure to her influence his efforts were successful.

Even though Borglum was an as-yet obscure artist, these activities together with his talent for stirring up verbal hornets' nests brought him newspaper coverage considerably greater than that given to his better known colleagues. And as might be expected, those colleagues were not pleased. "Borglum—I won't discuss him!" one of them tartly remarked. "That man is too much in the newspapers. He's always seeking publicity." Another, when later asked to comment on Borglum in those days, said, "Oh . . . he was a go-getter. He liked to be in the news. He followed important people." And a visiting English artist described Solon as "the famous Borglum," and Gutzon as "the notorious Borglum."

The thing was, Gutzon Borglum was absolutely determined to leave his mark on the world in every way he could, and especially as an artist. He said so himself, and said it often. He well knew that the best of artists often spend their lives in obscurity and poverty simply because they are not known and/or do not have "the right connections." Accordingly, Borglum intended to *be* known and to *have* the right connections, and in pursuit of that goal he was simply engaging in what now would be called "public relations." All too often, however, the methods he chose completely alienated those whom they did not completely win. Impetuous in approach, reckless in speech, inclined to fire public blasts at those with whom he had private disagreements, he left a host of enemies spluttering in his turbulent wake. But because Borglum was a man who found almost as much zest in a good fight as in a good friendship, and because this was a time when the current of his always powerful life-force was running at full flood, these may have been the most exhilarating years of his life. If they were not, it could only have been because running through them like a dark thread was his frustration at seemingly being unable, no matter what he did, to emerge from the shadow of Solon.

Gutzon and Solon both were doing outstanding work and turning it out in quantity. But Gutzon, in addition, was much in the news and often in the company of the prominent. Solon, on the other hand, was by nature quiet and withdrawn and kept pretty much to himself and his family. Hence, it would seem that Gutzon would have become the more prominent, but that was not the case. As late as 1911, when Gutzon had been a sculptor for nine years, the *Encyclopedia Brittanica* listed only Solon. It did mention Gutzon, but only in a line in Solon's biography that read, "His elder brother, Gutzon Borglum . . . also shows himself an artist of some originality." This was far more feeble praise than Gutzon's accomplishments deserved. But the truth was that despite Gutzon's very real sculptural achievements, to say nothing of the publicity he had received, when people in those days spoke of "Borglum the sculptor" they usually were referring to Solon. This was hard for someone of Gutzon's temperament to take. Moreover, it led to a serious rift between the brothers.

The problem was that prospective clients who did not realize there were two Borglum sculptors sometimes inadvertently called on Gutzon regarding projects they had meant to discuss with Solon. This led to a question of whether Gutzon had taken advantage of some such situations in an effort to secure the commissions for himself. Solon became convinced that in some cases, at least, Gutzon had done just that. Gutzon, on the other hand, insisted otherwise. He agreed that occasionally such situations did arise, but he declared time and again in letters and interviews that he was dedicated to helping his younger brother get ahead and would never dream of competing with him.

It is hard to say, now, just how much of Solon's suspicion, if any, was based in fact. There is some evidence to indicate, however, that Gutzon's contract for the Cathedral of St. John the Divine originally had been intended for

Solon. Also, there seems to have been a similar mix-up over a Monroe, Michigan, contract for a statue of George Armstrong Custer, with the result that neither Borglum received the assignment. But the situation that finally caused a complete break between the brothers, and which also indirectly led Gutzon to his greatest sculptural triumph up to that time, was not caused by this sort of confusion but rather by competition between them.

As it happened, the State of Nebraska was seeking a sculptor to do a massive statue of Abraham Lincoln for the Nebraska state capitol. Because it was a choice assignment and because the Borglums had grown up in Nebraska, both Gutzon and Solon applied for it and were eager to get it. Months then passed, during which the Nebraska committee remained unable to decide which of its several applicants to choose. Finally (according to a letter written by Solon), in early 1909 Gutzon invited Solon to come to his studio to discuss the matter. There, Solon reported, Gutzon asked him to withdraw his own application and to recommend Gutzon to the committee instead. Gutzon's reason, said Solon, was "that I had never made a Lincoln, and that I did not know the real soul of that great man." Upon hearing this, Solon was cut to the quick, stunned, and speechless. As far as he knew, Gutzon had never made a Lincoln either. The upshot of the affair was that neither brother received the assignment, and that they were no longer speaking to each other.

Meanwhile, although unbeknownst to Solon, Gutzon actually was "making a Lincoln." He was doing it on his own rather than on a contract, and he had begun it during the bidding for the Nebraska Lincoln. Hence, there can be little doubt that he had originally intended it as a model or demonstration piece to show the Nebraska committee. Whatever the case, from a block of marble in his studio Gutzon was carving a massive bust of the Great Emancipator. When the piece was finished it was exhibited in a Fifth Avenue store window in New York, where it was an instant success. Meanwhile, Borglum had written asking President Theodore Roosevelt if he would allow the bust to be displayed in the White House during the February, 1909, celebration of the centennial of Lincoln's birth. The president agreed, and once again the bust was a great success. It was then purchased and presented to the United States by Eugene Meyer, Jr., and was placed in the rotunda of the Capitol where it still may be seen today. It is a magnificent piece of work. In fact, when Lincoln's son Robert first saw it he exclaimed that it was "just like seeing Father again." As the first of Borglum's many Lincolns, it did much to establish him as a leading sculptor, and it was proof that he, indeed, was able to capture "the real soul of that great man."

It was while Borglum was working on the Lincoln bust that Liza at last divorced him. Shortly thereafter, on May 19, 1909, he married Mary Montgomery, who for some time had been his secretary. Borglum's career was shaped to a large extent by the influence of three remarkable, strong-minded women: Liza Putnam Borglum, Jessie Benton Frémont, and Mary Montgomery Borglum, and of these the influence of Mary was to be the greatest by far. Like Gutzon, she had a brilliant and wide-ranging mind. But, unlike Gutzon, she also was down-to-earth, practical, and organized, and thereby was able to serve as a counterbalance for her flighty and impetuous husband. She was so devoted to Gutzon and so dedicated to his welfare and advancement that, as one author was to put it, " . . . from now on, Mary Borglum made Gutzon Borglum her business. . . ." And in so doing she became and remained the stabilizer and mainstay of his life.

Her stabilizing influence, moreover, produced results almost immediately. As the first decade of the twentieth century came to a close, Borglum was embroiled in far fewer controversies than before; he and Solon were back on friendly terms; Gutzon and Mary had bought and moved to a beautiful wooded estate—which they named "Borgland"—near Stamford, Connecticut; Gutzon had plenty of work and was spending more of his time in attending to it and less in scattered and unrelated activities; and finally, as he remarked to a friend, he was "making a hell of a lot of money."

On April 9, 1912, Mary bore their first child, a son whom they named James Lincoln de la Mothe, and called "Lincoln." In 1912, also, Borglum became involved in national politics. Specifically, he became a key worker in Theodore Roosevelt's campaign against Woodrow Wilson for the presidency. Through an introduction by Mrs. Frémont, Borglum had met Roosevelt many years earlier, and during the 1909 White House showing of the Lincoln bust had visited with him again. Borglum liked Roosevelt and all that Roosevelt stood for. Accordingly, he now became the Stamford chairman of Roosevelt's new Progressive ("Bull Moose") Party. In addition, he stumped the state of Connecticut, appearing before student groups, factory workers, mass meetings, and in torchlight parades, speaking with all his oratorical power in praise of Roosevelt and in condemnation of Wilson. Roosevelt lost the election, but future events would show Borglum's time to have been far from wasted. For out of this experience he had gained a valuable understanding of a man whose face he one day was to carve upon the granite cliff of Mount Rushmore.

In 1917 the United States entered into the World War, and Borglum again embroiled himself in politics—this time as an investigator of the American aircraft industry. Long interested in aviation, and a member of the Aeronautical Club of America, Borglum believed himself to be an authority on airplanes. In later years, in fact, he would claim in his *Who's Who* biographies to be an "aeronautical engineer." Hence, when he heard rumors of mismanagement and inefficiency in American warplane production, he decided to look into the matter. Informally and entirely on his own, he visited a few aircraft factories and there saw enough to convince him that the rumors were true. Next, in November of 1917, he went to Washington to tell President Wilson about it.

Because of the sculptor's outspoken attacks upon him in the campaigns of 1912 and 1916, President Wilson already knew who Borglum was and did not think kindly of him—which probably explains the chilly reception Borglum received at the White House. A short time after he had arrived and stated his mission he was informed by the president's secretary that the president could not take the time to see him. Mr. Wilson was presently tied up in running a war and expected to be so occupied for some time to come, and he would therefore like Mr. Borglum to just leave a note stating the purpose of his call. Borglum did so and a short time later received from the president's office a suggestion that he go and explain the problem to the head of the National Aeronautical Board. Borglum promptly wrote back saying that the National Aeronautical Board *was* the problem, and that if it remained uncorrected it would bring "scandal and disaster" down upon the Wilson administration.

In response, the president asked Borglum to write a more detailed explanation of the problem, and to include suggestions for its solution. In a long letter, written on Christmas day, Borglum did so. He said that despite the government's enormous investment in it the aircraft industry had yet to deliver even one warplane (which was true), and he thought the president should appoint a board of three "competent, fearless, incorruptible" men to find out why. If done in time, Borglum continued, this would prevent an otherwise unavoidable "Congressional investigation of the aeronautical bodies" and the scandals that would arise therefrom. In volunteering himself to take charge of the investigation, Borglum said there were no "principles related to heavier-than-air machines" that he was not "thoroughly familiar with," and quoted Leonardo da Vinci in saying, "As for that art, I know all that is known." Moreover, Borglum continued, he was open-minded, unprejudiced, fearless, an accurate observer, and a good manager, and he believed he could straighten the aircraft industry out in time to avoid a public scandal.

At this point the record grows hazy. The president did not appoint the proposed board. He did, however, give Borglum a letter containing some sort of investigative authority, but the kind and extent of that authority is not clear. It did provide Borglum with a temporary office in the War Department, and with access to Stanley King, an assistant to the Secretary of War, for advice. On the other hand, strangely enough, there was no provision for expenses, and Borglum wound up having to pay most of the operation's cost from his own pocket.

Once appointed, Borglum moved quickly and within a month had produced a preliminary report. It was well done, and under other circumstances the president probably would have been grateful for it. As it happened, however, Borglum seems to have presented it to Mr. Wilson and his advisors with the indiscreet flourish of a cat bringing a mouse to its mistress while she is giving a formal tea. On top of that, while presenting the report he asked for blank subpoenas that would allow him to bring before the Senate Military Affairs Committee whomever he might choose to summon. And finally, during the brief time of his investigation, Borglum had stepped on so many official toes that his War Department contact, Stanley King, described him as "an uninhibited and unmitigated nuisance."

Taken all together, President Wilson found these things to be a bit more than he had bargained for. Accordingly, he told Borglum that he had misunderstood the extent of the authority given to him, and that now he would like for the sculptor to resign from the investigating business. When Borglum declined to do so, the president made a public announcement dismissing him. In turn, Borglum went public also. In a published letter he asked the president, "What is it . . . that you are afraid of? . . . What is it . . . that the President of the United States dares not face?"

Like many of Borglum's crusades, this one had somewhat resembled a comic opera, and yet it turned out to have done some good. As a result of it, President Wilson appointed a committee, headed by Charles Evans Hughes, to continue the probe. After a more orderly and detailed investigation, this committee reported that a number of Borglum's allegations were true. And this, in turn, led Borglum in his future biographical sketches to list as one of his major achievements that he had "investigated . . . and exposed the colossal aircraft failure."

At the time of that investigation, however, the event that was to lead Borglum to his greatest achievement and to alter forever the course of his life was already two years in the past. In 1915, members of the United Daughters of the Confederacy had asked him to carve on Georgia's Stone Mountain a memorial to the Confederate Army. Borglum accepted the job and thereby took his first step on the road that eventually was to lead him to Mount Rushmore and to the undying fame he so hungrily sought.

4. Stone Mountain Shootout

One day, no doubt, some scholar with a strong sense of humor and a taste for high-effort, low-yield research will patch together the complete story of the Great Stone Mountain debacle. Or, perhaps it already has been done and the result lies moldering in some forgotten file. Either way, one of the main conclusions reached through such an exercise would have to be that childishness is by no means limited to children. But even though the details of that ancient rhubarb are still considerably obscured by the dust it raised, we can with reasonable accuracy reconstruct some of its elements. Moreover, in any proper account of the creation of the Mount Rushmore memorial it is essential that we do reconstruct them, and at some length, for it was in the crucible of the Stone Mountain project that the Mount Rushmore project was forged. It was failure at Stone Mountain that produced success at Rushmore, and it was that failure, also, that very nearly destroyed the Rushmore project before it was really begun. Thus, to tell the story of Mount Rushmore without first telling the story of Stone Mountain would be to build a house without a foundation.

Just who first conceived the idea of carving a Confederate Memorial on Stone Mountain's granite flank is a fact now lost in the mists of time. Probably it was no single person. Considering how the mountain's cliffs stand like great blank billboards above the Georgia plain, and considering mankind's tendency toward carving its initials wherever such inviting empty spaces are found, the thought of carving *something* there must have occurred to many. Then, too, in the earlier years of the twentieth century, Southern memories of defeat in what the South called The War Between The States and the North called The Civil War were still bitter, and resentment of the subsequent humiliation of Reconstruction was still strong. Whereas the North at least had memories of victory to compensate for the bloody cost of that war, the once-proud South could only nourish the memories of glory long faded and erect monuments to a cause long lost. And wherever heroes to be commemorated and money to be raised could be found in the same place, the South *was* erecting monuments. It is likely, therefore, that the notion of carving some sort of Confederate memorial on Stone Mountain had been around for a long time. The first such suggestion on record, however, seems to be the one made in 1915 by an Atlanta newsman, John Graves. Probably because of its apparent impractibility, Graves soon dropped the idea, whereupon it was promptly picked up by another Atlantan, Mrs. Helen Plane. The national president of the United Daughters of the Confederacy and the widow of a Confederate surgeon killed in the war, Mrs. Plane at age eighty-five was still a pert little dynamo of woman who when she saw something that needed to be done set out to do it. And this, she thought, needed to be done.

As her first step, Mrs. Plane decided to get a sculptor's opinion of Stone Mountain as a place to carve a monument. This, in turn, brought Gutzon Borglum to Atlanta to see her. Just how this came about is not clear, but here again Gutzon's way seems to have been paved by Solon.

At that time, Georgians knew little about Gutzon but much about Solon. Several years earlier, the State of Georgia had decided to place on the capitol grounds at Atlanta a heroic statue of General John B. Gordon, and Solon Borglum had won the contract to do it. In The War Between The States, General Gordon had seen more action than any other commander, Northern or Southern. At "Bloody Angle" near Spotsylvania Courthouse he had led the charge that cost the Yankees more than 7,000 casualties. Later he had served Georgia as governor, then as senator, and had come to mean to that state in particular as much as Robert E. Lee meant to the South in general. Accordingly, the carving of General Gordon's statue was an important matter to the Georgians, and when it was unveiled in 1907 they could see immediately that Solon Borglum had given them even more than they had expected. In fact, when the general's daughter first saw the work she exclaimed, "The genius which could so catch the spirit of a man . . . is inspiration straight from God!"

By this means, Solon Borglum had made a name for himself in Georgia, and had become a close friend and frequent guest of the Venable family, owners of Stone Mountain and supporters of Mrs. Plane's dream of a Confederate monument there. Logically, therefore, it would have been Solon to whom Mrs. Plane directed her first inquiry, and she may have done so, for, years later, one of the Venable sisters told Solon's daughter, Monica: "Miss Borglum, when our family gave the land at Stone Mountain for a memorial to the army of the Confederacy, we did so believing that Solon and Gutzon would work on it together." Because of this, and because Solon did encourage Gutzon's effort at Stone Mountain but took no part in it himself, it seems likely that Solon was the first one approached; but not being as intrigued as his brother by the gargantuan and spectacular, he then passed the matter on to Gutzon.

In any case, on August 17, 1915, Gutzon Borglum arrived in Atlanta, met with the local chapter of the UDC, and found that the ladies had already settled upon a plan. They wanted him to carve upon the mountain a tablet twenty feet square, and upon that square to carve either a bust of Robert E. Lee or some written record of the war. Then, they showed him the mountain and asked what he thought about it. Borglum looked at its vast, curving granite wall—two thousand feet long, eight hundred feet high, and shaped like the side of an inverted bowl—and said, "Ladies, a twenty-foot head of Lee on that mountainside would look like a postage stamp on a barn door!" What did he think should be carved there, asked the Daughters. "I don't know yet," Borglum replied. "I'll have to think about it."

Borglum spent the next three days as a guest of the Venables at their home, "Mount Rest," close by the foot of Stone Mountain. During those three days he studied the mountain—its shape, texture, angles, and the way light and shadow played upon it. Then, as he sat one evening watching the mountain by moonlight, the inspiration came. He seemed to see drifting across the moon-washed cliff the shapes of that great gray army of long ago, its men marching strong and proudly as they had in the time when their hope was still bright and their cause still lived. In that moment he resolved to fix them there for all time, carved in stone for coming generations to see . . . and remember.

Next day, Borglum stood with Sam Venable before the mountain and described his vision and his plan. Up there near the top, he said, in that hollow just to the right of the crest, there would be artillery, its horse-drawn guns appearing to be coming over the horizon. Beginning immediately below the artillery, and sweeping down across the cliff from right to left, would be a stream of foot soldiers. And below that would be a column of cavalry, also marching from right to left. The infantry and cavalry would appear to be converging on a point directly ahead of the viewer and about two hundred feet up, where the cliff was at its maximum outward bulge. There, said Borglum, he would engrave the sculpture's crowning feature—a titanic grouping of mounted figures of the Confederacy's greatest leaders; say, Robert E. Lee, Jefferson Davis, and Stonewall Jackson. Venable looked at his mountain . . . then at Borglum (for whom he had developed a great liking) and said, dubiously, "It'll take an awful lot of rock!" It would indeed take a lot of rock, Borglum agreed, probably even more than Venable realized. "We-e-ell," said Venable, groping for a decision, "Well . . . All right! You can have it."

Upon returning to Atlanta, Borglum described his vision to Mrs. Plane and her sisters of the UDC, and they were delighted by it. But, they said, such a thing would require a great deal of money, and they could not imagine where that much money might be raised. No problem, Borglum assured them. No problem at all. This was to be a monument to the gallantry of the South and to the magnificent dedication of her men to a cause, and it was to be by far the grandest, most colossal piece of sculpture that had ever been carved anywhere at any time. The South would give massive support to such a monument—no doubt about it. Even the North would support it; Borglum, himself, would see to that. Delighted by these observations also, the ladies then asked if Borglum would come to the UDC national convention to be held in San Francisco in October and present his ideas there. He would. And when October came, he did.

While addressing that convention Borglum was at his oratorical best, which was very good indeed. In the sparkling language that flowed from the man with the rippling ease of water from a spring, he painted for the assembled Daughters a glorious vision. Upon that vast Southern cliff that once had been red-lit by the glow of Atlanta burning, and that had towered indestructibly above Sherman as he marched on his road of ruin to the sea, upon that cliff they now saw a carving of a valiant army of the Confederacy. In a massive pageant fifteen-hundred-feet long and four-hundred-feet high and covering more than twelve acres of vertical stone, he showed them a vision of that army and its leaders enshrined in eternal granite for future ages to see.

Naturally, the Daughters were spellbound. Many of them were old enough to remember the Carpetbaggered chaos of the Reconstruction, and more than a few were old enough to remember the agony and sacrifice of the war itself. One of the latter was Mrs. Plane. Seeking her missing husband after one of the war's early battles, she had driven a wagon over the field among the dead until she found his body, and she had by herself loaded his body in the wagon and taken it home. Thus, to the women at the convention, what Borglum was proposing was no abstract thing—no memorial to some intangible principle or ideal that, no matter how noble, had never been grieved over in the night. To those women, from whom the war had taken fathers, grandfathers, brothers, husbands, and sometimes even their homes, it was something personal, emotional, and immediate, and they were for it. Accordingly, they gave Borglum verbal authority to proceed with it.

During the winter of 1915–1916, Borglum worked in his Stamford, Connecticut, studio on preliminary plans and designs for the Confederate memorial. Disregarding the fact that he still had no tangible contract for the work and that as yet no one had raised any money for it, when spring came he gathered up his family and moved to Atlanta to start the work. Next, he hired an engineer named Major J. G. Tucker, from Bradenton, Florida, to serve as his assistant. Then he and Tucker began trying to figure out just how to proceed with this hitherto untried business of carving a mountain.

Their first problem was the matter of how even to get up to the stone to be carved; how to position men and equipment hundreds of feet up on a vertical wall in such a way that, once there, they could be safely and usefully employed. Borglum asked inventor Lester Barlow, of the Brown Hoist and Machinery Company of Cleveland, Ohio, for ideas. In response, Barlow dreamed up a great, complicated contraption of trestles, scaffolds, hoists, and elevators. Borglum was all for it at first, and even wrote a magazine article describing how he planned to use it. But when the cost of Barlow's monster turned out to be $200,000, whereas Mrs. Plane and the UDC had managed thus far to raise only $2,000, the idea was abandoned.

Next, Borglum and Tucker devised a system of lowering workmen to the carving area in sling-seats, with each seat suspended by a cable from its own individual winch. This, they found, was simple and inexpensive and it worked. To work well, however, this system required an operations and equipment base located on or very near to the actual carving area. For this, they proposed to affix to the face of the cliff a huge platform on which would be constructed a machine shop, power plant, and equipment storage. Access to the platform was to be provided by a long stairway of 480 steps leading down from the top of the mountain, and it was in the construction of that stairway that they began the actual work.

Just when the stairway was being completed, in the spring of 1917, the United States entered the first World War. Monument carving not being regarded as essential war work, that stopped the project. Tucker went into the army. Borglum moved his family back to Stamford and then went on to other endeavors—investigation of the aircraft industry being one of them.

When the war ended, Borglum was forced to contend with a distasteful set of financial realities. Before the war he had raised enough money for Stone Mountain to get the project started. He had not, however, raised it from among inspired Southerners and sympathetic Northerners, as he had told the Daughters of the Confederacy that he could. Instead, he had gotten it entirely from his own and Sam Venable's pockets, and he had had to put a heavy mortgage on Borgland, his Connecticut home, even to do that. Also, he had paid the cost of his aircraft investigation from his own pocket. Now he had a wife and two children to support (the second child, Mary Ellis, was born in Atlanta on March 25, 1916), as well as an elegant style of living that he was never willing nor probably even able to reduce, and he was deeply in debt. Thus, he found himself forced to forgo, for the time being at least, such exotic and financially risky enterprises as the carving of mountains, and, instead, he had to devote himself to finding and fulfilling those sculptural assignments more likely to produce prompt and cashable checks. Borglum did just that for the next four years, during which he produced some truly outstanding work.

The UDC, meanwhile, continued to seek financing for Stone Mountain but with no success. Finally, they gave up and turned the promotion of the monument over to a new group formed for that purpose—the Stone Mountain Monumental Association. In turn, this new association repeatedly asked Borglum to return to work on the project. At last, in 1922, he agreed to do so.

Just as before, he came with no firm contract for the work. Just as before, there was little money either in hand or in sight to pay for it. On the other hand, the eighteen members of the Association's executive board had been drawn from the cream of Atlanta's social and financial societies. Its roster read like a Georgia *Who's Who*, and to Borglum, who was always impressed by that sort of thing, that seemed to be security enough. Hence, he again moved himself and his family to Atlanta where, for a while, he again found himself financing Stone Mountain from his own pocket.

Borglum rehired Tucker and put him in charge of the project's engineering and construction work, and Tucker then set about repairing the old stairway, constructing the big platform on the face of the cliff, and installing machinery.

In his own part of the work, meanwhile, Borglum had run into a giant snag. A sculptor in a studio has an overview of the piece he is carving, and by his eye alone may guide his chisel as a painter's eye alone guides his brush. But sculpting a mountain is quite another thing. While working on the side of a mountain, a sculptor cannot see his overall design. He can see only the relatively tiny expanse of stone before his face, and his genius alone, no matter how great, cannot tell him what to carve there nor how to make that carving flow into his total plan. That information can come only from measurements and guidelines and paint-marked patterns. Thus, Borglum now had to figure out how to create from the pattern of his models a vastly enlarged duplicate pattern on the cliff, a pattern perfect in proportion and flawless in its details. Were this not perfectly done, the final carving would not be graceful and lifelike but soulless and coarse, and he would leave to future ages not a monument but a monstrosity—a giant cartoon etched on a stone billboard.

Borglum struggled with this problem for months. He kept returning to the idea of tracing the design from photo-slides projected upon the cliff at night. However, when he asked Eastman Kodak and similar manufacturers to build him a projector for that purpose, they all said it could not be done. He was asking for a machine of unheard-of power, one that would enlarge a slide image two-and-a-half *inches* square in the machine into a picture two hundred *feet* square on the mountain, a picture as tall as a twenty-story building and almost an acre in area. A light source strong enough to do that, they said, would generate an impossible amount of heat. In motion picture theaters, for example, pictures were projected over distances of perhaps a hundred feet and were shown, enlarged to about 50,000 times their original area, on a smooth, white, light-reflecting screen. To accomplish this, theater projectors required a light source so intense and so hot that only the rapid movement of the film past it kept the film from burning. Now, here Borglum was, asking for a machine that would project a *non*-moving picture *eleven* hundred feet, enlarge it to about a *million* times its original area, and have it show up clearly upon a wall of rough non-reflecting stone. It was doubtful such a lamp could be built, said the manufacturers; it was even more doubtful that a lens could be found that would withstand the heat from such a lamp; and it was certain that such a lamp would immediately burn up any photo-slide placed before it. No—the whole idea was ridiculous.

Had Borglum been sensible he would have agreed that the idea was ridiculous and would have given it up. However, when Borglum had his teeth locked on a problem he often was not sensible and so he did not give up. Instead, he persuaded E. S. Porter, of the Precision Machine Company of New York, to help him design and build such a machine. Together, they came up with a great ungainly contrivance in which the lamp assembly alone weighed a ton. And it worked. It did project from Borglum's small slides a picture covering almost an acre of cliff, and did it clearly and with no melting of the slide.

Next, Borglum traced on his slides with a fine, crow-quill pen the lines he wanted reproduced on the cliff. Then Tucker, dressed in white so as to be easily visible and carrying a bucket of white paint, was lowered in a sling-seat down onto the carving area. Borglum operated the projector, and by means of a telephone hookup he told the winch operator where to position Tucker on the cliff and told Tucker where he was and which lines to paint.

The system worked and worked well. Thanks to Borglum's stubbornness and ingenuity he now had a way of accurately transferring his designs from model to cliff, and that particular problem was a problem no longer.

During the time of this preparatory work, Borglum and the Stone Mountain Monumental Association both had been giving much thought to the overall scope of the Stone Mountain project and to what its ultimate limits should be. However, because Borglum tended to see himself as the commander of the enterprise and the association as being merely his assistant, whereas the association believed the opposite, their thinking was done pretty much independently of each other. As a result, they came to considerably different conclusions. And in so doing they planted in the Stone Mountain operation a time bomb that was to tick away undetected until the day when it would blow the project apart.

In Borglum's mind (as was usually the case when he thought about a project) the monument had been growing ever larger and grander. Thus, in addition to carving a gigantic frieze upon the mountain he was now planning also to excavate a huge cavern he called "The Hall of Records" within it. Conversely, and because of difficulties encountered in raising funds, in the minds of the association's executive committee the scope of the work had been growing ever smaller. Finally, they decided to limit the work (at least for the present) to the so-called Central Group consisting of the figures of Lee, Jackson, Jefferson Davis, and four other Confederate leaders not yet selected. The upshot of all this was that in the summer of 1923 the association offered Borglum a contract to complete the Central Group, to do it within three years and at a cost not to exceed $250,000; Borglum, with no intention at all of actually limiting his work to those figures, that time, or that cost, happily signed it.

As his final preparatory step, Borglum brought to the mountain an Italian artist named Hugo Villa. Formerly Borglum's assistant at his Borgland studio, Villa was himself a sculptor, and his job at Stone Mountain was to supervise routine carving operations. Then, with all the necessary equipment in place, and with Tucker and Villa to oversee the day-to-day engineering and sculpturing operations, on June 18, Borglum began carving the head of Lee . . . and hit another snag.

The problem this time was the efficient removal of stone. The studio sculptor removes stone by the ounce and the pound, but the mountain sculptor must remove it by the ton and tens of tons. Borglum began by having his workmen drill large numbers of closely spaced holes and then, with hammers and chisels and wedges, break away the stone between them. It took only a short time, however, for him to discover that by using this method he and his crew could hack away on Stone Mountain for the rest of their lives without leaving more than a few scratches to show for their labors. Dynamite was suggested as a possible answer, but a risky one. A misdirected blast could ruin the work of months. Even worse, blasting might fracture the underlying rock and thus render it unfit for carving, and whereas a studio sculptor can replace a spoiled block of marble, a mountain sculptor can hardly replace a spoiled mountain. Still, the choice seemed either to blast or to quit, so Borglum called on the DuPont explosives company for advice. In response, DuPont sent a blasting expert to the mountain. Experimenting, he and Tucker soon discovered that they could, in fact, safely adapt blasting to the needs of the sculpture, and could do it far better than they had hoped. By drilling lines of holes and loading them with light charges to be fired simultaneously, they could with one blast remove great sheets of excess stone. In doing the more delicate work, Tucker then found that by using mini-charges that sometimes contained no more than a half-ounce of dynamite, he could blast with safety to within a mere inch or two of the sculpture's finished "skin."

Once that problem was solved, the dam of difficulties that so long had restrained the work was broken, and all the hope and energy that had been pent up behind it were released in a powerful stream that picked up the work and swept it rapidly forward. Gone now were the hard days of doubt and frustration, replaced by days that were plump with confidence and accomplishment and that succeeded each other with the satisfied regularity of a procession of fat sheep. By day, the mountain's stillness was shattered by the iron clatter of pneumatic drills, and in the evenings by the whump and boom of exploding dynamite and the thunder of falling rock. And as summer passed into fall, and fall into winter, the head of Robert E. Lee began to appear on the mountain. Faintly at first, then more clearly, as if it had been there all the time, hidden inside, and was now floating slowly outward and pressing through the mountain's surface.

When they saw the profile of Lee emerging from the cliff, Georgians and others also began to see that the Confederate Memorial really was more than mere talk, and that it not only could be accomplished but was being accomplished. This, in turn, caused them to loosen their purse strings a little, although not too much, and a modest but steady stream of donations began flowing to the association.

The press, also, took note of the progress being made, and spurred by this evidence that the project actually was tangible and not just hot air, writers upended their thesauruses and poured out superlatives, which they arranged into feature stories that appeared in papers across the nation.

By late 1923 the technical problems had been solved, the work was progressing rapidly, publicity was flowing out and money was flowing in, and for those who were actively or emotionally involved with the great Confederate Monument these were days of satisfaction and harmony and hope. They were the golden days, and they lasted until just after the unveiling of the head of Lee.

The unveiling was held on January 19, 1924, which was the general's 117th birthday, and it was a spectacular event. It would have been so in any case; Borglum's unveilings always were. With his superb showmanship and flair for the dramatic, he saw to it that they were no less impressive than battleship launchings. Adding to the excitement of this one, however, were the size of the work, the publicity it had received, and the respect in which Lee's memory was held nationally and the reverence in which it was held in the South. And these things together made the event one of the most soul-stirring Atlanta had seen in a very long time.

For several days prior to the ceremony, newswriters and photographers, old Confederate veterans and young Confederate patriots, souvenir vendors, tourists, and an assortment of politicians and dignitaries all came swarming into Atlanta. On the day immediately prior, just before noon, Borglum led three southern governors and several other of the most prominent (and at the time perhaps the most nervous) visiting dignitaries down the long stairway from the mountain top, and then across a narrow catwalk to a platform mounted on the shoulder of the carving of General Lee. There they found a white-clothed table set with fine china and attended by waiters. And there, separated only by a plank floor from three hundred feet of vertical nothing, they were served a hot lunch of southern fried chicken.

The following day dawned mist-wet and chilly, which discouraged the curious crowd not in the least. By mid-morning the roads to the mountain were clogged with a damp tangle of autos, buggies, wagons, horses, mules, and pedestrians. The ceremony itself began just before mid-afternoon, and was opened with the inevitable speeches inherent in such occasions. Then Borglum picked up Mrs. Plane, who was now ninety-four years old and dressed in an 1860s costume, and carried her to the rostrum. She raised her hand. High on the mountain workmen pried away boulders securing two huge American flags. The boulders rumbled down and the flags parted to reveal a perfectly done head of Robert E. Lee. Across the throng of more than ten thousand gathered on the soggy plain there fell a stillness. Then, from a bent old man in a faded gray uniform came a piping cry, "By God! Hit's the Ginral hisself!" From somewhere there came a rebel yell . . . and then another

. . . and the crowd found its throat and its cheering was a rolling thunder. Leaning against Borglum, Mrs. Plane said, "I have waited long for this day," and wept.

That was the high point of the project at Stone Mountain—the culmination of its brief golden age of harmony and hope. Though imperceptibly at first, from then on it was in process of disintegration. Not because of technical problems, but because of human nature and the delicacy of human ego.

The first of the many conflicts now to plague the enterprise was probably the only one in which Borglum, himself, was not involved. It did, however, seem to involve almost everyone else who was in Georgia as well as some who were not. The question at issue was, who besides Lee and Jackson should be carved on the mountain? It was generally agreed that Jefferson Davis should be the third figure, and there agreement ended. Suggestions for the other four figures not only included all the most widely recognized Confederate heroes, but also a great many Kinfolks and Local Boys who had not been so recognized but should have been and here was a chance to do it. It was squabbled over in luncheon clubs, women's clubs, church groups, barber shops, pool halls, and in the Georgia legislature. Because he had yet to carve the rest of Lee, and Lee's horse, and Jackson and his horse—none of which were in dispute—the argument did not interfere with Borglum's work. But because donors were inclined to be generous only when assured that the monument would include their own chosen heroes, it did interfere with the flow of money to the project.

Soon, money became the basis of other problems. Not only was there not enough of it, but Borglum did not like the way it was being handled. The executive board was made up of gentlemen either to-the-manor-born or to-the-manor-risen, and they were accustomed to doing things in style. This included the operation of the association and its office, which in Borglum's opinion was soaking up a disproportionate share of the project income. Regarding any project dollar not spent by himself as being a dollar wasted, Borglum was put out and said so, bluntly. To these men, schooled in the old Southern courtesy that required arguments to be conducted gracefully and verbal daggers to be velvet-sheathed, Borglum's bluntness was more than distressing; it was "Yankee," which was synonymous with "crude."

The board also was upset by Borglum's frequent absences from the mountain following the unveiling of Lee. Borglum saw his relationship to the monument as that of a contractor to a building; so long as he produced it as and when promised, how he did so was his own business. He also felt that if he wished to carry on more than one project at a time, that, too, was his own business. He was right in feeling thus, for in truth he was a contractor with the association and not an employee of it. The board members, however, feared that Borglum's absences would damage the quality of the monument, or prevent him from finishing it on time, or both. Until it was completed, they argued, the memorial should be Borglum's daily business and his only business. Hence, when he left Stone Mountain more and more in the hands of Tucker and Villa while he, in the words of the board, "roamed at large" in quest of additional sculptural work and in political activities, the board became increasingly aggravated. He had even journeyed to South Dakota, they complained, and had even pulled Tucker off the job to go with him. And why? To look into carving on a mountain there a memorial which, according to rumor, was to be to the *Union!* Also, he had left Stone Mountain so as to wander about the country making campaign speeches for presidential candidate Robert LaFollette. And whereas Borglum's being a Republican was something these Southern Democrats thought unfortunate but could forgive, his leaving his work on the Confederate Memorial so as to campaign for a Socialist!—well, that was something they could not forgive.

Next, there came the half-dollar dispute. Like the idea of the monument itself, the idea of funding it by an issue of special coins is one of uncertain parentage. In the case of the coins, however, this is because the scheme ultimately succeeded and, therefore, was claimed by almost everyone connected with it, and especially by Borglum. The idea was to persuade Congress to authorize the minting of five million Confederate Memorial half-dollars that the association would then buy from the mint at face value and resell for a dollar apiece to collectors. As projected, the scheme would yield to the association, after expenses, a working fund of more than two million dollars.

Borglum, himself, took the proposal to Washington. He presented it to Senator Henry Cabot Lodge, who said it was "a good idea"; then to Senator Reed Smoot, who said it was "a noble idea"; and finally to President Coolidge, who said he would support it—and did. Unopposed in Congress, the ensuing authorization bill was signed by the President on March 24. Thereupon, Borglum settled down to preparing the coin's design, and found himself in a dispute with the National Fine Arts Commission (which was required to approve coin designs) over the proper shape for horses' legs and whether or not the legs of the American Eagle should be encased in feathered pantalets. The argument lasted six months and caused Borglum to redo his design nine times. In October, the design was at last approved, and coinage was scheduled to begin early in 1925.

To handle the financial end of the affair, the executive board meanwhile had persuaded the Federal Reserve Bank in Atlanta to purchase the coins when issued, and to hold them for piecemeal purchase and resale by the association. Borglum was not included in this negotiation, and there was no reason why he should have been. He, however, thought otherwise. Claiming he had been excluded so as to allow the board's members to rig the transaction in a way that would line their own pockets, he organized his own syndicate for the purchase and resale of the coins and then demanded that it, and not the Federal Reserve Bank, be appointed to handle the matter. This led the association's president, Hollins Randolph, to accuse Borglum of trying to rig the affair so as to line *his* own pockets. It appears, now, that both charges were without any foundation. Nonetheless, they had been made and they definitely were damaging.

December of 1924 brought still another blowup over money. Borglum claimed that the association still owed him for money he had spent on Stone Mountain prior to signing his contract, and that the association also owed him a fee for designing the memorial half-dollar. Altogether, he said, the association owed him $40,000.

The association claimed otherwise. It already had paid him $25,000 for those past expenditures and considered that debt settled. And the coin? Well, according to the executive board, Borglum, when promoting the idea, had said he would design it without charge. Therefore, said the board, the association owed Borglum nothing.

It did owe him!, Borglum responded. It owed him $40,000, and if he did not receive it immediately he would resign.

In that case, the board replied, there were some aspects of Borglum's contract that should be discussed. He had agreed to produce the Central Group, completely finished, for $250,000, and according to his contract this money was to be disbursed to him only in proportion to the amount of work completed at the time of payment. However, he had already been paid $77,000 for labor and materials, $50,000 for equipment, and $34,000 for himself. This came to $161,000, which was two-thirds of the total sum, and yet the work was no more than one-third completed. Therefore, the board told Borglum, even after adjusting for the cost of equipment (which was good for the entire job, but had to be paid for at the beginning of it), when we balance what you have received against what you should have received at this point, it appears that *you* owe *us* "something like $40,000."

It is hard to say, now, what the truth of the matter actually was. Later on, an audit was to reveal that the association's bookkeeping left much to be desired. Later on also, events at Mount Rushmore would reveal that when

Borglum was short of money he always managed to discover previously un-mentioned debts and fees and to demand that they be paid immediately. But whatever the case, the upshot of it all was that Borglum did not get paid and he did not resign, but he did continue to insist that he was being cheated out of $40,000.

Next, the executive board announced its intention to hire an associate sculptor for Stone Mountain. The reason, it said, was to have someone avail-able to carry on the job if anything should happen to Borglum.

No! Borglum flared back. He would tolerate no such arrangement.

Then, in January of 1925 the association voted to limit the Confederate Memorial to the Central Group alone, and to use the balance of the antici-pated two million dollars from the coins for unspecified "future purposes and causes." And that set off the time bomb.

Borglum blew up. Really blew up. Magnificently and completely. He had worked hard on the half-dollar project. He had contributed enormously to its success and probably had been essential to it. He had done so in the certain faith that the money would be spent on his work at Stone Mountain. But now, he declared, the executive board wanted to curtail the work just so it could steal the rest of the money from the coin issue. Being in no mood for half-measures, Borglum now wrote directly to President Coolidge asking him to hold up the half-dollar mintage until such time as the Confederate Memo-rial Association should come to its senses and allow Borglum to run the project in his own way and to build the monument just as he had originally designed it.

Time passed, and when it had become clear that the President was avoid-ing getting himself involved in the Stone Mountain spat, Borglum went to Washington to get the matter set straight. Shortly after his arrival there he held a press conference in which, with all his guns firing, he declared that: There were no funds left in the Stone Mountain treasury. . . . The Stone Mountain Confederate Monumental Association had "shrunk to a local habi-tation with scarcely a name." . . . The time limit for completion of the Central Group of the monument had expired (Actually, the Central Group contract still had two more years to run.) . . . "There is no contract for me to finish the work (That is, there was no contract for work other than the Central Group.), nor is the agreement [now] in effect equitable, or fair, or even [being] carried out as it is."

Delivered in Washington on February 21, Borglum's diatribe appeared in the Atlanta papers on the 22nd. Then it was the Stone Mountain executive board's turn to blow up, and it did. By the evening of the 24th it had drafted a resolution firing Borglum and had called for the following day a meeting for its formal adoption.

Upon getting wind of the board's action, Sam Venable wired Borglum in Washington, and Borglum promptly caught a train for Atlanta. He arrived in Atlanta on the 25th and was met by Tucker and Venable bearing the latest news, none of which was good. Tucker reported that the executive council had offered him a salary of $15,000 a year to take over and finish the Central Group according to Borglum's design, and that he had refused it. Following that, added Venable, the board had added to its resolution (at that moment being adopted) a provision for hiring "a sculptor of standing and reputation" to finish what Borglum had started.

Upon hearing that, Borglum flew into action. He was sure the board would require any new artist to proceed according to Borglum's design, and Borglum could not permit that. The result, no matter how poor, would still be known as Borglum's work, and he could not and would not allow that to happen. Accordingly, he rushed to his studio at the foot of the mountain, where he ordered a workman to take a hammer and destroy his big twelve-by-twenty-four foot model of the Central Group. Then he hurried up the mountain, climbed down to the working platform, and there pushed off working models of Lee's shoulders and Jackson's head onto the rocks below.

Next, the sculptor went to Venable's, where Mary was waiting. A few moments later, Tucker showed up with news that the executive board had already heard of the destruction of the models, and inasmuch as they regarded the models as being association property they had sworn out a warrant for Borglum's arrest, and a sheriff was even now on his way out to serve it. Taking Tucker with him, Borglum then jumped into an automobile and headed for North Carolina, some 120 miles away.

The details of their flight to North Carolina depend upon the storyteller. According to a later account by Mary Borglum, it was some time after they had gone that "a constable" appeared and "sheepishly produced" a warrant for the sculptor's arrest. According to the way Borglum told it, however, he fled with a sheriff's posse in hot pursuit:

I . . . picked up my personal effects hastily, got into a car, and got the hell out of there. I was pursued by these men who fired several shots at my car, punctured my gas tank, and only by the grace of God, Josephus Daniels—then a Raleigh newspaperman, and Angus McLean—then Governor of North Carolina (who said he would call out the militia if necessary), did I escape them.

Whatever the manner of his going, the next day found Borglum in North Carolina; the State of Georgia filing a $50,000 damage suit against him and calling for his extradition back to Georgia; and the governor of North Carolina refusing to grant it. It also found Borglum, who was in a fuming rage, and the executive board and various Atlanta political leaders, who had forgotten they were gentlemen, shouting insults across the border like children shouting across a schoolyard fence. The Atlanta City Council declared in a public resolution: "The City of Atlanta deplores the act of the sculptor in wantonly destroying the models and thus undertaking to prevent completion of this splendid effort. . . ." And Borglum retorted: "I destroyed the models for the greatest piece of sculpture in the world's history because I believe in the right of the artist to his own creation. I am ready to rot in jail before I concede this principle. Let the small provincial minds of my enemies contemplate the work of stone-cutters—or shoemakers if they wish. I am ready for a fight!" Said the Stone Mountain Executive Board: " . . . his loudly professed admiration for the valor of the soldiers of the South begins and ends at the door of the Association treasury. . . . His offensive egotism and his delusions of grandeur render it impossible to deal with him on any basis of fairness or common sense." To which Borglum shot back: "Why are they trying to crucify me! Think of their impudence! They fired me a fortnight after I served notice that I intended to ask for an accounting . . . of the Association's funds. . . ." "Borglum's lust for money is insatiable," cried the executive board. The board's actions constituted "the most remarkable piece of piracy in the history of the world!" shouted Borglum. And so it went, with neither side realizing that all their name-calling and wrangling was pointless because the Stone Mountain operation had already died—not with a bang nor a whimper, but with a snarl. Like the two Old Testament women brought before Solomon for fighting over the ownership of a child, the board and Borglum had been fighting over the "ownership" of Stone Mountain. Having no Solomon to bring them to their senses, however, they had pulled and hauled until they had torn the project apart, and whereas its body remained in Georgia its spirit had gone with Borglum.

Not realizing this, the association hired another sculptor to finish the work. He failed; possibly because, as it had been unable to do with Borglum, the executive board was continually peering over his shoulder and telling him what to carve and how to carve it. According to one usually reliable source, the board chairman even ordered this sculptor to chisel away the hat Borglum had carved on Lee. His reason: The monument was to be viewed by persons of both sexes, and "General Lee never would have worn a hat in the presence of ladies." This may or may not have happened, but it did happen that over a period of time Borglum's work on Stone Mountain was so butchered by the new sculptor that eventually it was removed altogether. Then, in 1928 the project was abandoned and not taken up again until after World War II.

Soon after firing Borglum, the executive board, to the astonishment of its members, found itself under attack from all sides. The nation's artists came to Borglum's defense, loudly proclaiming his right to destroy his models if he wished and roundly condemning those who would prosecute him for having done so. The national press, though conceding that Borglum was a hard man to get along with, generally came to his defense also. Moreover, many influential Georgians, including the Venables, sided with him and forced an audit that revealed that more than half of all the money the association had received had been spent for office and operating expenses instead of on the monument. As a result, the executive board began to feel about as unpopular as a skunk in a steam bath. Stung by this unexpected and (so they felt) unjustified disapproval, the board's members, together with a number of other Atlanta leaders, launched an expensive and almost hysterical campaign that appears to have been intended to preserve their reputations by destroying that of Borglum. And they made a special effort to destroy whatever chance Borglum might have had to go to the Black Hills to carve another mountain.

Borglum, meanwhile, was smarting, too, but for a different reason. He had the solid support of his fellow artists, the general support of the press, and substantial support in Georgia as well. But this was small comfort for his having lost his mountain and his dream of creating the world's most titanic piece of sculpture. He said in a letter to a friend that he felt like a mother who had lost her child, and that he was having days when "the world seems numb" and when he had nothing left "but the will to hang on." Even so, it was not in Borglum's nature to give up nor to allow such feelings to slow him down. Instead, he now set about trying to make sure of being engaged by those people who wanted a mountain-carving in South Dakota's Black Hills. For, he wrote to Doane Robinson, "I want the vindication it would give me."

5. Search for a Carvable Cliff

As the year 1924 grew old and white-drifted winter returned again to Dakota, snow settled upon the mountains in the Black Hills country and turned their dark-forested horizons to powder blue. Eastward, across the rolling golden-grassed plains, it gathered in the draws and in the lees of the hills, and the landscape became a broken, butterscotch pudding bathed in heavy cream. At Pierre, package-laden shoppers with smoking breath and quick, snow-creaking steps hurried gaily along the Christmas-crowded streets, streets along which Doane Robinson also walked—thoughtfully, however, and laden not with packages but with problems.

The reason for Robinson's sober mood (although he did not yet know it) was that he and all the others who were to become the reshapers of that as yet unknown mountain called Rushmore were, by that mountain, to become reshaped themselves. But whereas this reshaping was to be a future occurrence for the others, in Robinson's case it already had begun. When he first proposed the carving of a mighty monument in the Black Hills, he had never doubted that once his fellow Dakotans comprehended the greatness such a thing would thrust upon their state they would joyfully and unanimously spring to its support. Now, however, as he tramped the winter streets of Pierre, or sat in his office by the hissing radiator and gazed at the snow-dusted bluffs on the other side of the river, he was painfully coming to know that which politicians, preachers, and salesmen have ever known—to wit: no product, however beneficial, sells itself; and no cause, however noble, is self-sustaining. Such things, to be successful, must have behind them a steady driving force. In this matter of the Black Hills carving, Robinson had been trying to provide that force. Heaven knows he had been trying. He had talked about his envisioned monument wherever people had been gathered who would listen, and he had sent to the press a stream of releases that had inspirationally recounted the blessings to be derived from it. Occasionally, one of these would move some editor to produce an editorial on the subject. Generally speaking, however, after the first flood of headlines and stories following Borglum's September visit, press coverage of Robinson's proposal had dwindled to a mere trickle. In fact, about the only thing keeping the proposition alive in the press now was the clamor of those environmentalists who were trying to kill it.

As for the people of the state, at first they, too, had been stirred by the novelty of Robinson's proposal and by Borglum's eager endorsement of it. But their enthusiasm had not lasted very long and for a very good reason. Of all the states, South Dakota had been one of the latest to have been settled—so recently, in fact, that in 1924 most of its citizens were either children or grandchildren of pioneers, and there were many still living who had been the pioneers themselves. Understandably, therefore, they were still much influenced by the frontier philosophy that, as a matter of survival, no enterprise could be justified unless immediately productive or useful. Hence, their first excitement was soon replaced by a practical reality which said that *nothing* could be more pointlessly and expensively useless than a carved mountain. Accordingly, they soon dismissed the idea as a preposterous pipe dream and then forgot it altogether.

There were a few, to be sure, who were still pushing it. Out in Rapid City two civic-minded physicians, Doctors F. W. Minty and R. J. Jackson, were talking it up. The once-skeptical businessman Paul Bellamy had come around to supporting it, and Mayor John Boland was beginning to support it also. But these apostles were finding mountain-carving to be a difficult gospel to spread. Consequently, by the beginning of 1925, even in Rapid City interest in the project had become so slight that only twice in the preceding six weeks had the *Journal* even mentioned it.

On January 6, the *Journal* did finally carry another story on it—an interview with State Forester Theodore Shoemaker of Keystone. If Gutzon Borglum wanted to carve statues in the Black Hills, said Mr. Shoemaker, the folks at Keystone thought he ought to do it in their neighborhood because that was where the best granite was to be found. More specifically, he added, the best rock for carving would be found on Old Baldy Mountain, Sugarloaf Mountain, or on an obscure crag called Mount Rushmore. However, the story was not run to be taken very seriously . . . and it was not.

Thus, with the interest of both the press and the public having flickered out almost entirely, it was not a happy new year for Robinson. He felt as if he had been trying to start a fire with wet wood and was now about to run out of matches. Furthermore, the new legislature was to convene on January 6, and if he were to persuade it to pass the Mount Harney Memorial Bill now being prepared by Williamson and Norbeck, he needed a good deal more support than he now seemed to have.

That was how things looked before the legislature opened. Once it convened, they looked even worse.

The previous twenty years had been a period in South Dakota government that was later to be referred to as "the progressive era"—a period when the state, using public funds, had tried to be all things to all men and in so doing had gotten ahead of its time and behind in its budget. Some of the progressive era programs, such as workmen's compensation laws and mothers' pensions, had worked out all right; but others, such as the gasoline program, were now in trouble. A few years earlier, when the price of gasoline had gone to twenty-six cents a gallon, Governor McMaster had put the state, itself, into the gasoline business and had, thereby, forced the price of it back down to a more reasonable sixteen cents. Now, however, it had somehow crept back up to twenty-five cents, and irate voters were demanding to know why. Earlier still, Norbeck (during his governorship) had become concerned over the difficulty farmers were having in getting loans, and through an agency called the Rural Credit System he had put the state into the farm loan business. His program had worked well during the high-price years of the World War; but following the war, when crop prices plummeted and dragged land values down with them, the loans began to go bad. By 1925, the legislature had to face the fact that defaults on Rural Credit loans had put the state millions of dollars in the red. And that was not the worst of it. The worst was the bank insurance mess. In 1915, eighteen years before the Federal government was to get around to it, South Dakota had instituted a program for the insurance of bank deposits. But the same farm-value crash that had so hurt the Rural Credit System had been devastating to bankers. Caught with high-value loans on now low-value farms, South Dakota banks began tumbling like dominoes. Their failures had increased progressively from one in 1921 to 129 in 1924. Now, the 1925 legislature had to face the fact that the bank insurance fund was thirty million dollars in arrears—a sum which, in thinly populated South Dakota, was equivalent to sixty dollars for every man, woman, and child in the state. Consequently, confronted by a banking panic, Rural Credit losses, bank insurance losses, and the angry nagging of constituents demanding to know why gasoline cost so much, the legislators were feeling as flighty and full of woe as a herd of bull calves at branding time. Nor was it any easier to deal with the new governor, Carl Gunderson. He had inherited a mess, and in trying to deal with it he felt frustrated and harassed, and pulled in ten directions at once. Furthermore, because Norbeck had been a leader and spearhead of the Progressives, as well as the father of the Rural Credit System and godfather of the bank insurance plan, Gunderson held the senator personally responsible for the state's present predicament.

All things considered, there never could have been a worse time to ask the governor and legislature to appropriate $10,000 for such a tomfool project as surveying a mountain to see if it could be carved into statues. Nonetheless, Robinson proposed it anyhow and actually made some progress with it. As drafted, the Mount Harney Memorial Bill provided for (1) permission to carve a monument in Custer State Park, (2) establishment of a Mount Harney Memorial Commission to be headed by the governor, and (3) an appropriation of $10,000 for preliminary surveys and planning by Borglum. The bill was introduced in the second week of January and was referred to a committee for study. Then, such pro-carving forces as there were began to apply such political pressure as they could.

The strongest pressure, of course, came from the politically powerful Norbeck. He was a practical politician who had little hesitancy in granting political favors or, when the time was ripe, in collecting the debts arising from them. It was a characteristic dismaying to the straightlaced Williamson, who revered Norbeck in all other respects; and it led him to write in his diary that "[Norbeck's] worst fault was an effort to reward his political supporters. . . . He had much less scruples in reaching a desired end than I. . . ." Even so, Norbeck's influence now was not enough to budge Governor Gunderson, who figured he had already seen enough of Norbeck's spending schemes. With the legislature, however, it was a different matter. Without Norbeck's influence there, it is doubtful the Mount Harney bill could ever have been introduced at all.

Robinson was doing his bit also, buttonholing every lawmaker he could and trying with warm persuasion to melt their objections. And because Robinson was a much-loved and venerable old man, the legislators listened to him respectfully; but because they considered him to be more bookish than businesslike, they melted very little.

Meanwhile, three blocks down the street in the marble-columned lobby of the St. Charles Hotel, where most of the legislators stayed and where most of their vital decisions actually were made, Paul Bellamy was using a different approach. Bellamy, a pink-cheeked, big, blocky, busy kind of man, was a live wire and a go-getter. He was an argumentive extrovert and, as a first impression, a stranger might have thought him just another of those pushy and shallow small-town Babbitts whom Sinclair Lewis was currently immortalizing in his novels. Soon, however, such a stranger would find he had been mistaken. Bellamy was aggressive, a promoter, and a booster, but he was no Babbitt. He was a reader, thinker, dreamer, and at heart (though he tried to conceal it) an idealist. But, above all, Bellamy was a doer. His hero was Ulysses Grant, and in his home the red-and-green bound volumes of Grant's memoirs were always visibly displayed. Grant, Bellamy often remarked, was a dogged and determined man who when he had grasped the nettle of some difficult task, such as, say, the capture of Vicksburg, grasped it firmly, ignoring the pain, and never let it go until the job was done. Bellamy did the same. Years later, for example, Bellamy the visionary was to dream the impossible dream of getting the United Nations to establish its permanent headquarters in Rapid City. And unbelievable as it may seem, Bellamy the doer, with his Grant-inspired doggedness, was to keep little Rapid City in serious contention with such rivals as San Francisco, Philadelphia, and New York almost until the time New York was finally chosen.

At the moment, of course, that was still far into the future. And at the immediate moment, Bellamy was cornering legislators opposed to the Mount Harney Bill, and was attempting to demolish with a verbal snowplow the arguments Robinson had failed to melt with verbal sunshine. Unfortunately, his own dogged and determined efforts were not effective enough to get the bill moving either.

Stuck between forces neither strong enough to move it nor to kill it, the Harney Bill remained in committee throughout January. Also in January, Borglum again visited Norbeck in Washington, and again he caused the senator to arch his eyebrows. He had decided to have the Stone Mountain half-dollars sold for five dollars each instead of one dollar, and thereby raise twenty million dollars instead of five million. With that sum, he continued, he would expand the Stone Mountain Park from its present twenty-two acres to ten thousand acres in which he would build "assembly halls as large as any in the United States, also amphitheatres, highways, and whatnot."

"This stuff sounds too dreamy for me," Norbeck wrote to Robinson after the sculptor had gone. "Evidently he is not one of those artists who are going to die and wait a century or two for recognition. He is going to get a good deal of it as he goes along." Even so, Norbeck added, "He is one of the great artists of the world. . . . We must respond at this time or forget it until another opportunity comes along, which may be . . . in a century."

But back in Pierre, despite the efforts of its supporters, the Harney bill was killed early in February by the committee. The committee members had been willing to authorize the carving of a Dakota mountain, but they simply could not bring themselves to spend Dakota money on it.

As far as Robinson was concerned, that was the end of his dream. He had spent himself on it, he was tired, and there were other things he had to do. He had recently been given the job of preparing a special census for the state, and furthermore, his carving promotion had caused him to fall behind in his work on a South Dakota encyclopedia that he was also preparing for the state. So let the shortsighted legislators pass up this opportunity for greatness! He would quit. Hence he wrote Norbeck, "the conduct of the committee was the big legislative disappointment of my life. . . . Without committee support and with the governor unfavorable . . . the proposition is hopeless."

Norbeck replied by telling Robinson not to give up now, but instead to cut the requested appropriation down to $5,000 and get the bill reintroduced. This Robinson managed to do, and again the bill was referred to committee, but this time it received better treatment and was placed on the senate calendar for a vote on February 24. Unfortunately, however, this was precisely when, a thousand miles away, relations between Borglum and the Stone Mountain Monumental Association had reached the breaking point, and the Stone Mountain timebomb finally exploded.

The first noise from that explosion reached Robinson on February 22, as he was leafing through the afternoon paper. Suddenly, his eyes caught and froze on an account of that recklessly outspoken news conference Borglum had held in Washington on the previous evening. In shock, Robinson promptly wired the sculptor:

> ASSOCIATED PRESS SAYS YOU ANNOUNCED IN WASHINGTON LAST
> NIGHT THAT NO FUNDS REMAIN FOR CARRYING OUT YOUR PLAN
> AT STONE MOUNTAIN. THIS STATEMENT WILL BE FATAL TO OUR
> MOUNT HARNEY BILL NOW NEAR HEAD OF CALENDAR. WIRE
> SITUATION. . . .

Despite the fact that the report was true, Borglum replied on the following day by saying:

> THERE ARE PLENTY OF FUNDS AVAILABLE FOR THE MEMORIAL
> WORK. ACTUALLY MILLIONS HAVE BEEN OFFERED. THE TROUBLE IS
> THAT THE LOCAL COMMITTEE RESISTS NATIONAL REPRESENTATION
> ON THE BOARD. . . . THERE IS NO TROUBLE OVER THE WORK OR
> THE COIN.

Finding Borglum's message too brief to be helpful, Robinson wired back for more details—but it was too late. The Borglum story had come as a perfectly timed excuse for the legislators who did not really want to pass the Harney Bill anyhow, and on February 24 the bill was defeated.

Grasping at straws now, Robinson, Norbeck, and the memorial's other promoters decided to settle for whatever they could get; immediately they had the Harney bill resubmitted as simply an authorization for the carving— providing for no appropriation of money at all. A few days earlier this kind of bill would have sailed through the legislature unopposed, and except for the continuing eruption of news from Stone Mountain it still would have. But now stories of the Stone Mountain fuss were appearing daily on the front pages of South Dakota's newspapers. Typical were the headlines from the *Rapid City Journal*:

February 26
BORGLUM'S ROW WITH
STONE MOUNTAIN MEN
ENDS IN HIS RELEASE
Sculptor Says They Resent
National Aid; They Say
He Wrecks Plans

February 27
FOUR STATES
ARE LOOKING
FOR BORGLUM
Claim He And His Chief
Aide Have Destroyed
Stone Mt. Model

February 28
"I WILL ROT IN
JAIL BEFORE I
GIVE UP PLANS"
Borglum

March 1
(A false report)
BORGLUM FOUND
AND ARRESTED
Georgia Will Try Him For
Malicious Mischief

Such headlines and their accompanying stories were strong stuff. Daily they led more and more legislators to believe that Borglum was a wild man who should never be turned loose with his chisel in the Black Hills. At the same time, the monument's environmentalist opponents seized on the stories with such gleeful thunder that even the few strongly pro-carving legislators began to waver.

With this turn of events, Norbeck got his back up. Convinced that the proposed memorial would be of immeasurable benefit to the state, he now bowed his neck in determination to get it carved no matter what. In writing to prop up the wilting Robinson, he said:

> To say that I am disgusted with the Gunderson administration is putting it mild. The defeat of the Harney Memorial appropriation makes me feel like "going off the reservation."
>
> The Borglum matter seems to have come to a climax. . . . Borglum felt himself all-powerful and did things with a high hand. . . . His plans are not all sound, but he is a great artist.
>
> I am today in no mood of quitting: I feel like fighting all along the line. . . . I can make the politicians so darn much trouble they will be glad to take care of the park in order to have peace. . . . I am determined to take on a real fight.

At the same time, Norbeck told the Washington press:

> Borglum is one of the greatest, if not the greatest, sculptors in the world. . . . He could command vast fortunes every year with his chisel. . . . But Borglum has reached the stage in life where he wants to be in on the biggest task of its kind in the world . . . and to leave behind him monumental works that will stand for all time.

Just as Norbeck intended, the story was picked up by the South Dakota papers, and as he had hoped, most of the influential ones now joined him in endorsing both Borglum and the proposed monument. This, in turn, slowed the tide of opposition, and prospects for passage of the revised Harney bill again seemed fairly good.

Then the Stone Mountain Association took a hand in the game. After it had fired Borglum from its mountain, the association seemed determined to keep him from carving any other mountain, and at the end of February it sent to almost every public official and community leader in South Dakota a copy of the resolution it had passed when it dismissed the sculptor. In 2,600 words of purple prose the resolution charged Borglum with neglect of duty, "offensive egotism," trying to seize control of the association, "exploiting himself to the discredit of the Association," fault-finding, "delusions of grandeur," lying, and "being impossible to deal with." These were only a few of Borglum's faults, the resolution continued, but his others were not being listed because "the other particulars would require pages to catalogue."

To reinforce these accusations, the association also sent a roster that not only named the members of its executive council, but gave their pedigrees. All were Southern born; all were of Confederate descent; most had one or more distinguished ancestors; all but three of the eighteen were bankers, lawyers, corporation presidents, or "capitalists"; and therefore (so the roster implied) all were men of such impeccable credentials that neither their word nor their judgment could be doubted.

Surprisingly, considering the strength of this material, insofar as turning the Dakotans against Borglum and the Mount Harney Memorial was concerned, the mailing was a failure. Interviews with people who actually received the Stone Mountain mailing, together with research of correspondence concerning it, have revealed the probable reasons why. According to its own statements in the membership roster, the Stone Mountain executive committee was fairly dripping with aristocracy, and whereas in the long-settled areas of the South or East this might have counted in its favor, in recently settled South Dakota it was the other way around. Dakota's society was still grass-roots new and rough around the edges and consisted mainly of farmers, ranchers, sheepherders, cowpunchers, and shopkeepers. A large number of these were children of European peasants who had come to the United States for the precise purpose of escaping domination by an aristocracy. Thus, in a kind of reverse snobbery the Dakotans of that time were inclined to view the socially elite and all their works as being highly suspect.

Even more damaging to the association's case was the wording of its resolution condemning Borglum. The Dakotans of the 1920s (again probably because of their recent pioneer heritage) were generally a laconic people who thought understatement a virtue and overstatement a vice; and where overstatement was concerned, the Stone Mountain resolution was a masterpiece. It struck a great many of its Dakota readers as one of those childish temper tantrums that they found embarrassing when displayed in private and unforgivable when displayed in public. Hence, they concluded that if this were a sample of the Stone Mountain Association's usual behavior, no wonder

Borglum was having trouble with it. The upshot was that although the Stone Mountain broadside did agitate South Dakota's conversational waters, it did nothing to sink either Borglum or the Mount Harney bill. On the contrary, it may have sunk some of the opposition instead, for only a few days after its appearance the Mount Harney bill was passed by the legislature, and on March 5, 1925, the governor grudgingly signed it.

Once the bill was signed, Norbeck, Robinson, and the other supporters discontinued all public activity connected with the Mount Harney project. Like prospectors keeping a gold strike quiet until their claim can be recorded, they knew the bill was not yet out of danger. Its opponents had until June first to petition for a referendum. If they did so and were successful, the bill could not become law without first having been approved by a public vote at the next election. Otherwise, the bill would automatically become law on July first. Accordingly, the promoters now tried to avoid doing anything that would get their opposition stirred up.

No longer being prodded by the monument promoters, the local papers now turned their attention to such things as the alarming national increase in drug addiction, which one paper called "The Menace of Dope," and "the nation's number one problem"; and to the degeneration of youth, with one editor pointing to the latest hit song, *Doo Wacka Doo*, as yet another example of how low the younger generation, already debauched by rumble seats and hip flasks and dancing the "Charleston," had sunk.

Borglum, now living temporarily in North Carolina, was also keeping quiet about the project. In his case, however, this was because he was still so busily occupied in trying to take control of Stone Mountain, and he was not keeping quiet about that at all. In early March he reported by wire to Robinson:

THE GREAT SOUTHERN MEMORIAL HAS BECOME SO IMPORTANT TO BUSINESS THAT A GREAT FIGHT IS ON TO GET POSSESSION OF ITS ASSETS AND ROB IT AND BECAUSE I RESIST TO WRECK ME. . . . MY ANCESTORS WERE DANES SO I DON'T WRECK EASILY. . . .

Some time later he wired another report:

AM MAKING A GREAT FIGHT HERE AND SHALL WIN OUT. ALSO MEAN TO CARRY ON YOUR WORK IF IT IS DEFINITELY OFFERED TO ME.

Meanwhile, Stone Mountain was fighting back, and in mid-March fired a second literary broadside. This tirade filled an eight-page booklet and was sent to every Dakotan who might be considered a leader. "We hope it will not be necessary to say more about Borglum," the booklet began, then used 4,000 words to say more anyhow. It repeated the accusations in the previous resolution and added some new ones, such as that Borglum for his own benefit had planned to establish on Stone Mountain "road houses, dance halls and billiard parlors," that he was "subject to fits of ungovernable rage," and that "his objectives and methods are those of the Hun." This blast, however, proved to be even more of a dud in South Dakota than had the previous one. The *Daily Huronite* responded with an editorial strongly supporting the carving. The *Lead Call*, which previously had opposed the project, now came out in support of it also. Senator Norbeck gave *The New York Times* a statement strongly endorsing both the Mount Harney project and Borglum. And so far as Dakota was concerned, that was that.

In mid-April the Stone Mountain Association appointed a sculptor named Augustus Lukeman to finish the Confederate Memorial and thereby, so it thought, closed the door on Borglum's efforts to get the enterprise back. Borglum, however, took the association's action not as a defeat, but merely as a setback. At the same time, he thought it advisable now to try to get the Black Hills job nailed down; otherwise, instead of having two mountains to carve, he might wind up having none. Accordingly, he wrote to Robinson:

> I am writing to you to suggest we take up the Mount Harney work as soon as possible. . . .
>
> The Stone Mountain affair may not adjust itself in six months to a year. . . . No sculptor of standing would take the position, every able man in America refused, and thank God every Christian. They got an ordinary workman in New York. . . .
>
> The Association will probably be involved in frightful legalities and a feudal struggle. Then . . . it will send a Committee to wait on me and ask that I come back. No man can say what he will do after that length of time . . . [so] if you are wise you will get me absorbed in your subject as quickly as you can. . . .

Robinson replied that until the deadline for a referendum petition had passed he and the others were doing nothing but "sitting tight." Such being the case, Borglum then went to Omaha to bid on a job that, he said, might be "worth a quarter of a million," and from there went to Texas to negotiate a contract for a work to be called the Texas Trail Drivers' Monument.

As the weeks flowed past, the Mount Harney project remained shrouded in silence. June first came, with no petition for a referendum. Then it was July, and the Mount Harney bill was law, but that, too, passed almost unnoticed. The Norbecks were summering at Valhalla, their rambling mountain lodge near the Needles, where the senator was taking a much-needed rest. Williamson was at the summer home he was building in the Black Hills on Iron Creek, and he was too busy constructing a fireplace and a bathroom to concern himself with monuments. Robinson was tied up in finishing the special census the governor had asked him earlier to prepare. According to the Mount Harney bill, the governor now was supposed to appoint a Mount Harney Memorial Commission and serve as its chairman, but he was still preoccupied with the state's financial woes and with voters who were still giving him fits about the price of gasoline. The state's newspapers were engrossed in doing stories about a fiery and fascinating trial in Tennessee where the silver-tongued William Jennings Bryan and the brilliant Clarence Darrow were, respectively, prosecuting and defending John Scopes, a high school teacher charged with the crime of having taught the theory of evolution.

Thus, lacking money, action, organization, or public interest, the Mount Harney project drifted, hazy and formless as random smoke, into midsummer and beyond. Robinson and Borglum did continue to correspond about it, and Robinson in his letters spoke much about money—how much might be needed and where it might be found—and he thought that somewhere there might be prominent men who would be willing to finance one carved figure each in exchange for the immortality an accompanying carved inscription would give to their names. And since much of William Randolph Hearst's fortune had been made from Black Hills gold, Robinson thought Hearst might agree to underwrite, say, the figure of Washington.

Borglum, in his letters, gave estimates of the cost of the monument, but his estimates kept changing—$800,000, $400,000, $1,000,000. He seemed airily unconcerned about where the money was to come from and appeared to believe that at the appropriate moment it somehow would drop from heaven. When he did speak of raising it, he talked about having the government issue a memorial coin, a "Federal Dollar," to be resold to collectors for five dollars. His general attitude, however, was summed up when he wrote in late June, "I am not worried about the money—whether it costs half a million or a million-and-a-half will really matter not in the least."

What did matter to Borglum was getting the operation moving again. At the end of July, when the project was still stagnating, he decided to act. He told Robinson and Norbeck that in a few days he would return to the Hills, find a mountain to be carved, and begin surveying it. Unwilling to become morally bound by obligations for which there was as yet no money, organization, nor contract, they tried to talk him out of it . . . and failed. Then they tried to get him at least to wait until they could scrape together enough money to pay for his trip, and failed again. He was going to come now, Borglum said, and at his own risk.

That sort of attack on obstacles—a sudden cavalry charge with flags flying and bugles blowing—was typical of Borglum throughout his career. When it worked, it accomplished wonders. When it failed, it was disastrous. This time it worked. Without it, in fact, the Mount Rushmore operation might well have faded and died before it was ever started.

At Borglum's insistence, Robinson and Norbeck agreed to meet him in Pierre on August 10. There they called on Governor Gunderson, and before the day ended they had gotten him at last to organize and give life to the Mount Harney Memorial Commission. Next, on that same evening, accompanied by his son Lincoln and Senator Norbeck, Borglum boarded a train for the Black Hills.

His trip was beautifully timed. The public mood in South Dakota was inseparably linked to the fortunes of agriculture, and for agriculture the summer of 1925 had been a good one. As Borglum's train rattled westward on the morning of the eleventh, it passed herds of red cattle grazing plumply on olive-green hills, haystacks standing thick in stubbled alfalfa fields, and wheatfields studded with grain-heavy shocks. For a finishing touch, there had been a heavy rain at Rapid City the night before, and, because of it, Borglum's party stepped from the train at Rapid City into air that was sparkling clean and tangy with the scent of pine and with the mountains standing sharp-edged and blue against a cloudless sky. Altogether, both to Borglum and the crowd that greeted him, it was a day and season in which all things seemed possible.

As upon his arrival the previous year, a luncheon at which Borglum was to speak had been planned. This time, however, so many people were waiting to hear him that the meeting had to be moved at the last minute to the Baptist Church; it had the only auditorium in town large enough to accommodate them all.

Borglum's speech was a smashing success, and the reason was that he told his listeners exactly what they wanted to hear. Seven other states were "begging" him to carve one of their mountains, he told them, but he had chosen instead to carve one in the Black Hills. The Stone Mountain work would never be finished, he continued; its promoters had destroyed it with their own greed. And even though it was true that he was going to carve a great monument on North Carolina's Chimney Rock, it would be nothing compared to the one he was going to create right here in the Black Hills. For it was here, Borglum declared, that he had chosen to build the true "Great American Memorial." No, he was not going to deface the Hills, as some had charged. And, no, "the Needles must not be touched. . . . There never has been any intention of touching them. . . . Instead, we want to go back into the Hills, find some now unknown massive stone and carve these figures upon it." Then he said (even though the matter actually had not even been debated, let alone decided) that the figures to be carved were "to be those of George Washington, Thomas Jefferson, Abraham Lincoln, and Theodore Roosevelt." Once this had been done, he asserted, "The whole world will speak of South Dakota."

Had Borglum stopped at that point, the history of the Rushmore memorial would have been considerably different. Instead, unfortunately, he made a statement that for years to come was to cause an immense amount of trouble for both the monument and himself. "You are not asked to spend a dollar on this project!" he declared. "You are asked only to understand it."

After the luncheon, Norbeck drove Borglum and Lincoln to the Game Lodge, a luxurious little resort hotel some twenty miles by road southeast of Harney Peak, where the sculptor intended to stay while searching for a carvable cliff.

The story of that search has been told many times, and in the process has acquired a good deal of embroidery that was not present in the original fabric. As it is often told nowadays, and as Borglum himself sometimes told it, he and Lincoln, riding horses and leading mules loaded with camping gear, rode into the Hills and explored their way through (as one author put it) "a pathless . . . almost impenetrable wilderness." Then, after two full weeks of "clambering over seemingly inaccessible mountains," the sculptor found himself face-to-face with, and instantly recognized, the mountain to be sculpted.

The truth is, however, it took Borglum only three days to find his mountain; during that time he was "camped" not in the wilderness but in a hotel; and he was taken to his mountain by the state forester who, months earlier, had told the *Journal* it would be a good place for Borglum to do his carving.

As it happened, Norbeck, Borglum, and Lincoln arrived at the Game Lodge on the afternoon of the luncheon. Next morning, Norbeck drove them and the superintendent of Custer State Park, Colonel M. L. Shade, to

Sylvan Lake, which lies in a hollow at the edge of the Needles and a little below the crest of Harney Peak. On horses rented from the Sylvan Lake stables, they rode up onto the peak itself. From there, Borglum was able to survey the entire high granite area and select formations he thought worthy of close investigation. After descending from the peak, they spent the rest of the day inspecting those of Borglum's selections that lay nearby. On the next day, Borglum returned to investigate the Sylvan Lake area further. Senator Norbeck had been called to the eastern part of the state on business, but Colonel Shade returned with Borglum, and it may be that State Forester Theodore Shoemaker accompanied him also.

"Thee" Shoemaker was a small dark man who wore a big black moustache, rode a big black horse named "Highpockets," and who bore a striking resemblance to the famous Civil War general Philip Sheridan. Like Sheridan, Shoemaker was touchy about his size, and so even though in private he found it expedient to mount Highpockets from a stump or chopping block, he would never do so in public. Shoemaker was an old Black Hills hand who could spin colorful tales of such early day characters as Calamity Jane and Wild Bill Hickok. But the important thing about Shoemaker in this instance is that it was he who had first identified Old Baldy, Sugarloaf, and Mount Rushmore as likely sites for Borglum's monument.

Although we do not know for sure if Shoemaker was with Borglum at Sylvan Lake that Thursday, we do know that the two met at Keystone on the following morning so that Shoemaker could show Borglum the mountains he had been talking about.

Their trip was not a long one—at least not in distance. From Keystone they rode westward along the Battle Creek road for a mile or so, then rode southwestward up Lafferty Gulch. In its mere mile-and-a-half of length, Lafferty Gulch climbs almost a thousand feet, and rising from its western wall like molars from a giant jawbone are the three granite buttes that Shoemaker had in mind.

Borglum liked Old Baldy and said it had definite sculptural possibilities. He was less impressed by Sugarloaf, but when they reached the very top of Lafferty Gulch and there found themselves facing the great cliffs of Rushmore, Borglum became excited. The main wall, perhaps four hundred feet high and five hundred or so feet long, was big enough for the work he had in mind, and its granite appeared fine-grained enough to accept carving. The wall was divided by four deep angling fissures, but inasmuch as they were fairly evenly spaced it was probable that the carved figures could be fitted between them. The setting—as important to a sculpture as the frame is to a painting—was of stone battlements towering above wild-flowered slopes and green timber, and it had about it a feeling of both freshness and eternity. In addition, the cliff faced to the east, which in Borglum's opinion was the best of all directions for a favorable play of light and shadow upon whatever might be carved there. Adding it all together, Borglum decided he had found his mountain.

Upon returning to Rapid City that evening, he told the *Journal* that Mount Rushmore was perfect for his purpose and that he knew of "no piece of granite comparable to it in the United States." Therefore, it would be upon Mount Rushmore that he would create "The Great American Memorial." The work would cost a million dollars, he said, but that would be no problem. In fact, the money already had been found—"a number of eastern money-kings have already been interested and promises of large donations have been secured."

4. The original Rushmore cliff.

5. Borglum and his son Lincoln in Keystone, South Dakota, the day they climbed Mount Rushmore for the very first time.

His report to the *Journal* notwithstanding, Borglum knew that he would have to examine Rushmore a good deal more closely before he could really know if it were carvable. For this reason he began making arrangements to establish at the foot of the mountain a camp from which he could make detailed studies of the mountain's structure. To set up the camp he engaged Ray Sanders, a big, talkative cowboy who wore a hat so enormous that from a distance he somewhat resembled a long-stemmed mushroom. Although Sanders was later to become a remarkably successful businessman, his main claim to fame then (or so he loved to tell Custer Park visitors) was that, be-

cause of a certain piece of farm equipment bought by his father years earlier, he had been the first person ever to operate a manure spreader in Pennington County, South Dakota. The reason Borglum chose him, however, was because Sanders at that time was, in his own words, the State Park "horse, buffalo, and dude wrangler."

In preparation for Borglum's camp, Sanders amassed an impressive accumulation of outdoor equipment and a string of packmules to carry it. Next, he gathered up a string of saddle horses for use by the various people whom the sculptor had invited to ride along with him when he returned to the mountain. Then, on Sunday, August 16, Sanders led the whole collection to Keystone, where Borglum's Rushmore expedition was to be assembled the following day.

Early next morning, Gutzon and Lincoln Borglum, Colonel Shade, and "Thee" Shoemaker gathered at Keystone, where they were joined by the Reverend Carl Loocke of Keystone, a physician named G. S. Adams, Doane Robinson, and, of course, Sanders, who was already there with the horses and equipment.

The morning was still young when Borglum's little troop rode out of Keystone, and, as revealed in pictures taken by Loocke, they were all in a holiday mood. After perhaps an hour of riding, the party arrived at the base of the Rushmore escarpment, where everyone—including thirteen-year-old Lincoln and sixty-nine-year-old Robinson—set out to climb it. That was not an easy task, for even though the climb was made at the cliff's lower northern end, it still involved some scaling of vertical walls. Nonetheless, it was eventually accomplished, and when the climbers had reached the top of Borglum's chosen cliff and lay there resting on its sun-warmed stone, their holiday mood had changed to one of quiet wonder.

That portion of Rushmore's crest on which they found themselves was a small table some four hundred feet long and possibly a hundred feet wide at its widest. It was completely cut off from the rest of the mountaintop by a little canyon—a boomerang-shaped stone slot that was sheer-walled and grass-bottomed and was, perhaps, eighty feet deep and thirty feet wide.

6. Borglum planting the American flag on top of Mount Rushmore, with ex-cowboy Ray Sanders, who set up Borglum's first camp at Rushmore, and (possibly) Lincoln Borglum.

Bounded behind by this canyon and in front by the edge of the main cliff, the table was triangular in shape, and its naked stone surface, crosshatched by crevices of assorted sizes, was uneven and lumpy. But the striking thing about that part of Rushmore's crest was the view. The table on which they were resting was nothing more than the squared-off tip of a four-hundred-foot cliff, the cliff itself rising from a high shoulder of the highest mountain in the United States east of the Rockies—Harney Peak. Thus, it gave Borglum and the others a sense of standing on a platform in the sky and of being more above the world than in it. From there they could see more than five thousand square miles of mountains and plains stretching across western South Dakota, into Nebraska, into Wyoming, and on into the distance as far as the eye could follow. Nearby to the west, Harney Peak proper loomed, cliff-turreted and bulky, above ridges whose tangled ranks continued westward until they faded into the blue distance of Wyoming. To the east the rumpled mountains continued for a few miles, then abruptly tapered down to the floor of green-tan Dakota plains on which the mountains lay. Out on those plains they could see an occasional flash of sun reflecting from a ranch house window, the house itself too far distant to be seen. And beyond all—beyond the mountains and beyond the winking windows—the plains continued on like an amber ocean until, at their far horizon-rim, they appeared to curl upward to join the down-sweeping sky.

Later, Borglum recorded the feelings aroused in him on that day when he saw for the first time the view from Rushmore's crest:

> I was conscious we were in another world . . . and there a new thought seized me—a thought that was to redirect me and dominate all my carving—the scale of that mountain peak!

> We looked out over a horizon level and beaten like the rim of a great cartwheel 2,000 feet below. We had reached upward toward the heavenly bodies . . . and it came over me in an almost terrifying manner that I had never sensed what I was planning. Plans must change. The vastness I saw here demanded it.

After the group had finished their viewing and climbed down from the mountain, those who had come out only for the day went home. Gutzon and Lincoln Borglum, Loocke, Shade, and Sanders, however, stayed at the mountain and set up camp. They remained there for two days while Borglum climbed over Rushmore and studied it and sampled its stone, and while Loocke recorded its shape and lighting in photographs.

On Tuesday evening they returned to the Game Lodge, for by that time Borglum had convinced himself that Rushmore was the mountain he wanted to carve. He also knew that now he would have to sell Norbeck on the idea, and that it would not be easy. No roads, or even trails, led to Rushmore, and Norbeck, as a member of the Mount Harney Memorial Commission, had been doggedly holding out for a location easily accessible from an existing road. Therefore, even though Borglum was now fretting to return home to Borgland where pressing matters were demanding his attention, he went instead to Rapid City. There he passed the time by fishing in Rapid Creek while, with growing impatience, he waited for the senator to return from his trip.

6. The Chosen Stone

Despite his air of confidence, Borglum still did not know whether or not his mountain could be carved successfully. He had chosen it with care, but he knew that even when carving the most carefully selected block of studio marble (to say nothing of an entire mountain face) there was always a risk of encountering some disastrous hidden flaw. And the geological pedigree of the Black Hills granite was such that any of it was a risky proposition for massive sculpture.

The cliff Borglum had chosen for carving was weathered and old because the Black Hills themselves were old. When the Himalayas were still a reedy swamp and the Alps a level plain, the Black Hills were already standing in much their present form. Throughout sixty million years they have been standing thus; standing as an island surrounded in alternate ages by seas or by plains. Presently they stand as an island in plains—a rugged, pine-clad island some ninety miles long by sixty wide, rising from that vast, sunbaked, blizzard-swept grassy sea that tumbles crest and trough, ridge and draw, from the Missouri River to the Rocky Mountains. Like an island, they are surrounded by a reef—a ridge of foothills called the "Hogback"—from which they are separated by a narrow grass and red-earth valley that geologists have named "the Racetrack." The foothills ridge is notched by occasional narrow gaps through which the mountains' natural sculptors—the streams that splash and swirl down the canyons they have carved—escape to the plains and there rest from their labors in drowsy, moss-rimmed waterholes muddied by the hooves of thirsty cattle.

In the heart of the southern Black Hills, exposed by eons of wind and rain, stands their solid-stone foundation and core—the granite mass of the Harney Peak uplift. From the distance of the plains this uplift can be seen as the single massive mountain that it actually is. Viewed from nearby, however, it appears to be many mountains—the result of countless ages of wind and rain, frost and thaw, rushing streams, and the prying roots of pine trees, all having carved the great hump into a tangled wilderness of spires and domes, deep-cut canyons, and cliff-shelved peaks.

The very tip of the uplift is Harney Peak itself, which at 7,242 feet above sea level is the highest piece of land between the Rockies and the Alps. Rising from one shoulder of the uplift, a mile or two south of Harney Peak, is the forest of stone spires and columns called "the Needles." Rising from another shoulder, three miles east-northeast of Harney Peak and fifteen hundred feet below it, is a granite-walled mesa that towers some five hundred feet above the ridge on which it stands, and this mesa is called Mount Rushmore.

Like the other cliffs and crags on the granite uplift, Mount Rushmore shows its age. Its gray stone skin, seasoned by six hundred thousand centuries of weather, resembles the hide of an ancient elephant—deep-creviced, seamy, and wrinkled. To Borglum, these crevices were a matter for concern. Their depth and pattern would determine not only the design of his carving, but if it could even be done at all. Still, he could see and sketch the crevices and, to some extent at least, discover their depth, and so he was even more concerned about the things he could neither see nor measure: the condition of the stone inside the cliff, and whether or not nature, in its forging, had cast within it some hidden fatal flaw.

The forging of Rushmore's granite was begun some sixteen hundred million years ago, when the only life on earth was in the sea. And since the foundations of mountains, like those of buildings, are laid not on the earth but in it, the formation of the Black Hills granite began in layers of sandstone and limestone some ten or fifteen miles below the bottom of an ancient ocean. There, in a place where heat from the earth's internal furnace was somehow being trapped, a hot spot formed. As more heat gathered there, the stone in the hot spot became plastic, then it melted and lay like a white-hot liquid egg buried deep in layers of stone.

As the slow ages passed, the sea gradually laid down new sediments, adding their weight to that already pressing down upon the beds below. The deep layers, being thus compressed, squeezed against the pocket of molten rock (called magma) and forced it upward. Slowly—inches per century—it pushed through the layers of stone above it, and as it climbed, the character of its future granite was being formed. For even though it was liquid, this magma was stiff and heavy and its mixing action was sluggish. As a result, its different melted stone components did not always become thoroughly blended; sometimes they even remained in separate irregular bands and swirls, and the magma never did become uniform in its texture.

While creeping upward, the molten "egg" heated the edges of the beds through which it passed and made them plastic, and then twisted and deformed them with its dragging passage. It occasionally encountered pockets of shale, and with its heat and pressure transformed them into beds of mica. The hot mass also created mica in many of the formations it deformed while dragging past them—mica flecks and particles that caused those formations, in a future age when they lay exposed, to glint and glisten in the sun.

Under immense pressure, pushing ever upward, the hot mass thrust fiery sheets and fingers of magma into flaws and fissures in the stone formations surrounding it. Loosened by these intrusions, great chunks of those formations then broke free from their beds and were carried along as "xenoliths" or "float-blocks" in the molten pool. Some of the float-blocks then melted into the pool and became part of it. Others, although they became plastic and their layers were warped and twisted by heat and pressure, remained as foreign bodies within it. Eons later, when the mass had cooled, they would be there still—hidden lumps of easily shattered and therefore uncarvable schist, scattered unpredictably as raisins in a pudding, throughout the granite.

All the while the Black Hills' granite core was thus being forged, fluid "mineralizers" were at work weaving a golden necklace around it. Being under enormous pressure and extremely hot, these mineralizers, consisting mainly of water, quickly dissolved whatever particles of metal they encountered in the rock. They found and dissolved some lead and tin and silver, but more than anything else they found and dissolved gold. This produced a "mineral soup" that percolated outward from the molten pocket until, eventually, it came to a place where heat and pressure were so reduced that it could no longer hold its mineral burden in solution. There, in pores and crevices in the still-forming uplift, the mineralizers deposited their treasure.

More years passed, more years than the mind can comprehend: ten million, a hundred million, five hundred million. And as they passed the earth gradually came to life. The oceans grew seaweed, then shellfish, then fish, then amphibians. The land grew forests of ferns and then of trees, including oak, walnut, magnolia, and pine. The air began to swarm with insects, among them (perhaps in anticipation of future kitchens) some eight hundred varieties of cockroach. Amphibians crawled out of the seas and onto the land and became reptiles, and from the reptiles came the dinosaurs.

By the time of the dinosaurs, some seventy million years ago, the rising pocket of magma had come to within two or three miles of the earth's surface. Yielding to its upward thrust, the sandstone and limestone layers above it began to bend upward, and on the surface a mound appeared and grew. For more than thirty million years it continued to rise and swell. Inside, meanwhile, beneath its arched cover of layered stone, the magma cooled and hardened and became mica-spangled granite. Outside, wind and rain carved the surface of the uplift into mountains, then the cap of the layered arch became entirely weathered away, exposing its granite core. Exposed, too, were the now-granite sheets and fingers that had been thrust from the top of the magma, when still molten, into flaws and crevices in the sandstone and limestone above it. Now these rose from the granite mass to become the stone shafts and spires that men later would call "the Needles."

Streams flowing from the top of the uplift sliced canyons down its flanks. Near the granite core they exposed gleaming mica-schists; farther out, they cut cross-sections through the tilted layercake of sandstone and limestone covering the outer slopes. Then the streams escaped to the plains, where they deposited the debris from the eroding mountains into a shallow fresh-water sea.

At the edge of the sea and in its swampy shallows, dinosaurs died and their bones sank and were preserved in the mud. Then came the time when the dinosaurs were gone and the land became inhabited by ancestors of our modern mammals—tiny camels and three-toed horses and little long-fanged tigers—and some of these died at the edge of the sea, and their bones, also, were preserved in the mud.

Finally, the rising of the uplift slowed and then stopped. Later the fresh-water sea dried up, and its sediments—being soft and uncompressed—quickly eroded into the rugged earthen buttes and mesas of the Badlands. And at that point the Black Hills country looked as it did when man first saw it, and very little different from the way it looks today.

No one knows who were the first men to come to the Black Hills. Presumably they were Indians and presumably they came no more than thirty thousand years ago. But exactly who they were or exactly when they came, no one can say for sure.

Mankind's known history in the Black Hills country began in the mid-1700s, when the area was occupied by the Kiowa, Cheyenne, and Crow. Next came the warlike Sioux, who drove out the other tribes and seized the territory for themselves. Less than a century later, the west-flowing tide of white settlement began to press against the Sioux. The Sioux resisted until, after fifteen years or so of skirmishes and a few small battles, the United States and the Sioux signed the Treaty of 1868. Under the treaty, a large area that included the Black Hills was to remain the property of the Sioux forever. And had it not been for that golden necklace deposited there by the mineralizers so long before, the Black Hills probably would belong to the Sioux today. As it happened, however, "forever" lasted only eight years.

In 1874, during the first known exploration of the Black Hills by white men, gold was found on the slopes of the Harney Peak uplift. Newspapers picked up the story, sensationalized it, and described the Black Hills as "the world's new El Dorado." Inevitably, and despite the fact that the Treaty of 1868 forbade white men to enter the Great Sioux Reservation, the headlines set off a gold rush. The government attempted with army troops to prevent the gold hunters from trespassing on the Indians' land. But the gold hunters were too determined, too fleet, and too many. They filtered through the army's lines like gnats through a screen door, and by early 1876 there were more whites unlawfully in the Black Hills than there were Indians on the entire Sioux reservation. The Sioux fought back, attacking the invading whites at every opportunity. As a result of all this the government found itself faced with a treaty it was unable to enforce and the prospect of an Indian war it could ill afford to fight. It resolved its dilemma by forcing the Sioux to sell the Black Hills portion of their reservation—a transaction that the Sioux, more than a century later, are still protesting.

Once that sale was made, settlement of the Black Hills began in booming earnest. By early 1879, less than five years after the first exploration of the Black Hills by white men, the mining town of Deadwood had a telephone exchange, and three years after that it had electric lights.

Early in the 1880s, a blacksmith at the mining town of Keystone tossed a piece of ore into his forge and smelted from it drops of silvery metal that he soon discovered were tin. Searching prospectors soon made further tin discoveries that interested eastern investors, and in New York City the Harney Peak Tin Mining Company was organized. In 1885, the company sent a young lawyer named Charles Rushmore to the Black Hills to handle the acquisition of tin mining claims. Years later, Keystone resident David Swanzey, whose wife Carrie was the younger sister of Laura Ingalls Wilder of *Little House on the Prairie* fame, wrote a letter describing what happened next:

> On one of those spring mornings, typical of Keystone, which makes one feel in love with the world . . . a party consisting in part of Mr. Rushmore, Prof. W. Blake, with Bill Challis the famous prospector, hunter, and trapper of the bald-faced bear and discoveror of the Bob Ingersoll mine as guide, were driven in a Tally Ho Coach to the apex of Ingersoll Mountain. . . .

> Standing on the apex of "Bob Ingersoll" . . . we gazed upon Harney Peak and the whole Harney range. . . .

> Mr. Rushmore, viewing with awe and admiration the majestic gran-

deur and proportion of a high, rugged peak between "Bob Ingersoll" and Harney Peak, inquired its name.

Challis replied, "Never had none. But hereafter we'll call 'er Rushmore, by Jingo!"

Thus, because discovery of the "golden necklace" had caused the Black Hills to be taken from the Sioux, Borglum now had his mountain; and because of the discovery of tin, the mountain had a name. To be sure, Borglum was still far from certain of the quality of Rushmore's granite—the depth of its crevices, and whether or not float-blocks of uncarvable schist lay hidden within it—but in convincing others that the mountain was ideally suited to sculpture he had convinced himself. Now, he anticipated no difficulty in convincing Senator Norbeck of the same.

7. "The Statue of Washington Will Be Completed Within a Twelvemonth!"

Certain that Norbeck would simply take his word that Rushmore was the proper place for carving the monument and let it go at that, Borglum planned to spend only part of a day with the senator, and then he would board a train bound for Connecticut. But when, on August 23, the senator finally returned to Rapid City, Borglum found him to be a good deal less pliable than expected. The thing was, said Norbeck, Borglum might know all about sculpture, but he knew from long experience all about the cost of Black Hills roads, and the thousand-foot climb and the mile-and-a-half of jagged wilderness between Rushmore and the nearest existing road worried him immensely. Accordingly, before agreeing to the sculptor's choice he not only would have to be told, but be shown, why a more convenient cliff could not be used instead. So, rather than passing half a day with Norbeck, Borglum wound up spending four days.

They went to the Game Lodge and from there made daily expeditions into the high granite country until, on August 27, Norbeck reluctantly approved Borglum's selection. He then drove the sculptor and Lincoln to the railroad station in Rapid City, where the secretary of the Rapid City Commercial Club handed Borglum a check for $250 of expense money that the club had managed to scrape together. There, also, Borglum gave another interview to the press.

His Great American Monument, "the greatest thing of its character in the whole world," could best be carved on Mount Rushmore, he said, but added (perhaps because Norbeck's endorsement of Rushmore was still shaky), "We may have to go over on Old Baldy to get sufficient room." In two weeks' time he would return to the Hills to begin work, he continued, and he would bring with him "a staff of assistants" and "an airplane for use in getting about the country and to and from Rushmore."

Once aboard the train, Borglum began work on his Rushmore plans, and since he liked for all his projects to be dedicated early and often, he began with plans for the dedication of Mount Rushmore itself. By the time the train had reached Omaha, he had that part of his planning worked out and told the press about it. The mountain would be dedicated "in late September or early October," he said, and "while I am in the east I will arrange with President Coolidge to have a representative of his at the ceremonies." At the same time, he wrote to Robinson and Norbeck, telling them about his pageant plans and confirming his intention to return promptly to the Black Hills and begin his surveys. So that he might haul his surveying equipment directly to the mountain, he said (in a masterful understatement), "some slight work should be done in the way of road improvement." He concluded by saying, "I have only one prayer . . . and that is that we shall all continue in friendship and working together. . . ." Within a week that prayer would prove to have been timely and perhaps even necessary.

Robinson was pleased by Borglum's letter, and remarked to Norbeck, "The suggestion of dedicating the mountain is an extremely happy thought." Norbeck, however, was not pleased. In fact, the sculptor's letter had left him feeling a little dizzy, and he was beginning to think that working with this impulsive and unpredictable Borglum was going to be about like sharing a bathtub with a porpoise. In replying to Robinson, he said, "This man works so fast it is hard . . . even to keep track of him. . . . He seems to take it for granted he is going to build the great memorial and that there is no hitch in the program." Robinson, meanwhile, had received by wire another message from Borglum:

. . . I HAVE URGED DEFINITE ACTION CONTINUOUSLY AND TAKEN THE INITIATIVE AS STRONGLY AS DIGNITY PERMITS. . . . NOW I HAVE PROPOSED DEDICATION OF STONE FOUND, WITH HISTORIC CEREMONY, FULLER PLANS, SOME TESTS THIS MONTH, WITH AUTHORITIES OFFICIATING. POSSIBLE COST OF THIS, FIVE THOUSAND. HAVE TALKED WITH FRIENDS WHO . . . ASSURE ME OF TWO MEN WHO WILL PROVIDE THE MONEY FOR WASHINGTON AND

JEFFERSON. . . . BUT WE MUST DEDICATE THIS MONTH WHILE
PUBLIC EYE IS FIXED ON WEST. PERSONALLY HAVE NO INTENTION
OF MAKING ANY CHARGE AS SCULPTOR, BUT INITIAL ACTUAL
EXPENSE MUST BE BORN BY SOUTH DAKOTANS OR I CAN'T DO
ANYTHING FOR YOU.

Now it was Robinson's turn to feel dizzy, and as a consequence he and
Norbeck then set about comparing notes and trying to figure out who had
been told what, and just what exactly was going on. They knew that nothing
could be done without first finding some money somewhere, and although
Borglum kept making breezy assertions that money was no problem because
he knew where to find it, his statements were inconsistent, and he had never
produced evidence to prove any of them. During recent months the sculptor
had said much about the minting of a "Federal Dollar" to be sold to collectors. But at different times during the past three weeks he had told the press
that he had secured Rushmore financing from "eastern money-kings"; that it
would come from "large national memorial organizations"; and that the job
would be paid for by "popular subscription and certain government funds
especially laid aside for parks and monuments." And if all that were not confusing enough, Borglum at the same time had told Robinson repeatedly that
he had received commitments for all the money needed from John D. Rocke-
feller of Standard Oil, Judge E. H. Gary of U. S. Steel, and two unnamed
men, each of whom had agreed "to get in back of" $200,000. Now, according
to Borglum's latest wire, the number of these men had shrunk to two and the
promised money had shrunk by a half—or perhaps the wire referred to two
other men. Who could tell?

"The fact that Mr. Borglum talks so much about a special coin makes me
uneasy," said Norbeck. "I really do not know what financial support is back of
the proposition," Robinson replied.

The thing worrying Robinson and Norbeck at the moment, however, was
the cost of the surveys Borglum was planning to make. Originally he had
asked for $10,000 for that work, but when the legislature failed to grant it he
had returned to the Black Hills at his own insistence and expense. Upon his
arrival, moreover, Borglum had told a Black Hills audience, "You are not expected to spend a dollar on the project." Now it appeared that Borglum did
not consider his surveys as a part of the "project" and, according to his wire at
least, wanted the Dakotans to furnish $5,000 for them. So, what should they
do about all this expensive activity the sculptor was about to engage in now?
As Norbeck saw it: "His letter now indicates he is going to run up an expense

of several thousand dollars. . . . I have no idea how he expects to be paid: possibly he expects to pay it himself. It strikes me . . . it will probably give us nationwide publicity . . . and leave us a bunch of unpaid bills to worry about." To which Robinson replied: "I am sure it will be unfortunate if B. comes out and involves a considerable expense without first having a contract or understanding, and then expects us to meet it." Well, were there any "understandings?" Norbeck wanted to know. "Has anyone made any promises or commitments to Borglum?" "None whatever upon the part of the Mount Harney Memorial Commission, the only official source," Robinson answered.

That being the case, the two men now tried to persuade Borglum not to do anything more until money had been raised to do it with. But again Borglum insisted on going ahead, and pointedly observed that the Black Hills people could raise the money if they really wanted to. And again the sculptor's bullheaded persistence caused Rushmore's Dakota boosters to act when they might otherwise have let the project die.

Robinson asked Frank Hughes, president of the Rapid City Commercial Club, if the Black Hills communities might be able together to raise $5,000. Hughes thought they might. There was quite a bit of monument enthusiasm in the Hills at present, he said. Just the past weekend, for instance, the men of Keystone had on their own initiative gone out with axes and shovels and horse-drawn scrapers to open a road to Rushmore. The result, according to Keystone mayor Tom Hoy, was a road that was "passable" although it was no "speedway." On the other hand, that statement of Borglum's about not asking for a dollar from the Black Hills was going to be troublesome, but Hughes would take the matter up with the Commercial Club anyhow.

The club met on September 14, agreed to promote a fund-raising drive among all the Black Hills commercial clubs, and went into action. On the evening of the 16th, Hughes told Robinson that the club had managed to secure $2,000 in pledges, but no cash at all. Robinson relayed this information to Borglum, who promptly wired Hughes:

FOUR OF US WILL START FOR SOUTH DAKOTA SUNDAY [SEPT.
20]. . . . YOUR COMMITTEE SHOULD PLACE BY WIRE ONE THOU-
SAND DOLLARS AT MY DISPOSAL IN CHASE BANK NEW YORK BEFORE
SATURDAY NOON. . . . SHALL BRING SOME COSTUMES FOR
CEREMONIES. CAN YOU GET A FEW REAL INDIANS FOR
SPECTATORS. . . .

Now it was Hughes who felt a little dizzy. He had not raised any cash and the sculptor knew it, and yet the man was asking him to produce a thousand dollars and giving him less than two days in which to do it. Nonetheless, Hughes did manage to raise it somehow, and by Saturday noon it had been deposited in Borglum's bank. Thereupon, Borglum wired that he would arrive in Rapid City on the morning of the 23rd.

On the morning Borglum was to arrive, a crowd had gathered at the Rapid City depot where the Commercial Club had arranged a welcoming ceremony. When the train pulled in, however, Borglum was not on it. Embarrassed and upset, Hughes rushed over to the Western Union office and wired Robinson:

BORGLUM DID NOT ARRIVE. . . . DO YOU KNOW HIS PLANS. . . .
SPECTATORS AND INDIANS HARD TO HOLD.

Robinson did not know, nor did anyone else. Not, at least, until twenty-four hours later when Borglum wired from Mankato, Minnesota:

WE ARRIVE RAPID CITY IN THE MORNING.

This time, Borglum did arrive. He was accompanied by Lincoln, photographer Charles D'Emery, and an aide named J. Alan Giles, but without a staff of assistants or an airplane. And he was met by a delegation from the Commercial Club, but without spectators, Indians, or ceremony.

Upon leaving the train, Borglum announced that on October 1 (which was only six days away) he would stage a large dedication ceremony at Rushmore. Then he gathered up his party, hurried out to his Rushmore camp (which Sanders had maintained for him during his absence), and went to work.

On the following day Robinson arrived in town and plunged into the task of organizing the dedication Borglum had designed. This, in turn, stimulated a fever of monument excitement in the Black Hills. In fact, in all the monument's construction years this was probably the time when it enjoyed the greatest local interest and support. And one reason for that seems to have been that again the timing was good. It had been a summer of good crops and fat cattle. Now the harvest season was over and it was Indian summer and a good time to relax and have a little fun. Thus, as time for the dedication approached, a remarkable number of people became involved in it.

The commandant at Fort Meade agreed to send a troop of cavalry and a band to take part in the ceremony, and the troop and band marched the sixty miles from the fort to Rushmore, where they set up camp.

In Rapid City, thirty women volunteers labored day and night stitching together five huge flags, each eighteen feet wide by thirty feet long, which were to be used in the affair.

The commander of the National Guard in Rapid City, Colonel Earl Lewis, mustered his guardsmen and assigned them the task of controlling the traffic and crowds both at the mountain and en route to it.

Throughout the Hills, community officials announced that schools would be dismissed for Dedication Day.

The men of Keystone continued to work on their new Rushmore road and arranged to have teamsters and horses stationed along it to help autos over the bad spots, especially up a stupefying slope they called "Mica Hill."

The Keystone people also decided to help finance the ceremonies by selling barbequed elk sandwiches to the assembling crowd. They secured permission from Colonel Shade to kill an elk from the Custer Park herd, then asked Borglum if he would like to be the one to hunt and shoot the animal.

Borglum said he would indeed like to, and on the morning of the 28th set out to do so. The elk being uncooperative, the hunt took Borglum all day and made him late for a speech he was to give that evening in Rapid City. When he finally did arrive there, however, he was able to announce that he had bagged a four-hundred pound elk—"a splendid animal."

The *Journal* story about the event may have been set by the same typesetter who earlier had produced the headline "Sculptor Will Visit Bleak Hills," for it read: "The eelk was shot by Mr. Keystone."

Then it was Dedication Eve, and in a front-page box and in bold-face type the *Journal* proclaimed:

> Rapid City people who fail to attend the dedication of Rushmore will miss . . . the greatest historical event which has ever happened in the state.
>
> The carving of Rushmore is . . . the most stupendous undertaking of its kind in all history. It is conceived by admittedly the greatest living sculptor. . . . It is epoch marking.
>
> Every resident of Rapid City who can go should do so. Take the Keystone Road.

Dedication Day dawned overcast, chilly, and smelling of rain, but this seemed to be no discouragement. By mid-morning the stony roads to Keystone were jammed with automobiles joggling along in slow, solid lines punctuated here and there by exclamation points of steam hissing up from overheated radiators. Beside the road were other automobiles temporarily out of action while their drivers scraped, patched, and pumped to repair stonepunctured inner tubes. And occasionally on the steeper grades a Model T Ford could be seen traveling in reverse, the only way its gravity-feed fuel system would function on a steep slope.

At Keystone, crowds drawn by the aroma of roasting meat began to gather at the Congregational Church to buy sandwiches of barbequed elk and beef—and, as some believed, of buffalo and bear. "Of course, it was all either elk or beef," Keystonite Edwald Hayes recalled later, "but if somebody asked for buffalo or bear, why, that's what we gave 'em. It made 'em happy, and it sure sold sandwiches."

Beyond Keystone, pedestrians and automobiles were mingled in a stream that flowed up Grizzly Gulch to the new Rushmore road. After one look at the road, the more prudent motorists promptly abandoned their cars and joined the pedestrians on the trails. The more reckless drivers pushed on, however, and with the aid of the Keystone teamsters a number of them (four hundred and seventeen, according to one probably exaggerated account) actually managed to churn their way clear up to the dedication site.

The site itself was located on the side of a ridge a quarter of a mile southeast of the Rushmore cliff and separated from it by a shallow canyon. There, around a rough pine speakers' platform the crowd gathered and grew until, by program time, it numbered some 3,000 persons. Then, as if in honor of the occasion, the clouds broke up into scattered, slow-drifting whipped cream islands, and Mount Rushmore stood sunlit and sharp against a deep autumn sky.

At one o'clock, a thirty-piece band thundered out an overture that rolled out against the cliffs and came thundering back as a confusion of echoes, and the ceremony was under way.

A typical Borglum production, it contained drama and inspiration in flowing abundance. The band played; a group of Sioux Indians did a war dance and, later, a grass dance; and interspersed among these activities were speeches and more speeches. There were five major ones "and others," according to Doane Robinson, and none of them was restrained. Robinson, in his own speech, exclaimed, "Americans! Stand uncovered, in humility and reverence, before the majesty of this mighty mountain!" And Borglum in his oratorical offering, declared, "The hand of Providence has decreed that this monument be built! . . . The statue of Washington will be completed within a twelvemonth! Meet me here a year from today and we will dedicate it!"

Next, there was an intermission during which Borglum and certain other program participants made their way to the mountain and climbed it. Upon reaching the top, Borglum waved a signal. Thereupon, the band played a fanfare, and at the same time there appeared upon the top of the cliff the distance-dwarfed figure of a Sioux Indian chief, Black Horse, in full tribal regalia. Representing the land's original owners, he remained there, regal and unmoving, throughout the rest of the ceremony.

7. First dedication pageant participants on top of Rushmore cliff, October 1, 1925. Seated with Borglum are South Dakota Senator Peter Norbeck and State Forester Theodore "Thee" Shoemaker, the man who first suggested Rushmore as a carving site and later led Borglum to it.

Next, huge flags of the territory's other claimants—Great Britain, Spain, France, and the colonial United States—were successively raised and then lowered by a group of men dressed as early-day explorers. Each flag was saluted by a volley fired by the Fort Meade cavalry while it was being raised, and by the appropriate national anthem played by the band while it was being lowered.

Then came the climax of the dedication. While the band and audience joined in singing "The Star Spangled Banner" (Fort Meade's ceremonial anthem, but not yet the American national anthem), the "Stars and Stripes" was raised to fly for the first time over Mount Rushmore. Unlike the preceding flags, however, this one was not lowered. Instead, while the Reverend Carl Loocke pronounced a benediction and the crowd began to scatter, the flag remained there—streaming from the mountaintop in the lowering sun.

At that moment, in the afterglow of its dramatic dedication, the Rushmore memorial project seemed at last to be under way. The people now picking their way down the shadowed slopes from Rushmore had been impressed and inspired by the day's events, and their previous hope that the monument *might* be constructed was now being joined by a newborn faith that it *would* be constructed. Being new, it was a tentative, frail faith, but it was there and could be taken to indicate that Borglum at last had won for himself and his monument the solid Black Hills support he had for so long been seeking.

And had Borglum then let the matter rest for a moment, that probably would have been the case. Had he just kept quiet for a time and given the newborn enthusiasm time to spread, it is possible that his long-sought local support would have congealed into something solid and enduring. But, carried away by the heat of his own aggressive enthusiasm, Borglum did not keep quiet. And because he did not, within twenty-four hours his newly won support would become shattered almost beyond repair.

8. Where Often is Heard a Discouraging Word

On the evening of the dedication a celebration dinner was held at the A&F Cafe in Rapid City. Attended by Black Hills community leaders and their wives, it was a gala affair. The high-ceilinged, terrazzo-floored room echoed the buzz of table talk, and the talk was lively and exuberant. Until now, most of those present had doubted both the wisdom and the possibility of carving a gigantic monument on the side of one of their mountains. But no more. This marvelous thing *was* going to be created, and it would generate a tourist business that would bring the Black Hills fame and fortune—especially fortune. Borglum's dramatic dedication ceremony had convinced them of it.

Seated at the head table, Norbeck, Borglum, and Robinson were discussing the steps to be taken next. Earlier, Borglum had again told them that Judge E. H. Gary, chairman of the board of U. S. Steel, and a Mr. Webster had committed themselves definitely to contribute $200,000 each to the Rushmore work. In exchange for that, Borglum was now saying, he believed both men would expect to be appointed to the executive board of the Mount Harney Memorial Association and also would demand the right to name its treasurer. Hence, what Borglum wanted to know now was . . . would Norbeck and Robinson approve such an arrangement? They, being of the opinion that Gary's and Webster's donations alone would be sufficient to fund the entire project, said indeed they would approve it. On that happy note, Robinson then excused himself so as to catch the night train to Pierre—and thereby missed hearing Borglum's after-dinner speech.

On the next morning, shortly after Robinson had arrived in his office in Pierre his telephone rang. Paul Bellamy was calling from Rapid City, and he was mad as a wet bobcat. Had Robinson heard about Borglum's speech? Bellamy demanded to know; and, what kind of shell game was this Borglum running anyhow? Robinson said he had not heard and did not know. Whereupon Bellamy proceeded to enlighten him.

First, said Bellamy, Borglum had given his audience a tantalizing description of the financial and other blessings a mountain-carved memorial would shower upon them. Next he had stressed the fact that the sooner the job was begun the sooner its blessings could be harvested. By starting immediately, Borglum had gone on to say, he could have the Washington figure completed within twelve months. But *then*, said Bellamy, after dangling that bait Borglum had proceeded to sink a hook that was buried in it. For him to get started at all, he had then told his hearers, the Black Hills people must give him $50,000 to work with!

And so far as the Black Hills people were concerned, Bellamy concluded, that last statement of Borglum's had wrecked the Rushmore bandwagon.

Robinson suddenly felt numb and cold. In his own words, he was "completely flabbergasted." Throughout that day confused thoughts wheeled through his head, and later he recounted some of them:

> From the beginning, Borglum has given me to understand that his friends would contribute the money for the main works. . . .

> He said that Judge Gary and a Mr. Webster had agreed to back him to the extent of $200,000 each. . . .

> Based upon his statements, I have made very strong representations to the Black Hills people. . . .

That last thought was the one that hurt: "I have made strong representations. . . ." In his battles with Rushmore critics Robinson had said repeatedly that Borglum had arranged all the necessary funding and, therefore, the Dakotans need not be concerned about it. Quoting the sculptor's own statement made in August to a Rapid City audience, Robinson had been saying, "You are not asked to spend a dollar on the project," and he had been saying it not only in the Black Hills but all over the state as well. So now, assuming Bellamy's report were true, Robinson felt that Borglum had cut the ground from under him and had left him looking like a fool, or a liar . . . or both.

By day's end the old historian had decided "to just throw up my hands and quit." But during the sleepless night that followed, he, being Robinson, began to have mellowing second thoughts: "Bellamy's report probably was exaggerated. . . . Borglum doesn't mean to misrepresent. . . . In his enthusiasm he accepts a kind word as a pledge of aid. . . . He is a great sculptor . . .

can actually do the work. . . . To have it done is altogether worthwhile. . . . Consequently, I will continue to support Borglum and defend him against any prejudice he has incurred. . . . I will just have to take the blame and keep my mouth shut."

Despite all this mellowing, however, on the following morning Robinson still was so agitated that in writing to Norbeck he misdated the letter and then addressed the senator as "My Dear Governor."

By the time Robinson received Norbeck's reply, it had begun to appear that Bellamy *had* exaggerated a bit. The records of the matter are not clear, but Borglum seems to have made his $50,000 demand to various community leaders while the banquet was breaking up rather than (as Bellamy had said) in his formal speech. Either way, however, it had greatly damaged the Rushmore cause.

Even so, Norbeck had refused to let it bother him. He had ceased to count on Borglum's supposed contributors anyhow. He had a great and still-growing admiration for Borglum's artistic talents, but he had learned to let the man's big talk (especially about fund-raising) go in one ear and out the other. Besides, Norbeck was of the opinion that South Dakota *should* furnish some of the Rushmore funds, and he thought it should be done by state appropriation. It was Governor Gunderson's failure to agree that *did* have Norbeck upset. "The main stumbling block is the attitude of the State Administration," he wrote, and, therefore, "I am not as hopeful about this monument matter as I would like to be." Then he proceeded to put his blunt, well-driller's finger on the real problem. Before the Rushmore proposition could be advanced further, he observed, "we must have a definite plan."

There it was. Clear and simple. Lack of planning had kept the project semiparalyzed from the very start. Borglum and his Dakota supporters had put out a great deal of effort, but much of it had been uncoordinated and unorganized. This was understandable. Borglum had seemed so positive and so aggressively in control of the whole operation that his local supporters had allowed themselves to drift, willy-nilly, in his turbulent wake. It was clear now, however, that Borglum did not have all the problems under control and it was asking too much to expect him to. He needed and deserved a good deal more Dakota help than he was getting. But they needed most of all, as Norbeck put it, "*a definite plan.*" To begin with, they needed a definite plan of the monument itself. For as yet, no one, including Borglum, had more than a vague idea of how it was to look when finished.

Robinson, in a letter, passed Norbeck's ideas on to Borglum—especially the one about the need for a definite monument design. Robinson made only a passing reference to Bellamy's report, and called it "exaggerated." But he did go on to warn the sculptor, "I don't believe it would do any good for you to return to South Dakota until something definite is lined up."

By now Borglum's $50,000 request had become such a hot potato that the sculptor, in his reply, did not even try to pick it up. All he said about money was, "Regarding financing, I am not disturbed about that at all." He then went on to agree that planning was needed, and said he would begin immediately to prepare models and written specifications for the monument. And there the matter was left.

Now, through the end of 1925 and on into the summer of 1926, Borglum, Robinson, and Norbeck each worked on the project independently and quietly.

In his San Antonio studio, Borglum worked on Rushmore models and specifications. Also, in a number of major cities he made Rushmore fund-raising speeches, none of which raised any funds.

Robinson sent a stream of letters to prominent wealthy Americans, telling each that if he were to finance one of the Rushmore figures he not only would be performing "a great patriotic service" but, as well, would be "perpetuating his own name and fame to the centuries." However, he found no takers.

Norbeck made a strong effort to get the State of South Dakota to appropriate $10,000 for Rushmore and also to build a passable road to it. But both the governor and the legislature remained unmoved.

Encouraged by this faltering, Rushmore's environmentalist opponents now attempted to move in for the kill. Cora Johnson, of Hot Springs, wrote letters to a number of people for whom Borglum previously had done work, and openly encouraged them to say something nasty about him—something she could use to openly discredit him. However, she found none excepting the Stone Mountain people, and the Dakotans had heard enough from them already. Another critic, John Tjaden, of the University of South Dakota, then wrote a poem that was reproduced in several of the state's newspapers:

> When God made our matchless playground,
> He did not intend that man should
> even in his wildest ravings
> dare to come with hammer, chisel,
> block and tackle, pick and mallet,
> to profane His age-old record,
> to profane the face of Rushmore
> by his puny, pygmy scratches.

> Why should man presume to alter
> the Creator's masterpieces,
> wrought in everlasting granite,
> wrought by forces so titanic
> that no scientist can measure,
> that no human mind can master?
> And to think that man, presumptive,
> should deface and mutilate them!
>
> Men and women, 'tis your duty
> to lift up your earnest voices,
> to the end that all our people
> forthwith band themselves together
> to preserve from desecration
> finished products from God's workshop
> and placed by that Master-Artist
> in the playground of Dakota.

To the various Black Hills commercial clubs, who by now had agreed to try to raise at least $25,000 of the $50,000 Borglum had asked for, this sort of protest came as another unwelcome wave in an already choppy sea of opposition. Still, it was far from being their biggest problem. Their biggest problem lay in trying to explain why Borglum now was asking for all that money from the very people to whom he so recently had said, "you are not asked to spend a dollar." Frank Hughes, president of the Rapid City Commercial Club and fund-drive leader wrote asking Borglum for advice on how to deal with this objection. Borglum responded by airily saying his Dakota critics were merely "horseflies" that inevitably gather around the beginnings of "any big thing," and that the disturbance over his request for money was but "a flurry stimulated by malice" and would "soon disappear."

The difficulty, however, was deeper than that. And, stimulated not by malice but by local history, it was not about to disappear. As Borglum had done earlier, the fund raisers were telling prospective donors that money given to Rushmore would not really be a donation, it would be an *investment*. The monument, they declared, would return to its contributors—to the entire Black Hills, in fact—a golden bounty of tourist trade forever. It was a good argument and later history was to prove its truth, but the potential contributors were not buying it. To those (and there were many) who remembered the

Black Hills' gold rush days, it was an old familiar story: a surefire proposition in which a little money invested now could not fail to yield a rich reward in the future—that had been the pitch of the mining promoters. And, as the Black Hills people saw it now, about the only difference between this scheme and those of the earlier promoters was that this one was supposed to get money from a mountain by carving faces *on* it instead of by digging holes *in* it. Put that way, it sounded pretty shaky. Besides, many of the Black Hills people now being approached had once listened to the siren songs of those early-day mining promoters and had surrendered their savings to them. A few had profited thereby. But very few. The only return for most had been lost savings and shattered dreams, and that was a thing not easily forgotten. Especially if a person had been taken in a swindle, and there had been many of those. The Safe Investment mine, for example, had been an out-and-out fraud. Tigerville, according to its building-lot promoters, had been located on ground so rich that "even the chickens have nuggets in their craws." But whatever nuggets there were the chickens must have gotten; Tigerville's investors never found any. And who could forget wheeling-and-dealing Bob Flormann? By "salting" his barren Thunderhead mine with rich ore from elsewhere, Flormann had managed to sell its stock for a very fancy price. Then, a little later (or so the story is told), he had driven by the mine and asked the new foreman how things were going.

"Fine!" said the foreman. "We got about $3,000 worth out already."

"Hell!" snorted Flormann, "you're still $2,500 short of getting my salt back!"

Understandably, therefore, when listening to the sales talks of Rushmore promoters, prospective donors remembered similar sales talks by those earlier promoters. They remembered even now dozens if not hundreds of abandoned mine shafts, surrounded by rotting buildings and rusting junk, that remained as vivid monuments to wasted money and wasted hope. But most of all, they remembered that, once you stopped to think about it, this Borglum with his high-powered oratory and high-powered personality seemed much like those mine-stock hucksters of old—like Bob Flormann, in fact. True, Borglum *had* put a good deal of his own time and money into this thing. But, again like Bob Flormann, might he not be just "salting the mine" so as to line his pockets at the expense of gullible donors? So, the Black Hillers listened to the fund raisers because they were friends and neighbors . . . but they kept their wallets closed.

Because of these difficulties, by the summer of 1926 the Rushmore enterprise had sunk back into a now familiar pattern. No money nor prospects of any, and little planning despite all the talk about it. And again the project seemed to be drifting into oblivion.

Then, in July, Borglum announced that he was returning to the Hills, and this, too, followed a now familiar pattern. Just as before, his Dakota supporters had no money to pay for his expenses, let alone his time, and therefore they tried to persuade him to wait until they did have some. Borglum, in turn, said he was coming anyhow. He wanted to bring his newly finished models, he said, and to begin marking the mountain for carving. As for money? That was no problem. He knew of "swarms of malefactors of great wealth," he said, who would "gladly and readily contribute conscience money to popular public memorials."

Accompanied by Mary and the children—fourteen-year-old Lincoln and ten-year-old Mary Ellis—and by Major Tucker, he arrived in late August and moved himself and family into a primitive cabin in Keystone. Then, together with Tucker, he set out to measure and mark his mountain.

After about three weeks of painting white stripes on Rushmore's wrinkled old face, and thereby leaving it looking as if painted for war, they departed— Tucker returning to Florida and the Borglums to Connecticut and Borgland. En route, the sculptor made Rushmore promotional speeches in Minneapolis, Chicago, Detroit, and Pittsburgh. As in similar previous appearances, he stirred up much interest . . . and no money. Then, after having arrived back at Borgland, he fussed at Norbeck and the other Dakotans because they had not stirred up any money either. "I can do no more," he wired Frank Hughes, "until you act."

The trouble now was that Borglum was broke. The financial chickens Norbeck and Robinson had worried about for so long were coming home to roost. Despite the efforts of Mary, the financially responsible member of the family, this was not an unusual condition for Gutzon. To him, money was of little consequence. With his eyes always fixed on higher goals, he regarded money only as a minor means to major ends and could never understand why everyone else did not feel the same way. That is how he felt when he *had* money. When he did not have it, his distress (as the Stone Mountain people had discovered) was visible, audible, and awesome. And now the interest was due on his Borgland mortgage, and he did not have it. He had, however, spent a good bit of his own money on Rushmore and he figured it was about time he got some of it back. Accordingly, in late November he wired Hughes:

CAN YOU WIRE ME TWELVE TO FIFTEEN
HUNDRED DOLLARS ON ACCOUNT OF

EXPENSES ADVANCED. . . . ACTUAL
EXPENSES CHARGEABLE TO WORK
THIS YEAR MORE THAN TWICE THAT
BUT I DONT EXPECT TO NEED IT. . . .

Hughes, his secretary replied, was out of town for a few days. Immediately, Borglum wired back:

PLEASE SEND MY WIRE TO MR HUGHES   .
STOP MY TELEGRAM WAS OF COURSE
AN EMERGENCY AND URGENT TODAY

Five days later Hughes returned to Rapid City and replied:

MUCH AS WOULD LIKE TO WIRE MONEY
WE HAVENT IT ON HAND STOP SENATOR
NORBECK WILL BE HERE ON THURSDAY AND
WILL TRY HARDEST TO GET THIS DONE

Hughes, a wholesale grocer by profession, was a conscientious man, and, because he was, he now felt caught in a disagreeable corner. Borglum *had* been out a substantial amount of money and he *should* be reimbursed. But, doggone it! Until this moment he had given no indication of needing or even of wanting repayment, and now he wanted it instantly. As Hughes told Norbeck: "I really feel that if he wished us to compensate him for money already spent, that he should have brought this up in a definite way, and let us know to this effect."

Even so, Hughes tried to raise the money. Tried desperately. Time and again he received promises of help, but none who promised ever followed through. With a steady stream of messages—Borglum demanding, and Hughes apologizing and making excuses for his fellow townsmen—the affair rocked on into February of 1927. By then Borglum had found in the East a benefactor who had paid his mortgage interest, but he was still in need. Accordingly, he wired both Robinson and Norbeck:

HAVE EMBARRASSED MYSELF BY LONG
CONTINUED ADVANCES STOP CANNOT
GO FURTHER WITHOUT REIMBURSEMENT

This prompted Robinson to wire Hughes: "PLEASE SEND BORGLUM BY WIRE FIVE HUNDRED DOLLARS," but he made no suggestions as to where to get it.

Wearily, Hughes tried again, and on February 15 sent the sculptor $250. Also he sent a note, saying, "This may seem small to you, but I have spent a good portion of two days trying to get some of these people to come across." Even then, Hughes had not told Borglum the whole story, but he did tell Robinson and Norbeck. "I actually had to go out and beg for it, and not succeeding, had to put up $100 of the amount myself." The balance was furnished by Rapid City businessmen John Boland, Joseph Bennett, and E. M. Reeves, who put up $50 each.

Norbeck, meanwhile, had been having his own problems with Borglum, the first of which was keeping track of him. Said Norbeck: "He has no permanent place of residence—and what is worse, he seems to have no permanent address. He has spent most of the winter at the Metropolitan Club here in Washington, but letters sent to him at that address are not forwarded when he is out of the city." And, Norbeck told Hughes, he too had been caught up in the sculptor's financial problems:

Frankly. . . Mr. Borglum has been more of a problem to me this winter than I ever expected. It has been impossible for me to get him to see the Black Hills side of the matter. He was impatient because they did not send him money before he had ever rendered a bill. Then when he found out I was not going to try to scare anybody in South Dakota, he worked around and got others to try it. . . . He was desperately hard-up and didn't know which way to turn. . . .

Then the senator made two comments of far greater significance than he could have realized at the time. He said: ". . . but the amusing if not perplexing thing is to have him feel so good now that he wants to start right in working without delaying anything more on account of finances." and: "Mr. Borglum as an artist looms bigger and bigger to me, and one thing is certain, we need him more than he needs us. We are, however, responsible for the undertaking and we must proceed cautiously."

In so saying, Norbeck unknowingly pinpointed the reasons why the Mount Rushmore project, despite enormously greater technical and financial difficulties and substantially less local support, was eventually to succeed whereas the Stone Mountain project had failed. Between Borglum and the Stone Mountain executive board there had been little warmth, little cooperation, little compromise. That board had held an ill-concealed opinion of Borglum as a mere employee working only for his own financial gain. By the same token, Borglum had held an ill-concealed opinion of the board as a collection of cold-blooded plutocrats using the Stone Mountain memorial only for *their* financial gain. Accordingly, whenever disagreements arose between them, each side tended to take a position that was hostile and unbending. And on that rock of mutual suspicion and animosity the Stone Mountain enterprise had been irreparably shattered.

At Rushmore, however, things were quite different. There were disagreements to be sure, and sometimes they were tempestuous. This is normal in any enterprise, and it was absolutely unavoidable in any involving Borglum. In resolving them, however, the members of the Mount Harney Commission did not treat Borglum as a mere employee. They considered him to be possibly the world's greatest sculptor and believed with Norbeck, "We need him more than he needs us." Therefore, not only did they allow him always to occupy the center of the Rushmore stage, they encouraged it. And in their statements and news releases they regularly played up Borglum's importance to the project while, just as regularly, minimizing their own.

Borglum, on his part, had long been obsessed with the idea of creating upon some mountain the world's most colossal carving. Now, Mount Rushmore seemed to offer his best and possibly last opportunity to do so. Norbeck's opinion notwithstanding, therefore, Borglum needed the Mount Harney Memorial Association fully as much as it needed him. Moreover, he had come to regard its members—Norbeck, Robinson, and the others—as honest and unpretentious men who, though maddeningly overpractical at times, were willing to work, listen, compromise, and recognize his importance.

From these elements of mutual need and mutual respect for each other's abilities there was forged between Borglum and the members of the Mount Harney Association a bond of cooperation and tolerance, and of forgiveness, too, (when forgiveness was required) that had been lacking at Stone Mountain. Time and again the bond was to be severely tested; later it would weaken, and eventually it would fail. But in the beginning it was strong, and that was why Borglum now was willing not only to forgive the Dakotans for not having reimbursed his expenses to date, but also was willing—was eager in fact—to get on with the job.

At this point, unfortunately, mere eagerness was not enough. At the beginning of 1927 the Rushmore venture was near death and failing fast. About the only recent events favorable to it had occurred in the November elections. There Senator Norbeck, Rushmore's most powerful friend, had been re-

turned to office, and Governor Gunderson, one of its most powerful opponents, had not. Gunderson had been unseated by a Democrat, William Bulow,
who was at least mildly favorable to the monument. At best, however, these
events by themselves could have done no more than to slow the project's de-
cline. To revive it and restore it to health, something bigger was needed. And
just in time, it came.

9. From Dream
to Contract

Calvin Coolidge, born and raised in a backwoods hamlet in the hills of Vermont, liked mountains, small towns and their people, and privacy. He did not like, among other things, flies, mosquitoes, and curious crowds. He was a rockribbed Republican, suffered from chronic bronchitis, and in 1927 was President of the United States. And if any one of these things had not been true, Mount Rushmore National Memorial probably would never have been created.

For anyone, summer in Washington, D.C., before the days of air conditioning was uncomfortable. For Mr. Coolidge, whose bronchitis was aggravated by muggy heat, it was almost intolerable. Accordingly, in the summer of 1925 he had sought relief on the cool coast of Massachusetts, and in the summer of 1926 he had gone to New York's Adirondack Mountains. However, in the damp sea air of the former his bronchitis had continued to act up, in the latter he had been plagued by insects, and in both places he had been annoyed by curious crowds trying to get a peek at their president. And so now he had decided that in the summer of 1927 he would seek escape from bronchitis, bugs, and crowds by vacationing "somewhere west of the Alleghenies but east of the Rockies." Exactly where? . . . Well, he was open to suggestions, and the South Dakotans had one: the Black Hills.

It was not a new suggestion. Borglum had invited Mr. Coolidge to the Hills in 1925 to dedicate Mount Rushmore, but the invitation had been declined. Next, the publisher of the *Hot Springs Star* had talked the South Dakota congressional delegation into inviting the president to vacation in the Black Hills, and their proposal also had been declined. Now, however, the president had said he *wanted* to vacation in the West. Whereupon the Dakotans launched another and more intensive effort to get him to come to their Hills.

On January 7, 1927, the South Dakota legislators passed a resolution formally inviting Mr. Coolidge. They spared no adjectives when drafting it, and indulged in no false modesty. They spoke with eloquence of the Black Hills' "lofty peaks," "ideal climate," "magnificent forests," and "sparkling streams." They mentioned "wildflowers abounding in infinite variety," the abundance of "buffalo, deer, elk, and mountain sheep," and "splendid fishing, golf, polo, and tennis." And to make sure that Mr. Coolidge did not believe—as so many Easterners did—that the Black Hills country was still an untamed land of gunslingers, rustlers, and scarlet women, the legislature went on to assure him that "the population in and about the mountains are intelligent and moral," and that "neighborly relations" there were "safe and pleasurable."

The resolution was delivered personally to the president by Senator Norbeck. After reading it, Mr. Coolidge reflected for a moment, then dryly observed, "Senator, I can't tell whether this is a chapter from Revelations or Mohammed's idea of the seventh heaven." Beyond that, however, he would not commit himself.

During the following months the Dakotans bombarded the president with pictures, literature, and general propaganda. Other states, trying to lure him to their vacation spots, did the same. He listened to all, encouraged none, and remained noncommittal.

As time passed and the presidential silence continued unbroken, the Dakotans became increasingly anxious. Then, on March 12, the *Chicago Tribune* announced that Mr. Coolidge definitely had chosen to go to the Black Hills. Immediately, the Dakotans began to remodel the Game Lodge for his quarters and to whittle from a nearby mountaintop a golf course for his entertainment. Two weeks later, papers in Washington, D.C., broke the news that he had elected to go to Colorado Springs instead. Whereupon, Paul Bellamy—with his Grant-inspired belief in direct action—drafted a letter to Mr. Coolidge and traveled by train sixteen hundred miles to Washington to deliver it personally. On April 1, in an appointment secured by Congressman Williamson, Bellamy delivered his letter. More restrained and informative than the florid invitation submitted by the South Dakota legislature, it was a good letter, and the president told Bellamy so. But that was all he would say about it. Soon afterward, however, he asked Congressman Williamson, "Why do *you* think I should vacation in the Black Hills?" After hearing Williamson's reasons, Mr. Coolidge then asked, "How are the flies and mosquitoes out there?"

"In the mountains proper, few or none," Williamson assured him.

"That's good," said Coolidge. "Last place I went they nearly pestered me to death. I'll send a man out to look at your Hills."

The "man"—Colonel Edward Starling, head of the White House Secret Service—came to Rapid City in early May, looked around for two days, then returned to Washington. Still, the president said nothing.

Finally, on May 31, the suspense was ended. The first hint of the president's decision came when, at Rapid City, Colonel Starling and several members of his staff arrived, unannounced, on the morning train. Then, later on that same morning, South Dakota's major newspapers all received a triumphant telegram from Senator Norbeck. As a result, when the *Rapid City Journal* hit the streets that afternoon it carried a screamer headline:

COOLIDGE WILL ARRIVE JUNE 16!!

The news brought joy to the hearts of Rushmore's boosters, who by that time, surprisingly enough, already had quite a bit to be joyful about. During the past two months the Mount Harney Association had actually managed to raise some money. Borglum, no longer peeved at his Dakota supporters, was so full of energy and optimism that he was moving, in the words of one observer, "like a man with his shirt tail on fire." Since late April, Tucker had been at the mountain preparing to install carving equipment. Thus, the prospects that had seemed so dismal at the beginning of the year now seemed to be growing brighter by the day.

The raw material of this happy situation had been provided almost entirely by the Coolidge affair. Even though until now there had been no assurance that the president would vacation in the Hills, the fact that he might do so had given the Black Hills much favorable publicity abroad and had created a mood of sunny optimism at home. This raw material had been converted into an effective force for Rushmore mainly through the efforts of a new player on the Rushmore stage: a human dynamo named Herbert Myrick, of Springfield, Massachusetts.

Myrick, a prominent and successful publisher, owned a string of farm magazines, one of which was the *Dakota Farmer*. A self-made man who took great pride in his country and its history, he had been a major contributor to Stone Mountain and thereby had come to be acquainted with Borglum. Myrick liked Borglum, was awed by his sculptural ability, and called him "the Michael Angelo of our era." He was not impressed, however, by the sculptor's business sense, and said Borglum was inclined "to 'blow in' in one way or another" any funds at his disposal. But Myrick also said this was a failing common to "creative geniuses," and that when such persons were in need it was the duty of the more affluent to come to their rescue. Which was why, in the past November, Myrick had paid the interest on the Borgland mortgage when Borglum, himself, could not. In turn, the grateful sculptor had insisted on sculpting a bust of his benefactor.

Myrick "sat" for the bust in early January, and during that sitting Borglum sold him on the Rushmore project so thoroughly that from that moment until his death six months later, Myrick devoted most of his waking hours to the Rushmore cause. Because of a heart condition that kept him bedfast during much of each day, Myrick had to confine his Rushmore activity to correspondence, but he produced a flood of that. He wrote to prominent men by the dozens, urging them to contribute to the work. He urged President Coolidge, who was a personal friend, to choose the Black Hills for his vacation—and there is reason to believe that Myrick, whose magazines could influence the farm vote, was partly responsible for the president's decision to do so. Daily, Myrick peppered Norbeck, Robinson, Hughes, and Borglum with letters of advice on every aspect of Rushmore. Get out more publicity! he prodded. Ask more people for contributions! Pay Borglum for his past expenses! Send more fund-raising letters! "How can Borglum be expected to work without a contract?" Myrick asked. "Prepare a contract for him!" Act! Act! Act!

The Mount Harney Association's executive committee (Norbeck, Robinson, and Governor Bulow) thought that preparing a contract now would be putting the cart in front of the horse. Of what use would it be, with no money to back it up? Nonetheless, prodded by Myrick, they and Congressman Williamson together set about drafting not one contract, but two. The reason for the second one was that Borglum had no intention of making Rushmore a full-time job nor of tying himself down to supervision of its routine work. He intended to deal with it as an architect deals with a building: he would create the design and provide the supervision necessary to assure that the work was done according to that design, but the work itself could and should be done by Tucker under a separate contract. The Association agreed with that, and began preparing contracts accordingly.

This, in turn, forced the executive committee to decide exactly what it was that they were hiring Borglum to carve. Heretofore this had been an open question, subject to much debate and mind-changing. In drafting these contracts, however, they had to be able to define precisely what they were contracting for.

The world has known for more than half a century what their final decision was, but the world seems not to know, even yet, how and why that particular decision was reached. For that matter, the members of the executive committee, themselves, seem not to have known just how they reached it either. The reason is that it was not a decision they "made" so much as one they muddled into, over a period of time; it became crystallized only when they had to write it into Borglum's contract. And this, in turn, probably explains why the association never produced any clear statement of: (1) how the monument came to be a memorial to United States presidents instead of a war memorial, for example, or a memorial to other national leaders or events; (2) why four presidents were included instead of, say, two or three or five; (3) how this particular combination of presidents came to be selected and, especially, how Theodore Roosevelt came to be included.

These are the questions that persons interested in Rushmore probably ask most often even today, and almost certainly are the ones to which they receive the haziest answers. This is unfortunate, for without knowing why these things were decided as they were the story of Rushmore cannot be fully understood. And to understand just how these decisions were made, it is necessary to retrace the paths followed by the association in making them.

In the beginning, it must be remembered, it was the monument itself that was important to its creators and promoters—not what was to be carved on it. They did not set out to build it for its meaning nationally, but for its usefulness locally and/or personally. (Later, this would change. As the work progressed, all who were connected with it became increasingly dedicated to it for its own sake and for its meaning. But that was later, and here we are speaking of the beginning.) There was nothing wrong with those motives. Indeed, they probably are the ones from which most of the world's great works have sprung. The Pharaohs of Egypt, for instance, gave the world the Pyramids when all they had intended was to make themselves tombs. And Mark Twain gave the world some of its finest literature at a time when, in his later life, all he was trying to do was to write himself out of debt. Similarly, those who promoted and built the Mount Rushmore Memorial gave the world one of its greatest sculptural treasures, but their original purpose was something far less exalted.

The Dakotans wanted a monument that would bring recognition to their obscure state and generate a prosperous tourist industry. Borglum wanted a monument that would enable him to do something never before accomplished; he wanted to create a work that would give him artistic immortality; and he wanted one from which he could earn a large fee (he always denied this, but the evidence to the contrary is indisputable).

If a monument were to fulfill all of these aims, it would have to be, first of all, a one-of-a-kind showpiece; and it ought to be an unprecedented sculptural wonder. A solid mountaintop carved into a memorial would be such a showpiece and such a wonder—regardless of what it had been carved to memorialize. Even so, the selection of a proper subject was important. The more apt, impressive, or intriguing the monument's subject, the greater its public impact and appeal would be. With this in mind, Robinson originally had envisioned a cowboys-and-Indians carving that would include the figures of various Wild West characters. There can be little doubt, however, that he would have been happy to settle for figures of, say, Santa Claus and his elves had he thought they would serve his purpose better. Borglum, being more experienced in such matters, realized that without national interest and support the monument could not be financed, and he knew that to get that interest and support the monument must memorialize something of great national significance. "If we pitch the note high enough," he told Robinson, "we will arouse the nation." Hence, in September of 1924, when he and Robinson first met, Borglum declared that if they were to carve statues of the nation's two greatest heroes, Washington and Lincoln, they would indeed pitch the note high enough and as a consequence would be able to attract both the money to build the monument and tourists to look at it.

Robinson agreed. And so, at that moment and for that reason, the decision was made to create a monument dedicated to American presidents rather than to someone or something else.

It was not until almost a year later that inclusion of a figure of Jefferson was first proposed. There seems to be no clear record of how this came about, but it appears to have been Borglum's idea. For one thing, just as he had at Stone Mountain, Borglum was always pushing to make the Rushmore project as big as possible. For another, it was Borglum who, in August of 1925, first told the public that a Jefferson figure might be carved (*would* be carved, according to Borglum). Regardless of how it came about, it was an excellent suggestion, for, as Borglum explained, Jefferson not only had been the architect of the Declaration of Independence, but by his Louisiana Purchase (of which the Black Hills were a part) he had more than doubled the nation's territory. It was a selection few people could argue with, and few did.

They could and did argue, however, with the fourth selection for Rushmore, which was the figure of Theodore Roosevelt. The suggestion of carving Roosevelt was made almost immediately after the proposal of Jefferson, and it was controversial right from the start. There was a feeling that regardless of how great a president he might have been, Roosevelt somehow did not fit into a pattern with Washington, Lincoln, and Jefferson. Accordingly, the choice of Roosevelt was challenged and questioned then, continued to be challenged throughout its carving, and is often questioned, although more mildly, even today. "How *did* Roosevelt come to be carved on Rushmore?" people ask, "and why?"

The "why" is easily answered. The Roosevelt figure was included because Borglum and Norbeck wanted it included. It has been said that it was done at least partly because Roosevelt once had lived on a ranch some two hundred miles north of the Black Hills and therefore sort of "belonged" to the territory. It has been said also that Roosevelt was chosen for Rushmore because the Mount Harney Memorial Association hoped this would inspire well-to-do members of the Roosevelt family to make large contributions to the work. And there may be a grain or two of truth in both statements, but no more than that. The truth is, Roosevelt's likeness now appears on Mount Rushmore because Borglum and Norbeck both were ardent Roosevelt fans. Both had campaigned for him in his 1912 bid for reelection to the presidency, and it was partly due to Norbeck's efforts that Roosevelt had carried South Dakota in that election. Roosevelt had been a "trust buster" who sought to curb the powers of big business. He had championed the cause of those whom he called "the little people . . . the forgotten people," and in his 1912 campaign he had roared out to them, "I am strong as a bull moose! You may use me to the limit!" Norbeck and Borglum, too, believed in trust busting and in consideration for "the little people," and they, too, believed a man should use himself to the limit. Hence, they believed that the "Bull Moose" deserved to be immortalized in the everlasting stone of Mount Rushmore. And so, he was.

Just *how* the selection of Roosevelt was brought about, however, is a rather foggy matter. Although Borglum was always to claim credit for selecting Rushmore's other figures, he usually said that Roosevelt was Norbeck's idea. This creates a faint suspicion that Borglum did this because the Roosevelt selection drew a good deal of criticism, whereas the others did not; for it appears that Borglum himself first suggested Roosevelt even before he had suggested Jefferson. In October of 1924, just after his first inspection trip to the Black Hills, Borglum told Robinson that he was thinking of "colossal figures of Washington, Lincoln, and Roosevelt. . . ." It was Borglum, also, who made the first public mention of Roosevelt when, in the summer of 1925, he told the Rapid City Lion's Club that the monument would include figures of Washington, Lincoln, Jefferson, *and* Roosevelt. That speech, moreover, seems to have been Norbeck's introduction to the notion of a Roosevelt carving. For, upon hearing of it he wrote to Robinson, "I am much impressed with his latest idea . . . the Roosevelt subject would make a very strong appeal . . . especially in the Northwest."

However it may have come about, the Roosevelt suggestion created another problem. If the figure were to be included in the monument, it would be necessary to produce a reason for doing so that would fit the memorial's theme—for, by this time the memorial did have a theme. Soon after the selection of the first two figures Borglum had pointed out that if the monument were to be promoted successfully it would have to be promoted as something more than a pair of giant statues. It would have to be a monument "to" something. It needed, Borglum said, "to be given a real purpose . . . predicated upon clear and definite statements. . . ." In the beginning, that was easy to do. Washington had been the Union's most prominent founder, and Lincoln had been its foremost preserver. Thus, originally this was to have been a monument to "the foundation and preservation of the United States." When Jefferson was brought into the picture, there still was no problem. Jefferson had added vast territory to the nation through the Louisiana Purchase, and therefore the theme was simply expanded to include the term, "continental expansion." But how could Roosevelt be fitted in? Should the theme be tailored to fit Roosevelt, or should Roosevelt be tailored to fit the theme? It was Borglum who got around the problem, and he got around it via the Panama Canal. By building that canal, Borglum said, "Roosevelt completed the dream of Columbus, opened the way to the East, joined the waters of the great East and West seas." This had contributed to the nation's commercial expansion, which sort of tied in with "continental expansion." Therefore, Roosevelt could be included without changing the Rushmore memorial theme, which was and would remain, "in commemoration of the foundation, preservation, and continental expansion of the United States."

Once the executive committee had accepted the idea of carving four presidential figures instead of two or three, it never considered adding more. Which raises the often-asked question, "Why not? Why did they stop at four?"

There are two answers: the problem of money, and the nature of the mountain. In allowing themselves to be persuaded to authorize the carving of four figures when they did not even have money to start the first one, the association members felt they had gone pretty far out on a limb and they would go no further. As for the mountain; its face was divided by several deep, diagonal fissures, and whereas Borglum was certain he could fit four figures in among them he was not certain he could work in any more. Thus, it was decided to limit the Rushmore memorial to four presidential busts.

The executive committee did agree, however, to one other addition to the monument. Some of the stone that was too flawed to accept deep-carved human statues could be made to accept something shallower, and Borglum did not intend to let that space be wasted. Instead, he proposed to fill it with an inscription. He wanted to smooth off a space 120 feet high by 80 feet wide, and in giant letters carve upon it a brief history of the United States. It would not cost much to do that, he said, and it would add infinitely to the monument's future value. Without it, he said, archaeologists of the future might well be as baffled by the carved faces on Rushmore as those of the present were by the carved faces on Easter Island, and that could not be permitted. "You might as well drop a letter in the postal service without an address or signature," he said, "as to send that carved mountain into the future without identification." This inscription, which Borglum called "The Entablature," was to become the source of a bitter controversy and would never be carved. It was included, however, in the Rushmore plans he submitted in late 1926 to the Mount Harney executive committee.

With these plans before them, the executive committee early in 1927 set about deciding how much of Borglum's plan they were willing to undertake, and to draft his contract accordingly. They were worried about the cost of the venture, but Borglum kept sending them new estimates, each lower than the last, until he finally got the whole thing, including the entablature and his fee, down to $400,000. Whereupon, the committee voted to accept the project just as he had planned it, and wrote into his contract the association's intention to: "obtain the necessary funds and to create upon Rushmore Mountain . . . a memorial . . . of figures in heroic size of Washington, Jefferson, Lincoln and Roosevelt, also a suitably inscribed tablet. . . . "

The contract also stated that: The memorial was "to be carved . . . by . . . and/or under the direction of Gutzon Borglum, sculptor"; Borglum was to enjoy "full, final and complete freedom and authority in the execution" of the monument's design, but that he must consult with the executive committee before making any "great changes" in the design; Borglum, at his own expense, must furnish "all designs . . . all sketches and models . . . all enlargements in plaster . . . [and] all information or instructions required by the contractor"; and if the association should "require the sculptor to make journeys for lecturing, for propaganda or for other purposes," it would reimburse him for his expenses but not for his time.

As a fee for his services, Borglum was to receive a sum equal to twenty-five percent of the cost of the work itself. According to his estimates (which were written into the contract), the four figures and the entablature together would cost $312,000. This would produce a sculptor's fee of $78,000, and thus a total cost of $400,000. The contract further provided, however, that in no case could Borglum's fee exceed $82,500. He was to receive his fee in monthly installments, each being computed from the cost of the previous month's work; and in case "there should not be sufficient funds" to pay an installment when due, Borglum was to be paid twenty-five percent of whatever money the association actually did have, and was to be credited with interest at an annual rate of six percent on the balance until paid.

Then, there was the matter of those past expenses for which Borglum had not been paid and for which, at last, he had submitted a formal bill for $5,900. In the contract the association acknowledged that debt and stated that "not less than $2,900 of this amount" would be paid to him before the contract was signed. "The balance of $3,000," the contract continued, in a very strange statement, "shall be paid . . . by the association at its very earliest convenience out of funds it receives *from other than South Dakota Subscribers.*" (Emphasis added.)

In a similarly strange statement, the contract stipulated that the first $25,000 of funds contributed by Black Hills people could be spent only for "the plant and equipment required for the work," which meant, of course, that none of it could be paid to Borglum. Both of these unusual provisions were included for the same reason: to make it easier to raise money in the Black Hills. The people there were still smarting over Borglum's request for large sums of money after first having said he would not ask them for any, and they could be expected to give more readily if assured that their contribution would go to the actual work rather than to Borglum himself.

Tucker's contract was less complicated. It authorized him to install and operate the plant and equipment needed for the job, and to perform the actual construction of the monument according to Borglum's designs and instructions. In exchange he was to be paid $7,500 per year plus five percent of whatever he might save on the cost estimates listed in the contract.

While the contract was being prepared, Borglum began to get cold feet about signing it. Still smarting from his difficulties in trying to collect for his past expenses, he told Myrick that he was doubtful of the good will and honesty of the Mount Harney Association's leaders. In response, Myrick stated firmly that they *were* men of good will and *were* honest. As evidence, he recalled the fact that when Borglum had asked for a sculptor's fee of twenty-five percent instead of the twenty percent originally discussed, the association's executive committee agreed readily to the higher figure. Thus reassured, Borglum replied, "I am sure now of these good men and true . . . and [that] you (HM) . . . will suggest nothing unfair to me," and said he was ready to sign.

By its terms, however, the contract could not be signed until Borglum had been paid $2,900 for past expenses. And whereas fund raising committees in the Black Hills had managed by this time to get $12,000 in pledges from their fellow citizens, they had only pledges and no cash. To get the thing off dead center, Myrick pledged his *Dakota Farmer* magazine to give $2,500, one thousand of which would be paid immediately provided it were paid to Borglum. With that as a start, the fund raisers managed to scrape up another $1,900 in cash, Borglum was paid, and in mid-March the contract was signed.

A few days later, Tucker wrote from Florida to say that he had received his contract but could not accept the $7,500 per year it offered. He had to have $10,000 or it was no deal. The association then sent him a contract that provided the salary he was asking for, and in late March Tucker signed it.*

Doane Robinson, meanwhile, had suddenly been inspired to ask for a donation from the man for whom the mountain had been named, Charles Rushmore, now a prominent attorney in New York. On the first of April he received Mr. Rushmore's reply—a check for $5,000.

Later in April, a delegation that included Norbeck, Borglum, and Hughes went to Chicago to solicit donations from each of the three railroads serving the Black Hills, and was successful. Each road promised to give $5,000, payable whenever the association should request it.**

Now the Rushmore fund raising campaign began to develop momentum locally. John Boland joined Frank Hughes in pushing the local drive, and the Black Hills pledges increased steadily until in mid-May they reached $25,000, which was the campaign goal. It seemed likely, however, that a number of these pledges would prove to be "soft"—uncertain and to some extent uncollectable. To remove that uncertainty and thus give the association a figure it could count on, a group of Rapid City businessmen led by John Boland volunteered to guarantee the Black Hills pledges. Very quietly, so as not to encourage defaults among those who had made pledges, Boland and his group agreed to make up personally any difference between the amount actually given by Black Hills people and the $25,000 they had pledged to give.

---

* Some years later Borglum was to insist time-and-again that before signing his contract he had voluntarily reduced its sculptural fee provision from thirty-five to twenty-five percent so that Tucker's demand could be met. Hence, the sequence in which these events actually occurred is important.

** The delegation's Dakota members practiced the frugality they preached. During these three days on a train and a day and a night in Chicago, Frank Hughes spent $39.87 for train fare; $13.50 for meals; $3.50 for a hotel room—total, $56.87.

During this same time, the total of cash and solid pledges received from outside the Black Hills and South Dakota had grown to $23,000. Thus, after paying Borglum the $3,000 balance of the expense money due him, the association was still able to enter June with dependable assets of $42,000 with which to get the Rushmore work actually under way.

And there was still more good news. After William Bulow became governor, Norbeck had managed to persuade the state to build a road to Rushmore, and work on it was now about to start. On top of that, Borglum had persuaded utilities magnate Samuel Insull to lend to the Rushmore project a large, diesel-powered electric generating plant. And as a finishing touch, the Coolidge visit was now confirmed, which meant that for the next few weeks the Black Hills would occupy the center of the national stage. For Rushmore's promoters, considering all they had gone through, it was a time of well-earned euphoria.

8. The power plant, about October, 1927, which utilities magnate Samuel Insull donated and which Borglum later declared had been "maliciously wrecked."

10. The Trout and the President Play

hen the president announced his decision to visit the Black Hills, Governor Bulow at first felt nothing but pleasure. Then he discovered the announcement had a catch to it. Having chosen the Game Lodge for his summer White House and Rapid City High School for his summer capitol, obviously Mr. Coolidge had to be able to travel between them in any weather. Colonel Starling had just now discovered, however, that twelve miles of the thirty-mile road connecting them was a dirt trail, ungraded, unsurfaced, and, he correctly suspected, bottomless when wet. That, said the colonel, would never do. The governor must guarantee an all-weather road or the president would cancel his visit. Governor Bulow, who at that point would have promised anything, guaranteed it. Then he called the state highway engineer and told him to get busy grading and graveling those offending miles.

"Hell, Governor!" the engineer protested, "in the time we've got we can't even get it surveyed!"

"Do it first and survey it later!" retorted Bulow. "How's the president going to know he's riding on an unsurveyed road?"

And so it was done. The road was graded and graveled at the rate of a mile and a half a day and was ready ahead of time.

On June 13, President and Mrs. Coolidge—together with the presidential staff; a sizable covey of newspaper reporters; the Coolidge's white collie dogs, Rob Roy and Prudence Prim; and a pet raccoon named Rebecca who belonged to Mrs. Coolidge and lived in a wicker basket—rolled out of Washington, D.C., on a special train bound for the Black Hills.

The Presidential Special was due to arrive at Rapid City at half-past five on the afternoon of June 15, which had started out as a poor day for the president or anyone else to get a good first impression of the Black Hills country.

Heavy rain during the night had left behind a mass of lead-colored clouds that enshrouded the Hills and extended eastward in a dark, gloomy sheet over the town. A sharp little breeze was blowing down from the mountains, and it had a cheek-pinking bite to it and smelled of wet earth and wet pine, but it failed to stir the flag-and-bunting decorations, which sagged, limp and water-heavy, above the puddled streets.

As the day progressed the town became increasingly crowded with Dakotans who, despite the weather, were gathering to get a look at their president. By late afternoon when they began streaming across Main Street to congregate around the Chicago & Northwestern depot there were some ten thousand of them, which was twenty percent more than the population of the town, and they were quietly but thoroughly excited. Few incumbent presidents had ever visited the Hills, and this gave the occasion much importance. Most important, however, was the *kind* of president who was coming. South Dakota, and especially western South Dakota, was and always had been a rock-solid Republican fortress. True, Dakotans did sometimes elect a Democrat to office—Governor Bulow, for instance—but they were inclined to do it apologetically, as if it were a fall from grace they hoped would not be held against them. And Calvin Coolidge was Republican through and through. Moreover, he believed government should be kept small and inexpensive, and should hold its voice down and not meddle unnecessarily in the affairs of its people; and the Dakotans, their ideas of government having been frontier-forged, believed the same. Also, Calvin Coolidge was said to be a close-mouthed, close-fisted, down-to-earth man who minded his own business— characteristics that Dakotans generally admired in others and looked for with considerable success in themselves. All things considered, therefore, this Coolidge visit promised to be the most exciting Black Hills event since statehood.

To top it all off, while the crowd was gathering at the depot the clouds began to break in the west. Thus, when at last the Presidential Special rumbled across the Rapid Creek trestle and came to a stop beside the station, both it and the crowd were touched by shafts of sunshine.

John Boland, now president of the Commercial Club, and Vic Jepsen, who had replaced Boland as mayor, boarded the train to greet the president. The white collies, Rob Roy and Prudence Prim, appeared in the door of the Presidential Coach, dainty-stepped down to the station platform, and then, following them, came Calvin and Grace Coolidge.

From the National Guard artillery range in the Box Elder breaks to the northeast there came the distance-muted thunder of a twenty-one-gun salute.

9. *President and Mrs. Calvin Coolidge are met at Rapid
City, South Dakota, by Senator Norbeck on June 15, 1927.*

10. *The Game Lodge, in the Black Hills, where Borglum stayed
while hunting for a mountain to carve, and where President
Coolidge maintained a Summer White House for three months in 1927.*

While it was being fired, the crowd, craning and rustling, was sizing the Coolidges up.

The President was a bit more slightly built than they had expected . . . hair was a little more reddish. . . . Otherwise he looked about as they had thought . . . businesslike, sober, unpretentious. Mrs. Coolidge, well, she was pretty stylishly rigged out . . . looked kind of sophisticated . . . but she did have an engaging smile, and when smiling she looked like a warm, motherly kind of woman who probably liked to knit and to make apple butter. Actually, she looked like a smartly dressed farm woman . . . looked like a *Dakotan* in fact, and so did her husband. . . . And now the president was smiling! He was said to be a dour man who never smiled, but now he was actually grinning!

The crowd roared its approval. The Coolidges beamed. The National Guard band began thundering *Hail To The Chief.* And at that moment a love affair between Grace and Calvin Coolidge and the South Dakotans was begun.

The Coolidges lingered only briefly at the depot and then were driven to the Game Lodge. Behind them, Rapid City celebrated their coming. There was a big dance that night at the Fairy Garden and another at the Alfalfa Palace, and at both, couples danced to such recent hit songs as "Bye-Bye Blackbird," "Blue Skies," and "Sweet Georgia Brown."

At the Game Lodge, meanwhile, things were considerably more restrained. At a table set before a pine fire crackling in a massive stone fireplace, the Coolidges enjoyed a quiet dinner of elk steak, then settled down for the night.

A few days later, Borglum returned to the Hills, having driven by car from San Antonio. And he came determined to get the president to make a formal dedication of Mount Rushmore. The fact that it already had been dedicated once was no reason for not dedicating it again—not when you considered the publicity a dedication by the President of the United States would generate. However, there were two problems. First, the Coolidges had come for only a three-week stay, and almost a week of that had passed, which left too little time for arranging a proper ceremony. Second, Mr. Coolidge had stated flatly that he would make no formal appearances while on this vacation. While Borglum was pondering ways to change the president's mind, the South Dakota legislature, on June 22, changed the name of one of the Black Hills' peaks to "Mount Coolidge." With that in mind, Borglum on the following day opened his campaign of persuasion.

At that same time, as it happened, the president was involved in a very serious matter. The Governor-General of the Philippines, General Leonard Wood, had just arrived, having been summoned by Mr. Coolidge for discussion of a threatening insurrection in those islands. At the Game Lodge on the morning of the 23rd, the president and General Wood were deep in consultation when the morning stillness was suddenly shattered by the clatter of a low-flying plane. Flown by veteran Black Hills pilot Clyde Ice, and occupied by Gutzon and Lincoln Borglum, the plane roared low over the Game Lodge lawn. As it passed, Gutzon pitched out a huge wreath of flowers. Attached to the wreath were two Indian moccasins—one labeled "Mount Rushmore" and the other, "Mount Coolidge"—and a card that read, "Greetings from Mount Rushmore to Mount Coolidge."

This event is a matter of record; the reaction of Mr. Coolidge is not, and perhaps it is just as well. In any case, Borglum did manage to get an audience with the president a few days later, and to make his request. Though favorable to the Rushmore work, Coolidge would not be moved. He would make no formal appearances and no speeches while on his vacation, and that was that.

Borglum and Tucker both were at Rushmore now, Tucker having been there since late April, and between them they were kicking up a whirlwind.

Near the base of the mountain, a studio for Borglum was under construction, and from dawn until dark the mountainside itself echoed to the hammers of carpenters building a stairway to the top.

Early in July the power plant lent by Samuel Insull—two railway carloads of it—arrived in Keystone, where it was to be set up. A concrete foundation seven feet thick was poured to accommodate it, and a crew was set to work at putting it together. Another crew, meanwhile, began setting up a line of poles to carry power from the plant to the mountain.

By mid-July Tucker was working a force of sixteen men, and was heading his daily memos to them with "RUSH MORE!"

Also in July, the association received two more substantial donations. On July 1, as a result of a solicitation by Borglum, Robinson received a check for $5,000 from Senator Coleman DuPont, of Delaware. A little later Senator Norbeck obtained $5,000 from the Homestake Mining Co., of Lead, South Dakota.

The Rushmore road, however, was still in bad shape. Money had been appropriated and plans and surveys were being prepared, but the work was not going fast enough—at least, not from Borglum's point of view. Determined to get it speeded up, he went straight to Governor Bulow. As the governor told it later:

Almost every day he would demand that the road be built, and after each demand he expected the job to be completed before breakfast the next morning.

I especially recall one telegram he sent me. . . . It was the longest telegram I ever received and it contained the most expressive language. There were three hundred words in that telegram and Gutzon didn't repeat himself. Every word meant something. It was a masterpiece. . . . He said that he had just returned from the mountain. That it had rained. That he had worn white dress shoes and a new pair of white dress pants. . . . That he had ruined his shoes and his new white pants. I wired him suggesting that the next time he went to the mountain he ought to put on a pair of overalls and go barefooted. This advice held him down for several days, but in a short time he was lambasting again.

In mid-July the lambasting stopped. By then the state had two crews actively at work on the road. Also, Borglum had gone back to San Antonio to do further work on his Rushmore models and to catch up on other projects he had under commission.

The Coolidges, meanwhile, were having a delightful time. True, the sitting room and bedroom that comprised their private quarters in the Game Lodge were modest in both size and furnishings, and the bathroom was down the hall, but if this bothered them they never mentioned it. For the fact was, they were at ease and comfortable. Mrs. Coolidge, it turned out, did indeed like to knit, and she spent long hours on the spacious Game Lodge veranda just knitting and visiting.

Mr. Coolidge found Williamson to have been right about the absence of flies and mosquitoes, and the mountain air was doing wonders for his bronchitis. Before the president had been at the Game Lodge even a week his physician, Major James Coupal, was able to announce, "The warm days and cool nights, freedom from insects, and altitude . . . of the Black Hills are improving the health of President Coolidge."

Churchgoing Congregationalists, the Coolidges had found a church and pastor whom they liked. The church, located in the village of Hermosa some twelve miles east of the Game Lodge, was a plain, white clapboard affair attended by local farmers and ranchers. The pastor, a twenty-year-old blond giant named Ralph Lium, was a student-minister who had been sent to Hermosa only for the summer and had arrived there just in time to preach the very first sermon of his ministerial career, on June 19, to a congregation that included the President of the United States. In reporting the event, the *Rapid City Journal* said that as the congregation was filing out of the church after the service, an elderly lady approached Mr. Coolidge in hope of shaking his hand. Whereupon (or so the reporter worded it), "The President . . . shook her hand cordially, and then passed out . . . where he was shortly joined by Pastor Lium."

With churchgoing as a start, the Coolidges began mingling with the local people in other ways. They still would make no formal appearances, but, as they and the locals discovered how well they fitted in with each other, the Coolidges began to do a lot of just plain visiting. In the process, Mr. Coolidge began to adopt the local customs and local color. His Dakota hosts gave him a Western hat that, one observer said, "pointed a full ten inches into the air, and had a brim so wide he had to bend it slightly to get into his limousine," and the hat promptly became his off-duty headgear. On the president's birthday, which was the fourth of July, he was given a Western saddle and a spirited horse named Kit to go under it, a pair of chaps, and a pair of Western boots. Like the hat, the boots immediately became a part of his off-duty costume.

The Coolidges visited Nebraska's ex-governor, Samuel McKelvie, at his Black Hills cabin on Slate Creek, and because of the rugged terrain they went in a horse-drawn wagon. Along the way the wagon got caught in going so rough that the horses, alone, could no longer pull it; and later much was made of the fact that the president then rolled up his sleeves and joined the other male passengers in the sweaty task of pushing it.

A delegation of Sioux Indians, led by Chief Chauncey Yellow Robe, made Mr. Coolidge an honorary Sioux and named him *Wanbli Tokaha*—Leading Eagle.*

He took up horseback riding, and under the tutelage of "Dakota Clyde" Jones, a national rodeo champion, became a pretty fair horseman.

The thing the president was doing most and enjoying most, however, was fishing for trout. This was unexpected—at least on Mr. Coolidge's part. He had never taken up trout fishing, nor had he planned to. Nonetheless, urged on by his Dakota hosts he reluctantly agreed to make a stab at it. From his very first cast, he was successful. Remarkably so. He caught fish, a lot of fish,

---

* Later, other tribal members objected, saying that Yellow Robe had not been authorized to do that. Hence, there is some doubt as to whether Calvin Coolidge really did become an honorary Sioux Indian named Leading Eagle. He thought he did, however, and that was the important thing.

11. President Coolidge chose, during his stay in the Black Hills, to attend this country church in Hermosa rather than the big brick Congregational Church in Rapid City.

12. President and Mrs. Coolidge entering the Hermosa Congregational Church on June 19, 1927.

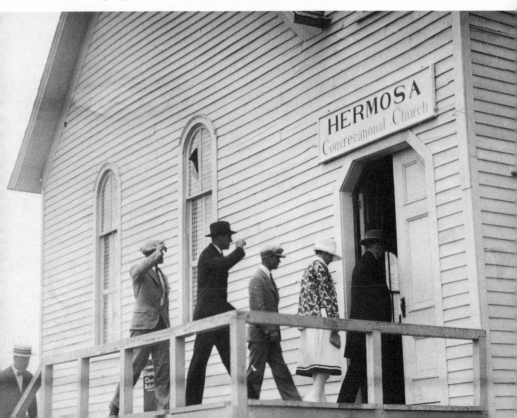

13. *President Coolidge traveled by wagon to visit Samuel McKelvie, ex-governor of Nebraska, at his cabin on Slate Creek. When the going got too rough for the horses alone to budge the wagon, the President rolled up his sleeves and helped to push it.*

14. *President Coolidge becomes* Wanbli Tokaha, *Chief Leading Eagle . . . maybe.*

and all of them big. Soon he had become a fishing addict—one who never knew failure; which, although he was never aware of it, was no accident. The Dakotans had stacked the deck.

Upon learning that the president actually was coming to visit, his hosts-to-be had begun thinking up ways to keep him interestingly occupied during his stay. The superior choice, if he could be made to enjoy it, seemed to be trout fishing. It would have a double advantage. Not only would it keep Mr. Coolidge entertained, but, as a valuable by-product, the attendant publicity ought to lure a host of fishing-minded tourists to the Hills. Accordingly, Governor Bulow and a few close-mouthed cohorts set about seeing to it that if the president could be persuaded to fish he would fish successfully.

By consulting the state game-and-fish warden, Bulow found that the State Fish Hatchery at Spearfish, in the northern Hills, had a lot of tired old breeding-trout it would be glad to part with—in fact, the hatchery had been planning to get rid of them anyhow. Years of lazy living on ground liver and horsemeat had left them fat and flabby. But they were big, fearless, and emi-nently catchable.

Next, across Squaw Creek, which was the stream running past the Game Lodge, two wire-netting fish fences were stretched—one hidden beneath a bridge near the lodge and the other concealed beneath a bridge two miles downstream. The section of creek between them was reserved for presidential fishing only—so, as he was told later, that the president might enjoy pri-vacy—and it was stocked with the fat old "liver-feds" from the Spearfish hatchery.

State records show two thousand fish to have been put into that section of creek during the summer of 1927, but not all at once, for there would not have been room. Instead they were put in gradually, and stealthily. On the back roads of the Black Hills in those days of prohibition there was much late-night traffic of automobiles running bootleggers' furtive errands. And on every fourth night of that summer one of those automobiles, an old Dodge truck with a tank on the back, was driven by hatcherymen Al Atcheson and "Dutch" Gleason "fishlegging" trout to the presidential fishing waters.

On the very first morning after his arrival, the president's hosts persuaded him to try catching a trout. He did so reluctantly, dressed in a business suit and only as a momentary pause on his way to his Rapid City High School offices. It was a morning no true fisherman would have chosen. The water, high and muddy from recent rains, was the kind no self-respecting trout would bite in. But the Game Lodge trout were not self-respecting. Snatched from a life of egg-to-grave security, cut off from their dole of liver and horse-

*15. President Coolidge learning to fish,
in the Black Hills, June 16, 1927.*

*16. President Coolidge after catching his first fish,
but before he decided whether he liked to fish or not.*

meat and cast into the wilderness, they did not care about the water nor that the president handled his fishing rod as gingerly as he might a red-hot poker. They were ready to snap at any reasonable-looking proposition, and Mr. Coolidge's hook looked reasonable. Within a few minutes five hefty fish were resting in the presidential creel.

The president fished again that evening with similar results, and returned, according to Mrs. Coolidge, "as pleased as a boy with his first pair of red-topped boots." Next morning, the Coolidges breakfasted on his catch and it seems not to have discouraged them, though perhaps it should have. In describing a dinner to which the Coolidges invited him later, Governor Bulow explained why. "Trout was served," he said, "and the first bite I took I could taste the liver and horsemeat on which that trout had lived for years, and I had never liked liver. . . . " Looking at the plump specimen on his plate, Bulow had then murmured, "Seems to me I've seen you before."

"What did you say, Governor?," asked Mr. Coolidge.

"I said, Mr. President, that I've not seen trout like these before."

"Came from right here at the Game Lodge," Coolidge proudly responded. "Caught 'em myself!"

These things might seem to have had little to do with Rushmore, but the fact is, they had everything to do with it. Through such experiences, Grace and Calvin Coolidge had come to regard the Dakotans as their friends. And as a favor to those friends, in mid-July, the president yielded to the urging of Williamson and Norbeck and agreed to dedicate Rushmore. He still could not have done it had the Coolidges not stayed longer than they had planned (they had come for three weeks, but stayed three months). They did stay on, however, and there can be little doubt that the remarkable Game Lodge fishing was a large part of the reason.

When Borglum was told of the president's decision, he announced August 10 as the dedication date and began preparing to return from San Antonio to the Black Hills. Meanwhile, Tucker began getting things at the mountain set up for the affair, and, as in 1925, Robinson together with committees of local people began preparing the ceremony itself.

While all this was going on, Mr. Coolidge was involved in two other events that may not have much to do with Rushmore but somehow still seem to belong in its story.

The first took place in July, when an automobile caravan bearing members of the National Womens' Party rattled over the dusty roads of Dakota to the Black Hills. They came to seek the president's support for a constitutional amendment that read, "Men and women shall have equal rights throughout the United States in every place subject to its jurisdiction." Accompanying them was Stephanie Dolgorouski, a Russian princess and sister-in-law to the late Czar Nicholas II. She had come, she told the *Journal*, to help her "sisters in their just and sacred cause," and to see the scenery.

The women were cordially welcomed by Mayor Vic Jepsen, and were told that the city attorney would gladly see to any arrangements they wanted made. They wanted to stage a mass rally, the women said; whereupon the mayor lent them Halley Park to hold it in, and the Rapid City Military Band to provide them with music.

The women held their rally, they saw the president, and there, unfortunately, the story ends. What the Women's Party delegates and the president said to each other seems to have gone unrecorded. The name of their proposal, however, *is* known. They called it, "The Equal Rights Amendment."

The second event occurred at Rapid City High School on August 2, the fourth anniversary of Mr. Coolidge's succession to the presidency following the death of President Harding. The day was unseasonably damp and cold, the temperature was some thirty degrees below the eighty-seven degrees normal for the date, and a soft gray mist was falling. The usual crowd of onlookers was standing outside the school hoping to get a glimpse of the president, and today they wore topcoats and carried umbrellas. Inside the building, the thirty-odd reporters assigned to covering the president were waiting, listless and bored, for the gloomy morning to end. Then, unexpectedly, they were told that Mr. Coolidge wanted to see them at twelve o'clock in his office. This was extraordinary. Mr. Coolidge held his press conferences on Friday and *only* on Fridays, and this was Tuesday. Suddenly their boredom vanished.

Exactly at noon the correspondents were shown into the president's office. Mr. Coolidge, smoking a long thin cigar, rose to greet them and asked, "Is everyone here now?" Upon being told that everyone was, he motioned them to file past his desk. As they passed he handed each a slip on which was typed, "I do not choose to run for president in nineteen twenty-eight."

The reporters were stunned. Not for a moment had the nation doubted that Coolidge would seek another term. Then one correspondent found his voice and asked, "Can you give us some further comment, Mr. President?"

"No," said Mr. Coolidge, and putting on his coat he left the building. The reporters, however, left it faster. Coats and hats forgotten, they clattered down the stairs and jostled their way through the crowd outside. In a Keystone Kops steeplechase, in cars and on foot they dashed and scrambled the four blocks to the telephone and telegraph offices downtown.

Mr. Coolidge spoke but five words during that conference, and his written message contained only twelve more. But the correspondents explaining those seventeen words wired 50,000 words of copy that afternoon, according to Western Union's records, and sent 40,000 more the following morning. How many more words were sent by telephone is anybody's guess. Whatever their number, the reporters' words were soon forgotten, but the phrase "I do not choose to run" was to live on as a part of the American vocabulary. In fact, on the very next morning a Model-T Ford abandoned on Rapid City's outskirts bore on its side a sign reading, "*I* do not choose to run in *1927*."

II. "Were We Afraid? Of Course We Were Afraid!"

Augustgust 10, 1927, was a golden day in the Black Hills country: warm but not really hot, occasional cotton-puff clouds lazy-drifting in a sky that was deep blue and endless, and the plains and mountains, freshened by summer rains, lying green and fragrant in the sun.

Considering it was that kind of day, that the roads to Keystone had been much improved since the summer of 1925, and that the President of the United States was going to speak, the 1927 dedication of Rushmore could have been expected to draw a much larger crowd than the one in 1925. Actually, however, it drew a substantially smaller one. One reason was the timing. The earlier dedication had been held after harvest season while this one was right in the middle of it, and because of the wet season the harvest was heavy. Accordingly, few farmers or the merchants supplying them could see taking the day off to attend the dedication of a 'mountain that had already been dedicated. Besides, they had not been hearing much lately about Rushmore, anyhow. The president's visit had pushed it out of the news and out of their minds. Moreover, many of the country people, and others as well, still regarded this mountain carving as a proposition entirely too cockeyed ever to amount to anything. Hence, most who did attend the affair went not for the dedication but to see the president.

The upshot was that between 1,000 and 1,700 people showed up—half, or a few more than half, of the number that had attended the dedication in 1925. There were enough, however, that all through the morning the Keystone road lay under a sun-shimmering trail of dust kicked up by Rushmore-bound autos. For autos to continue on to Rushmore from Keystone, however, was another matter. The state was in the process of making the Rushmore road into a real road, but at the moment it was in mid-construction and a real mess. On the assumption that some bold visitors would travel it anyhow, a parking lot had been set up at the dedication site, and young Howdy Peterson, of Keystone, had been stationed there to direct parking. However, as Howdy told it later, "The first car up got stuck and stayed stuck all day. It had the road bottled up, and so that was that." Anyhow, most people had chosen to leave their cars on the only sizable flat spot in Keystone—the baseball diamond. From there, carrying baskets of fried chicken and potato salad and jugs of iced lemonade, they walked two steep miles up to the hillside facing the Rushmore cliff from across the head of Lafferty Gulch. Then, in cool pine shade beside the little brook that chuckles past the foot of the cliff, they picnicked and waited for the president.

Mr. Coolidge has chosen yet another means of getting to the mountain; one in keeping with his newly acquired Western image. He had elected to go on horseback, and his mount, along with others for his secret service escort and special guests, had been sent to Keystone ahead of him. With Coolidge-like prudence, however, he had chosen not to ride the horse he had been given on his birthday. Kit was spirited and skittish and in the disturbing presence of a crowd might become so disrespectful as to dump the United States President into the dust of the road. Accordingly, he had decided to ride Mistletoe, a sedate old Game Lodge plodder whose philosophical serenity could not be disturbed by man or nature.

Clad in his big hat, Western boots, and a business suit, the president arrived in Keystone by limousine. Being thirsty from the dusty drive, he stopped at the pool hall, where he drank a bottle of cold soda pop. Then he drew on a pair of extravagantly fringed buckskin gloves, mounted Mistletoe, and led his small cavalry troop of secret service men and presidential guests up the hill to Rushmore.

The ceremony was much like the one in 1925—an abundance of speeches followed by a flag-raising pageant on the crest of the cliff—but with the notable addition of the presidential salute. It was "a salute of 21 guns fired under the direction of H. W. Zolper, highway engineer . . ." according to the *Rapid City Journal*, and although the *Journal* did not explain why it was conducted by a highway engineer, there was a reason. It was not a twenty-one *gun* salute at all. It was a twenty-one *stump* salute, accomplished by blasting that same number of troublesome pine stumps from the new roadway. As such, it may have been history's first salute to a head of state that accomplished something

17. *President Coolidge, in new cowboy boots, dedicates Mount Rushmore while Borglum shades his face with his hat, August 10, 1927.*

useful while being given—a point the frugal Mr. Coolidge could have been expected to appreciate, and probably he did.

With typical Norbeck simplicity, Senator Norbeck introduced Mr. Coolidge to the crowd by saying, "The President of the United States will now address you." Responding with an eloquence that belied his laconic reputation, Mr. Coolidge then said (in part):

> We have come here to dedicate a cornerstone laid by the hand of the Almighty. . . .
>
> The union of these four presidents carved on the face of the everlasting Black Hills of South Dakota . . . will be distinctly American in its conception, in its magnitude, in its meaning. . . . No one can look upon it without realizing it is a picture of hope fulfilled.
>
> Its location will be significant. Here in the heart of the continent, on the side of a mountain which probably no white man had ever be-

held in the days of Washington, in territory acquired by the action of Jefferson, which remained an unbroken wilderness beyond the days of Lincoln, which was especially loved by Roosevelt. . . .

The people of South Dakota are taking the lead in the preparation of this memorial out of their meager resources. . . . Their effort and courage entitles them to the sympathy and support of private benefi- cence *and of the national government.** They realize fully that they have no means of succeeding in the development of their state except a reliance upon American institutions. They do not fail to appreciate their value. There is no power that can stay the progress of such a people.

Mr. Coolidge concluded by presenting to Borglum six steel drills with which the sculptor would today formally begin the carving of Rushmore. Next, to the horror of his secret service escort and to the delight of his Dakota onlookers (who reveled in every Coolidge display of the common touch), the president stepped to a water bucket sitting on the corner of the speaker's platform and drank deeply from the community dipper suspended in it. Then he clapped his big hat back on his head, sat down, and with folded arms listened to Borglum's response.

Always a master orator, Borglum outdid himself that day. He had been hoping for presidential endorsement of a government contribution to Rush- more, and now inspired by the remark the president had made about the work deserving the sympathy and support of the national government, he set about trying to get that support nailed down.

"I am getting old," exclaimed the sculptor, "but I may yet live long enough to put the bust of *Coolidge* alongside those of Washington, Jefferson, Lincoln, and Roosevelt!" Next he spoke of Rushmore's meaning: "a memo- rial to the first modern republic in the Western World." He spoke of the en- tablature and how, by its message, it might instruct future generations in the meaning of the United States; and by way of the entablature he then returned his focus to the president. In a grand flourish of seemingly extemporaneous oratory, Borglum concluded by exclaiming:

Mr. Coolidge! As the first president who has taken part in this great undertaking, please write the inscription to be carved on that moun-

---

* Emphasis added.

tain! We want your connection with it shown in some other way than just by your presence!

I want the name of Coolidge on that mountain!

It was a dramatic pronouncement that drew a cheering response from the crowd, and it probably aroused some response in Mr. Coolidge also, although by no flicker of expression did he reveal it. The passage of time would reveal, however, that in making it Borglum had again sowed the dragon's teeth of future conflict.

Next was the flag-raising pageant, which gave Borglum time to carry his six drills to the top of the mountain. Then came the climax of the affair. Looking tiny as a fly on the side of a barn, Borglum was lowered by cable onto the face of the cliff. The spectators, silent now, heard the metallic chatter of a pneumatic drill. A tendril of rock dust drifted away from the tiny figure. Then Borglum was hoisted successively to five more locations on the cliff, and at each for a few moments he drilled. And with this drilling, it said in the program, he had begun the carving of Washington.

Carrying the six drills, Borglum then returned from the mountain to the speakers' platform, where he presented one drill each to President Coolidge, Senator Norbeck, and Doane Robinson. Ralph Lium, the boy-minister from Hermosa, pronounced a benediction, and the dedication of the mountain was done.

After three years of effort, six token holes drilled in the mountain. Not much, but something. A beginning. That is, it was a formal beginning. Actually, Borglum and Tucker still had far to go before any real carving could be done, and Borglum had been able to do his token drilling only because a portable, gasoline-powered air compressor rig had been brought in for that express purpose.

The time following the dedication was one of intense effort at Rushmore, and for those involved in it the effort was all-absorbing and all-important. For the rest of the population, both local and national, however, it was neither. Public attention had been diverted to more exciting events. The first of these occurred on the very evening of the dedication and was a violent confrontation between what today would be called the "establishment" and the "anti-establishment."

As it happened, when President Coolidge rode up to Rushmore that day, there was on his desk a clemency appeal from Nicola Sacco and Bartolomeo Vanzetti, political radicals and World War draft evaders who had been sentenced to die for the robbery-murder in 1921 of a factory paymaster in Massachusetts. Over the years members of the political left had been insisting, sometimes violently, that Sacco and Vanzetti were innocent and had been condemned only because of their politics. Then many liberals, Gutzon Borglum among them, had taken up the Sacco-Vanzetti cause and had made it intellectually fashionable. But even as the far left and numerous liberals had come to believe that since Sacco and Vanzetti were radicals they must therefore be innocent, members of the far right and many conservatives had come to believe that because the two were not only radicals but draft dodgers as well they must therefore be guilty. Caught in a political bind between these two forces—both of which were motivated more by emotion and bias than by actual knowledge—the governor of Massachusetts finally had appointed a committee, headed by the president of Harvard University, to make a thorough investigation of the case. Early in 1927 the committee reported having found Sacco and Vanzetti "guilty beyond reasonable doubt." Accordingly, the governor had confirmed their death sentences, and Sacco and Vanzetti, in turn, had appealed directly to the president.

On the same afternoon that he dedicated Rushmore, President Coolidge denied the Sacco-Vanzetti appeal, and touched off a firestorm. That evening rioting leftist mobs stoned United States embassies in London, Paris, Geneva, and even in South Africa. At home, violence broke out in a number of major cities, and the United Press reported, for example: "5,000 people, shouting defiance to capitalism and the law, singing 'The Third Internationale,' and shouting "Sacco and Vanzetti must not die," battled 400 Chicago police in a savage outburst of radicalism." And similar but less ferocious demonstrations in various American cities were to keep the Sacco-Vanzetti pot boiling until well after the two were executed in late August.

In the Black Hills, the Coolidges, by extending their stay into late August, and then on into September, continued to be the center of attention, with but one exception. In May, Charles Lindbergh had made world history by flying his tiny *Spirit of St. Louis* nonstop from New York to Paris; and, on September 2, he made local history by flying the *Spirit of St. Louis* to the Black Hills where, upon his arrival, he circled the Game Lodge in salute to the president.

Then came the excitement of the Coolidges' departure; a departure embellished by every kind of ceremony the local people could think up and the Coolidges would stand for. (Before leaving, the president told his secretary to secure from Governor Bulow a bill for the Coolidges' three months use of the Game Lodge. "You tell the President," Bulow retorted, "that I never invite a man to dinner and then charge him for the meal! He'll get no bill from me!" And he never did.)

This sudden diversion of public attention from himself and Rushmore did nothing to improve Borglum's disposition, which had become difficult, to say the least. Norbeck and some others were of the opinion that Borglum's head had been turned by the attention he had received from the president. It seems more likely, however, that his peevishness was caused by a collection of worries that he was prudently keeping to himself. But whatever the reason, Borglum's associates during that autumn were finding him to be a heavy cross to bear. He was carping at the association's executive committee for being inept in its own work and for interfering in his, and for what he regarded as their remarkable stinginess with money.

Borglum, himself, was in no danger of being called a penny pincher. He was disposing of the project's funds at a rate the executive committee was finding to be both alarming and hard to control. It was not supposed to be that way. Myrick, before his death in July, had warned the committee about the sculptor's ways with money and had said he should not be allowed to spend Rushmore funds except through use of vouchers that had been previously approved by the executive committee. This, however, was turning out to be easier said than done. Just as at Stone Mountain, Borglum at Rushmore felt it was demeaning for him, the project sculptor, not to be the sole judge of where, how, and for what the project's expenditures were made. Moreover, because he was a man who regarded the goal ahead as being more important than the details underfoot, he tended to think of vouchers and similar paperwork only as pettifogging obstacles created for the entertainment of bookkeepers. As a consequence, he was committing the association to expenditures first and obtaining authorization for them afterward, if at all. When association treasurer Doane Robinson spoke to Borglum about this, and asked him not to be so "free-handed," the sculptor snapped back by saying that if the association expected him to do a proper job it would have to quit bothering him with its "trifling economies."

Another thing upsetting Borglum was his lack of a proper studio. The one being built was nowhere near ready, and he was operating meanwhile from a log cabin, remodeled as a studio, down on Grizzly Creek. This studio, he said, was too small and too far from the job, as indeed it was. He also said it was incomprehensible that the association should not have realized his need for a proper studio and have had one ready for him. Now it was Robinson who was stung, and who snapped back. He said that in requesting structures and equipment Borglum had made no particular point of the studio nor submitted any specifications for one. "I am not worth a damn at divining what a man has in the back of his head," said Robinson. "You may think it is artistic temperament, but to me it seems childishness, pettiness, unworthy of a man of your great gifts."

This sort of thing was kept within the Rushmore "family" as much as possible, of course. Even so, some of its flavor began to seep out and affect Borglum's image in the general community. That fall, for example, the *Journal* reported that one of the world's rarest birds was to be found in the Hills and was called a white-winged junco. This prompted a letter to the editor from a local resident, who said, "We've got another one down by Keystone that is just as rare—they call it a Borglum."

It must be said, however, that if ever there was a time when Borglum had reasons for being touchy and out of sorts, this was that time. He had many things on his mind, all of them unspoken and all of them heavy. Talking about this job had been one thing. Performing it was going to be quite another. Like a matador facing a bull, Borglum, after much preliminary fanfare, was now facing the mountain. For Borglum, as for the matador, this was the moment of truth. The challenge of Stone Mountain had been great, but it had been as nothing compared to this challenge at Rushmore. There, Borglum had been carving shallow bas-relief figures on stone that was relatively smooth and unflawed. Here, he would be carving much larger figures, deep and in-the-round, on a fissured crag containing heaven only knew what kinds of defects. And how deep were those fissures? Dr. C. C. O'Hara, the geologist-president of the School of Mines, had warned him that they were likely to be very deep, but in preparing his cost estimates for the association Borglum had ignored that warning. Now, he could only hope that Dr. O'Hara had been wrong. And, were there float-blocks of uncarvable schist hidden in that granite cliff? Dr. Joseph Connolly had pointed out, and indeed it could be seen with the naked eye, that much of the bottom half of the cliff consisted of the exposed edge of such a float-block.* Were there others, or an extension of the one visible, lying beneath the surfaces to be carved? Also, there still was a question about the granite itself. One reason Borglum had chosen Rushmore was because its visible granite was a fine-grained biotite-muscovite, which was workable. Most Black Hills granite, however, was a pegmatite that was too coarsely crystallized for carving. So . . . was the Rush-

---

* In looking at Rushmore or a picture of it, you will see, just below the Washington carving, closely spaced lines sweeping upward from right to left. These are the edges of twisted strata in the float-block.

more cliff fine-grained inside? Or was there coarse pegmatite behind its fine-grained surface?

The safest way to tackle these problems, of course, would have been for Borglum to peel off the entire surface of the area he intended to carve, remove whatever unsound rock he might find, and then reshape the cliff to fit his models. It would have been a sensible thing to do and likely that which most sculptors would have done. His artistic integrity would not permit it, and now we begin to see why it took a Borglum to make a Rushmore. As he later explained:

> The one successful way to proceed . . . is to adapt the sculptured forms to the existing stone formation, and *not* to convert the mountain into an architectural form and then transform the sculpture to fit it. Sculptured work on a mountain must *belong* to the mountain as a natural part of it; otherwise it becomes a hideous mechanical application.

That was how Borglum saw it, and to the everlasting benefit of Rushmore, that was how he did it. He chose to carve one head at a time, and not to locate the next one until he could see how it would blend with the previous work as well as with the mountain itself. It was a gamble that time would prove to have been time-consuming, expensive . . . and correct. In speaking of it, Borglum said, "Were we afraid? Of course we were afraid . . ."; but he did not say that until much later. At the time, the public was skeptical enough as it was. Thus, if he had spoken of fissures and of schist float-blocks and of the unknown quality of the rock; if he had admitted that to get the project going he had overstated the probable quality of the stone and had understated the probable cost of carving it, he would likely have killed the project even before it was begun.

Having decided to make Washington the monument's dominant figure, Borglum decided to begin with the Washington head and to place it on the highest and front-most dome of the cliff's irregular crest.

Next, he had to solve the problem of transferring his design from the model to the mountain. Borglum had said publicly that he would do this as he had done it at Stone Mountain, which was by use of a photo-projector. But even while saying it he had to have known it could not be done that way. Projection would work for flat figures but not for those to be carved in-the-round. Besides, Rushmore's face was too lumpy for accurate projection. It would have been like trying to project a picture onto the side of a sack of potatoes. Rushmore demanded an entirely different approach, so naturally the ingenious Borglum invented one.

What he came up with was a system whereby a given point on either the model or the mountain could be precisely located in terms of horizontal distance, vertical distance, and angle from a fixed "master point"—the master point being the center of the top of the head of the figure being measured. For simplicity in transferring these "points," as he called them, from model to mountain, Borglum built his models on a scale of one-to-twelve so that one inch on a model was one foot on the mountain. To make these measurements

18. Chief Pointer Jim LaRue (left) and Lincoln Borglum operating the vertical mast, horizontal boom, and protractor plate of the Rushmore pointing machine.

he constructed devices called "pointing machines," and the men he trained to use them were called "pointers."

In constructing his first pointing machine he installed at the top and center of the head of the Washington model a horizontal protractor plate so positioned as to measure degrees of right and left angle from the centerline of the model's face. To the center of the protractor he attached a horizontal swinging boom thirty inches long. The boom was calibrated to measure in inches the distance from the master point and was equipped with a sliding device from which, on a line also calibrated in inches, a plumb bob could be lowered. Thus, when the tip of the plumb bob was placed in contact with a given point on the model, that point could be described in degrees of right or left angle as determined by where the boom lay across the protractor, and in terms of horizontal and vertical distance from the master point as indicated on the scales on the boom and plumb-bob line.

Locating on the mountain what he believed would be the top center of the Washington head, Borglum there constructed a similar device. In this case, however, the protractor was a steel slab four feet across. The boom, also of steel, was thirty feet long—its tip being supported by a cable running from the top of a mast erected on the master point. The plumb-bob fitting was carried along the length of the boom by a crank-operated endless cable, and the plumb bob itself was raised and lowered (to mark a point) by another hand-cranked cable.

This system of transferring measurements from one pointing machine to another, and thus from model to mountain or vice versa, proved to be so simple and effective that it would be the only measuring system used throughout Rushmore's construction.

Finally, Borglum laid out for Tucker a procedure to follow in roughing out the Washington head. First, he was to locate the "rough points" that would determine the outline of the head. Next, he was to "peel off" the surface of that area until he reached sound carving stone. Then he was to carve the stone into a "great egg-shaped mass . . . from three to six feet larger than the final head." By this method Borglum could preserve maximum sculptural flexibility. Once the "egg" had been formed he could study the play of light and shadow upon it and observe its relationship to the mountain around it before deciding just how the finished head should be positioned within it.

Tucker and his assistant, J. C. Denison, had started many things at the mountain during the summer, but by the time of the dedication they had completed only a few. Now, with a crew of twenty-two men, they buckled down to getting them finished up.

19. The mountain has been marked for the start of the Washington head and the tramway cable is in place, but the carving has not yet begun.

20. The beginning of the Washington head, October, 1927.

21. *At work on Washington's head, autumn, 1927. The man in the foreground is the pointer, and the vertical tape is suspended from the pointing machine boom mounted atop the head.*

22. *A driller, in the sling-seat designed by Borglum, begins to cut away the excess stone on the Rushmore cliff, probably in October, 1927.*

In honor of Doane Robinson, the pine-clad knob across the gulch to the south of Rushmore had been named "Mount Doane," and on the slope of Mount Doane facing the Rushmore cliff the project's operating base was established.

To lift materials from there to the top of the mountain, Tucker and his men now installed an overhead tramway—a heavy cable 1,300 feet long from which a steel mine-bucket was suspended on a trolley. This was for supplies only; its five hundred-pound load limit was considered too low for the safe hauling of men. The men would go to work by means of the stairway now being completed; it would have 506 steps interspersed with forty-five inclined ramps, and climbing it would be equivalent to climbing a forty-story building.

Crews installed two big air compressors on Mount Doane, dammed the brook to provide cooling water for them, and laid a half-mile steel pipeline to carry the compressed air to the clifftop.

On the top itself they emplaced eight hand-cranked winches for lowering workmen onto the cliff. Around the winches, a building, anchored to the naked stone, was built to shelter the winch operators and to serve, as well, as a warehouse and workshop.

By fall the base had become a village. There was an air-compressor house, a house for the tramway hoist and its operator, a blacksmith shop fitted with special drill-sharpening equipment, a bunkhouse, a dining hall and kitchen, and there was under construction a large log studio for Borglum.

At last the planning was done, the buildings were built, the equipment was in place, and on October 4, 1927, the real carving of Mount Rushmore was begun. Considering all the time and money and planning and politics that had gone into bringing this to pass, one would have thought it would have been a much celebrated affair. As it happened, however, it was nothing of the kind. Tucker simply set men with jackhammers to drilling on what was to become Washington's forehead, and that was that. No press coverage, no fanfare, no celebration. Even Borglum was not present for it. After having finished locating the Washington head and working out the pointing and carving procedures, he had turned the work over to Tucker and had gone back to San Antonio to take care of assignments awaiting him there.

But even though the beginning of Rushmore was less than impressive to the public, it was more than impressive to those men who now began to work on the face of the cliff. Most had had experience in mines and quarries, and so it was not what they were going to do that they found impressive. It was where they were going to do it. Instead of working on solid ground as man was meant to do, they would be working suspended in space, where man was

not meant to be. And because of man's instinctive fear of heights and of falling, this kind of "mining" was going to take some getting used to.

To understand their feelings, imagine for a moment that you have just
now begun work on Rushmore as, say, a driller. Your place of business has a
stone wall on one side and empty air on the other. You hang suspended there
in a seat like that of a child's swing, only it is longer and is made of leather
covered steel. Your business is the drilling of holes by means of an air-driven
jackhammer that weighs half as much as you do and is attached at one side to
a cumbersome air hose. The hammer is suspended by a chain from the same
cable that supports you, so you cannot lose it. Nonetheless, its weight and
shape and the drag of its air hose makes the hammer an awkward tool to ma-
nipulate for a man suspended in a swing-seat. Hence you find that for one
who is not yet accustomed to it, wrestling with that hammer is about like
wrestling with a live hog.

You will do your drilling while hanging on the side of a stone wall so lofty
that you will feel at first like you are hanging on the back fence of Creation.
From where you sit you can look down upon mountains and plains that
stretch farther than your eye can see. Two miles to your right some of Keystone's buildings are visible in a canyon bottom, but they do not look like
buildings in a canyon. They look like cracker crumbs scattered in a fold of a
rumpled green blanket. Directly below you are pine trees, and just beyond
them are the buildings of Rushmore's village, but from where you sit the
trees are toy trees and the buildings are dollhouses. As you look out over
these things they all seem remote and not quite real, and you feel a little as if
you were viewing them as a spectator from another world. Surrounded by
these vast spaces, suspended against a stone cliff that is vast also, you feel
dwarfed and insignificant . . . and uneasy.

The cable from which you are suspended is attached at its other end to a
winch in the cliff-top winch house. However, you cannot see the winch
operator, nor he you. Therefore, signals are passed between you by a "call-
boy"—a young man secured by a safety harness to the lip of the cliff in a
position where he can see you both.

Your seat and its rigging were designed by Borglum himself. At either end
of your seat, welded to it and rising some six inches above it, is a steel arch.
Attached to each arch by buckles and rings are the heavy leather straps by
which the seat is supported. Some six feet above your head the two straps are
connected by steel rings to the end of your lifeline—your cable. About four
feet above your head a spreader bar of the same length as your seat is mounted
horizontally between the straps, pushing them apart so that they rise ver-

23. *A view into the winch-house, showing the winches from which drillers were suspended on cables over the mountain face. The men are Alfred Berg and Jack "Palooka" Payne.*

tically beside you and are thus kept out of the way of your work. Also fastened to the arches on your seat is your safety belt: a broad leather strap that passes across your lower back and another that buckles across your front. This harness is perfectly safe. Once buckled in, there is no way you can fall out of it; you know this in your head but not in your gut. The same with your cable —three-eighths of an inch in diameter, made of mild steel, capable of holding a three-ton load—which your head knows but not your gut, not yet anyhow. When you look up at that cable after first having taken a dizzying look into the canyon below, it seems a slender thread to hang a life on. Especially if that life is your own.

These are things you must get used to if you are to work on the Rushmore

cliff, and chances are that you will. Others, however, will not. As one workman told the author:

> They gave me my jackhammer and they gave me my drills, and I
> went down over that mountain and stayed 'til noon. Then I went
> back and stayed 'til night. But, God! It scared me! No two ways
> about it. But I did that for three or four days and, no foolin', I'd
> wake up in the night and grab that old bed and hang on for all I was
> worth, thinkin' I was fallin' off that mountain. Somehow you never
> had any faith in that cable, and you could look down and see just
> where you'd fall to, and it looked so damned far! So I told Mr.

*24. Call-boy Jimmy Payne on the forehead of Washington, sitting
beneath the horizontal boom of the pointing machine. His job was to
relay movement instructions from the driller to the winch operator.*

25. Robert "Bob" Himebaugh starting his descent over Washington's forehead while carrying the detonator box for dynamite charges.

26. Powdermen Alfred Berg (left) and Clyde "Spot" Denton preparing dynamite charges for fine-blasting. Note how small the charges are.

Denison, "God! I just can't do that! I can't sleep at night and I'm scared to death hangin' out there on that dinky cable." So he give me a different job and I stayed at Rushmore until it was finished.

Also, there are special techniques you must learn in order to work down on the cliff. Among these is the business of simply getting up and down on it. You will do this by leaning back in your seat, with your feet firmly thrust against the rock, and by "walking" up or down at the same rate that your winch operator is taking in or letting out cable. If you "walk" down too fast or up too slowly your body angle relative to the cliff will become too steep and you will lose your footing. Then you will find yourself hanging flush against the cliff while being dragged over its rough stone. Making this mistake is sometimes painful and always embarrassing, and therefore you will learn early not to make it. You must learn, too, how to handle your jackhammer in awkward positions and never to become absentminded while using it. You will find each day, at your particular place of work, marks and numbers that the pointers have painted there to tell you just where and how deep to drill. If a hole is to be drilled from a difficult angle or on sharply sloping rock, when you turn on the drill the bit will bounce and skitter over the stone like water over a hot skillet. Then you will learn to place your heels together and your toes apart, with the mark between them. By placing the bit in the vee thus formed you can control it with your feet until it has dug a pocket that will keep it from wandering. And above all, you must never absentmindedly drill too deep. Stone can be removed but it can never be replaced, so this would be a cardinal sin.

These, then, were the kinds of things Tucker's crew had to learn and to get used to, and they did. But while they were at it they discovered something else they were going to have to do if they were to be effective. They would have to use dynamite. Borglum had not planned on that. It is hard to say why, considering his experience at Stone Mountain, but he had not. In his formal Rushmore proposal he had written: "The stone will have to be drilled, hand-plugged, and machine cut by what are known as air drills. I shall use no explosives . . . this is unnecessary and unsafe at Rushmore." However, less than three weeks of drilling and "plugging" (a method of breaking away stone between closely placed holes) revealed that at Rushmore as at Stone Mountain the job would last forever if done by this method alone. Accordingly, the project log for October 25 reported, "The chief event of the day was the trying of dynamite in blasting off rock." These were only "experimental" shots, the project clerk told the *Journal*, and though they had been "highly satisfactory," he said, "blasting won't be used often, and to avoid cracking portions to be used for figures it will be used with the utmost caution." But this attitude, too, was to change almost immediately. This may have been because there were at least two highly skilled powdermen on the job. Denison was expert in the use of dynamite generally, and Tucker was expert in using it in mountain-carving. Anyhow, dynamiting soon became a daily occurrence at Rushmore, and although it may have been used "with utmost caution," one of the first blasts was so powerful that a boulder flew 186 feet through the air to strike and snap the tramway cable.

Now, with the crew getting broken in and dynamite coming into daily use, the results were becoming increasingly visible. Dark-weathered exterior stone was stripped away, fresh mica-spangled granite was revealed, and at the top of the Washington dome a white spot appeared. Then the spot became a patch, growing daily, creeping down to the hairline and then the eyebrow-line of the future Washington face. As the patch grew, its whiteness contrasting starkly with the gray-brown of the surrounding stone, it more and more began to resemble a blob of plaster of paris that had been placed there, perhaps to repair a nick in the cliff's upper rim. Then the top of the patch became rounded, and became the top of that "egg-shaped mass" Borglum had told Tucker to carve.

But even as this was going on and the work was gaining momentum, two forces were conspiring to stop it. One was weather. The other, as usual, was money—or, rather, the lack of it.

Borglum had gone to San Antonio expecting the Rushmore work to be continued throughout the winter. As late as the end of September, Tucker, too, had said this would be the case. But even while he was saying it, weather and the bank account both were giving warnings to the contrary.

Borglum and Tucker had expected the weather to be troublesome but by no means impossible. True, Black Hills winters are mountain winters. They are unpredictable, subject to vast and rapid temperature variations, and occasionally they are severe. Moreover, the worst place to be in any kind of winter, severe or not, is high on the side of a windswept cliff. Borglum and Tucker knew that, of course. But they also knew that as mountain winters go, Black Hills winters were a great deal milder than those unfamiliar with them commonly suppose. Accordingly, they decided that if they were to build across the carving area an enclosed scaffold heated by stoves, the crew would be able to work on all but the worst of days. In later years this was to prove to be a fairly satisfactory arrangement, and if the forthcoming winter had been an ordinary one it might have proven satisfactory now. However, as the weather began signaling early and often, this was not to be an ordinary winter. Snow fell on September 24. It was light and quickly melted, but it was unseasonal and a warning. On September 29 the temperature at Rapid City fell to an all-time low for that date of twenty-four degrees Fahrenheit. October began with cold wind and cold rain, snow on the 6th and again on the 10th, and so it went. In November there came another stretch of record-breaking cold. Even so, there were nice days sprinkled among the bad, and enough of them that Tucker persisted, continuing the work on all days when it was possible. December opened with heavy, blowing snow, and following that the mercury dived down into the bulb and hid. Twenty-two degrees below zero, another record low for the date. And that did it. Tucker gave up and shut the job down for the winter.

It was a good thing that he did, for when the executive committee then got its accounts together and got its financial position figured out, it was all bad news. Borglum, although he had been paid about $7,700 in sculptural fees, had about $8,800 due him. Tucker had not drawn all of his pay; there was a sheaf of unpaid bills—and no money with which to pay any of them. On top of that, Tucker, to keep the job going, had borrowed $2,000 on his own signature to so as to meet the November payroll.

It is hard to understand how the money-cautious members of the executive committee had allowed this situation to develop. Borglum could hardly be blamed for it; he had been gone since the middle of September. But regardless of the reason, optimism or carelessness or whatever, the fact was that the association now had about $20 in cash and owed about $20,000.

So, in Washington, D.C., Norbeck and Williamson, both of whom hated debt like cats hate water, set out to try to get the project out of the hole and going again. Specifically, they set about trying to get some of that "support of the national government" President Coolidge had talked about at the Rushmore dedication.

12. Government Aid—
Half a Loaf,
But Better Than None

When, in 1938, a congressional committee asked Gutzon Borglum to explain just how, ten years earlier, the Federal government had been persuaded to invest in the carving of Rushmore, the sculptor had a ready answer.

"I personally secured that help," he declared, and went on to tell how he had managed to do it. At the dedication of Rushmore, back in 1927, he recalled:

> President Coolidge whispered to me, "Who's paying for all this?"
> I said, "These farmers are paying for it. . . ."
> He said, "These people cannot do this and they ought not to be asked to do it. . . . You come see me when I get back to Washington . . . and we will set down and work out a plan."

Borglum said he had then discussed the matter with Norbeck, who "warned me to ask for the whole amount." However:

> I did not like that; I did not want to do it; and when I got to Washington and talked with Mr. Coolidge he sent me right over to [Treasury Secretary] Mellon. I saw Mr. Mellon and went over the whole matter and told him what I thought it would cost [$500,000]. . . .
> He said, "What do you want us to do?"
> I said, "I want half the cost to be carried by the Federal government and the rest by us."

He said, "That is not fair to you."

"Well," I said, "I want to get the people's teeth into this thing."

[Then] Mr. Coolidge told me, "Go to the Capitol and talk to your senators and put in a bill. . . ."

And that was all there was to that.

Borglum's account contained the gist of the story, all right, but that was by no means "all there was to that." The passing years apparently had caused him to forget that the matter had not been that simple, that it had not occurred in quite that way, and that in his eager helpfulness he had managed to contribute about as much to the problem itself as he had to its solution.

As it happened, the quest for Federal money actually was begun and Borglum's visit with Mellon actually took place some six months *before* President Coolidge first appeared in the Black Hills. It began in January 1927 in Norbeck's office, where Borglum, Williamson, and the senator had met to discuss the money problem. And it was Norbeck who then came up with the idea of asking the government to cover the entire cost of Rushmore, which Borglum was now estimating to be $500,000. The senator knew, however, that such a proposition would not get far in Congress unless it had first received the blessing of Treasury Secretary Andrew Mellon. Accordingly (in a decision he was to regret frequently and vocally ever afterward) Norbeck arranged for Borglum to see Mellon and try to secure that blessing.

Borglum saw Mellon in February, and their conversation seems to have gone about as Borglum later described it. After having sold the secretary on Rushmore so thoroughly that he seemed willing to have the government pay for all of it, Borglum then told Mellon he wanted the government to pay for only half of it. He wanted, said Borglum, to have the government contribute one dollar for each dollar contributed privately. And since that is what Borglum asked for, that is what Mellon approved.

When Borglum told Norbeck what he had done, the senator was dumbfounded. "You could have gotten it all!" he exclaimed. "Now I don't know what you'll get!" Even so, Norbeck knew that a half a loaf was better than none, and he asked Williamson to draft a bill authorizing the government to match, up to a maximum of $250,000, any private funds spent on Rushmore.

Because Norbeck meanwhile had been injured in a taxicab accident, the bill was introduced by South Dakota's other senator, ex-governor McMaster, and it got nowhere. Not that it would have fared any better under Norbeck's management. For, as Norbeck himself said, the time just had not been right for it.

Now, in the early months of 1928, the time did seem to be right. Now, thanks to his past summer in the Black Hills, President Coolidge was solidly behind Federal aid to Rushmore, and that made an enormous difference. Accordingly, Norbeck resubmitted the Rushmore bill in the Senate, Williamson did the same in the House, and both began a do-or-die campaign to get it passed. Senator Norbeck rallied his senatorial friends behind it, cashed political IOUs among other senators less favorable to it, and, though few of them either knew or cared much about the Rushmore project, on May 16 they passed the Rushmore bill.

Elated by what he had accomplished, Norbeck wired the good news to Borglum, and on the next day he received the sculptor's reply. If this Federal money was to carry with it any Federal control of how it was to be spent, said Borglum, he wanted no part of it. Besides, he knew where they could get all the money they needed, a million dollars in fact, from private sources. Upon receiving this response to "the hardest day's work I have done since I came to Washington," Norbeck hit the ceiling. "He does not want the $250,000 from congress now!" the senator wrote to Doane Robinson, "He wants to go to New York, London, Jerusalem or Heaven and get a million dollars. He is quite sure that a million is more than $250,000, but that is all he is sure of."

In the House, meanwhile, Williamson had run into hard sledding. Borglum's dedication day remark about hoping one day to carve the bust of Coolidge on the mountain had been twisted by a Massachusetts newspaper into a story that Coolidge *was* to be carved there. This, in turn, had caused a bloc of congressmen to rise in opposition to the spending of even a dime of Federal money on the monument. Finally, however, Williamson managed to get that rumor killed, then cashed a few political IOUs of his own, with the result that on May 29 the bill was passed by the House. Even so, it could not go to the president for signature until after a joint committee had smoothed out the differences between the House and Senate versions of bill, and there was no time for that now. Congress was about to adjourn, and until it reconvened late in December the bill must remain in limbo. Meanwhile, of course, there would be no Federal money for Rushmore.

Upon hearing that news, the Black Hills commercial clubs decided in a joint meeting that until the matter of the congressional bill was resolved, there would be little use in trying to raise more private donations. Consequently there was no private money, either, for the monument in 1928, and the Rushmore project, like the Rushmore bill, remained in limbo throughout that year.

Tucker did return to the mountain for a little while during that summer, but that was because he was being paid $10,000 a year whether or not the job was in operation, and he felt honor-bound to do something to earn it. So, he hired a few men and did a little work on the Rushmore water system, but because he had to pay for it out of his own pocket he did not stay very long or do very much.

Borglum, on the other hand, did not return to Rushmore at all in 1928, but he had a busy year, nonetheless. He was working on a Vicksburg battlefield memorial for the State of North Carolina, and on a statue of General John Greenway for the State of Arizona. He had conceived and was trying to sell a plan for redecorating and to some extent remodeling the entire state of Texas, and as a start was working with Lorine Spoonts, a wealthy Corpus Christi civic leader, on plans for redecorating and remodeling the city of Corpus Christi. On top of all that, he received the following letter from the great Polish pianist Ignace Paderewski:

> My Dear Great Friend:
> . . . During my hard fight for Poland you showed me a great deal of favor and sympathy. . . . [Now] a group of my compatriots have decided to erect in the city of Poznan a monument to . . . . Poland's most generous benefactor, President Wilson. The statue should be done . . . by the greatest living sculptor in the whole world. I now take the liberty of asking whether you are willing and free to do Woodrow Wilson.

Borglum replied that nothing would please him more, and accepted. However, he was so busy with his other projects that he could not go to Poland himself to make the necessary arrangements. Instead, in the summer of 1928, Mary and Lincoln went to Poland in his place.

Dull though the year was at Rushmore, it was exciting elsewhere. In a Schenectady laboratory in February a marveling audience saw on a three-inch screen "radio pictures" (some called it "television") being broadcast from a studio three miles distant. In the spring the moving pictures found their voice in a film called *The Jazz Singer*, in which its star, Al Jolson, exclaimed, "You ain't heard nuthin' yet!"; and Jolson was right. All across the land theater owners hastened to install Vitaphone and Talkaphone systems and began to advertise their cinemas not as "movies" but as "talkies." Henry Ford came out with a revolutionary automobile he called the Model A; the first Ford to have an enclosed body, it had a "self-starter" and thus did not have to be hand-cranked, came "in a choice of four colors," and was "capable of doing 55–60 mph with ease." Times were good and even the air smelled of prosperity, and in November people sang, "You're The Cream In My Coffee" and "I Can't Give You Anything But Love, Baby," as they drove in their new Model As to the polls to elect Herbert Hoover (rather than Alfred "The Happy Warrior" Smith) as the thirty-first President of the United States. Then, through a revolutionary "nation-wide radio hookup" they were able for the first time to hear national election votes reported the moment they had been counted.

Then the year was over. Congress was again in session, and a joint House and Senate committee began work on the Rushmore bill. It worked slowly, however, and while it worked the apprehension of Rushmore's backers grew. If and when the committee released the bill, President Coolidge was sure to sign it, but Coolidge's time was growing short. On March 4 Herbert Hoover would become president, and who could say what he would do? So Norbeck and the others counted down the critical days, and Williamson recorded those days in his diary.

> Feb. 18, 1929
>
> Norbeck came over to the house several times today to see me about the Rushmore bill. He fidgets like a nervous girl as it goes the slow process of adjustment in conference. Every hitch throws him into a cold sweat. But for him I guess the project would have been dead long ago.
>
> Feb. 21
>
> To the relief of everybody . . . the conference report was today disposed of by the House.
>
> Feb. 22
>
> The Senate agreed on the conference report. . . . The Senator could hardly contain himself with joy. . . . The project now seems assured if the vagaries of the sculptor do not wreck it.

The bill thus approved by both houses of Congress was entitled Public Law 805 of the 70th Congress, and said, in part:

> A commission is hereby created . . . known as the Mount Rushmore National Memorial Commission . . . to consist of twelve members who shall be appointed by the President . . . a treasurer may be selected from outside the commission. . . .

> The commission is to complete the carving of the Mount Rushmore

National Memorial, to consist of heroic figures of Washington, Jefferson, Lincoln and Roosevelt, together with an entablature upon which shall be cut a suitable inscription to be indited by Calvin Coolidge. . . . Such memorial is to be constructed according to designs and models by Gutzon Borglum. . . . No charge shall ever be made for admission to the memorial grounds or viewing the memorial.

Not more than one-half the cost of such memorial and landscaping shall be borne by the United States, and not to exceed $250,000 is hereby authorized for the purpose. . . . The appropriate proportionate share of the United States shall be advanced to said commission from time to time . . . to match the funds advanced from other sources.

Next, the bill went to the president, and on February 25, when only six days remained in the Coolidge presidency, Williamson was able to write in his diary, "The President signed the Rushmore bill today."

At the time he signed the bill, Mr. Coolidge also appointed ten of the twelve commissioners it called for. The other two positions, he said, should be filled by President Hoover. He made the appointments from a list of recommendations he had requested earlier from Norbeck and Borglum. When they were preparing that list, Borglum had said that the commission should be "loaded with millionaires." Norbeck had partially agreed, but added that six of the twelve should be South Dakotans who, because of Dakota's shortage of millionaires, were not likely to fall into such an exalted financial category. Norbeck partially got his way, but only partially, with three of the ten appointees being Dakotans. These were:

John A. Boland of Rapid City: owner of Rapid City Implement Company.

Delos B. Gurney of Yankton: president of House of Gurney, a large supplier of seeds, feeds, livestock medicines, etc.; also owner of WNAX, South Dakota's most powerful radio station.

Charles M. Day of Sioux Falls: publisher of the *Argus-Leader*, South Dakota's largest newspaper.

The other members appointed by Mr. Coolidge were:

27. *The National Commission meeting at Mount Rushmore, July 17, 1929. Front row, left to right: John A. Boland, Rapid City, S. D.; Julius Rosenwald, Chicago, Ill.; Doane Robinson, Pierre, S. D.; Gutzon Borglum, the sculptor; William Williamson, Custer, S. D.; Frank O. Lowden, Oregon, Ill.; Fred W. Sargent, Chicago, Ill.; Royal C. Johnson, Aberdeen, S. D.; Mrs. Lorine Jones Spoonts, Corpus Christi, Tex. Rear row, left to right: Delos B. Gurney, Yankton, S. D.: Joseph S. Cullinan, Houston, Tex.; Charles M. Day, Sioux Falls, S. D.*

Charles Crane of New York City: businessman and friend of Borglum.

Joseph Cullinan of Houston: president of the Texas Company (Texaco) and friend of Borglum.

Hale Holden of New York City: Railroad executive and friend of Borglum.

Lorine J. Spoonts of Corpus Christi, Texas: social and civic leader and friend of Borglum.

Frank O. Lowden of Oregon, Illinois: an Illinois political leader.

Julius Rosenwald of Chicago: board chairman of Sears, Roebuck & Co., and a noted philanthropist.

Fred W. Sargent of Chicago: president of Chicago & Northwestern Railway.

The prize appointment seemed at the time to be that of Julius Rosenwald. He was a public-spirited man of almost unbelievable wealth and had already given almost forty million dollars to various worthy causes. Hence it seemed likely that, as a commissioner, he would give lavishly to Rushmore. Unfortunately, however, that was not to be. He would give but $2,400, attend only three or four commission meetings, and then resign. Crane and Holden would prove to do even less. They would attend no meetings, give nothing, and resign within the year. On the other hand, if judged by money and prominence the weakest appointment had to be that of John Boland. And yet it was Boland who would turn out to be the commission's one indispensable member, and a man without whom the Rushmore monument probably could not have been constructed. Rushmore was to gain much from the services of several of the commission's other members as well, but that gain was to be accompanied by a serious loss—the loss of the dedication and services of the monument's original parent, Doane Robinson.

Most of the commissioners were chosen simply because they were rich and influential. Gurney and Day were chosen because of their local influence through press and radio. Boland was chosen to give the commission an on-the-scene representative with proven business ability. Robinson was none of these. He was the father of Rushmore, he had put his whole heart into keeping it alive when it was failing, and, far more than any of those actually appointed, he had hungered to serve on its governing body. But he was not rich, controlled no news medium, was not a businessman, and Borglum and Norbeck had not included him in their recommendations.

Robinson was crushed, and in a letter to Borglum he said he felt "eliminated" and that "South Dakota has already forgotten that I ever had anything to do with the matter." What hurt Robinson even worse was that his old and close friend Peter Norbeck, who was usually so considerate, would have allowed such a thing to happen.

In a letter to Robinson, Norbeck tried to soften the blow, but he did not try to pretend that he had not been responsible for it. His "main thought," he said, had been: "to put on somebody who can get the money . . . regardless of who is entitled to credit for the onerous burden that has been carried for four long years. . . . I will gladly endorse Jews, Gentiles, or Mohammedans if they will only come forward with the necessary money."

What the senator did not tell Robinson was this: it was mainly because Robinson had not been appointed to the commission that Norbeck, himself, was not appointed. Coolidge had offered him an appointment, and both Borglum and Coolidge had urged him to accept, but the senator had refused. "I could not accept such a position," he said, "when so many of my South Dakota friends, who have sacrificed much for this undertaking, desire to be members and must be left off."

Borglum, too, tried to soften the blow to Robinson, although in a somewhat different way. "I told Norbeck some time ago that you should be on the commission," he wrote, and then added: "I'm going to get the head of Washington unveiled this year. I want you to see it unveiled and help unveil it. . . . At that time a most suitable record and statement should be made of your part . . . in conceiving this great memorial. The Black Hills may forget that you ever had anything to do with it, but America will never forget."

Robinson swallowed hard and tried to accept the situation with grace. He told both Borglum and Norbeck that he was still in full support of the work and added, simply, "Let me serve where I can." Nonetheless, it was not the same for him now. Richer and more important men had been given his child to raise. He was being consulted less and less on Rushmore affairs, and he felt that when he was consulted it was more from courtesy than a desire for his advice. And so Robinson, feeling like excess baggage, in the spring of 1929 stepped back from the Rushmore work and for all practical purposes was lost to it.

Once the bill had been signed and the commission appointed, Norbeck looked forward to a respite from his efforts and frustrations concerning Rushmore. "I am very much relieved," he said, "to have unloaded it on Uncle

Sam and stronger shoulders." His feeling of relief, however, was premature. Rushmore could not actually receive any Federal money until the commission had been organized. By the terms of the Rushmore bill, it could be organized only at a meeting called by the President of the United States. When President Coolidge signed the bill his term was so near its end that he had had no time to call such a meeting. Now, it was up to President Hoover to do so, and Mr. Hoover did not seem to be very concerned about Rushmore. Shortly after his inauguration, it was true, he had appointed William Williamson and South Dakota's other congressman, Royal Johnson, to fill the commission's two vacant seats. However, he did nothing about convening the commission, and as the weeks of spring dragged by it began to appear that unless someone built a fire under him he never would.

Finally, Norbeck asked Williamson to call on Mr. Hoover and try to get him to move. That, Williamson soon discovered, would not be easy. When Williamson had wanted to see Coolidge he had been able to simply go to the White House and see him. Not so with this president. Now Williamson had to apply for an appointment, and when he did receive one it was set for a date some distance in the future. Norbeck, in the meantime, had expressed in a letter to Borglum his frustration at the president's delay. Instantly, Borglum wired back:

WILL BE IN WASHINGTON MONDAY AND DO WHAT I CAN TO BRING
MATTERS TO A HEAD

William Williamson, in his autobiography, later described what happened after the sculptor arrived: "Borglum . . . went directly to the White House and asked to see the President without a prior appointment. He got into an altercation with the President's secretary, with the result that *my* appointment was temporarily cancelled.

Norbeck was very unhappy and told Gutzon, 'We had better leave this matter to Williamson.'"

In late May, Williamson finally saw the president and presented his case so effectively that only a few days later (on June 6, 1929) the president held the meeting that brought the Mount Rushmore National Memorial Commission formally into being. During the meeting an election was held in which Joseph Cullinan became the commission's president; Williamson became secretary; and Boland and Williamson became president and secretary, respectively, of the executive committee with Gurney, Sargent, and Rosenwald as additional members.

The moment the meeting was over, Borglum wired Tucker to resume work on the mountain, and that evening he celebrated by giving a dinner party for some twenty-five senators and other Washington notables.

On the following morning, Boland and Williamson went to the office of Secretary Mellon to see about the government money for which Rushmore was now eligible. There they were told that the commission would be given a check for $54,670.56 to match a like amount of private funds already spent by the old Mount Harney Association.

And so it was done, and just in time. For, as events were soon to prove, if Rushmore's backers had not gotten Federal funding when they did, they could never have gotten it at all.

13. Miners Who Carved a Mountain

The year 1929 was not only the end of a decade, it was the end of an era. It was a turning point year—a year following which things never again would be as they had been before.

Had the 1920s not been the kind of times they were, there would be no Mount Rushmore Memorial today. It was a child of those times, of those cocky, we-can-do-anything years in which it was possible to dream of carving mountains and to gain the necessary support for actually doing so. And only because those also were times when prosperity seemed assured forever was it possible to persuade the government to invest in a piece of natural furniture that contributed nothing to national productivity, national defense, or the national pantry, and which was, therefore, purely a luxury item.

During those years the general population had developed a sense of everlasting prosperity and of national economic infallibility. As a consequence, by the time of President Hoover's inauguration America's economic checks had become over-flushed and its economic eyes had become over-bright, and its people kept telling each other that these were signs of health when actually they were signs of fever—the fever of speculation—and with each passing day the fever rose. President Coolidge had said when leaving office, "The nation's prosperity is absolutely sound." The governor of New York, Franklin D. Roosevelt, agreed and said, "The nation is in a healthy and prosperous condition." President Hoover, however, was not so sure. He was troubled by all the frantic financial activity he saw going on. His advisors, Treasury Secretary Mellon and Owen Young of the Federal Reserve board, also thought the current investment frenzy was liable to have drastic consequences. However, Mr. Hoover was a cautious man who would not holler "Fire!" in a theater before he had actually seen the flames, and he feared to voice his concern publicly lest he set off the very panic he intended to avoid. Instead he called to the

White House the publishers of various leading papers and magazines and asked them to try with their publications to stem the "easy profit" craze that was sweeping the country. Unfortunately, the publishers were not receptive. This president was an engineer by profession, so what could he know about the state of the economy? Surely not as much as the great financier, J. J. Raskob; and Mr. Raskob was saying that even a small investor could expect a return from the stock market of better than twenty percent per year, and that an ordinary workman investing fifteen dollars a month could expect in twenty years to have accumulated $80,000. So the butcher and baker and candlestick-maker continued to invest their life savings in down payments of ten percent on stocks they bought with ninety percent borrowed money, and the market continued its dizzy climb. In only three months General Electric and AT&T stocks rose seventy percent, and other stocks followed. Every day more "paper fortunes" were made . . . and every day the fever rose nearer to the crisis point.

While the nation's condition was daily growing more perilous, Rushmore's condition, on the contrary, was becoming more sound. Not only had the Rushmore bill given the project money, but a great psychological boost as well. Even though the government had been known to invest in some pretty silly things at times, the fact that Rushmore was to be given Federal support and was to be supervised by a commission appointed by The President Himself, gave it an aura of stability and respectability far greater than it had had before. Moreover, the operating equipment was now in place, a road had been built to the work, and there actually was some carving visible on the mountain. Hence, to the external observer the enterprise was no longer a pipe dream but a going concern.

Rushmore became a going concern internally, as well, in 1929. It was a shakedown year, a year of creating and breaking in the organization that was ultimately to make the Rushmore memorial a reality. By now there had been some casualties among those who had brought the project to its present point. Myrick, the great motivator, had died in the summer of 1927; Frank Hughes, who had raised funds against almost impossible odds, had moved from the Hills in that same year; and now Robinson, the originator and one of the most dedicated promoters of the monument dream, was being lost. Without the contributions of these men it is likely that the monument would never have come into being, but their contributions had been made now, and it was time for men with other talents to take their places on the Rushmore stage.

Foremost among these others was John Boland. As the commission's field

*28. An autumn, 1927, view of the original Rushmore powerhouse
at Keystone, and of the tank (lower left) that Borglum accused
John Boland of unlawfully selling.*

representative and president of its executive committee, he was, in effect, general manager of the entire project, excepting the actual design and supervision of the sculptural work itself.

Boland, forty-five years old in 1929, was short, slender, quick-moving, dapper, and shining bald. He had long, narrow eyes and thin lips that, had he been of a more somber nature, would have given him a rather sinister appearance. As it was, however, they merely gave a pixie quality to this outgoing, effervescent little man who loved life, people, parties, good stories, and who was, therefore, a natural born salesman.

On the other hand, Boland had one quality that in many men would have been disastrous. Periodically he surrendered to an urge to go on a monumental drunk. When he did, he tried to do it discreetly and out of public view. Nonetheless, there are few secrets in a small town, and so everybody knew about it. But because Boland was so greatly esteemed by his fellow townspeople, this weakness for which they would have ostracized many and severely criticized most was in his case regarded only as an interesting peculiarity.

The only Black Hills native on the Rushmore executive team, Boland was born at Keystone, in the very shadow of the mountain. In 1899, he enrolled in the School of Mines at Rapid City, but two years there convinced him that the exotic calculations of the engineer were not for him. He preferred the simple arithmetic of profit and loss—particularly profit. Therefore, he returned to Keystone where he contracted to buy out his father's general store. Being at that age when young men perceive most keenly the mistakes of their elders, Boland replaced his father's old-fashioned merchandising with more up-to-date methods. As a result, his business boomed . . . for about six months. Then a number of the surrounding mines were closed down, and when that happened Boland's store was forced to close down also. His modern merchandising, consisting simply of credit lavishly and indiscriminately extended, had left him with large debts, few assets, and a new and permanent respect for the arithmetic of profit and loss. This, in turn, led Boland to attend a Lincoln, Nebraska, business college, after which he returned to Keystone and opened another store.

For the next eleven years, during which he wooed and won a peppery, pint-sized school teacher named Ethel Winne, Boland prospered. Then, on a flame-filled night in 1917, an entire block of Keystone went up in smoke, and with it went Boland's store. The Bolands then went to Rapid City where they invested their savings in a down payment on the purchase of the Rapid City Implement Company (International Harvester farm machinery, Chrysler automobiles, Maytag washing machines).

Now Boland found himself in his true element. He could sell—really sell—not just groceries and hardware as before, but big ticket items such as threshing machines and tractors and automobiles. He was still lavish with credit, but farmers were far better credit risks than miners, and, besides, he had developed a talent for distinguishing the good risks from the bad. Also, Boland had become a stickler for record-keeping and waste control and preparation for the unexpected. Thus equipped, he soon raised his Rapid City Implement Company to almost total dominance of the local market, and caused his fellow townsmen to say admiringly and often, "Johnny Boland sure knows how to run a business."

The other key men who came to Rushmore that summer were workmen. Of course, not all who came stayed to become key men, and not all who were to become key men arrived in 1929, but many did and formed the essential nucleus of that rowdy and weather-beaten crew who actually constructed the Rushmore monument.

When Borglum wired Tucker on June 6, telling him to resume operations, Tucker told his assistant, J. G. Denison, to hire a work force. Most of the men Denison hired were miners, though not all were. In either case, none of them knew anything about carving mountains. They knew only that they needed jobs, and since no one had told them they were not qualified to carve faces on mountains they learned to do it, and neither then nor later did they think it remarkable that they had managed to do so.

One of those who came to the mountain that summer was Otto "Red" Anderson. Anderson's wife Dorothy had only recently been discharged from the State Tuberculosis Sanitorium; he also had their seven-year-old daughter Audrey to support; and he had no money and no job. He had heard, however, that an outfit called Keystone Consolidated Mines was planning to re-open the famous old Holy Terror gold mine, whose headworks stood right in the town of Keystone. Accordingly, Anderson arranged for his family to stay with Dorothy's parents while he went to investigate the situation, packed his necessities in a cardboard suitcase, and with three silver dollars in his pocket walked eleven miles to Keystone.

A night at Alexander's rooming house in Keystone reduced his capital to two dollars, and breakfast at Rumple's cafe reduced it twenty-five cents more. Being less than two dollars away from complete destitution, however, is likely to give a person both alertness and initiative, and thus it was with Anderson. While he was having breakfast he heard another patron saying to Rumple, "Well, I guess I got to go to Rapid and hire me a couple of guys to mix mud [plaster] for the studio they're building for that sculptor fella up at Rushmore."

"Hey, Mister!" interrupted Anderson. "Did you say you want a couple of mud mixers?"

"That's what I said," the man replied.

"Well, Sir," Anderson said. "You're lookin' at both of 'em!"

The man, who was a plastering contractor, doubted that anyone could mix fast enough to supply three plasterers, but it would be a long, hot trip to Rapid City and back; and . . . well, this big, rawboned Scandinavian looked pretty husky. If Anderson would agree to take the job for forty-five cents an hour and would wait until the job was done to be paid, the contractor said he would give him a shot at it. Rushmore provided quarters for live-in workmen, and although the bunkhouse was full at present Anderson could find a cot in one of the big platform tents, and Chuck Hallstead, who ran the Rushmore boarding house, would let him charge his meals.

So Anderson went to Rushmore, and for three days he managed to mix mud fast enough to keep up with the plasterers. Then the job was over, but when the contractor was paid he went on a spree and spent all he had received. Anderson wound up with nothing but three days' experience and an unpaid bill at the boardinghouse. Fortunately, Bod Perry, contractor for the studio's two fireplaces, now offered Anderson a job. And since Perry was a man of more responsible habits than the plastering contractor, this time Anderson got paid for his work.

It was while he was working for Perry that Anderson first saw and came to know "The Old Man," as Borglum was called by the crew (although never to his face).

29. Borglum's studio at Rushmore, replaced in 1940 by a larger one.

He was working on the models of Rushmore, and the first thing that struck me was how lively the guy was. The models were maybe ten feet high and he had to work on 'em from a ladder. But when he came down off that ladder he didn't climb down—he *jumped*.

He wasn't the sort of guy you'd "howdy" and start talking to. You waited until he started talkin' to you. So at first I just saw him and that was all. Then, one day he saw the Bull Durham tag hanging from my shirt pocket and he hollered down, "Hey Red! How about rolling me a cigarette?" So I did, and we started talking, and right off we seemed to strike some kind of rapport.

That was the beginning of a friendship that lasted until Borglum died. We had ups and downs, but we were always friends. He was a bear to get along with sometimes, and temperamental as the very devil, but underneath it all he was really a good man and a great man. I always respected him, and I think he always respected me.

After a month or so of working on the fireplaces, Anderson was approached by Denison, who said, "How would you like to work as a rough-driller on the mountain? I'll start you at fifty cents an hour, and if you can really do the job I'll raise you to fifty-five cents." Anderson accepted, proved able to do the job well, and shortly thereafter received the promised raise.

At about the same time, a space became available in the bunkhouse, and Anderson moved in to share a room with another young man who, along with Anderson, was to become a mainstay and twelve-year veteran of the Rushmore crew: Alton "Hoot" Leach. And from this beginning there developed a strong friendship that endured until, in 1956, Leach died of silicosis contracted from granite dust while working on the mountain.

Two other future key men who were hired that summer were Howard "Howdy" Peterson and his brother Merle. They were members of a whole pack of Peterson brothers who lived in Keystone—all of them athletes, and all of them so aggressive that they were occasionally referred to by their neighbors as "Them fightin' Petersons." In 1928, when Howdy was only twenty and Merle was even younger, these two had quit mining and become logging contractors supplying shoring timbers to the mines. Then, when the construction of Borglum's studio was begun, Denison said to the Petersons, "If you fellows will contract to supply me with logs for the studio, when you're done I'll give you jobs on the mountain." That appealed to the boys, so in 1929, when all the logs had been peeled and delivered, they took Denison up on his offer. Howdy served as a mechanic and as overseer of the equipment on the top of the mountain, and Merle became first a laborer and ultimately a driller.

James Champion, the carpenter, was not new to the job in 1929—he had been there before, helping to build the stairway up the mountain. Now, however, the stairway was done, and henceforth Champion would build sheds and scaffolds and do any other carpentering that was needed. A bookish man and a fun-loving prankster, Champion was a long, lean Englishman who looked much as Edward, Prince of Wales, was to look when he, too, had reached his fifties—except that the Prince of Wales did not chew tobacco. Champion lived a few miles southeast of Keystone, near Glendale over in Little Elk gulch, where he had a mining claim. He called the claim The Expectation, and the name was apt, for no matter how much he worked it, it remained only an expectation. And "expectation" might have been an apt name for his household as well, for James and Mrs. Champion had fourteen children.

Another returnee, also an older man, was Keystone miner Ray Grover, known to everyone as Uncle Ray. Uncle Ray was no great shakes for looks—he'd never have been asked to pose for a collar ad—but he was something better. He was a good, kind man who, as one workman put it, "was one of the nicest fellows ever to work on the mountain." And because Uncle Ray was that kind of man, another of the workmen, Bert Kinsey, lived when otherwise he would have died. This happened one day when Kinsey was down on the face of the cliff in a saddle, and a winch-man accidentally released the brake on Kinsey's winch. The drum started spinning out cable and Kinsey began free-falling to the canyon below. When the drum started spinning the iron crank attached to it started spinning also, and since Kinsey was a big, heavy man it was spinning with great force. Nonetheless, instantly and with great presence of mind Ray Grover walked into that spinning crank. Somehow he managed to endure its vicious battering of his shins and thighs and held his ground until his legs had so blocked the crank as to stop the drum and Kinsey's fall.

Two who joined the crew that summer were from the East. William "Bill" Tallman was a young man who had studied art in New York City, then for a time had worked for Borglum (who was a family friend), and now had been asked by Borglum to work at Rushmore as chief pointer. Young Matthew ("Matt" or "Matty") Riley's father had worked at Borgland, and young Matt had grown up in that vicinity and had known Borglum most of his life, and now, at the adventurous age of eighteen, Matt Riley was going to work on Mr. Borglum's mountain as an assistant pointer.

Following the commission's organizational meeting with President

Hoover, Borglum had gone directly to Vicksburg, Mississippi, to prepare for the July 3 unveiling of his North Carolina Confederate memorial. Accordingly, when on July 10 he did at last arrive at Rushmore he found the mountain much changed. When he had last seen it, in September, 1927, no carving had been done at all. Now, however, Tucker had developed the granite "egg" of the Washington head to the point where Borglum could begin to rough in its facial features. Borglum did that, and soon the mass began to become recognizable as a Washington head.

When shaping the rounded mass for the head, Tucker had cut its edges back into the cliff without removing the surrounding stone either at the sides or at the bottom. As a consequence, vertical walls now extended from the face of the cliff back to the sides of the emerging head, and at the bottom these walls were connected by a flat ledge that ran just under and in front of Washington's chin. Thus, to an observer on Mount Doane the Washington head appeared to be looking out of the open side of a snug-fitting stone box.

During this time of beginning and of learning for the crew, there were problems, frustrations, and accidents, and from these there came new techniques, new solutions to problems, and new precautions.

Red Anderson, Hoot Leach, Merle Peterson, Walt Wilkerson, and other drillers were learning, with efforts that were always intense and often profane, how to handle their Chicago-Pneumatic jackhammers. The hammers weighed eighty-five pounds; they were cumbersome, and before a hole was drilled deep enough to swallow a substantial length of the drill, or "steel," they stood awkwardly tall. Awkward also were the locations in which the holes were to be drilled, and it was not easy for a man to get into a position from which he could "buck" the hammer with enough pressure to make the drill bite into the rock. "You'd find yourself bucking the hammer with your shoulder," said one of them, "or maybe with your thigh, and sometimes even with your butt." A man trying to drill a horizontal hole while suspended in a saddle could not even do that. By pushing against the hammer he would succeed only in pushing himself backward in space. In these cases, therefore, they learned to drill first two other holes, vertical and shallow, about three feet apart. "In these we'd wedge steel pins to which we'd attach a loop of chain. Then we'd put our feet against the cliff and push back against the chain, and we'd get enough traction to buck the hammer in a horizontal hole."

When going down on the cliff each driller took along enough steel to last for two hours or so. Then, as his bits grew dull a "steel nipper" would come down in a harness with fresh drills to exchange for the dulled ones. At first, however, the drill-bits were dulling entirely too fast. The problem turned out

30. Roughing in Washington's nose and eye sockets, 1929.

to be that the blacksmith was not putting enough flare on their tips, hence the holes they drilled were too snug to allow the drills to turn as freely as they had to do to work properly. Yet, neither complaint nor cussing nor gentle persuasion could get the blacksmith to change his ways, until one day:

A salesman for screw-bits showed up at the mountain. A screw-bit would drill about seven feet before getting dull, as compared to about two feet with the solid drills we were using. Of course, the screw-bits were more expensive because when you dulled one you replaced it with a new one, whereas the ones we were using could be sharpened over and over again. Well, Borglum said he was going to buy 'em anyhow, and if he had it would of put the blacksmith out of a job. When the blacksmith saw that hand-writing on the wall he asked for one more chance, and Borglum gave it to him. After that you just couldn't wear one of his bits out!

At the same time, mechanic Howdy Peterson was encountering a problem that was to plague him throughout the entire project. "That granite dust was just as sharp as hell, y'know, and just as abrasive as emery, and it'd get into those hammers and eat out the cylinders and pistons somethin' terrible. Then the air would just blow by, and you couldn't get any power. So we were constantly buyin' and replacin' cyclinders and pistons."

As might be expected, there were some close calls during Rushmore's shakedown period. Howdy Peterson had one of the first when, one morning, he went down onto the ledge in front of Washington's chin . . . and fainted. "I just passed out right there, but I was lucky. Instead of falling outward and into the canyon, I fell in towards the head. When I came to I got out of there and went home and saw the doctor. He said I had chicken pox. Imagine, chicken pox at that age! Anyhow, I got over the chicken pox OK, but if I'd of fallen in the other direction . . . well I wouldn't of got over that!"

Red Anderson also had a disconcerting adventure on that same ledge. He had gone down there in a saddle to remove a steel pin that had been used as an equipment anchor. The pin proved to be hard to remove, and Anderson became so involved in tugging on it that he failed to notice that, through some mix-up in signals, his winch-man was continuing to reel out cable, and loops of the slack cable were piling up on the ledge behind Anderson. When he did discover it, Anderson did it the hard way. After a particularly vicious yank the pin suddenly ceased to resist and:

I just flipped backward right out into space. I fell free for about twenty-five feet, then I hit the end of the slack. The jerk darn near snapped me in two! Then I slammed into the face of the cliff and just sort of bounced back and forth against it. Somehow I'd had sense enough to fold my arms in front of my face when I started falling. My hands and arms got skinned up pretty bad, but if I hadn't done that the Lord only knows what kind of a face I'd be wearing now. And I can tell you this: If you fall off a cliff and expect to be supported by a cable that isn't there it'll surprise you some.

Then there was the day when the A-frame collapsed, and had it done so five minutes earlier the resulting tragedy probably would have ended the Rushmore project forever. The A-frame, a wooden structure some twenty feet tall and shaped like a letter "A," was built to support the mountaintop end of the tramway cable. The weight of the cable, together with that of the tramway bucket and the small "haulage cable" that pulled the bucket back and forth, created a force of more than four tons constantly tugging at the top of the A-frame, where the cable was attached. Accordingly, the structure was built of massive timbers and was anchored in the rear by another heavy cable that ran from the top of the frame back to a steel pin embedded in the granite mountain. Extending forward from the base of the frame to the edge of the cliff was a wooden loading platform some fifteen feet square, and in the leading edge of the platform a U-shaped notch served as a pocket for the bucket to come up into. This platform, with its smooth surface and breathtaking view, was the crew's favorite lunching place on nice days. And it was just after lunch on such a day, with a loaded bucket on its way up from below, that the A-frame guy cable suddenly snapped. Instantly, the pull of the tramway cable snatched the A-frame off the mountain. As one crew man remembered: "We'd just finished eating—hadn't been off that platform three minutes— when the A-frame came loose and down she went. It took the platform with it; just wiped it right off the mountain, and the whole business went sailing down into the canyon. Three minutes earlier and all of us would have been wiped off with it."

Howdy Peterson escaped the A-frame disaster by an even narrower margin. When the other lunchers left the platform, he remained behind to unload equipment that was coming up in the bucket: "Then somebody hollered, 'Hey Howdy! You're wanted on the phone'—we had a telephone hookup with the bottom of the mountain—so I started off to answer it. I swear I hadn't got more than about two steps off that platform when the A-frame

31. On the face of Washington, 1930, left to right:
John Arthur "Whisky Art" Johnson, Otto "Red" Anderson,
and Howard "Howdy" Peterson.

went! Man oh man! When it went the whole damn thing went. A-frame, platform, everything, flyin' out over the edge and down into the canyon."

Since these and the few other near-disasters turned out all right and produced no injuries, they probably were blessings in disguise. They demonstrated dramatically the kinds of things that could happen, and caused steps to
be taken to see that they did not happen. Besides, although Borglum took
reckless chances on the mountain himself, he was a stickler about safety for
the men and refused to allow them to do as he did. As a result, the Rushmore
job was to produce a safety record far better than anyone could have expected
from such an operation.

At about this same time there occurred another accident, although of
quite a different kind, that also turned out to have been a blessing in disguise.
On mornings, especially cold ones, when Borglum was not around to catch
them at it, the crew would take a break and gather in one of the mountaintop
shacks to have coffee. When they did, they would station a call-boy where he
could see the stairway and, if he saw the "Old Man" coming up, could give an
alarm in time for the crew to scatter and look busy. Then came a morning
when the crew gathered in the shack without having posted a sentry. Just as
they had gotten comfortably settled, Borglum and his chauffeur and personal
handyman Charlie Johnson appeared in the doorway. There was a startled
hush-before-the-storm while Borglum glared at the assembly. Then, in a
voice like sudden thunder he roared, "WHAT THE HELL IS GOING ON
AROUND HERE?"

After a moment, one crew member found his voice and said, "Well . . . uh
. . . we were just . . . uh . . . havin' a little java."

"So I see!" snapped Borglum. Then he turned to Johnson and said with a
mischievous twinkle, "Charlie, see to it that at about ten o'clock every morning we get some doughnuts and hot coffee up here for these bums!"

And that, or so Rushmore's veterans will tell you anyhow, was the birth of
that national institution known as "The Coffee Break." And even if that is not
actually true, it is true that it was one of the things that caused the crew to
develop a growing loyalty to both Borglum and his mountain.

Another benefit of the work and learning and close calls of this shakedown period was that it was drawing the crew together. At first these men
had just been a collection of individuals who happened to be in the same
place and doing the same work because it was where they had chanced to find
a job. Now, however, they were becoming a solid unit—a fraternity of the
mountain. And as they grew ever more loyal to each other they also grew
more loyal to the job they were doing. As Red Anderson put it: "At first,

Rushmore was just another job and a crazy kind of a job at that. It was just a place to earn some money and nothing more. Anyway, that's how I felt about it, and I think it's how most of the others felt, too. But the longer we were there, the more we began to sense that we were building a truly great thing, and after a while all of us old hands became truly dedicated to it."

The more the crew grew together and became a fraternity, the more a newcomer could expect to undergo an initiation before becoming one of them. The ingenious and devilish ways in which this was done would fill a small book. One, for example, would take place when the new man was down on the cliff-face in a saddle:

> You'd take hold of his cable where it ran over the rock on top, and if you went at it real slow you could just gradually raise him up a foot or so without him knowin' he'd ever been lifted. Then you'd let go of the cable and of course he'd drop with a helluva jerk, and, why, it'd just scare the waddin' out of him. I've seen more than one guy come boilin' up over the edge of the cliff and hollerin', "I'm done with this damn job!"
>
> Then you'd tell him what happened, and he'd grin kinda sheepish like, and it'd be OK. Then he'd start itchin' to pull the same stunt on somebody else.

And so as the face of Washington took shape and the work progressed, Borglum and the crew drew closer together as a working unit. Then, suddenly, they lost Tucker.

There was no question of Tucker's loyalty to the job. He had even spent his own money, at times, to keep it going. Now, however, he was having trouble with Borglum. In a disagreement between Borglum and Boland over whether or not Rushmore should buy electric power or produce its own, Tucker had sided with Boland. Borglum then told Robinson that Tucker was becoming disloyal. Robinson insisted otherwise. "If ever I found one man loyal to another," he said, "Tucker is loyal to you. . . . If you can suspect his loyalty then you are in a hopeless state." Nonetheless, a rift had been created, and now Borglum was criticizing Tucker for little things and was saying that Tucker had cut too many corners when constructing such things as scaffolding and stairway railings. This upset Tucker, for, as Robinson said later, "His main weakness was a sensitiveness to criticism," and it may well have been what caused Tucker to resign. The reason he gave for resigning, however, was an action by the commission at a meeting it held at Rushmore on July 17.

This was the meeting at which the commission formally took over the affairs of the old Mount Harney Memorial Association, and never again would a Mount Rushmore Commission meeting be so well attended. Many of the commissioners were there, of course, because of the meeting's importance, but a number of others seem to have come to enjoy the honor of serving on a presidentially appointed body, and also to enjoy an expense-paid outing. We may assume this from the fact that when the commissioners found that they were expected to contribute time and effort to the project, and heard it suggested that they might contribute some money as well, there was a rash of resignations. But the thing that seems to have brought a number of them to the meeting—as indicated by the fact that they brought their families—was the prospect of enjoying in luxury a Black Hills vacation. And the reason for this, in turn, was Rapid City's new Alex Johnson Hotel.

Decorated in American Indian motif, with a great stone fireplace in its balconied lobby, resplendent with lush carpeting and red-capped bellboys and even with that new marvel called air conditioning, the Alex had been built to be the finest hostelry between Minneapolis and Seattle, and probably it was. Anyhow, by the evening of the 16th all commissioners but Holden, Crane, and Boland had checked in at the hotel, and Boland had not simply because he lived in Rapid City. At a banquet that evening, they sat beneath the murals and tall tapestries of the Alex Johnson dining room and feasted on mountain trout while Borglum painted for them a glowing picture of what, with their assistance, Mount Rushmore would become.

On the next afternoon, they met at Borglum's half-finished Rushmore studio and took up a tangled mass of problems.

First, they voted to take over Borglum's contract, unchanged, from the expiring Mount Harney Association. Borglum agreed, so that was no problem.

Then they took up the matter of the Mount Harney debts, and that did create a problem. Those debts, amounting to about $32,500, were a burden the commissioners were far from eager to assume. Most wanted the commission to disclaim the debts, as legally it could, and start with a clean slate. Boland and Williamson balked at that. Perhaps the commission could repudiate those debts legally, they said, but how about morally? Others countered by saying that honoring the debts would leave the commission only about $20,000 with which to go forward, and that just was not enough. But Boland and Williamson, now joined by the other Dakota members, refused to bend. About $9,000 of that debt was owed to Borglum; an even larger amount was owed to Tucker, and were these men to remain unpaid for their past services?

Should not Tucker be paid for his out-of-pocket expenditures to keep the job going? Finally, the commissioners agreed to assume the Mount Harney debt if (1) it were to be retired by a series of annual installments, and (2) if Tucker's contract were to be rewritten.

Under his present contract, Tucker was receiving a flat $10,000 per year even though, due to shutdowns caused by weather and lack of funds, he had spent fewer than twelve of the past twenty-four months actually on the job. Henceforth, the commissioners now decided, Tucker would be paid $833.33 per month, which was at the rate of $10,000 per year, but only for those months when he actually worked. After all, $833 per month was still an enormous sum in those days, and they figured Tucker surely would be satisfied with it.

At first, Tucker did seem to be satisfied. Two months later, however, he announced that he was resigning as of September 23 because he had been asked to take an unacceptable cut in pay. Thereupon, Boland and Williamson asked Borglum if something could not be done to change Tucker's mind. Borglum, however, did not want it changed. According to the sculptor, "Tucker's services have been decidedly unsatisfactory," Williamson wrote in his diary; therefore, Williamson added, "we made no effort to keep him on."

Tucker said, when leaving, that the commission owed him more than $11,000. When Boland then replied that the debt was not that large, Tucker filed suit against Borglum and the commission jointly and managed to garnishee the commission's bank account. A certified audit was performed and showed Tucker to be owed $8,289, and in December Boland finally got Tucker to accept $7,500 provided it were paid immediately. To pay it, Borglum volunteered to lend the commission $5,000 from his own pocket, and Boland persuaded the Rapid City Chamber of Commerce (formerly the Commercial Club) to donate the remaining $2,500. And thus the painful matter was finally settled.

The Tucker affair, however, left Borglum with another problem. He had trusted Tucker to perform without supervision all of the rough carving, and he had planned to spend his own time only on the finishing work and on those subtleties and refinements by which he, as an artist, could give the carvings vitality and character. When Tucker left, Denison, with Borglum's approval, had been appointed (at $4,000 per year) to take his place. But even though Denison was dependable, capable, inventive, and more able than Tucker to command the loyalty of the crew, he simply was not trained in mountain sculpture.

Much as he hated to be tied down to any one job, Borglum decided the only way to solve the problem was for him to move to the Hills and thus be available to give Denison close supervision. Accordingly, and with typical Borglum impetuosity, he bought a ranch and did it so suddenly that even Mary did not know what he was up to until after he had done it.

On September 24, the day after Tucker actually left the job, Borglum announced his new purchase and his plans for it. His purchase was the 1,200 acre Rhodes ranch, which lay along Grace Coolidge Creek six miles east of the Game Lodge and twenty miles southeast of Rushmore. He planned, he said, to make this ranch his permanent home. He was going to begin immediately to construct a native stone house with a living room that would measure forty by sixty feet and contain three fireplaces, and at the same time he was going to convert the ranch barn into a studio.

His idea was good, but his timing (although he could not have known it) was absolutely terrible and was to cause him years of distress. He bought the ranch precisely when the nation's fever was at its peak and land prices were soaring. Then, just one month to the day after he had made his announcement, the Associated Press reported: "The most terrifying panic of selling since the war scare of 1914 dealt a crushing blow to the leading stock markets today . . . all records for wild and frenzied trading were broken . . . the ticker tape was more than 2½ hours behind in printing quotations."

It was the beginning of that long darkness known as the Great Depression. It was a darkness that was almost to destroy the nation, and, paradoxically, was to assure the survival of Rushmore.

14. Dedication of Washington

etermined to have the head of Washington ready for dedication in the following summer, Borglum was also determined to continue working in 1929 as long as the money held out. Summer faded and fall came on, and grass and the roofs of buildings gleamed frostily in the morning sunrise. Above the mountain, great honking vee's of cranes and wild geese flapped southward across the Indian summer sky, and then were gone. The aspen groves in the canyons turned yellow, then brown, and then were bare. Light falls of snow dusted the mountains, melted, fell again and melted again, each time falling a little more heavily and melting a little more slowly. The days grew short, and Rushmore's workmen left home in the darkness of morning and returned in the darkness of evening. And still the carving continued.

As the days passed, the weather came more and more to control both the progress of the work and the lives of the men performing it. Black Hills winters not being nearly as ferocious as the uninformed believed, there were many good days—and those that were good were the best of days. Facing to the southeast, the Rushmore cliff enjoyed maximum exposure to the sun and minimum exposure to the northwest winds, which were the coldest ones. Moreover, to the northwest of the carving cliff and immediately across the little canyon behind it, Rushmore's main crest rose sixty feet or more above the clifftop where the winch-house and shop were located, thus providing additional shelter. In the heat of summer, this sheltering together with the reflection of sunlight from the white, fresh-cut rock created temperatures on the cliff's working face that were almost unbearable. But on the nice days of November and December when temperatures were in the 40s, 50s, and 60s, these same conditions provided a working climate that was almost ideal. In fact, on a day that was sun-bright and still, one could even work without suffering on the cliff in temperatures as low as, say, fifteen degrees above zero. On mornings that were nice it was a pleasure just to go up on the mountain. A man would climb through the morning-fresh canyon where night-shadows still lingered, and then would arrive on top just in time to see the rising sun flood gold across the plains to the east, then touch with gold the peaks and high ridges of the mountains and cause them to stand sharp-chiseled and bright above the shadowed network of gulches and canyons from which they rose. And old Rushmore hands recall with an awe that approaches reverence the splendor of those occasional mornings when the mountain stood above a cloud-layer blanketing the hills and valleys below. Then the stairway was enshrouded in a fog-muffled stillness, the trees were frosty ghosts but dimly seen, and the clatter of heavy shoes on the wooden steps was also fog-muffled and softened. But when they reached the top and were above the layer of cloud, they would see it stretching away below them forever, a fluffy sea broken only by the scattered dark islands of other peaks protruding through it. Then the rising sun would touch the layer with rose, then gold, then bright silver. And *that*, Rushmore's veterans will tell you, was a sight to be remembered.

There were bad days too, of course, and just as the good days could be very, very good, the bad ones could be absolutely terrible. When the air was damp and raw and the sky was gray and the wind was a hostile living thing that probed the thickest clothing and made eyes water and turned feet into numbly aching lumps, working on the mountain became a matter of blind endurance. To make it as bearable as possible, Borglum had erected in front of the Washington face a sturdy scaffold that rose for several stories from the ledge in front of Washington's chin. By fastening tarpaulins to this framework, canvas "rooms" could be created where needed in front of working areas. To heat these "rooms" he had provided "salamanders," which were steel oil drums that had been converted into coke-burning stoves. This arrangement did give substantial relief from the cold; even so, its disadvantages were such that at best it was but the lesser of evils. Coke was burned because it gave off far fewer fumes than wood or oil. Still, it gave off enough that after a few hours work in a heated enclosure a man was likely to develop a dull headache and perhaps a queasy stomach. And even worse than the fumes was the fog of granite dust that drilling in such an enclosure created. Consequently, on any day warm enough to be endurable the workmen usually pulled back the tarps and worked in the open air. And as a result, Red Anderson recalled, "Many times I'd come home so cold I wouldn't even eat supper. I'd just take a bunch of hot-water bottles and go to bed and try to get warm."

Then, there were those days when the weather would permit no work at all, and these were the most unwelcome because no work meant no pay. The general rule was, "No work when the temperature is ten above zero or lower," but that required additional interpretation. On a day that was considerably warmer but happened also to be a day of wet or heavy snow or one with a stiff, raw wind, work still might be impossible. Thus, on all but the obviously impossible days the men usually went up to project headquarters on Doane Mountain and there drank coffee in the mess hall or idled around the compressor house while waiting to see if the weather would improve. If it did not, the usual thing was then to go down to Tom Hoy's pool hall in Keystone and there, warmed by a roaring fire in the round-bellied stove, play Kelley pool and small-stakes games of gin rummy. "We'd have our lunch boxes with us," remembered Edwald Hayes, "so we'd stay there the whole day." And Howdy Peterson added, "You didn't dare leave the card table to go to dinner. If you did you'd lose your seat, and you might even lose it if you went to the bathroom."

Just before Christmas the job was finally shut down. The money was all spent and there was no prospect of getting any more. This time, however, nobody seemed particularly disturbed by that. True, the economy was showing signs of distress; the stock market was swooping up and down like a kite in a wind, and always seeming to swoop down more than up. Still, no one knew what that meant, if anything, and the experts were all saying it was only a temporary adjustment. And regardless of what it might mean, Rushmore's promoters were approaching the coming year with more optimism—and with less reason for having it—than ever before.

They did solve the money problem (temporarily at least) by two brainstorms—one by Commissioner Joseph Cullinan and the other by Borglum. Why not create some sort of honorary Rushmore association? asked Cullinan. Call it, say, the Mount Rushmore National Memorial Society. Sell memberships for, well, a hundred dollars apiece and give each member a certificate signed by Borglum. And, asked Borglum, why not publish and sell a well-illustrated and well-written Rushmore booklet? Maybe even sell advertising space in it?

Both ideas were adopted. The society was organized, Doane Robinson was elected its secretary, and he sent letters inviting some 2,000 prominent Americans to join it. Borglum, himself, produced the booklet and did a superb job of it. Robinson's effort resulted in seventy-two memberships (many bought by commission members), and thus, $7,200. Sales of the booklet yielded about $10,000, and the result of these two enterprises, when matched with Federal funds, provided sufficient money for yet another season's work.

The project's chief pointer, Bill Tallman, returned to the mountain in late April, 1930, and began transferring Borglum's design from the models to the cliff. Denison then started the crew to work. Two weeks after that, Borglum showed up, full of energy, optimism, and ideas.

He intended to dedicate the Washington head on the Fourth of July, but the head was far from ready for it. Hence, he decided to take full advantage of the season's sixteen hours of daylight and ordered Denison to set up two shifts—the first to work from four in the morning until noon, and the second from noon until eight in the evening.

Borglum was also eager to begin the entablature—the brief history of the United States to be written by Calvin Coolidge and carved in letters three feet high on the face of the cliff. He had been in touch with Mr. Coolidge in regard to the text (which was to lead to an imbroglio that will be discussed later), and he now started a crew preparing a place for it on the mountain.

At the same time, the sculptor was promoting another inscription that was not in the present Rushmore plans. He wanted to smooth off the walls of the little stone canyon behind the carving cliff and there inscribe another message repeated in "English, Latin, and some Asian language." The Asian language he mentioned most often was Sanskrit, probably because Mary, during her European studies, had become proficient in it. This inscription would explain more fully than the one on the cliff, Borglum said, the meaning of the monument and the nation it had been carved to commemorate. Also, its repetition in several languages would give linguists of future ages a key—a "Rosetta Stone"—for deciphering scripts that by then would have been long dead.

As if this were not keeping him busy enough, Borglum had now gotten into the cattle business and had stocked his ranch with two hundred whiteface Herefords. Also, he had a crew at work preparing his new home and studio at the ranch, and meanwhile he and his family were living in a suite at the Alex Johnson Hotel. And in the process of getting his ranch in order, Borglum had acquired the services of a couple who were to become perhaps the most devoted and loyal of all his employees during his Rushmore years and who were to remain with him until his death: Emil and Christine Flick.

During the World War Emil Flick had so distinguished himself as to have won a battlefield commission, and he had been so badly gassed that he would suffer from it for the rest of his life. Following the Armistice he had served in the army of occupation in Germany, where he met and married a pert young lady named Christine Dietrich. Christine's parents owned a small but elegant hotel, and this fact was to be of some importance many years later at the Borglum ranch.

Upon coming to the United States the Flicks settled on a small central South Dakota ranch. But the 1920s were about as lean for farmers as they were fat for most everyone else, and in the spring of 1930 the Flicks sold out and started for California. In passing through the Black Hills they stopped to help a man get his car out of a muddy ditch on the Keystone road. The man introduced himself as E. C. Howe, said he was "clerk of the works" at Rushmore, and offered Emil a job there. Liking the Hills and having friends in Keystone, the Flicks accepted the offer. Shortly thereafter, Borglum hired Emil away from Rushmore to work for him personally at the ranch, and thus their long association was begun.

Flick was a quiet, smiling man, slow to anger, and so self-effacing that people were inclined to underestimate him. He was, however, amazingly capable at a wide variety of tasks, and he had a way of quietly appearing wherever he was needed and doing what needed doing without being told. Altogether, therefore, Emil Flick was a perfectly constituted foil for the volatile, impatient Borglum. Consequently, Flick became Borglum's ranch manager and caretaker, often served as his companion, and occasionally as his driver as well. Borglum already had a driver—his personal chauffeur Charlie Johnson—but every now and then, to Mrs. Borglum's consternation, he took a notion to drive himself. One of Emil's jobs, given him confidentially by Mrs. Borglum, was to prevent this whenever possible, and for good reason. Borglum, with his busy mind, never allowed driving to interfere with his examination of passing objects or the jotting in his notebook of such inspirations as might come to him. Behind the wheel, therefore, Borglum was one of the Black Hills' most terrifying citizens, and it was Emil's task to see that he was behind it as little as possible.

Christine's talents, acquired at her parents' *pension*, were also soon discovered by the Borglums. She knew good food and how to prepare it, how to set and serve a table for the most sophisticated company, and how a house should be cleaned and kept. Therefore, running the house and kitchen, under Mary Borglum's general supervision, became Christine's responsibility.

At first, people at the Borglum ranch found it hard to understand Christine, for she spoke very broken English. As it happened, however, soon after moving to the ranch the Borglums had hired a highly educated young Englishman named Teddy Sodon to act as a private tutor for Lincoln and Mary Ellis. While he was at it, Sodon also tutored Christine, and some forty-five years later she would still glow in recalling that experience. "I had my very own tutor," she said. "And pretty soon I could talk to all the VIPs who came to visit, and I could speak to them in good English. I was so proud!"

When June returned to the Hills, so did the tourists, and despite the deepening depression they came in greater numbers than ever before. It was not an easy trip in those days. South Dakota's arterial highways were as yet unpaved, and tourists coming from the east, as most of them did, had to cross the entire state on dusty gravel. This was a substantial part of their journey, for South Dakota is a wide state. In fact, when Black Hills-bound travelers from New York City or Washington, D.C., crossed the Dakota border, a quarter of their trip still lay ahead of them; and those from, say, Chicago or St. Louis were but halfway to their destination. Nonetheless, they came by the tens of thousands, and even though by present standards they traveled under hardship conditions, there is reason to believe they found in their touring a richness of experience unknown to the tourist of today.

Today's tourist rides in an air-conditioned box whose tightly closed windows wall him off from the smell of sun-warmed grass and pine trees and new-mown hay; he eats in chain-franchised restaurants identical in menu and appearance to those of yesterday and tomorrow; he sleeps in chain-franchised motels also identical; he drives on interstate highways whose straightened curves and whittled-down hills, whose breadth and routing and bulldozed artificiality give them, too, a sense-deadening uniformity and isolate him from exposure to the towns and life and even the scenery along his route. And this tourist is but a pale, pampered, and probably (though he may deny it) underprivileged imitation of his touring forebears of the 1920s and 1930s.

We are not speaking now of the few affluent travelers of that era. We are speaking, rather, of those ordinary people whom Lincoln said God must love because He made so many of them; the ones for whom development of the automobile first made long-distance touring possible.

For those people and at that time, a vacation tour was an adventure as eagerly anticipated and planned for as an African safari. Before Starting Day the family flivver was given a physical examination and its real or potential ailments were treated. Then it was loaded. In the interior, in the trunk, behind latticed metal fences on the running boards, and sometimes on the top as well, were stored a tool kit, tire chains, second spare tire, inner tubes and a patching kit, towrope, shovel, spare fanbelt, extra oil, and a can of water for the radiator. Also, there was likely to be a tent, blankets, towels, soap, cooking utensils, a water bucket, adhesive tape, iodine, and milk of magnesia. And there would certainly be a grocery box containing bread, cheese, ham, cans of pork and beans, and a can of coffee. If Father were a smoker he would have picked up some "makin's"—eight-cent bags of Bull Durham and five-cent books of papers—for tailor-made cigarettes cost fifteen cents a pack and sometimes more, and it only made sense to roll your own. Another necessity was a Brownie box camera for producing those treasured, sun-squinting snapshots of Ma or Pa or The Kids, or all of them together, standing in front of a mountain, waterfall, statue, or stuffed buffalo. And *always* there would be suspended somewhere on the outside of the automobile a canvas bag of drinking water, kept cool by the evaporation of water seeping through its fabric.

Thus equipped, Americans who a generation earlier would have been unlikely to venture more than fifty miles from home set out in search of memories to last a lifetime.

To know the feeling of that kind of travel in that kind of time, imagine for a moment that you are one of the half-million tourists who will motor to the Black Hills in the summer of 1930. . . .

If you have come from the east you will enter the Hills through Rapid City, and probably you will arrive at "Rapid" (by now you will be using the native abbreviation) late in the afternoon. As you approach, you see no indication of the town other than increasingly numerous signboards. Then you sweep up over one more prairie hill and there it is, lying along Rapid Creek and tucked against a ridge of foothills to the west. In fact, when you pop over the hill you not only see the town, you are in it—rolling along a street lined with tourist cabins and tourist courts.

If by some magic you had been instantly transported from the lush greenery and towering trees of the East, Rapid City would look rather dry and its trees rather short. However, since crossing the Missouri River some 250 miles and seven or more hours ago, you have followed a dusty ribbon of gravel across rolling, treeless, sun-beaten rangeland. Hence, with sprinklers swiveling in rich green lawns and cool evening shadows sliding from the foothills eastward across the town, Rapid City looks like the Garden of Eden. Even so, you and the rest of the family are gritty and sticky from the day's travel, and until you have found a place to stay and have washed up and changed clothes you are likely to be cranky and short of temper.

Once you have cleaned up and have stepped out into the crisp air of evening, you feel a sense of adventure and exhilaration that tourists of the future will rarely know, at least not to the extent that you feel it now. You feel a luxurious freshness you could not have known had you not earlier been so sweaty and grimy. And you feel an explorer's excitement at having arrived at an alien destination. In the days before World War II the population had not yet become mobile nor the nation homogenized, thus it is a destination where food, customs, speech, and perhaps even the architecture are different from those at home. At least you hope they are, because one of the pleasures of travel lies in the local flavor of the places you visit.

To gather some of that flavor you will stroll downtown and perhaps you will idle through the lobby of the Harney Hotel and admire the stuffed heads of deer, elk, and buffalo that line its walls. In frontier days the Harney was a gathering place for cavalry officers, mining investors, cattlemen, and men involved in Indian affairs. Now, many old-timers from those days come here to sit in the deep leather chairs and reminisce, seeking to hold on to a past that, like the buffalo herds, lives now only in their memories. In this year of 1930, with its airplanes and talking pictures, it is hard to realize that there still are men around who took part in the gold rush and the Indian wars and who well remember when, just northwest of the Hills, the Sioux rubbed out Custer and his troopers. But there are, and some of them are probably in the Harney lobby now. If so, you will have no trouble engaging them in conversation, for they know that when they were young they lived in historic times, and now that they are old much of their pleasure comes from sharing the memory of it. Thus, they may speak to you of Generals Crook and Custer, Red Cloud or Sitting Bull, Calamity Jane or Wild Bill Hickok, all of whom are a part of local history. Or perhaps one of them will tell you how the Rockerville flume just might have left a mark on the nation's literature.

Rockerville lies in a gulch a few miles southwest of town; if you go out to where that Borglum fellow is trying to carve a mountain you'll pass right through it. It is not much now, just a few shacks, but in its time it was a real gold town. It was placer gold, and to get it you had to wash it out of gravel and clay. That was done with "rockers," hand-agitated washing boxes about the size and shape of a child's cradle, which is how the place got called Rockerville. Trouble was, rockers have to have water and the gulch had none, which was why it was first known as Captain Jack's Dry Diggins. To supply the needed water, a group of promoters built a wooden flume from a creek seventeen miles away. When they got it finished it leaked so badly that it was almost useless, so they started experimenting with ways to seal it. Finally they discovered that a wagonload of horse manure dumped in the upper end of the flume each morning would keep the cracks sealed and the water flowing. *
But now they had another problem. Rockerville's miners were happy, but its citizens who looked to the flume only for drinking and washing water were

---

* Actually, this system was used to seal flumes in many mining communities throughout the West.

not happy at all. The middleman in the controversy was the flume manager, a young fellow named Ambrose Bierce, who had abandoned a literary career (or thought he had) to go into the gold business. When he found himself unable to settle the argument, Bierce gave it up as a bad job and went to San Francisco. There, he resumed his writing and became famous for a biting style that caused him to become known as "Bitter Bierce." And some folks will tell you that what made Bierce bitter was trying to reconcile the pro- and anti-horse manure factions in Rockerville, South Dakota.

If you should stroll from the Harney over to the Rex Theater, and if the Rex is showing a Western—say, a Tom Mix or Hoot Gibson film—you may find that not all of the Hills' colorful characters lived in the past. If your timing happens to be right you will see entering the theater, probably with a companion or two, a stocky, dark-moustached, quick-moving man. You will be struck by two things about this man: he radiates so much energy that even his moustache seems alive; and he and whoever is with him will march right in without bothering to buy tickets. The lobby attendant may tell you, if you ask, that this man is a nut about Western movies, and if he likes one he is apt to see it on two nights in succession. His name is Gutzon Borglum, the fellow who is trying to carve a mountain, and he never buys a ticket. He figures the monument he is building will do so much for local businesses, including theaters, that they should do something for him in return. Moreover, his personality is so powerful that few theater owners care to argue the point with him. So, when Borglum wants to see a movie at the Rex or any other theater in the Hills, he simply walks in and sees it.

What the attendant does not tell you, because he does not know, is how good these shows are for Borglum. Not only do they give him pleasure, but they seem to provide a sort of therapy as well. In public, Borglum is always on stage. He is by nature an actor who strives to play every part and assume every image that he thinks may be expected of him. Yet, underneath this facade there is a warmth, a sentimentality, and a kind of out-reaching that Borglum seems to find hard if not impossible to release in public. In the anonymous darkness of a theater, however, he can lay aside his mask and let his emotions flow. And he does. One of his most frequent movie companions was Emil Flick, who, just before his death in 1976, recalled:

Borglum loved those Westerns, especially those double features they used to show at the Rex. He'd insist that we sit right down in front, and if he missed a line he'd poke me and ask, "What'd he say, Emil, what'd he say?"

He'd ask me afterward how I liked the show, and I had to be careful how I answered. If I said I liked it he was liable to say, "Good! We'll see it again tomorrow night!"

He was just like a big kid at the movies. He'd just drink 'em in and laugh out loud at all the funny scenes and he'd cry in all the sad ones. Once he said to me, "Emil, a man has a *right* to cry at a movie."

While in the Hills you could go out to see Rushmore. Probably, however, you will not if you have come before the dedication of the Washington head, for not until after that will Rushmore be much of a drawing card for tourists. You will rely on local people for sightseeing information, and they will direct you first of all to the Game Lodge—"President Coolidge was here in '27, you know, and that's where he stayed, and you've got to see that." They may send you to the Needles, or the big gold mine at Lead, or to Deadwood where Wild Bill got himself shot. Rushmore? Possibly, but most of those whom you talk to have not been there themselves. They can tell you, though, that Rushmore is not so much a place where there is something as it is a place where there is going to be something: they have been saying there will be for the last six years, but without much to show for a lot of money spent. Besides, they say the road up there is terrible.

Should you go to Rushmore anyhow, you are apt to find it disappointing. You will be impressed by what Borglum is trying to do, but you will not realize the magnitude of it. The head, set back in its stone box, will appear to be resting in a little niche in a very big cliff. This is the kind of country that dwarfs itself, so that large things seen from a distance do not look large. Thus, even if the head had been cut free from the surrounding stone it would still look far smaller than it actually is. Also, it is not yet finished enough to be a very good likeness. You can tell that it is supposed to be Washington, but the face is heavy-featured and lumpish and the eyes are not yet alive, nor the mouth. It appears that way to others, too, and as William Williamson has just noted in his diary, "It lacks expression. . . . It is little more than an image in its present state. Power is lacking." You must not let Borglum hear you saying such things, however. Others have, and he has resented it powerfully. He has told Norbeck only recently, "The head 'Washington' is so fine that I don't care a damn what anybody says. . . . The dignity of its features, the calmness of it, the uprightness of it, is perfectly astonishing to me."

Undoubtedly, Borglum said this not realizing that he and the lay viewer do not see the same things. The layman can see it only as it is and not as it will

32. *Scaffolding on the face of Washington in May, 1930.*
Twisted strata in the lower center of the cliff represent
the edge of a "float-block" of uncarvable schist.

be. Borglum, with his sculptor's vision, can see it only as it will be and not as
it is. Because he sees it that way, and has a genius for translating sculptural
vision into sculptural fact, the Washington head one day will be all that
Borglum sees in it now, and more. But not yet.

As the Fourth of July and the Washington dedication approached, a committee of Rapid City women headed by Mrs. C. C. Warren worked tirelessly
at constructing the dedication flag. It was a gigantic thing; when finished it
measured forty by seventy-two feet, and to publicize the dedication it was suspended lengthwise above Sixth Street. With one side attached to the eighth
story of the Alex Johnson Hotel and the other to a mast atop the Duhamel
building across the street, and with its lower hem just high enough to be clear
of passing traffic, it hung as a spectacular Stars and Stripes curtain that could
not possibly be overlooked.

Apparently the flag served its purpose—or something did—for the dedication was attended by more than 2,500 people. One reason may have been that this time the visitors did not have to choose between walking or trying to drive their cars from Keystone to the mountain. They were able instead to ride up, free of charge, in buses lent by Paul Bellamy's Black Hills Transportation Company.

Senator Norbeck could not attend this dedication, and for a sad reason. The previous September, he had gone to Johns Hopkins Medical Center to see about a bothersome growth affecting his lower jaw and tongue. The verdict—cancer! Surgeons had then removed the growth and said they probably had gotten all of it, but . . . you never could be sure. Norbeck had kept this

33. Borglum speaking at the dedication of the Washington head, July 4, 1930: ". . . let us place there, carved high, as close to heaven as we can, the words of our leaders, their faces, to show posterity what manner of men they were. Then breathe a prayer that these records will endure until the wind and the rain alone shall wear them away."

secret from all but his immediate family, but the knowledge of it had plunged him into a deep depression. To make matters worse, he had suffered throughout the winter from a variety of other ailments. Hoping that a change of scene would restore him in body and mind, Norbeck took his family on a summer tour of the Scandinavian countries, and at the time of the Washington dedication they were in his ancestral Norway.

In most respects the dedication was very similar to the two previous ones at Rushmore. It was the usual Borglum affair: dramatic and well-staged. There was, however, a difference in the unveiling. Heretofore, Borglum's large works had been unveiled in the manner of Lee at Stone Mountain—an instant dropping of flags and the impact of sudden revelation. The revelation of the Washington head, on the contrary, was to be gradual.

The huge flag now draped over the head was attached at the top to cables from the mountaintop winches. At a signal from his grandfather, Doane Robinson's four-year-old grandson, Billydoane Robinson, pressed a button on the speakers' stand. This sounded a buzzer in the winch-house on the mountain, whereupon the winch-men began reeling in cable. Slowly, the great flag began to slide upward and expose the features of Washington.

To keep the flag moving smoothly without snagging, Red Anderson, Merle Peterson, Walt Wilkerson, Jack "Palooka" Payne (so-called because he had been a prizefighter), and perhaps some other workmen as well, were suspended over the mountain in saddles. There, they held the edges of the flag and "walked" up with it as it rose, and in so doing encountered an unexpected problem. Occasionally a gust of wind would balloon a portion of the flag outward from the cliff, and when it did the men holding the flag at that particular place would be swung outward also, then bang back into the cliff when the gust had passed. From their viewpoint on Doane Mountain the audience could not see that, but they could see how small and antlike the workmen looked against the giant Washington face, and they were mightily impressed.

A small by-product of the ceremony was the sense of self-importance young Billydoane Robinson gained from having pushed the unveiling button. His grandfather wrote to Norbeck, "The young man's head is badly swelled but his mother thinks if we give strict attention to the business we can spank it out of him in about thirty days."

A large by-product of it, an extremely important one, was the immense amount of publicity it received. Aside from Borglum, himself, no nationally known personalities were involved in the ceremony. Even Governor Bulow was not in attendance. Nonetheless it was filmed by cameramen from Fox,

34. Workmen removing the American flag at the dedication of the Washington head, July 4, 1930.

Pathé, Paramount, Universal Studios, and Kinogram. Many newspaper reporters were present also, and *The New York Times* gave the event a front page spread. Moreover, the publicity was all favorable, with a few inevitable exceptions, such as the editor who remarked that if enough of "these tombstone chiselers" were allowed to infest the land, "instead of lifting up our eyes to the soft, restful hills whence cometh our help, we shall instead contemplate the hard features of Henry Hokum, president of the First National Bank."

Once it was over, the all-out effort to get the Washington head ready in time for its dedication turned out to have had a price tag on it: the loss of Denison. In June, Borglum had described Denison as "an able, resourceful, indefatigable worker, tireless and loyal," and Denison was all of that and a skilled practical engineer and handler of men as well. Unfortunately, however, he knew little of sculpture, and this had thrown an extra burden of supervision upon Borglum. Under the high-pressure sixteen-hours-a-day hurry-up effort on Washington, nerves had become ragged and tempers had grown short. This had created between Denison and Borglum such a strain that two weeks after the dedication Denison resigned.

Now Borglum decided to try another approach to the superintendent problem. What he really needed was one who was both an engineer and an artist, but these were almost impossible to find. In Denison he had had an engineer who was not an artist. Now he would try an artist who was not an engineer. And by this means young Bill Tallman, the project's chief pointer, became the third man in ten months to serve as the Mount Rushmore construction superintendent.

Another problem created by the two-shift operation was that it had drained away the money that was to have lasted all summer, and late in July the job had to be shut down. When it was, Borglum and Borglum alone, came to its rescue. To the commission he made an outright donation of $1,500, and from the society he purchased five one-hundred dollar memberships. When matched with Federal funds this $2,000 was sufficient to get the work going again and to keep it going until the society could raise some money through membership sales.

At this point one begins to wonder when, in that summer of 1930, Borglum ever rested and if he ever slept. For, in addition to everything else, he now was engaged in trying to get back his original mountain-carving project—Stone Mountain. The sculptor hired to replace him there had botched the job and been fired. At the same time, the Atlanta people had learned from the progress at Rushmore that it *was* possible for a commission to work with Borglum and that Borglum *could* get the job done. Accordingly, in September they had him come to Atlanta to talk about reviving the Confederate Memorial. As it turned out, however, the Atlanta people were facing the same problem the Dakotans had been fighting for so long: money. And with the economy now looking grimmer every day, and with investors becoming increasingly nervous, the problem appeared almost insurmountable. Even so, they told Borglum, they wanted to keep the idea alive and negotiations open. In return, Borglum (still an incurable optimist about fund raising) said he thought he knew where the money might be found. And for the time being, there the matter rested.

The Black Hills country, too, was having economic problems that fall but they were not depression problems—not yet anyhow. The newspapers, it was true, were showing pictures of bread lines in New York and were saying three-and-a-half million Americans were seeking work, but all this seemed remote. It was happening "back east" where most Dakotans had never been. Back there people were known to gamble on the stock market and indulge in all sorts of other foolishness, and therefore no doubt they had brought their troubles on themselves. In Rapid City, on the other hand, "help wanted" ads in the *Journal*'s classified section were outnumbering "employment wanted" ads by about ten to one. Dakota's problem that fall was drought. The 1920s had been for the most part lush growing years, but in 1930 the heavens dried up. The soil had turned to powder, wells were dangerously low, waterholes were turning to mud and the farmers were mowing their stunted wheat for hay because the grain in its shriveled heads was not worth harvesting.

Conditions being what they were, both nationally and locally, at their fall meeting the Rushmore commissioners were little inclined to try another general drive for funds. Instead, they came up with a novel campaign for what came to be known as "the schoolchildren's fund." The idea was to ask each of South Dakota's grade school children to give a dime to Rushmore, and each of the high school students to give a quarter. According to the commissioners' projections this campaign should produce at least $10,000 and probably more. The state superintendent of schools approved it, Governor Bulow approved it, and during the week of October 19th—designated by the governor as Mount Rushmore Week—it was carried out.

During that week the teaching in history, geography, citizenship, and art classes was centered around Rushmore. Students engaged in Rushmore study projects, made Rushmore posters, wrote Rushmore essays, and heard (and sometimes made) Rushmore speeches. By the time it was over there were few Dakota pupils who had not learned all they had ever expected or wanted to know about Rushmore, and then some. In fact, few Dakotans of today who were in school at the time have ever forgotten that fund drive—which yielded, after expenses, only $1,700 of the $10,000 hoped for.

The commissioners were more than disappointed. They were shocked and unable to understand what had caused the dismal difference between what they had received and what they expected. Viewed in retrospect, it appears that the culprit, at least in part, was that little toy called a yo-yo. As it hap-

35. Borglum, center, directing Superintendent Bill Tallman and powderman John Johnson on the face of Washington, late in 1931 or early in 1933. Note that the head has not yet been freed from the surrounding granite and that a ledge of stone remains beneath the chin.

pened, precisely at the time the schoolchildren's fund campaign was getting under way the yo-yo craze struck, and it swept the nation with an intensity even greater than that of the hula hoop mania some twenty-five years later. It was, as the *Journal* reported just before Rushmore Week, "an epidemic. . . . citizens walk the streets with hypnotic gaze fixed on a little wooden ball attached to a string. . . . Young men, old men, women and children all have contracted the malady." Hardest hit, of course, were the children, and right at the time when they were being asked for dimes and quarters for Rushmore. A basic yo-yo cost a dime, the big fancy model cost a quarter. Dimes and quarters were hard to come by, and if it came to a choice—well, Rushmore was something remote and abstract; a yo-yo was a necessity of life. Hence, it seems likely that because of the drive's unfortunate timing, a good deal of money was invested in yo-yos that otherwise would have been invested in Rushmore. But in any case, John Boland pointed out, the drive had "brought the story of Rushmore to all of the schoolchildren and teachers in the state." And he was right, for it certainly had done that.

Once the schoolchildren's fund drive had proved a failure, the commissioners, as a last resort and under heavy pressure from Borglum and Boland, looked to themselves for funds. Their giving was reluctant, to say the least. As one commissioner tartly observed, they thought they had been appointed to manage the Rushmore work, not to pay for it. They did come up with money enough (when matched with Federal funds) to carry the work well into the coming season. As a consequence of it, however, a few commissioners then resigned, and one or two others so completely lost interest that they might as well have.

To those, and they were many, who long had been predicting the total collapse of the Rushmore project, it must have appeared the collapse finally had begun. From its very beginning almost four years ago the operation had been in a state of seemingly perpetual crisis. So far it had managed somehow to survive—which in itself was something of a miracle—but now that various commissioners were abandoning it, it was beginning to look very much like a sinking ship. As it happened, however, just the reverse was true. The project was growing stronger, and rather than having been harmed by the loss of those who resigned it had been helped. For, just as in Gideon's army of old, among the commissioners and all the others involved with Rushmore as well, the inept and faint-of-heart and less than dedicated were being weeded out.

Remaining, both on the commission and on the work force, were those stalwarts who were determined to carry on the work, and who in surviving the crises of the past had become confident of their ability to survive the crises yet to come. On the commission the foremost of these were its Dakota members—William Williamson, Royal Johnson, C. M. Day, John Boland and Chan Gurney—together with Borglum's friend Lorine Spoonts and the president of the Chicago and Northwestern Railway, Fred Sargent. Then, in March of 1931, the commission received an additional member whose strength more than made up for the commissioners who had resigned. President Hoover again asked Norbeck to serve on the commission, and this time Norbeck accepted.

15. One of the Foxiest Men in the Senate

I n July of 1931, Borglum's statue of Woodrow Wilson was to be unveiled in Poznan, Poland. This called for the sculptor's presence, both as the statue's creator and to see that it was erected properly—which meant that Borglum would have to be away from Rushmore for most of the summer. Such being the case, when he returned in April to the Black Hills from San Antonio he brought with him a sculptor named Hugo Villa. Years earlier, Villa had worked with Borglum at Stone Mountain and then, like Borglum, had established a studio at San Antonio. Now Borglum was enlisting Villa to carry the Rushmore work forward during his absence.

The season's main project was to be the roughing out of the Jefferson face. This was begun early in June, at which time the sculptor and his family departed for Europe. (Which prompted one editor to observe that if the Europeans did not want to see the Alps carved into statues, they had better guard them carefully until Borglum had returned home.)

On his way to Poland Borglum visited Denmark, home of his ancestors, and there was knighted by King Christian X. In that same summer, Harold Gatty and Wiley Post, in a little airplane named Winnie May, made history by flying around the world in eight days and sixteen hours. Also in that summer a group of German scientists said the day would soon come when men would orbit the earth in space stations; Italian dictator Benito Mussolini told the United States Secretary of State, Henry Stimson, "There is a road toward war and a road toward peace—I have chosen the road toward peace."; and the distinguished American economist Roger Babson declared that the worst of the current depression was over and that soon the nation could expect "unparalleled prosperity."

Back in Dakota, however, people were not worrying much about the depression; it would have been like a drowning man worrying about a hangnail.

Last year's drought had been bad, but this year's was the worst in the history of the local weather bureau. Last year the old-timers had said, "If you think this is bad you should have been here in ought-'leven." But they were not saying it now. Compared to this year, 1911 had been wet. In this spring farmers had plowed in dust and planted in dust. Now, they longingly watched the cumulus clouds that built up almost every afternoon over the Hills, and let their hopes build with them. But always the clouds sailed lazily eastward, like great silver ships, taking their precious cargo of moisture with them. And there were grasshoppers. "Possibly the worst infestation in the nation's history," one entomologist said. Whether or not this was true, it was true that the grasshoppers were eating whatever crops the drought had not killed, and for dessert they were nibbling on fenceposts and pitchfork handles.

In the Hills, ordinarily kept green by mountain rains, the pine needle ground-carpet became tinder dry and the resinous pine trees became torches waiting for a spark. Then, by lightning and carelessly discarded cigarettes, the sparks were provided. In late July more than 2,000 men were fighting fires in various parts of the Hills. On the Rushmore cliff, Borglum's men worked in air that smelled of burning pine and looked out over the mountains dimmed by drifting smoke. And as they worked they worried that the next fire might be one that would take their homes.

The good news in the Hills that summer was the increase in the tourist trade. Despite the depression, nationwide tourism was up fourteen percent from the previous year, and the increase in Black Hills tourism was much larger still—which may explain why a fall survey showed Rapid City to have only 250 people seeking jobs, and most of these (according to the report) were farmers who had been "dried out" or "hoppered out" and needed income to carry them over to the next season.

Thus, when Borglum returned to the Hills on August 27, he found the prairies dust-hazed and swarming with grasshoppers and the Black Hills smoke-hazed and swarming with tourists; and he found Villa in trouble with the head of Jefferson. There are different stories about that trouble, the most common one being that Villa had made a cut that was too deep and thereby had removed some irreplaceable stone and ruined the head. The mistake was so obvious, the story continues, that when the returning Borglum reached the site of the Keystone baseball diamond, still two miles from the mountain, he already could see what had happened. Whereupon, he stormed up to the mountain, called in Villa, and demanded an explanation. Villa then admitted that a mistake had been made in pointing, which had caused too much stone to be removed from Jefferson's forehead (according to one version) or from beneath his eye (according to another). Then, so one author tells it, "Villa hastily left the scene" and went back to San Antonio.

This account of the affair seems to stem from the way Borglum described it years later, and, more often than not, is the accepted version. However, to those who well know that from nowhere in Keystone would it even have been possible for Borglum to have seen Rushmore cliff, the story is suspect, and properly so.

As it actually happened, Villa *was* in trouble with the head, but the extent of that trouble was not determined until quite a while after Borglum's return. Also, Villa did resign shortly after Borglum came back, but not because of the Jefferson problem. In fact, Borglum, upon his return, said he was "well pleased" with the work done during his absence, and told the press that thanks to the remarkable abilities of Villa and Tallman, "we are accomplishing as much for one dollar this year as we did for three dollars in 1929."

The real Jefferson problem was that the head had been located where there would have been barely enough stone for it if all the stone there had been sound, which it proved not to be. Hence, not only Villa but many of the

36. Men at work, in 1931, on the first Jefferson head, which was to have been on Washington's right. Faulty rock was encountered and the unfinished head was blasted down.

workmen as well were of the opinion that, located where it was, the head could not possibly be finished. Borglum seems at first to have disagreed with them, for when rumors of the Jefferson trouble began to circulate through the community he condemned them as "evil-tongued gossip."

The dispute between Villa and Borglum actually was over wages. Villa claimed that when Borglum asked him to come to Rushmore he had promised him more pay than Villa was in fact receiving. Borglum denied it. Villa then lost his temper and resigned. After arriving back in San Antonio, Villa, still in a huff, unburdened himself by writing a letter to the governor of South Dakota. Trying to carve the Jefferson head in its present location, he wrote, was a pure waste of time because the stone there did not fit Borglum's model. If Borglum did not start doing a better job of fitting his models to the cliff, Villa Continued, Rushmore would never be finished. Besides, he added, Borglum was gone too much, and when he was gone he never left adequate instructions for those who were to carry on in his absence.

Although Villa and Borglum had been friends and sometimes associates for many years, this sort of thing could have been expected to destroy that friendship. Interestingly, however, it did not. Borglum was a man who found it very hard to forgive the other party for having been right in a dispute, and Villa had been right in this one. On the other hand, when Borglum liked someone enough, he could forgive him much, and in this case he did. He continued to speak well of Villa, forgave him for having been right, and remained his friend.

Work at the mountain was continued well into the fall of 1931. Then the hard times of the '30s caught up with it. At the end of November the commission had $16,000 in debts, $500 in assets, and no prospects at all of finding more money. The deepening depression had closed such purses as once had been open, and the flow of money, like Dakota's creeks, had gone dry.

Borglum, too, was deep in financial trouble. When he moved to South Dakota he had brought a large amount of savings with him—usually he said $40,000, but sometimes claimed it was $60,000—yet his income from Rushmore had been far smaller than he had counted on. He had expected to receive from $15,000 to $17,500 per year from it, but the work had proceeded far more slowly than he had anticipated. Hence, from 1927 to the present it had paid him an average of only $5,000 a year. (Adjusted for inflation and tax-rate differences, the equivalent today would be an expected gross income of from $140,000 to $175,000 a year and an actual one of $45,000.) In addition, of course, he had income from other sculptural contracts and from lectures, so to the casual observer Borglum appeared to be a lot better off than most

*37. Borglum with his model at the time when Jefferson was
to be carved on Washington's right. At the left is Charlie
Johnson, Borglum's personal handyman and chauffeur. To the
left of Johnson is Borglum's first model for the memorial.*

people in 1931. Both his obligations and his style of living had been constructed, however, on an assumption of an income much larger than he was
receiving. Most of his savings had gone into down payments on his ranch,
cattle, new home, and studio, and the rest had been used to cover the difference between his income and expenditures. Now, the savings were gone and
Borglum was broke. Remembering that the commission still owed him about
$6,000 in sculptural fees plus $3,500 on the loan he had made it when Tucker
quit, he wrote to Boland: "If one half the amount due could be paid me . . . I
would be able to carry my obligations . . . without disastrous loss to me."

Unfortunately, Boland could not help him. The commission had no
money, either. Boland did suggest that Borglum might cut his expenses here
and there and that, for example, he might not actually need to be driven
about by a chauffeur in a most expensive automobile. Borglum seems not to
have resented that, for he then wrote to Norbeck that Boland was "loyal to his

38. Borglum's first model for the Mount Rushmore Memorial.

duty and faithful to his trust." He did, however, go on to admit that people were saying, "Oh, hell, Borglum spends money recklessly," and then to add, "I don't spend money recklessly . . . I spend it in keeping with what I do in my life and not . . . in gambling, speculation or feasting."

Borglum managed in one way or another to scrape by until February. Then he wired Norbeck:

THE FINANCIAL SITUATION . . . IS SUCH THAT I AM OBLIGED
UTTERLY AGAINST MY PERSONAL WISH . . . TO SHUT DOWN THE
WORK INDEFINITELY AND TAKE UP WORK AWAITING ME
ELSEWHERE. BOLAND HAS DONE EVERYTHING HUMANLY POSSIBLE
TO AVOID THIS. I HAVE RISKED ALL I HAVE, BUT I MUST BE
FINANCED AT ONCE OR I SHALL HAVE TO GO AWAY.

But, since Rushmore, too, was out of money and in debt, there simply was no way for Borglum to be "financed." Therefore, he did go away and began to work on a statue of William Jennings Bryan that was to be erected in Potomac Park in Washington, D.C. Behind him he left a mountain that was silent, its buildings deserted, its machinery covered and still. It was to remain that way throughout the spring and summer of 1932, and well into the fall.

As might be expected, this shut-down worked a great hardship on the Rushmore crew, and this, in turn, further endangered the future of the work itself. These men had learned their jobs, had become used to working with Borglum and each other, and thus had become a working unit that was almost irreplaceable. But this shut-down—which was for no one knew how long, and might be forever the way things looked—seemed likely to cause the crew to become scattered and lost. However, these were tough-minded men who did not want to become scattered, and since they also were scramblers it turned out that they did not have to be. Some found work on the Iron Mountain road, a scenic drive under construction in Custer State Park. Others got jobs at the Holy Terror and Golden Slipper gold mines. Two of them returned to their original occupation of barbering. The Peterson boys leased and reworked some abandoned feldspar mines and "took out enough to make eating money." And one family, that has asked to remain anonymous, survived by making and bootlegging home brew. One thing that helped, also, was that in 1932 rains came abundantly and at the right time to create bumper crops (in fact, this was about the only good agricultural year in the entire decade of the '30s), and farmers who still had any money left were hiring help. Thus, fortunately for Rushmore's future, its builders managed in one way and another to stay in the neighborhood during the shut-down, and to survive. "Need is a great incentive," one of them was to say later. "We had to have something to do, so we found something to do, and we all made it through."

Norbeck, too, was a tough-minded scrambler, and because he was he now got Rushmore through its last truly critical financial crisis. As it happened, in the spring of 1932 there was in Congress a bill to authorize distribution among the various states of a $300 million "unemployment relief fund," and Norbeck thought this just might answer Rushmore's money problem. As originally drawn, however, the bill was not flexible enough to allow any of the South Dakota share to be diverted to Rushmore. Therefore, on June 21 Norbeck asked Williamson to draft an amendment that would create the needed flexibility. Williamson had the amendment finished on the very next day and said it was a "sleeper" designed to accomplish the desired end without revealing to Congress just what that end was. Then, only two days after that, Williamson wrote in his diary, "Peter Norbeck . . . called up with victory and jubilation in his voice and said, 'I got your amendment in without a change!' He is one of the foxiest men in the Senate."

The bill passed in July, the funds were distributed to the various states, then Norbeck hit a snag with Governor Green. South Dakota's share of the fund was $150,000, and Green had promised Norbeck earlier that he would give $50,000 of it to Rushmore. Once he had received the money, however, Green tried to back out. South Dakota is divided approximately in half by the Missouri River, and for reasons both topographical and historic, the river is not only a sharply defined boundary between the Midwest and the West, but also between areas that are politically competitive. Although East River contains only about forty percent of the state's land, in 1932 it contained almost eighty percent of its population. Thus, to Governor Green, himself an East River man, diverting a full third of the relief fund to a single West River project smelled of political suicide. On the other hand Green was a Republican, and when Norbeck spoke Green listened. Even so, he would not listen to Norbeck now. Finally, as Norbeck confided later to John Boland, "I had to get rough about it." When he did, Green surrendered, and on September 22 gave the $50,000 to Rushmore.

Green did manage, however, to attach a restriction to the fund. It must be used to give jobs to the needy, and for nothing else. Since the Rushmore operation could not function without also having electricity and supplies, this meant that the carving still could not be resumed. It meant also that those crew-members who now had other jobs could not be rehired because they could not be called "needy." The upshot was that more than forty new men, and a few of the old hands, were put to work on Rushmore's roads, trails, and landscaping, and on enlarging its parking lot.

But Norbeck was not finished. Not yet. Living up to Williamson's description as "one of the foxiest men in the Senate," Norbeck now executed his greatest Rushmore coup of all. The wording of the Rushmore Act was clear: "Not more than one-half of the cost . . . shall be borne by the United States." It was also clear in providing for disbursement of Federal funds only when matched by "funds from other sources." Even so, Norbeck, by means never fully explained, managed to get the $50,000 relief fund matched by another $50,000 from the Rushmore appropriation. In so doing, he managed to get the government to match its own money. Even more important, he saved the Rushmore project from almost certain death.

The matching money arrived on the 9th of December, whereupon John Boland set about cleaning Rushmore's financial house. He cleaned up the remaining obligations of the old Mount Harney Association, then paid all of the present commission's bills. Included in this were checks to Borglum for his unpaid sculptural fees and his previous loans to the commission, together with interest accumulated at six percent on both. When finished, Boland still had plenty of money left that could be used for electricity, equipment, dynamite, etc.; and since the relief-fund money could be used for salaries, this meant that Rushmore would enter 1933 free of debt and with money for another season of work.

As it looked then, this had been accomplished just in time. President Hoover had tried to end the depression through government spending, and in so doing had created a five billion dollar deficit in the Federal budget. In the 1932 elections, as a consequence, the Democrats' campaign slogan had been, "Throw the spenders out!" Hoover's opponent, Franklin D. Roosevelt, had declared that if he were elected he would cut government spending by twenty-five percent. Now, Mr. Roosevelt had been elected, and it looked as though government money in the future would be extremely hard to get.

In that election, South Dakota broke its Republican habit. Except for William Jennings Bryan, who in 1896 had carried the state by a margin of 180 votes, a Democrat had never received South Dakota's presidential vote. As if to make up for that history, the state gave Mr. Roosevelt a larger percentage of its vote than he received from the nation as a whole.

Indestructible politician that he was, Norbeck survived the 1932 Democratic landslide and was returned to office. Congressman Williamson, on the other hand, did not. Which bothered him very little—probably because by his own admission he was not temperamentally suited to the Congressional life anyhow. After the election he noted in his diary, "My defeat probably was a godsend. . . . I had no sense of depression." Then he promptly set about establishing a law office in Rapid City, where he was to serve Rushmore more diligently than before.

16. Lincoln Borglum— Pointer Without Pay

Nineteen thirty-three, and in the world and the nation the winds of change were blowing, overturning old concepts, sweeping out old problems and sweeping in new ones, reshaping the future. Abroad, Adolf Hitler gained dictatorial control of Germany, and at home Franklin Delano Roosevelt became the 31st President of the United States; both of these events were to affect profoundly the future of Rushmore.

In March, President Roosevelt was inaugurated, and across the land orchestras played the Democrats' new theme song, "Happy Days Are Here Again." Then came the famous "hundred days" during which Black Hillers and all other Americans learned a new vocabulary and new alphabet. In a style of speech he called the "fireside chat," Mr. Roosevelt told Americans they were to receive a "new deal," and it would come to them through a collection of alphabetic agencies: the PWA (later the WPA), NRA, AAA, and CCC. In the Black Hills country, as elsewhere, the New Deal began to appear shortly thereafter. The Public Works Administration began hiring the unemployed for work on public projects. Clad in the forest green uniforms of the Civilian Conservation Corps, formerly unemployed youths from the South and East began arriving in the Hills to work on bridges, dams, picnic grounds, and scenic trails. Placards bearing the Blue Eagle of the National Recovery Act began to appear in Black Hills business places, testimony that the owners thereof had agreed to work their employees no more than forty hours per week and to pay them no less than thirty cents per hour. In the surrounding countryside farmers-become-agents for the Agricultural Adjustment Act were explaining to their neighbors the government's plan for paying them *not* to raise grain and livestock.

Sudden, radical, these programs created a shock wave in the West River country. Here in the most conservative region of conservative South Dakota, at least as many people opposed the New Deal as supported it. Either way, these usually laconic and understated people were expressing their opinions so vigorously that tempers flared, friendships grew strained, and there was loud contention between those who thought the New Deal a blessing and those who thought it a curse.

One of the latter was George Reeves, a sheep rancher in the Elk Creek breaks just north of Rapid City. Years later, as a professor of literature at the University of Michigan, he wrote an award-winning book, *A Man From South Dakota,* in which he recalled his response to Mr. Roosevelt's first fireside chat:

> There was a blizzard raging and lambs were dropping in my lambing shed. . . .
>
> Uncle Harry called to me from over the corral fence. "Roosevelt is talking," he said. "You'd better come up and hear what he's got to say."
>
> The living room was filled with thousands of voices cheering the hero of the New Deal. . . . Listening to him was an ordeal, because I did not enjoy being patted on the head like a dimwitted child by a man who talked as if I were a fool. I could grant no awe to his insight nor long submit to his elaborate simplicities.
>
> He was, he said, going to drive the money-changers from the temple. . . . Government was going to protect its little citizens from their bad elder brothers.
>
> The three of us sat there and listened to those crazy people yell. . . .
>
> "If he thinks he can do all those things he's a damned fool," I said, "and if he doesn't think he can do them he's a damned liar. Personally, I think he's both."
>
> I wasn't ready to accept patronage from this man's hands. . . . Pulling on my jacket, I went back to the lambing shed.

It was not the PWA, NRA, or CCC that upset the New Deal's Black Hills opponents so much as it was the AAA. They had struggled for years to grow crops and livestock on a stubborn land, and now the AAA wanted them *not* to grow crops and livestock. It made no sense. If the government were to buy their produce at a good price . . . well, that might be all right. But to hear that because of a "farm surplus" they were to be paid not to produce food when all over the land people were going hungry—that, they thought, was a tale told by an idiot. Again, George Reeves summed up their feelings:

An emissary of the New Deal appeared in my barn. The man was a neighbor. . . . I didn't recognize him as an emissary of government. I thought he had come to borrow some machinery . . . but I soon learned he was a Greek bearing gifts. He had come, he said, to offer me money for not raising hogs, for reducing my wheat acreage and for refraining from planting corn.

I didn't think there was a farm surplus as long as there were people anywhere in the world who didn't have enough to eat. And how were these textbook politicians . . . to know that Famine might not come next year in a bad drought? . . . bins empty all over the United States. . . .

"I don't raise hogs," I said shortly, "and not much corn."

"You don't have to raise hogs to get the money," he pointed out. "All you have to do is agree *not* to raise hogs, and to plant less corn and wheat."

"My wheat acreage is just the way I want it," I said. . . . "And if Roosevelt doesn't like it he can go straight to hell."

Extending even to Borglum and Boland, this contention was to contribute to the serious rift soon to develop between them. Borglum was a New Deal enthusiast, which confirmed Boland's long-held opinion of the sculptor as a starry-eyed dreamer and economic illiterate. Boland was adamantly anti-New Deal, which confirmed Borglum's opinion that he was an inhumane businessman with ice-water blood.

Nonetheless, the New Deal had come to stay. And even though it was to be some time yet before anyone realized it, the New Deal was to secure the future of Mount Rushmore National Memorial.

The memorial had been conceived in the only kind of times when such a thing could have been conceived—in the effervescent, optimistic 1920s. But even in those times money sufficient to complete the job had been impossible to raise. Now, in the somber, depressed 1930s, just the opposite was true. Now, it would have been impossible to get such a nonessential and nonedible enterprise approved and under way, but since Rushmore was already under way when the New Deal's make-work attack on unemployment came along, it was to become yet another place where Federal money could be spent to create jobs. Thus, the memorial was begun in an era when it could not have been finished, and was finished in an era when it could not have been begun. Nor could it have come into being even then if Senator Norbeck had not cleverly finagled the emergency relief-fund money for the project, and then managed to get that sum matched by the Rushmore appropriation. That was the critical bridge. It brought the work into the days of the New Deal as a going concern and as a project whose bills were paid, and that was important. For even though the New Deal Congress could be persuaded to spend money on creating new jobs, it was not too willing to spend it on the payment of old bills.

In another notable Rushmore event of 1933, Borglum's son Lincoln became a full-fledged member of the crew. He already had done some work on the mountain, but only on an off-and-on basis and without pay, and he had never intended to make a full-time job of it. Instead, he had planned to study engineering at the University of Virginia, where he had been accepted, but now Borglum had other ideas. He doted on this son of his, and all through Lincoln's growing years had kept him close by his side. Now Lincoln was a man, and Borglum still wanted him by his side, helping to build Rushmore. Accordingly, Lincoln postponed his college plans (temporarily, he thought; permanently, as it would turn out) and became a full-time, though still unpaid, Rushmore workman.

Whether or not he realized it, Borglum was taking quite a chance when he put Lincoln on the crew. Independent as hogs on ice, the crew-members set their own standards for those with whom they worked. By means both overt and subtle, they would make life so miserable for anyone not meeting these standards that even in those days of scarce jobs he would quit—and it had to be that way. The work was dangerous, demanding, exhausting, and much of it was done in physically punishing positions and in temperatures either too hot or too cold. Some of it was work no one had done before, even at Stone Mountain. It presented frustrating problems that even Borglum had not previously encountered. It strained nervous systems, bodies, and tempers. Hence, it demanded a crew that could work in harmony and that had a feeling of fraternity and esprit de corps; and one way or another, anyone disrupting that harmony had to be made to shape up or quit.

Lincoln came to the crew as a big, rugged young fellow who was no shirker and no sissy, and that was in his favor. But it was about all that was, for he also came as "the boss's son." From the crew's point of view he was a "rich kid" whose background was "ritzy" and "high-toned," he had traveled widely and in high style, had had much association with the rich and famous, had always had (again from the crew's point of view) a great deal of money to spend, and had grown up under the influence of a father who was much less than democratic in his associations.

Nor was that all he was up against. As one of the Rushmore veterans remembered, "The Old Man was always trying to push Lincoln along—to make him important." Accordingly, instead of starting Lincoln at the bottom of the Rushmore ladder, say as a roustabout or mechanic's helper, Borglum made him a pointer. This was a prestige job that required experience, concentration, and careful judgment. Although Lincoln was to receive no pay for it, it was a top-of-the-scale position that his presence kept someone else from filling. And for the boss's son to receive without effort this job for which other men had struggled to qualify was not the sort of thing likely to endear him to the crew. All things considered, therefore, Borglum's placing Lincoln on the work force as he did should have been about like putting a housecat in a cage full of coyotes.

And yet . . . it did not work out that way at all. To Lincoln's everlasting credit, it turned out very well indeed. He had inherited his father's talent for art, and years of watching his father at work had given him a good basic understanding of sculpture, both mountain and otherwise. Thus, he very quickly developed competence in his new job. That would not have helped, of course, if the workmen had found him to be obnoxious personally. But as it happened, they found him to be the opposite. He was quiet, considerate, and as one of the crew later recalled, "Lincoln always acted like a gentleman." And the man who had spoken of Borglum's trying to make Lincoln important, ended that comment by saying: "Lincoln never let it go to his head. He didn't know much about what he was doing at first, but he was such a nice kid that all the other pointers helped him out until he learned to do it by himself, so it all worked out OK. Lincoln was a good guy to work with."

Rushmore got another bonus that summer: the opening of the Iron Mountain road. The road was not a part of the memorial, but it turned out to seem as if it were. Running northwestward from a point near Borglum's ranch on the Game Lodge Road to the Rushmore road just west of Keystone, this new road had been intended by the highway department only to provide a more direct linkage between the Game Lodge and Rushmore areas. Its purpose was not scenery but convenience. Senator Norbeck, to the highway department's distress, thought it ought to be the other way around. He loved this wild section of the Hills, knew the spectacular scenery to be found there, and wanted a road that would expose it to public view. And he got it. With strong backing from Paul Bellamy and some others of like mind, the senator first maneuvered himself into a position where he could pretty well dictate where the road was to run. Then, or so the story is told, accompanied by a state highway engineer, Norbeck walked over his proposed route, driving stakes to mark key points along the way. To the engineer's dismay, instead of marking a route around the base of Iron Mountain, Norbeck went right up over its crest. There was no sense in going over the crest, protested the engineer. It would cost too much. It would be a slow road to drive. It would be dangerous. Besides, the senator was putting those darned stakes in places where a road would be impossible to build. "I know it's impossible," Norbeck is reported to have said, grinning, "but put it there anyhow!"

Over a period of years and the continued protests of the engineers, the impossible road had been built. Where there was no room for a two-way road it was built as two one-way roads sometimes running as much as a quarter-mile apart. In places on the north side of the mountain where the slope was too steep for a road to climb, the ascent was accomplished by building spiral pine-log ramps called "pigtail bridges." But Norbeck's pride and joy was the

39. View of Rushmore through one of the tunnels on Peter Norbeck's "impossible road"—the Iron Mountain road.

road's three tunnels. He had had an enormous amount of trouble in getting them dug, for the reason that all were entirely unnecessary. His files reveal many letters in which the state's engineers imply (politely, of course) that he had been out of his mind even to ask for them. Norbeck had responded by declaring that when it came to scenery, engineers "don't know a park from a ranch," and he continued to insist that the tunnels be built.

Before the road was finished it had become a severe aggravation to everyone connected with it. Borglum had become furious with the highway department for taking so long in finishing it. Norbeck had almost exhausted himself in getting it built as he had planned it. The highway engineers were constantly frustrated by what they considered its unnecessary difficulties. The governor and other state officials had become alarmed by the cost of it—especially when Norbeck insisted on expensive extras such as padding the trunks of giant pines along the route so as to protect them from blasting damage.

But when the road was opened it proved to be so beautiful that its problems were forgotten, and everyone agreed it was worth all that had gone into it. Especially Norbeck's tunnels! Each was so aligned that motorists entering it would see, framed like a picture in the tunnel's far end, the carvings on Mount Rushmore.

In the summer of 1933, Norbeck also strengthened Rushmore's position by getting President Roosevelt to place in under the jurisdiction of the National Park Service. Signed on June 19, the order directed the commission to account to the Park Service for all expenditures of Federal funds, and charged the commission's executive committee chairman, John Boland, with the task of seeing that Rushmore's Federal funds were spent in accordance with Federal regulations.

The order did not affect the actual conduct of the work, but it did imply some measure of government control. Accordingly, the senator wrote asking John Boland to break the news to Borglum tactfully, "at some opportune time." This was unlike Norbeck, for he was the one Rushmore official who, when necessary, could tell the sculptor unpleasant things without causing him to blow up. Now, however, even Norbeck was handling Borglum gingerly, and the reason seems to have been his fear that Rushmore might go the way of Stone Mountain. That project had overcome its money problems, Norbeck had often reminded the commissioners, but it had not been able to overcome the breakdown in relations between Borglum and the Stone Mountain Association. Norbeck had always worried about the same thing happening at Rushmore, and it looked to him now as if things were moving in that direction. There was clearly a deterioration taking place in the relationship between Borglum and the commission, the executive committee, and even the Black Hills community in general. It seemed to have begun rather suddenly but with no one particular cause. Once started, however, the breakdown rapidly grew worse. Until now Rushmore's main problem had been financial, and for some time to come those connected with the work would still see that as the main problem. The hindsight of history, however, shows it otherwise.

The year 1933 was a turning point. From that time forward, money would become progressively easier to get, and the struggle would become a human rather than a financial conflict. As Norbeck now feared, the story of Rushmore was to become more and more parallel to the story of Stone Mountain—but with one exception. The human struggle had destroyed Stone Mountain, but it would strengthen Rushmore.

17. "Don't These Crazy People Know What I'm Doing For Them?"

N
ow Gutzon Borglum was entering his most tempestuous and triumphant years—years in which he struggled endlessly against obstacles created both by himself and by others, years in which his name became an American household word and in which he transformed the rough granite carvings on Rushmore into figures of such grace and character that they might have been carved from marble inside a studio. He was sixty-six years old, claimed to be sixty-two, looked fifty, and depending on the circumstances acted anywhere from four to forty. Age had neither mellowed him nor slowed him down. He was as much a fighter as ever, and in his impact on others he still left no one neutral. Those with whom he dealt still wound up either loving him or hating him, but they were always fascinated by him. And because he was still the brilliant, contradictory, many-faceted man he had always been, his associates found him no easier to understand or predict than they ever had.

The perspective of history, however, discloses much more about him than was obvious then. From the tracks he made in those sixty-six years, from his accomplishments and failures, speeches, articles, and the reactions of others to him it is possible to construct with confidence a blueprint of the man Gutzon Borglum had become. And examination of that blueprint reveals that it was almost entirely by the nature of Borglum himself that the final years of Rushmore's construction were shaped.

He was intense and serious, hard to joke with and impossible to joke at. Excepting wine with his meals he drank very little. He had no use for nightlife and never gambled. Self-centered though he was, he was a devoted family man who if he ever philandered left no trace of it. When in a rage his language was intemperate, but only mildly profane and never obscene. His work absorbed his energy, and aside from occasional fishing he seems never to have played very much nor even to have needed to. Exasperating as he often was to those around him, Borglum had an astonishing ability to hold their loyalty. Thus, even when his relations with them were stormy and strained, Norbeck, Williamson, Boland, Robinson, the crew at the mountain, and others continued to support him.

These characteristics, however, only explain *how* Borglum was, and not *why*. To understand his inner motivations and, thus, why the later years at Rushmore turned out as they did, it is necessary to examine the inner Borglum as revealed by the record of his life.

Childlike. That was Borglum. He was Peter Pan, the boy who never grew up. The wear and tear of sixty-six years had not tarnished his youthful zest for life nor his belief that by wishing hard enough he could make any dream come true. Like a child, he saw with fresh eyes those things that had become mundane and commonplace to others and found in them new dimensions and new beauty, and he retained the sense of wonder that is the wellspring of creative genius. He never lost the belief that somewhere there were dragons to be slain and that he would be the one to find and slay them. To be sure, these things often led him into trouble. But they also led him to triumph, for with his fresh vision and the magic of his believing he routinely accomplished things others had said were impossible.

His emotions, too, were childlike—untamed and uninhibited, quick to be aroused and quick to change, and this was reflected in his dealings with those around him. One veteran of the Rushmore crew spoke for all when he said: "You could stand very high with the Chief one minute and be at the bottom the next. It all depended on his mood, and his moods changed real fast. But the guys all knew he was like that and didn't let it bother them." His moods were so mercurial, in fact, that there were few crew-members whom he had not at least once fired in fury and then rehired after he had cooled down. This happened to Merle Peterson eight times, which Peterson claimed was the record number among the crew. Borglum's secretary at Rushmore, Jean Peters, seems however to have held the overall record. After being fired and rehired ten times she had lost count, she said, but thought the grand total was seventeen.

Childlike, also, was Borglum's lack of interest in saving for tomorrow any treats he could partake of today. Not only was he determined to enjoy the good life whether or not he could pay for it, but he seems to have felt that he had a natural right to do so. Together with his lavish generosity when he did have money, this kept him in financial hot water throughout his life and contributed much to the friction that developed between him and the Black Hills community. Because of his charm and commanding personality, local businessmen found it hard not to give him credit, and they found it even harder to collect from him after they had done so. A onetime friend of the sculptor recalled his suddenly exclaiming: "Don't these crazy people understand what I'm doing for them? Just because I have an unpaid grocery bill at Hermosa, they're calling me a deadbeat! My God! I'm giving them something that will bring a billion dollars into these hills, and they carp at me because I haven't paid for a piddling parcel of groceries!" And a filling-station operator remembered a time that Borglum had appeared at the station in his chauffeur-driven Cadillac and said, "Fill 'er up!"

"I'm sorry, but I'll have to have some money first," the station operator replied.

"Young man!" Borglum snapped, "Don't you know who I am?!"

"Sure do," said the operator, "that's why I need the money first!" "I never got any of Borglum's business after that," the operator recalled, "but that was all right with me. The station men who did sell him gas said it was usually a losing proposition."

Finally, Borglum had a child's hunger for attention and praise and to be at center stage. Some of that desire is present in all of us, of course, but in Borglum it was a demanding, egocentric drive so strong that it may well have been the core of his personality and the mainspring of his accomplishments. Late in life he wrote a recollection (mentioned earlier) of himself as a toddler running to capture a rising Nebraska moon. Running, falling, running again, yearning to hold that moon and crying because he could not catch it. Throughout his life he had been pursuing that moon, he wrote, "but I have never reached it."

He never said what his moon was, probably because he did not know. By looking at the full sweep of Borglum's life now, however, we can see what it was. We can see, too, that long before his death he had already captured his moon but did not know that he had, and so kept chasing it. There can be little doubt now that Borglum's moon—the shining goal that lured him on and caused him to fall and be hurt time and again, and that ultimately led him to greatness—was recognition, adulation, and universal fame. He had to be the center of every gathering, recognized as the dominant figure in every group or undertaking, and to receive total credit for the success of any venture with which he was associated. At Rushmore, Borglum not only wanted credit for every achievement, he demanded it so insistently that Norbeck, in exasperation, finally wrote to him:

> Isn't the fact that all future time will view this work as Borglum's work sufficient unto you? Why not let the men who do little things get credit for their little things? . . . Big men should . . . be content with the ultimate vindication instead of trying to hog it all.
>
> Isn't it sufficient to be known as the world's greatest sculptor without also craving the handclapping of those who live in the styx [*sic*] and don't know what it is all about?

Aggravating as Borglum's demand for recognition and dominance may have been, however, the world is richer because he had it. Without it he might well have become just another in that army of gifted artists who despite their talents live unrecognized and die unknown. And without Borglum's driving desire to achieve greatness at Rushmore mountain and his aggressive assumption of leadership when others were faltering, there almost certainly would be no Rushmore monument today.

At the same time, it was this egocentricity of Borglum's that caused most of the conflict that characterized the project's later years. In an excellently researched book, *Mount Rushmore*, published in 1952, historian Gilbert Fite recounted some of those conflicts and thereby caused Borglum's widow to become greatly distressed. "So great an undertaking produced on such a lofty scale," wrote Mary Borglum, should never be "cheapened" by public disclosure of "petty disagreements" or "clashes of wills" occurring during its construction. In so doing, Fite had painted a false and "seamy side to Rushmore," she said, and had attempted to belittle her husband's character. Besides, she added, Rushmore's creators "all ended up as friends, and that was all that was important."

Mary Borglum's feelings are understandable and from her viewpoint entirely justifiable, but they were hardly objective. She was a gentle, peace-loving woman, devoted to the memory of her husband and to his creation at Rushmore and unable to stand hearing either of them criticized. Borglum himself, however, probably would have taken a different view. During his lifetime he had been an exuberant scrapper who would fight for his convictions and objectives at the drop of a hat—sometimes even dropping the hat himself—and it is hard to believe that he would have wanted history to remember him otherwise. In fact, he had once said to an author preparing to do a story on him, "For heaven's sake, don't cover me with twaddle and gush!"

Moreover, the nation Rushmore was built to honor—also "a great undertaking produced on a lofty scale"—was born in conflict, shaped by conflict, preserved through conflict. Whig versus Tory, South versus North, Labor versus Management, Republican versus Democrat; by such opposing forces, each struggling to curb what it saw as the excesses of the other, were the practical paths between impractical extremes hammered out, and the nation was thus enabled to survive and to grow. It was the same with the building of Rushmore. Borglum, with his keen sense of history, would have known that, and he would have known also that just as the American Nation is not cheapened by having been forged in conflict, neither is its Mount Rushmore monument.

Although disputes between Borglum and the Rushmore developers were nothing new, heretofore they had arisen only occasionally and usually singly, and could be handled accordingly. Now, however, they were coming in bunches and piling up until it was hard to know where to start in dealing with them. They took many forms, but their common base seems to have been Borglum's growing disenchantment with the Dakotans, particularly those in the Black Hills. So far as he could see, they did not comprehend the greatness or meaning of what he was doing, the difficulty of doing it, or the genius it required. Despite his barrage of biting letters to the governor and to newspapers, the state was not improving its highways to the Hills—it seemed determined to remain in "the oxcart age," he said—and thus the state was keeping his monument from being properly accessible to tourists. On top of that, most Black Hillers did not even seem to understand or appreciate how prosperous Borglum, through his carving, was going to make them. The more he thought about it the testier he got, and the testier he got the more he let his feelings be known—which did not help things at all.

In his assessment of the people's attitudes, Borglum was right. Most Dakotans, and those of the Black Hills in particular, did not appreciate him or his work nearly as much as he thought they should. Many of the Black Hills people, perhaps even a majority of them, still thought this mountain carving was a crazy idea, and that in trying to do it Borglum had to be a little crazy, too. Furthermore, the farmers and ranchers, who were definitely in the majority in that agricultural land, saw no blessing to be gained from increased tourism. Tourists did not earn them a dime; they only made highways dusty and rough and parking places hard to find in the towns.

What it all came down to was this: the local people were becoming about as disenchanted with Borglum as he had become with them. And from Borglum's point of view, although he never would have admitted it, this was a distressing thing. Not only did Borglum want the Black Hillers to admire and praise him, he wanted them to like him, too. Had they been able to, his Rushmore years might have been easier and they certainly would have been happier and less tempestuous. Unfortunately, however, he and the Black Hills people never did manage to develop much in the way of warm feelings for each other. It was neither side's fault; it was just that their natures were so different as to be entirely incompatible. Although Borglum had lived the first fifteen years of his life in the West and loved the West he simply was not a Westerner. Not any more, at any rate. He had long since become a sophisticated man of the cities—New York, London, Paris, and especially Washington—where his chosen associates were the financial, social, and political elite and where, in 1933, status was a golden social coin that purchased a great deal of deference for those who had it.

West River Dakota, on the other hand, was the last section of the United States to have been invaded and settled by white pioneers and was an entirely different world from that of cities. Here, Borglum's neighbors were the spiritual heirs of a frontier society that had been egalitarian to the point of reverse-snobbery, and where "puttin' on airs" produced reactions that were instant and hostile. One of the stories of the early days, for example, told of an adventuring English aristocrat who asked a cowpuncher, "I say, my man, is your master at home?"

"At home, hell!" the puncher retorted. "The sunovabitch ain't even been born yet!"

Now worn by its second generation of inheritors, that spirit had by now become a somewhat faded hand-me-down, but it was still visible enough to prompt writer and war correspondent Robert J. Casey, who had grown up in Rapid City, to remark that where persons of prominence and wealth were concerned, "nobody in this region has ever been very much awed." Calvin Coolidge had proved to be an exception, but Borglum had not—and therein lay the nub of the problem.

During the preparation of this book, dozens of Black Hills people who had known Borglum were asked to recall their impressions of him, and although their ways of expressing it varied, the first thing they recalled, almost without exception, was that Borglum had been a man of regal manner whose way of mingling with them left the impression of a grand duke mingling with the commoners. The unfortunate thing about this was that Borglum clearly seems not to have meant to be that way, nor even to have known that he was, and to have been trying a good deal harder to win the Dakotans' affection than they were trying to win his, but he was just not equipped to do it. He had an enormous number of worthy attributes, but the warm, relaxed common touch and the old-shoe easiness with others was not among them.

As Norbeck had said, Borglum truly did "crave the handclapping of those who live in the [Dakota] sticks," and craved their affection as well. But because they were the kind of people they were, so long as the Dakotans thought Borglum was trying to stand on a lofty, self-constructed Olympus above them, they would give him neither applause nor affection. And because he was the kind of man he was, no matter how lonely Borglum's Olympus became, he could not climb down from it. He did not know how to.

18. Borglum and Boland— The Gathering Storm

Assembling the largest Rushmore crew so far, Borglum set out to make up in 1933 for the time he had lost to the shut-down in 1932. He cut back the cliff under the Washington head and there roughed in the outline of Washington's chest. He removed the stone boxing in the head itself, began shaping the left side of Washington's wig, and worked at refining the features of the face. At the same time, he was wrestling with the problem of the Jefferson head. At present it was a coarse, ghostlike mask immediately to Washington's right, where, in 1931, Villa had roughed in its hair, forehead, eyesockets, and nose. However, it seemed the head could not be completed where it was, although in the minds of all excepting perhaps Borglum, himself, there was some confusion over why it could not. According to some, it was because the stone in that site had proved to be faulty. Villa had said it was because Borglum had not modeled the head properly to fit the location. Borglum was blaming it on Villa, saying that in molding the head Villa had ruined it by cutting too deep. Still others were saying the problem was simply that the Jefferson head was too close to Washington and did not look good there. Too crowded. In fact, a story was making the rounds about two dowager-type tourist ladies who were viewing the work when one of them said: "That's George in front, so the other one has to be Martha."

"No," protested her companion. "They're putting only presidents up there."

"Rubbish!" the first lady retorted. "Mr. Borglum would never carve two men snuggled up to each other like that!"

Anyhow, regardless of the reason, Borglum was now seeking a new site for Jefferson, and the task was not easy. Working within the limitations imposed by the cliff, he had to come up with an entirely new monument design that would still meet his exacting standards of artistic composition. Making dozens of sketches and models, he shuffled and reshuffled the monument's four figures until at last he settled upon an arrangement that placed Jefferson immediately to Washington's left, where until now he had intended to carve Lincoln.

To establish the new location on the mountain, however, was far different from establishing it on paper. This required peeling away the cliff's rough outer rind and continuing to peel until a sound carving surface had been uncovered, and it turned out to be a suspenseful operation. Separated by the little boomerang-shaped canyon from the rest of the mountain, the top eighty or so feet of the cliff was actually a free-standing wall. Its face was seamed with fissures and crevices, some of which could possibly be so deep that excavating beyond them would leave the remaining wall too thin to accept a carving. And as the peeling progressed, it began to look as if this might be true in the new Jefferson site. Layer after layer of stone was blasted away, and still some of the fissures persisted. Finally, sixty feet back from the cliff's original face a surface was uncovered that could be considered sound, although it was by no means ideal. There was a deep vertical crack perhaps five inches wide that ran all the way up the side nearest the Washington head, and there were some smaller cracks as well. Even so, Borglum decided it would have to do. Further excavation would upset the artistry of his new design and also might make the remaining wall too thin. He would accept this surface, and he would figure out a way to deal with its cracks. And so, the matter was ultimately settled.

As the days of summer passed, the monument's appearance became dramatically changed. The head of Washington began to stand out ever more boldly against the sky and to dominate the cliff rather than to be dominated by it; excavation of the new Jefferson site on Washington's left was creating a great bay of fresh white granite that grew steadily deeper; and all this was causing people to say this was a season of most remarkable progress. But not Borglum. For Borglum it was a season of discontent. He felt himself to be entangled in a thicket of aggravations from which there was no escape. Most particularly, Borglum felt he was not being allowed to accomplish all that he could be accomplishing, and he complained that he was deliberately being "hamstrung." And the more he thought about it the more certain he became that all his aggravations were rooted in a single source, and that the source was named John Boland.

Boland would not let him spend money as fast as job efficiency required, Borglum declared. There was plenty of money in Rushmore's treasury, he said, but Boland, who held the purse strings, was just too stingy to let him

have it. He also needed to hire more men, Borglum said, but Boland would
not let him do that, either.

Nor would Boland let him have all the electric power he wanted. Originally, Rushmore's power had come from the generating plant donated in 1927
by Samuel Insull. It was a tired old generator whose salad days had been spent
in service to a town in the eastern part of the state, and after one season at
Rushmore it had needed so much repair that Boland had arranged instead for
Rushmore to buy power from Keystone Consolidated Mines. Now Borglum
wanted more power than Keystone Consolidated could furnish, and he
wanted to get it from the old Insull plant. He had once been "a master machinist in the American Federation of Labor" and was able to repair the plant
himself, the sculptor told Norbeck, only Boland would not let him do it.

On top of all that, said Borglum, he was not being paid enough for the
work he was doing. As superintendent, Tucker had been paid $10,000 a year.
The present superintendent, Bill Tallman, was competent to do only a part of
what Tucker had done and was receiving $3,000 a year for it. The rest of
Tucker's work had fallen upon his own overburdened shoulders, Borglum declared, and he ought to be receiving the other $7,000 of Tucker's salary for
doing it.

In that last complaint Borglum laid bare the real cause of his discontent.
He had a mountain of debts and (in his opinion) a molehill of income. He
even owed his chauffeur Charlie Johnson so much back pay that Johnson had
secretly asked John Boland for assistance in collecting it. As Boland was to tell
it years later: "I said, 'What do you do for Mr. Borglum?' and Charlie said,
'Well, I drives him around and I rubs him down, but what I does too much of
is not git paid!'"

Borglum was never to know about that particular incident, but he did
know that he had creditors all over the Hills and they were giving him fits.
He, in turn, was fuming inwardly at those shopkeepers for letting their petty
invoices blind them to the greatness of what he was doing for them. He kept

ON FOLLOWING PAGES:

*40. Stone at Washington's left is being peeled away in search of
sound rock on which to carve the new Jefferson head. The old
Jefferson head on Washington's right already has been blasted down.*

saying he would pay when he could, and that by carrying his accounts in the meantime they would enable him to create an attraction that would bring glowing prosperity to them all. His creditors, however, saw it otherwise. They had creditors of their own to satisfy, and in these hard times they, too, were just hanging on by their fingernails. Besides, when they saw him being driven about in his Cadillac and read in the papers about his hobnobbing with senators and financiers, they found it hard to believe he actually could not pay his bills. They believed instead that he just would not, and so they continued to bedevil him with duns and even, sometimes, to call him a "deadbeat."

Proud and sensitive, and hard up as well, Borglum found this to be a cross almost too heavy to bear, and he denounced Boland and the commission for having forced the situation upon him. They should have been paying him for

41. Lincoln Borglum measures "points" from the Jefferson model for transfer to the work on the mountain, about 1934.

doing Tucker's old job. They should have been spending more on Rushmore (which would have increased his sculptor's fees). Then he could have paid his bills. Because of "the stupid penurious practices of the Commission," he wrote to Norbeck, his income had been reduced to "an almost negligible amount."

Borglum exaggerated a bit when making that statement. His 1933 Rushmore fees came to a little over $16,000 (the equivalent after taxes and inflation of about $150,000 today) and could have been called "negligible" only, perhaps, when compared to his debts. Nonetheless, the sculptor's discontent continued to grow, and so did the bitterness with which he expressed it. He said he was being "stopped whenever and wherever there is an excuse" so that Rushmore's funds could be "hoarded and not used." Borglum accused John Boland of being a "petty politician" with a "Keystone mentality" and the commission of being "the most useless and uninformed political body that ever attempted anything," and he said that together Boland and the commission were forcing him to "suffer beyond all reason or belief." Even worse, said the sculptor, was the sordid truth behind his electricity shortage. The Insull plant had not been shut down because it was worn out, as Boland had claimed. It had been shut down after being deliberately "wrecked" to give Boland an excuse to throw Rushmore's power business to Harold Eyrich, Keystone Consolidated's manager and Boland's longtime friend. And it was to force the commission to continue "meekly" buying power from "racketeers," thundered Borglum, that Boland would not let him fix up the Insull plant now.

Norbeck was one of the beneficiaries of Borglum's complaints, but paid little attention to them at first. He knew that Borglum when disturbed was like a tin barn in a hailstorm—he made a noise all out of proportion to the seriousness of the occasion. Also, Norbeck's health was not good, and he felt burdened enough in just doing what the taxpayers were paying him to do without getting involved in another Rushmore wrangle as well. By early fall, however, Borglum had become so strident in his complaining and so irresponsible and even vicious in his accusation that Norbeck decided he had to be hushed before he tore the project apart and Rushmore wound up in the same wastebasket as Stone Mountain. Norbeck also knew that to get Borglum quieted it would be necessary to sit down on him so hard that he might walk off the job in a huff and never come back. Believing himself to be the person most likely to be able to accomplish the first result while avoiding the second, Norbeck decided to take a direct hand in the affair after all. Acting accordingly, he asked Boland and Williamson to join him in meeting with Borglum on September 17, at Borglum's studio.

Had she been present at that meeting, Mrs. Norbeck would have known just from the way her husband was pacing the floor that indeed it was going to be, as Norbeck had told Boland and Williamson, "a showdown." Norbeck's immigrant father had walked as the fishermen of his native Trøndheim, Norway, walked—with solidly planted steps and a wide, invincible stride developed on the heaving decks of fishing trawlers. As a boy, Norbeck unconsciously had picked up that way of walking from his father; as a man he just as unconsciously fell back into it when he was troubled, and Mrs. Norbeck had often been heard to say, "I always know when Peter is upset because then he walks his Trønder walk." And in Borglum's studio that day, Norbeck walked his Trønder walk while, with words as solid as his steps, giving Borglum a verbal spanking.

Borglum ought to know better than to keep telling everybody that "we are long on money, when the truth is that we are short on money," said Norbeck.

Also, Borglum should know better than to keep vilifying John Boland for not letting him spend all he wanted for whatever he wanted. These were Federal funds they were dealing with. They had to be spent according to Federal rules. Also, Norbeck said, no dollar could be spent from the congressional appropriation that had not first been "matched" by an equal expenditure from the Emergency Relief Fund, and there were severe government restrictions on how the Emergency Relief Fund could be used. Keeping all this straight and legal was a tough job, and it was Boland's job. Mishandled, it might get them all into more trouble than they could ever get out of and would certainly prevent them from ever getting any more government money. However, Norbeck continued, Boland had been handling it splendidly, and Borglum had no business in accusing him of "Keystone mentality" (whatever that was) for doing so.

As for the matter of electric power, said Norbeck, if Borglum continued his present fussing about that he just might convince the Federal authorities that "we're all a bunch of crooks," and what would happen to Rushmore then? Besides, what were the facts? Well, one was that Borglum wanted more power so he could hire more drillers, and he already had all the drillers the budget could stand. Another was that repairing the Insull plant would take a big chunk of money that otherwise could be spent on carving. And for what? Operating and maintaining the plant, and hiring a crew to run it, would probably make their power cost more than it did now. And what about those times when the plant would have to be shut down for repairs? Then there would be no power at all. No, Boland had hurt neither the project nor the sculptor by handling it as he had. On the contrary, Borglum and Rushmore both would be a good deal worse off now if Boland had done otherwise, and Borglum had no right to call him a "crook" because of it.

Borglum was calling the commission "useless," and Norbeck agreed that some of its members might be. But which ones? Its Dakota members were the only ones not chosen by Borglum himself, but with the exception of Fred Sargeant and Borglum's friend Lorine Spoonts, the Dakotans were the only ones doing any work.

Borglum was complaining that Boland and the commission were trying to run the Rushmore project as they would a business when it was not a business but a work of art, and he claimed that their Philistine meddling in his artistic affairs had slowed him to the point that "it will take twenty years at this rate." Norbeck agreed with the "twenty years," he said, and agreed also that "meddling" was the reason. But meddling by whom? The way he saw it, said Norbeck, the problem was that Borglum was spending entirely too much time in interfering with the work of Boland and the commission and too little in attending to his own.

Borglum was a great artist, Norbeck continued bluntly, but he certainly was no administrator. He was no more qualified to run the business end of Rushmore than the commissioners were to carve its figures. Therefore, he would like Borglum henceforth to confine himself to that which he did so magnificently, which was to sculpt, and leave the rest of the job to people who knew how to handle it.

Finally, said Norbeck, he wanted this confounded squabbling stopped! Now!

As later events would prove, Norbeck's "showdown" accomplished its purpose, but at a price. Borglum did quiet down for a while, and he did not quit the job. However, he was furious at Norbeck for having unfairly sided with Boland and the commission in matters wherein Borglum believed himself to be totally in the right, and a few days later he wrote to the senator, "Your utterly unwarranted attack on me has unjustly hurt a friendship this work will fail without." And it was true that the friendship had been hurt. Borglum had a great capacity for forgiveness, but attacks on his ego did not fall within its limits, and thus the relationship between him and Norbeck was never again to be quite as warm as it had been in the past.

It was not long after the meeting that Borglum's irascibility became a good deal easier to understand. Unable to meet his mortgage payments, he was on the verge of losing his ranch and was casting about frantically for ways to save it. He asked Boland for an advance of $3,200 from the commission, and although Boland was sympathetic to his plight, as were Norbeck and Williamson also, his request was impossible to grant. Federal rules would not permit such a disbursement by the commission. Neither could any of these men make Borglum a personal loan, as he had hoped they might. Though he likely did not realize it, he was probably making more money than any of them, and they were in trouble, too. They just were not making any noise about it.

Norbeck's $10,000 senatorial salary had been reduced by a government economy move to $8,500 in 1932, $7,500 this year, and to $7,000 in 1934. Because of this and some other financial reverses, he wrote to Borglum, "I have turned much of my property over to creditors."

The frugal Williamson had thought to build his future security from far farmland, and over the past quarter-century had acquired 16,000 acres of it. Now, drought and depression combined had caused him to lose all but a thousand acres, and those acres were earning barely enough to cover their taxes. Hence, his only income now was from his law practice, and it was yielding only about $200 a month.

According to his books, John Boland was in the best shape of them all— but only according to his books. His assets consisted mostly of accounts receivable from farmers and ranchers who at present had no money. Boland knew his customers, knew that they hated debt like the devil hates holy water and that they would pay when they could. Accordingly, during those lean years when they could not pay he still kept their credit open and rarely pressed anyone for collection. He had seldom lost anything by this policy, and it had won him a host of devoted customers. Now, however, it just about had him strapped. During the drought and grasshopper years of 1930 and '31 Boland's accounts receivable had soared to a new high. Then had come the bumper year of 1932, when his customers had the greatest grain crop ever in their fields and no money in their pockets to pay for the binder twine necessary for harvesting it. Boland mortgaged his home and thereby got them the twine— again on credit—and old farmers in that area still remember how Johnny Boland had gotten them twine when they had to have it but could not pay for it. But that same bumper crop, unfortunately, created such a surplus of grain that the price of wheat dropped to forty cents a bushel, and even after harvest Boland's customers still had little money to pay him. As a consequence, Boland, too, was now wondering just how much longer he could hang on.

Even so, and despite the things the sculptor had been saying about him, it was Boland who saved the day for Borglum. He guaranteed a note for Borglum at the First National Bank and made him a personal loan as well.

Thus, Borglum was enabled to remain financially afloat, for the moment at least, and to save his ranch.

Once that had been done, Borglum's disposition became marvelously improved, and he threw himself enthusiastically into the development of a new idea he had come up with for publicizing Rushmore.

19. No Tomahto Juice
on the Mountain

L ike Borglum, the men who did the actual work of building Rushmore were men who lived fully and enthusiastically. They worked
hard when they worked, played even harder when they played, and
(again like Borglum) they were little disposed to taking much back talk from
anybody. Most were natives of the Keystone district and had been molded by
its heritage, and those who were not from there were of much the same type
as those who were. To know just what type that was, it is necessary to know
something of Keystone's past.

The first white men in the vicinity had come in search of gold; rugged,
rowdy transients who had flowed restlessly back and forth across the area as
they heard of new places in which to try their luck—places like Sitting Bull
and Hoodlum Gulch and Giltedge Bar. Their nationalities were varied, but a
good many of them seem to have been Irishmen and "Cousin Jacks"—Cor-
nish immigrant miners or sons thereof. By and large they were men whom
others often regarded as hard-case toughs, but who regarded themselves as
exuberantly uninhibited and who, no doubt, were actually an interesting combination of both. In any case, they were men whose ways of dealing with life's
problems were disconcertingly direct.

One time around 1900, for instance, there came a Saturday when one of
the district's mines was unable to meet its payroll. Whereupon, the unpaid
and aggravated miners gathered to lubricate their thinking in a local saloon
while they figured out what to do about the matter. After a time they hit
upon a simple solution. They would take the mine's paymaster out and hang
him. The paymaster, however, a young graduate of the University of Michigan named Stewart Edward White, was a man of words. So much so, in fact,
that while standing on a barrelhead with a rope draped disconcertingly
around his neck, he talked the peevish assembly into turning him loose.

Probably they did not actually intend to hang him anyhow; but, whatever their intentions, when they let White go he kept right on going, and for many years the Black Hills saw him no more. Meanwhile, however, he was having the last laugh. He used his Black Hills experiences as the basis of three novels, *The Westerners, The Claim Jumpers,* and *The High Graders.* All turned out to be best-sellers, and they started White on his way to becoming a prominent American author.

Keystone itself did not amount to much in the district's earlier days. A hotel and a few stores and a scatter of cabins along the creek, and that was about it. But then, on a spring afternoon in 1894, William "Rocky Mountain Frank" Franklin went for a walk along the lower slopes of Mount Aetna, and that walk changed everything for Keystone. Picking up a stray piece of quartz and idly examining it, he saw a speck of gold streaked through it—which must have been perfectly astonishing to him. After all, how often is a gold strike made within spitting distance of main street and on ground prospectors had been tramping over for the past fifteen years, and made by someone who was not even looking for it?

Franklin and his partner, Thomas Blair, filed a claim on the site, named it the Holy Terror in honor of Franklin's wife, and went to work. Soon the Holy Terror was yielding ore worth $500 a ton, miners were flocking to Keystone, and the town was booming.

Keystone never was as unruly a place as White's novels might have led one to believe (White, after all, had good reason to be prejudiced), but for a time it was unruly enough. Shortly, though, under the influence of its more stable citizens, it began to settle down. After the town had acquired sixteen saloons, one for every 125 citizens, its residents decided it ought to have a schoolhouse as well. So they built one; and not being people who did things by halves, they built a big two-and-a-half story frame structure so solid that ninety years later it was still serving Keystone as a schoolhouse.

By the time Rushmore's future crew-members were old enough to attend that school the gold boom had died away, and Keystone had shrunk in size and become considerably more sedate. As was usual with old mining towns, it still had a rowdy reputation, but the reputation now substantially exceeded the fact. Thus, even though it was often said that Keystone's kids were so tough their playpens were fenced with barbed wire, and so ornery that any cat in town who still had a tail was a tourist, it was not really true. Nonetheless, their boyhood was still flavored with enough frontier aggressiveness that fistfights were a favored form of recreation. When they turned the other cheek it was usually in connection with the delivery of a left hook, and any potential shrinking violets among them soon learned, as a matter of self-preservation, not to shrink.

It is often said that when the Rushmore job came along Keystone was dying and almost deserted, and only by Rushmore was it saved from eventual extinction. That statement has always been fiercely resented by Keystone's natives; they prefer to think their town was just too stubborn to die—and, to a substantial extent, they are right.

In 1903 the Holy Terror shut down—not for lack of gold, but from insolvency due to lawsuits filed by the families of miners killed and injured in accidents there. Once it was shut down the mine flooded and became almost prohibitively expensive to rehabilitate. Gradually, other gold mines in the area began to play out and close, as did the tin and silver mines. Next, Keystone was plagued by fires. A part of the town burned in 1913; in 1917 fire destroyed an entire block, including John Boland's store; in 1921 fire claimed the hotel, Methodist church, and two more stores. Still, Keystone hung on, its economy supported by logging and by the mining of feldspar, beryllium, and lithium ores. Then, at about the same time as the early Rushmore activity, a firm called Keystone Consolidated Mines began trying to pump out and rehabilitate the Holy Terror. Thus, when the Rushmore job began Keystone was still a going concern. It had shrunk, however, to about fifteen percent of the population of its heyday; which meant there was no shortage of housing for Rushmore workmen, even though that housing might need some repair. In recalling their own experience with Keystone housing, Red and Dorothy Anderson had this to say:

> David Swanzy owned an old house that had been abandoned for years. The windows were all smashed out and there were holes in the floor, and cattle had been wandering in and out through the open doors.
>
> He told us, "If you'll fix it up, I'll rent it to you for five dollars a month for just as long as you want to stay."
>
> Well, we rustled up scrap lumber and some old packing cases and stuff and fixed it up to be a right comfortable place. We spent several happy years in it, and we sure couldn't complain about the rent!

To see the Keystone community as the Andersons saw it in 1933, picture a scatter of buildings lying along two miles or so of the bottom of Battle Creek canyon, with the main part of town—the central city, as it were—being about four blocks long and two blocks wide. It is bounded on the west by the big white frame schoolhouse standing low on the slope of Mount Etna, on the north by the headworks of the Holy Terror standing on a flat bench just above the foot of Mount Etna; and on the east by Main Street and by Battle Creek, which runs south to north just to the east of Main Street. Lining the sloping dirt streets between the schoolhouse on one side and Main Street on the other are tall Victorian houses with scrollwork trim and low frame houses that are small and plain, and most of the houses need paint. Main Street is a gravel road between rows of false-front wooden buildings, and the rows are gap-toothed because of the buildings lost to the various Keystone fires. By 1933 there is no longer a bank at Keystone, nor a hotel. There is still a cafe, however, and a rooming and boarding house. John Hayes, Edwald's father, has a store where you can buy hardware and gent's furnishings, and Ernest

42. A view of Keystone a few years before the start of the Rushmore project. The open space in the foreground is where, in 1917, fire consumed an entire block, including John Boland's store. At top center is the headworks of the Holy Terror mine—named for the owner's wife.

"Peggy" Haas (so named because of a peg leg) still does a good business at his blacksmith shop. Prospering, too, is the town's bootlegger, whose drink and dance joint across the creek has no identifying sign but is known to all as "The Honky-tonk." One of the most important businesses is Halley's Store. It smells of leather and denim and oranges and kerosene; and you can buy a sack of flour there, or a pair of overalls, a stove, a bag of candy, a saddle—you name it and Halley has it. Art Lyndoe's Store is an important establishment, too, especially when you need groceries and are short on money, because Art is good about giving credit. (One of the Rushmore wives would say later, "There were times when a lot of us couldn't have gotten by without credit at Lyndoe's.") Things were different at Halley's. As a workman later remembered, "Jim Halley was a great guy to drink home brew with, but he sure was hell to get credit from." (Which may explain why Halley's was to remain open for another forty-seven years while Lyndoe's, with $40,000 in uncollected accounts, closed in 1936.)

On workday mornings in Keystone, the Rushmore families begin stirring early. The men are expected to be on the mountain and ready to work at seven o'clock in summer and at half-past-seven in fall and winter. In summer they arise when the sun has just begun to touch the ridge-tops and the town itself lies deep in the cold dawn shadows of the canyon, and in winter they must arise when the town still lies hushed and dark under ice-bright stars. Their arising is first announced by the clatter of grates and stove lids as ashes are shaken down and breakfast fires are lit, and then by the fragrance of pine smoke and coffee and frying bacon. Along the quiet streets radios may be heard broadcasting the early news, weather, sports, and the singing of the WNAX Yodeling Cowboy, George B. German. The weather is important because the men need to know what to expect on the mountain and how to dress for it. The sports news is even more important, for this is a sports-minded town—especially about baseball. Tiny as Keystone is, its baseball team, made up mostly of Rushmore men, is a power in the state's amateur league. Almost as avidly as the fortunes of their own team, the Rushmore men follow those of the big leagues. In fact, on days when a particularly important game is to be broadcast they ask Lincoln Borglum if he will park his car beside the hoist-house. That way, hoist operator Edwald Hayes can follow the game on Lincoln's radio and report its progress by telephone to the men up on the mountain.

Now a starter can be heard grinding somewhere, and then another, and another. Automobile engines sputter reluctantly to life, horns honk as drivers stop to pick up riders, and a scattered caravan of cars, most of them elderly, heads up the canyon to Grizzly Gulch and the climb to Rushmore. Behind them, the Rushmore wives get the breakfast dishes cleaned up and the kids off to school. Then they gather here and there to visit over coffee and play cribbage until ten o'clock or so, when they have to return to their housework.

Upon arriving at the parking lot behind Borglum's studio on Doane Mountain, most of the men walk across the canyon and up the stairway to the top of Rushmore, but not all do. It depends on how they feel about riding the aerial tramway. It was not designed to carry men, and every now and again John Boland posts a bulletin to that effect. Nonetheless, Borglum rides it all the time. It provides him with an ideal viewpoint for studying the carving and also, of course, it saves him much time and exertion. A few of the men, too, prefer this effortless (though dizzying and possibly dangerous) three-minute ride to the fifteen-minute hike and four-hundred-foot climb they otherwise would have to make. Most, however, do not. The old hands, especially, remember the day the A-frame collapsed and the tramway bucket plunged to the bottom of the canyon.

Once the men have arrived at their stations the job comes noisily to life. On the slope of Doane Mountain the big air compressors begin to pound, up on the carving the jackhammers begin to chatter, and from a distance the cliff looks and sounds as if invaded by machine-gunning ants. In a shed on the mountaintop, powderman John Arthur "Whiskey Art" Johnson and an assistant begin to prepare dynamite charges they will shortly place in the holes now being drilled. To avoid the risk of shattering any carving surfaces, each blast consists of many very small charges—as many as sixty or seventy in a shingle shot. These charges are prepared by cutting sticks of dynamite into lengths as short as an inch or even shorter, depending on the delicacy of the shot, and carefully tying into each length an electric detonator cap. It is tedious work and must be done with great care. Cutting the sticks like this exposes the naked dynamite to the powdermen's touch, and there is something in the stuff that, if you are not wearing gloves, will seep through the pores of your hands and cause a dull, pounding ache at the base of the skull that is aptly called a "dynamite headache." The dynamite itself is not dangerous to work with unless it is old. In old dynamite the nitroglycerine tends to gather and crystallize until it becomes as treacherous as a rattlesnake. This is why Johnson and the other powdermen at Rushmore will never carry over unused dynamite from one season to the next. Fresh dynamite, however, can be dropped, stepped on, thrown, even burned, without exploding. It can be detonated only by a mighty shock, and that is the purpose of the caps. These tiny copper cylinders, each attached to a pair of four-foot-long electric wires, are

43. *Some of the support structures on Mount Doane, opposite Mount Rushmore. Lower left, compressor house; upper center, hoist house; center right, blacksmith shop.*

packed with an explosive so powerful that a cap detonated inside a steel barrel will blast bits of its copper jacket clear through the barrel's walls. Unlike the dynamite, moreover, the caps are touchy and do not forgive carelessness. The powderman who forgets that is likely to lose a finger, hand, eye, or his life.

As the morning wears on and the drillers' bits begin to dull, workmen called "steel nippers" move up and down the cliff exchanging fresh drills for old, and then send the old ones down by tramway to the blacksmith shop on Doane Mountain. There, sweating in the fierce heat of a forge, blacksmith Matt Cindel, assisted perhaps by Basil "Bake" Canfield or Lloyd "Lively" Virtue, resharpens the drill-bits at a rate of literally hundreds per day.

At last it is lunchtime, and when all workmen have returned to the top of the cliff and out of harm's way, it is time to blast. During most of the morning Whiskey Art and his helpers have been down on the face of the work loading drill holes with charges and carefully tying each charge into an electric detonator cord. Now Johnson throws a switch and all charges fire as one single explosion. Swarms of granite chunks bound and clatter down to the muck-pile in the canyon; a cloud of dust rises and drifts in the breeze, and that ends the morning's work. The afternoon's work will be just like it.

The job is tedious, muscular, dusty, and usually either too hot or too cold. Whenever possible, therefore, the crewmen lighten the grind of it with humor and horseplay. Most of the humorous incidents are enjoyed and then forgotten. A few, however, are so rich that they are recounted and chuckled over time and again. One time, for instance, Borglum's secretary misspelled the work "winch" in a bulletin-board notice that read:

From: The Sculptor   To: All Employees
Subject: Wenches

> Starting as of now, the following rule will be strictly enforced. Upon arriving at the mountain in the morning, each operator will be assigned a wench and helper. The wench will be under his supervision for that day. The helper will be responsible for the proper functioning of the wench, and will be in constant attendance when the wench is in use. One wench will be kept available at all times for the exclusive use of the sculptor.

And there is another oft-recounted incident involving Borglum's secretary. In this case she had accompanied the sculptor to the top of the mountain, and while there had slipped away unobserved to visit the outhouse, which was situated down a flight of steps from the clifftop proper. Bob Himebaugh, who was preparing dynamite charges at the time, later recalled:

> All of a sudden one of the winchmen had to answer a call of nature. He charged down the steps, yanked open the privy door, slammed it shut again, and came charging back up even faster than he had gone down. I hollered, "What's the matter, Shorty?" Well, he was so embarrassed that he could only stutter and so flustered he couldn't remember "secretary." So, finally he managed to sputter out, "There's uh . . . the . . . uh . . . the *typewriter*'s a'settin' in there!"

The crew's horseplay takes a hundred forms, but the seemingly best-remembered incident was so wildly improbable in both occurrence and result that only after careful confirmation was it included in this book. It happened one day at the end of work, while the men were undergoing a daily process called "blowing-off." This was done to remove the coating of rock dust they always wore when coming up from work on the cliff, and it was accomplished by blasts of high-pressure air from a nozzled hose. Howdy Peterson was handling the hose when a workman whom we shall call Abner (though that was not his name) came along and, in Peterson's words:

> As he came by he gave me a kick. Well, in return I reached out and speared him in the butt with that air hose. And, why, I just blowed him up tighter'n a drum! I sure didn't mean to. It was a freak thing. How you could hit a guy that square-on I don't know, but it happened. Ol' Abner looked almost like air was gonna start comin' out of his ears. Scared? Man oh man! I was never so scared in my life!

Abner, of course, was scared also, mainly because his abdomen was not in very good condition anyhow. A year earlier he had undergone surgery for removal of an abdominal cancer, and this had left him troubled by intestinal adhesions. Red Anderson witnessed the incident and later recalled:

> When that hose connected you could just see Abner's belly swell up. He yelled, "My God, Howdy! You've killed me!" Then he started passing the air, and when he did he passed some blood, too. That *really* scared him, and us too!

Next day, Abner went to Rapid City to see his doctor and find out how much he had been damaged. After examining him, the doctor said with some amazement, "Abner, that shot of air didn't hurt you one bit. The fact is, it may have done you some good because, the way it looks to me, it has loosened up your adhesions!"

And that was the way it turned out. Abner never had any bad effects from the experience, nor did he suffer again from adhesions. "And when that proved to be the case," said Peterson, "the guys all kidded me and said I ought to go into that business. But I told 'em, 'Not on your life! It'd scare me too much!'"

When four o'clock comes and the whistle blows, the winchmen strain at the cranks of their windlasses, and the drillers and carvers being hoisted thereby begin to appear at the lip of the cliff. When all are up and accounted for, the powderman pushes his detonator button and again there is dust and thunder as the afternoon's charges are fired. The workmen, meanwhile, are being blown off, putting away their tools, and beginning to troop down the long stairway.

As they go they leave behind all the job's problems but one. Dust. The pesky, miserable granite dust. Blowing off has removed some of it, but not all. The remainder, clinging to hair and skin, the men wear home with them. The dust makes hair dry and strawlike and almost impossible to pull a comb through, and it makes clothing rasp against the skin. A man can wash it off, once he gets home, but even that is not easy. It catches at the soap and resists being lubricated by it, and only with much soap and effort can it be dislodged. And that is but the dust's exterior effect. The interior effect of that which a man has breathed is something he cannot yet know, but in years to come he likely will find it out. Many of the men, Lincoln Borglum among them, will wind up with permanently scarred lungs. Some will ultimately develop silicosis; in 1948 James Champion, Jr., will die of it, and in 1955 Elton "Hoot" Leach will do the same. At the moment, however, that lies in the unknown future. Presently the dust is only an irritating nuisance to be dealt with before enjoyment of the evening can begin.

For these men whose day has been spent in heat and dust and the clamor of drills, evening is a rich time—a time of luxurious relaxation. About the time supper is over, the sun sinks behind Mount Aetna and evening shadows flow swiftly up the mountainsides and become twilight, and just as swiftly the twilight becomes darkness. For here, as in all mountain gorges, the night comes on with a rush, and with it comes air that is crisply cool and night-spiced with pine and the wet stone smell of the rushing creek. Now, on darkened porches the firefly glow of cigarettes punctuates murmured conversations as families visit among themselves or with friends. From the earthen streets lit only by bars of light from doorways and windows comes the sound of shouting and laughter and the running feet of children playing Run Sheep Run. From Tom Hoy's pool hall down on Main Street there comes the sound of laughter also, and the rattle of billiard balls and the slap of playing cards. The pool hall is to Rushmore's men what a country club is to an executive— social center, recreation center, information center. If you do not find a particular man at home, try the pool hall. Probably he will be there. If he is not, those who are will know where he has gone, why he went, and when he is expected back. Whether or not they tell you these things, however, will depend on who you are and why you are asking.

But because the working day at Rushmore begins early, these evening activities end early. And so by nine o'clock, or ten at the latest, the town's windows are dark and its streets are hushed, and the only sound is that of Battle Creek chuckling in its stony bed.

That is Rushmore life on weekdays, but not on weekends. On weekends this crew plays just as hard as during the week it has worked. The holiday mood first appears at about noon on Friday, and during the afternoon it grows; on the mountain there is increasing boisterousness and a feeling of anticipation. When the whistle blows, men hurry to put away their tools and to be blown off. Then they clatter down the stairway with a boyish exuberance that recalls a line by James Whitcomb Riley: "The feet that dragged so slow to school go storming out to play." The 506 steps of the stairway are in flights separated by forty-five ramps and platforms. On Friday evenings, especially, some of the crew will attempt to descend these by "mountain-goating," the objective of which is to get to the bottom by leaping down from platform to platform without touching any intervening steps. No one has ever accomplished it, but neither has anyone broken a leg while attempting it; so they keep on trying.

The first stop beyond the stairs is the office on Mount Doane where they collect their paychecks, and for many the second stop is in the parking lot where the bootlegger is waiting. He sells sour-mash whiskey of his own manufacture, and any deficiency in its quality is more than made up by its remarkable authority. Swallowing the first drink of it is like swallowing a hot brick, but the second drink is no problem because by then your tongue and throat are numb. And a rancher who knows little of either whiskey or mathematics has been heard to say of this bootlegger, "he makes his stuff a hunnerd and ten percent alkyhol!" In any case, even at a price of two dollars a pint his product is popular with the crew.

Not all the money for the bootlegger comes from the crew's paychecks, however. Some is produced by sale of "honeycomb specimens." In removing the final layer of granite from the "skin" of the monument's faces, carvers drill a grid of holes two or so inches deep and so closely spaced that only an inch of stone separates a hole from each of its surrounding neighbors. Then with hammers and chisels the carvers ordinarily break away the granite membranes between the holes and thus create an almost finished final surface. They have discovered, however, that if they first break out the stone between holes in rows surrounding a square or rectangle of this perforated rock, and then tap with hammer and chisel at the bottoms of the holes enclosed within it, they can often lift out the enclosed perforated piece in one solid sheet. By this

44. Approximately 50 of the 506 stairs the crew climbed each morning on the way to work.

45. Merle Peterson "honeycombing," to remove rock in relatively thin layers as the carving nears the "skin" of the faces.

means they can produce collander-like granite slabs about two inches thick, one to two feet wide, and from one to three feet long. And these perforated "honeycomb specimens," the men have found, are much prized by tourists. In fact, about all a man has to do is carry one through the visitor observation area and some tourist will offer to buy it. There is a more subtle marketing technique, however, that usually produces a higher price. The way this works is this: the specimen is sent in the tramway bucket down from the mountain to hoist operator Edwald Hayes, who then hangs it on a peg in the hoist

46. Carver Otto "Red" Anderson breaks away the stone after "honeycombing."

47. Hoist operator Edwald Hayes standing outside the hoist house, where, the sign notwithstanding, he managed to sell "honeycomb" specimens to tourists. Rushmore's only serious accident occurred when the drivewheel seen at lower left came loose from its axle.

house. Since at this time the working areas have not yet been declared out of bounds to sightseers, pretty soon a tourist peering into the hoist house will notice the specimen. Then, so Hayes will observe later, the conversation will go something like this:

"Hey! What's that funny looking rock with all the holes in it?"

"Oh, just a freak piece one of the carvers is saving."

"Sure is unusual. They get many like that?"

"We-e-ll, one like that is pretty rare."

"Um . . . uh . . . don't s'pose you'd consider selling it?"

"Don't hardly see how I could. It belongs to another guy."

"Well, I'd really like to have it. You *sure* you can't sell it?"

"Golly! I just don't see how. . . . Oh well, I guess for, say, six bucks I might sell it and just take my chances with the owner."

"At this point," Hayes will chuckle in recalling, "the guy figures he's really pulled a fast one. So he shoves the money in my hand and runs like a burglar! Then I phone up to the mountain and say, 'OK boys, send down another one!'"

"Depending on size and quality," Red Anderson will remember, "we sold those pieces for two, four, or six dollars. A pint of moonshine cost two dollars, so we just naturally thought in those units."

In years to come, buyers of those specimens will find they got a bargain far greater than they could have imagined at the time. Eventually Rushmore's honeycomb specimens will become collector's items commanding prices a hundred or more times their original cost.

On Friday night there is a good deal of card playing. Also there is some drinking and partying, but only as a warm-up for Saturday night, which is the main event. It is the hard-drinking, rip-roaring, go-to-a-dance-stomp-and-holler night. The dance may be in Keystone at the Legion Hall or the honky-tonk, or it may be at Hiseiga, Pactola, or Rockerville. But wherever, Rushmore's people go expecting a high old time and some delightfully bloody brawls, and often as not they find both.

"I guess you could say fighting at dances was sort of a hobby with us," one of them will recall.

"It was one of our more enjoyable forms of recreation," another will add. "We seldom fought each other, but we were always happy to fight anybody else."

And according to a story told by Ed Coad, a Keystone native and onetime Rushmore call-boy, their opponents in these battles felt much the same way:

There was one specially busy night at Rockerville, about six fights going on outside the hall all at the same time, when one of our guys found a fellow lying about halfway under a car. He was out cold. I mean, he was out like a light and stiff as a board. Well, some of us thought we'd help him, but we couldn't seem to do him any good. Then somebody felt of him and hollered, "My God! He's dead! Let's get the hell out of here!" and we all cleared out real fast.

Later we found the guy was an epileptic, and when he recovered from his seizure he was madder'n hell because we'd all run off and he wasn't ready to quit fighting yet!

Rushmore's frequent and favored antagonists were the Homestake boys—miners from the big gold mine at Lead. "They came to dances at Pactola a lot, and the fights we had there were somethin' to see!" But in dealing with the boys from the CCC (Civilian Conservation Corps) camps, Rushmore and Homestake became allies:

> Them Cee Cee's would come to a dance in a gang, figuring to take it over. Quite a few were from city slums and knew every dirty fighting trick in the book plus a few they'd invented themselves, and they were a tough outfit to handle. Just the same, they weren't tough enough to take over one of our dances, and they never did.

Remarkably, those turbulent Saturday nights seemed to have little effect on the crew's ability to play baseball on Sunday. Baseball was *the* sport in South Dakota in those days, and by the time a boy had learned to handle a knife and fork he usually had also learned to handle a ball and bat and was dreaming of the day when he would become the new Lefty Grove or Rogers Hornsby. Towns and rural communities alike all fielded teams and supported them with fanatic fervency. Many of these teams were very good, but most of the better ones, naturally, were from the larger towns. But there were exceptions, and the Rushmore team was one of them. It was remarkably successful, and just as remarkably unorthodox. According to one of its members, "Red Anderson was good at making home brew, and every Sunday morning he'd have a batch on ice for us. So the way we got ready for a game was by all sitting around in Red's garage drinking that home brew."

And there was Borglum's startling habit of interrupting games. There was nothing official about it. Borglum was an ardent Rushmore rooter, but at its games he was only a spectator and nothing more. Even so, as a veteran of that team later recounted:

> A ball game's got rules, y'know, but Borglum never figured they applied to him. If he wanted to go out on the field and talk to one of our guys, why, they just had to stop the game while he did it, and he did it pretty often. It wasn't that he had anything important to say—sometimes it wasn't even about baseball. I think it was his way of letting the folks know, "I'm Borglum, and I'm here, and I can do this if I want to."
>
> Funny thing was, all the other teams seemed to figure he could, too. Anyhow, they never tried to stop him.

Moreover, according to another team veteran, this disconcerting habit may have had something to do with the team's success:

> That man had a commanding presence. He really did. When he'd stride out on that field and halt a game it made you think of Joshua commanding the sun to stand still. I think it sort of demoralized the opposition because it was like we had Jehovah visibly on our side.

Anyhow, despite all these things—or maybe because of them—Rushmore was a baseball power. In 1939 it won the right to represent the Black Hills in the state championship playoffs held at Aberdeen, South Dakota. Unable to accompany the team to Aberdeen, Borglum sent it a telegram of encouragement, and because of a mistype by the Western Union operator the wire read:

STICK TO IT. WE ARE ROTTING FOR YOU.
GUTZON AND LINCOLN BORGLUM

They did stick to it, and even though they did not win the championship, they had become one of the tournament's four finalists before going down, six to five, in a sixteen inning game.

To the extent of the whiskey and home brew left in the bottles and the stamina left in its consumers, there was partying again on Sunday night. Consequently, by the time the weekend was over the stamina was pretty well exhausted, and Monday morning on the mountain was a time of suffering and woe. "Some guys would be too hung-over to come to work at all. Finally it got to the point where the Old Man had to make a rule that any man not showing up on Monday morning would be laid off for the whole week." And another old Rushmore hand remembered:

> All along the stairway you'd see guys resting and holding their heads and trying to work up strength to finish the climb. When everybody finally was on top who could get there, we'd phone down to the boarding house to send a gallon of tomato juice up in the hoist.
>
> Once when Bill Tallman was superintendent and we did that, he happened to answer the phone, and in that New England accent he had, he said, "There'll be no to*mah*to juice on the mountain today!" Well, that was one of our inside jokes from then on. When all the fellas would get to the top, all headachy and sick, don'cha know,

why, some joker would pipe up, "There'll be no to*mah*to juice on the mountain today!"

Battles, bottles, and hangovers notwithstanding, these men were not irresponsible boozers, bums, or hard-case toughs—not by any means. Not all of them engaged in that sort of thing anyhow, and for most who did it was a form of recreation and not a way of life. It was a part of their frontier mining-camp heritage, and was far outweighed by another part of that heritage—by the great gift that the settlers of all frontiers usually passed to their immediate descendants—the gift of responsibility, self-sufficiency, and a strong desire to get ahead in life.

Every frontier attracted great numbers of drifters and drunkards and wastrels, but only in the beginning. Being what they were, they did not stay to settle the land, build the communities, raise the children. Those who did were of an opposite breed. They had to be. Most frontier families were hard-pressed to provide their own necessities; they had no safety nets of welfare or unemployment benefits to catch them should they fall. Neither was there enough community wealth to allow for assistance to those who could not or would not assist themselves. In short, the frontier was a place of "root, hog, or die," and those unable to "root" effectively could not long remain there. Thus, as the settlements evolved and became communities, their populations evolved also and more and more were made up only of those who were competent, industrious, and responsible.

Impressed upon Rushmore's men as children, these virtues were reimpressed upon them as adults during the Great Depression. For in those years, families again were hard-pressed and had no margin for sharing with others more needy. In tight-knit and interrelated communities such as Keystone this created an especially distressing problem, for there the needy were never anonymous. The hungry family was a neighbor family, and the hungry child a cousin's child. Hence, not sharing with those in greater need, or being able to, was painful indeed. But sharing with them at the cost of depriving one's own family was painful, too, and to the receivers as well as the givers because they knew the cost of what they had been given. Accordingly, those who were most admired were the "scramblers" who in one way or another—by diligence in keeping their jobs if they had them, or by diligence and resourcefulness in finding or making jobs for themselves if they had none—managed to avoid becoming an embarrassing problem to their relatives and friends.

So stamped by their heritage and times, the people of Keystone and similar communities generally believed it all right for a man to raise Cain on Saturday night, but only if he otherwise strove to be self-reliant, to give a day's work for a day's pay, and to accept the fact there is no such thing as a free lunch. And this no doubt explains, also, the achievements of many of the crew after their Rushmore days had ended.

They came to the job, most of them, as unskilled and semiskilled workers who of necessity had drifted from job to job according to which mines or construction projects were opening or closing. After leaving Rushmore, some, of course, returned to that sort of thing. A look at their records some forty years later, however, reveals that most did not. A substantial number went on to become successful entrepreneurs—merchants, salesmen, real-estate developers, ranchers, farmers. Several went on to get college degrees. One eventually became a general in the United States Air Force, one became an official in the South Dakota State Police, and yet another became a National Park Service Ranger who gave his own life in saving the life of a careless Yellowstone Park tourist.

Perhaps this heritage-bred and depression-tempered inner fiber also explains how these men were able to build the world's most massive sculpture, and why they persevered until they had done it.

The leaders of the project—Borglum, Robinson, Norbeck, Boland, and Williamson—all came to the mountain in the grip of a dream. They came knowing what they had to do, and each came equipped with some special talent for doing it. The men of the crew came only because they needed jobs. They did not know what they were to do or how to do it, nor were they properly qualified even to learn to do it.

There was public recognition of the leaders. Borglum was made a national figure because of his Rushmore work, and he knew that so long as the monument should endure, he would be immortalized as its sculptor. Norbeck, Boland, and the others also received public credit while the work was going on, and knew, as well, that their names would be indelibly written in its history. Rushmore's workmen, on the other hand, were anonymous. The newspapers did not know their names, nor would the monument's future viewers. They were Rushmore's unknown soldiers, and they knew it.

These things probably would have made no difference, however, if the job had been a steady one, but it was not. All too often, and for too long at a time, the work was shut down because of weather or lack of funds, and the men were laid off. By the time the job was ended, in fact, these shut-downs would have consumed an astonishing seven-and-a-half years of its fourteen-year existence, and one lay-off would have lasted for an entire year. Rushmore workers received far better than average wages, but only when they worked, and obviously they did not get to work nearly as much as they needed to. Consequently, not one of the longtime crew was able to support his family by his Rushmore work alone, and all of them knew periods when keeping nothing but bread on the table was difficult indeed.

And yet . . . they persisted, and they carved the mountain. Unrewarded by recognition, enduring financial hardship time after time when the work was shut down, those who became the longtimers of the crew—the real crew—stuck to it. When they were laid off they found other things to do, depression or no. "Need is a wonderful incentive," one of them would say later, "so when we had to find other things to do, we found them." But each time the work was resumed, they abandoned whatever security their interim jobs might have provided and returned to their carving.

That they could and would do all this was no doubt due to their heritage-bred belief that a man can learn what he has to learn, and can accomplish what he wants to accomplish—if he wants to enough.

Why they did it is another matter. When asked, Rushmore's veterans give a variety of answers, but with one central theme. "More and more we sensed that we were creating a truly great thing, and after a while all of us old hands became truly dedicated to it and determined to stick to it," said Red Anderson.

"Yes," added Howdy Peterson, "and we had a hell of a good time while we were at it."

20. Tempest in the Entablature Teapot

I n 1934 the rains again did not come to Dakota, but the grasshoppers did come, and dust clouds rose and boiled on the arid wind, and grasshoppers ate whatever the drought had spared.

The New Deal was trying with massive Federal expenditures to "prime the pump" of the American economy, but so far the economic pump remained as dry as the weather. In the spring President Roosevelt increased the price of gold and thereby devalued the dollar, hoping to create a surge of new money that in turn would create new jobs. But that was not working very well either, and twenty-five percent of the country's wage earners remained unemployed.

In Italy, Benito Mussolini was, he said, "making the trains run on time," but he was doing it with a type of government he called "fascism" and at the price of Italian freedom.

In Germany, on a June night known as "the night of the long knives," a onetime coffee-shop radical and anti-establishment protester named Adolf Hitler led his storm troopers in the bloody assassination of several hundred of his political opponents and thereby completed his seizure of dictatorial powers. Now he was saying that through a type of government he called National Socialism he would create for the German working class a "Thousand-Year Reich" of peace and prosperity.

In the Soviet Union, Joseph Stalin also was using bloody assassinations to further tighten his already iron grip on that unhappy land. And although Mussolini, Hitler, and Stalin all were plotting by means of arms or intimidation to gain control of various of their neighboring countries, all three were declaring themselves to be men of peace and good will and were calling on the nations of the world to disarm.

Thus, from the viewpoint of Dakota's farmers, American job-seekers, and world democracy, 1934 just was not a good year.

On the other hand, for each American who was unemployed there were three who were employed, and these and their families were traveling as never before. Tourism was increasing all over the nation, and in the Black Hills it was up an astonishing fifty percent from 1933. And so, despite the state of the national economy, 1934 was for the Black Hills tourist industry the very best year so far.

And for the Rushmore monument, now coming to be known as "The Shrine of Democracy," this also was the best year so far—and also the most turbulent. And both its gains and its turbulence in that year were produced by Borglum: by his determination and drive and endless energy; by his conviction that every issue had two sides (his and the wrong one); and by his habit—especially when pursuing an improbable goal—of disregarding the counsel of cooler heads.

This human dynamo came into the new year promoting, simultaneously, the revival of Stone Mountain, new government financing for Rushmore, and a scheme for publicizing Rushmore as it had never been publicized before.

Borglum's publicity scheme was centered on the Entablature—the five-hundred-word message that was to be carved alongside Rushmore's faces. This was not his first attempt to make publicity from the Entablature, but his first effort had backfired. In fact, it had created a good deal of bad publicity and had cost him the friendship of Calvin Coolidge as well.

That had occurred back in 1930, and it started out well enough. Borglum asked ex-president Coolidge to draft the Entablature's wording, and, as he had promised at the 1927 Rushmore dedication, Coolidge said he would. Then Coolidge started writing and Borglum started publicizing. The sculptor set out with a stream of press releases to create public anticipation of what Mr. Coolidge would produce, and he did it successfully. By the hundreds, newspapers both at home and abroad picked up the story and discussed it. Some were derisive, and the *London Daily Telegraph*, for example, loftily observed that it must be "quite jolly" for a nation to be able "to tell its history in five hundred words." Most of the stories and comments, however, were pleasingly positive.

In April, Borglum released what he said were Mr. Coolidge's first two paragraphs, and the mood of the papers changed. Printed nationwide, the paragraphs stimulated a flood of comment that was no longer pleasing. All too many editors and columnists assumed the role of literary and historical authorities and amused themselves by picking the paragraphs apart.

48. *Borglum's plan for the Entablature, carved in three-foot high letters, on a background the shape of the territory gained in the Louisiana Purchase.*

ON FOLLOWING PAGES:

49. *The high-relief numbers, 1776, in the newly begun area to the right of the Washington head were the start of the Entablature, which, despite President Coolidge's disapproval and contrary to the Commission's orders, Borglum commenced carving.*

Reading their comments, Calvin Coolidge became mightily displeased. He was the target of this barrage of criticism, but the paragraphs for which he was being criticized *were not the paragraphs he had written*. Borglum had edited them. Characteristically, Coolidge said nothing about that in public, but he did say plenty about it to Borglum in private. "The publicity," he wrote, "is exceedingly distasteful to me, it misrepresents me, and I should like to have it discontinued. . . . You can see where your improvements, published without consulting me, have landed me." In reply, the sculptor said he had been given permission by Mr. Coolidge, himself, to make "minor changes" in the text. This was true, but Coolidge thought it was beside the point. The point was that Borglum had not consulted him when making the changes. Even worse, he had told the press the much-criticized words were Coolidge's own when they were not, and Borglum had had no business doing that without permission. Moreover, he would not have approved those specific changes anyhow, Coolidge said, "because it breaks up the thought I was trying to convey."

Undaunted by this exchange, Borglum began to carve the edited text into Rushmore's granite. He had to have done so in the belief that Mr. Coolidge eventually would give in and approve the edited version, because otherwise such carving would have been wasted effort. The Rushmore Act passed by Congress in 1929 clearly stated that the Entablature text was "to be indited by Calvin Coolidge." Mr. Coolidge, however, was not about to give in.

When a month had passed and the matter was still deadlocked, Borglum went public with the story. He released Coolidge's original paragraphs to the press, admitted having edited them, and gave his reasons. Coolidge's first line, "The Declaration of Independence—the eternal right to seek happiness through self-government," Borglum had changed to read, "In the year of our Lord 1776 the people declared the eternal right to seek happiness through self-government." Mr. Coolidge's second paragraph:

> The Constitution—charter of perpetual union of free people of sovereign states establishing a government of limited powers—under an independent President, Congress and Court, charged to provide security for all citizens in their enjoyment of liberty, equality and justice under the law.

Borglum had overhauled it to read:

> In 1787 assembled in convention they made a charter of perpetual union for free people of sovereign states establishing a government

of limited powers under an independent President, Congress, and Court charged to provide security for all citizens in their enjoyment of liberty, equality and justice.

The reason he had made these changes, Borglum said, was to establish more clearly the historical periods involved and to give the text a narrative flow.

It appears that Borglum released the story and gave his explanations in hope of gaining enough public support to cause Mr. Coolidge to change his mind. Whatever Borglum's reason, however, it proved to be a colossal mistake. The newspapers had another field day, but this time Borglum was the victim. Whooping and chortling in print, they wrote the story under such headlines as, BORGLUM SHOWS COOLIDGE HOW; and in articles that ranged from scathing to ridicule they called Borglum's editing "high-handed" and "presumptuous" and suggested that now perhaps Coolidge should edit Borglum's designs for Rushmore.

Viewed in retrospect, the whole thing appears very much like a tiny tempest that should not have been allowed out of its teapot. Had it not been brewed by Borglum and Coolidge in pouring hot water on each other's ego, probably that is all it ever would have been. Borglum's editing consisted only of a little rearranging and the substitution of seventeen of his own words for nine of Coolidge's. Besides, probably neither version was of a quality to be immortalized in granite.

Nonetheless, the tempest did escape its teapot, and when it did Calvin Coolidge said he was withdrawing from the unfortunate affair. The Mount Rushmore commission then drafted a resolution asking him to reconsider and submit another text, but to no avail. Coolidge was, he said, washing his hands of the whole thing. He did not, however, forget it. In January of 1931 he was visited at his Massachusetts home by Paul Bellamy, and during their conversation Borglum was mentioned. Whereupon (so this author has heard Bellamy tell it) Mr. Coolidge asked, in his dry New England twang, "About how far would y' say 'tis from here to the Black Hills?"

"Oh, I don't know, Mr. President," Bellamy replied. "I'd guess maybe fifteen hundred miles."

Coolidge twinkled, took a thoughtful puff on his cigar, and said, "Well . . . Y'know, Mr. Bellamy, that's about as close t' Mr. Borglum as I care t' be."

Calvin Coolidge died in 1933. So now, in 1934, Borglum felt free to take up the Entablature matter again and to use a different approach to it. His idea now was to hold a national contest offering substantial prizes to those who produced the best Entablature manuscripts, with the grand winner enjoying the honor of seeing his or her composition carved for all eternity in Rushmore's granite. This, Borglum figured, ought to produce an outstanding inscription, and it surely would produce a blizzard of publicity.

Borglum took his idea to the Hearst newspaper chain, whose combined circulation exceeded five million and whose founder, William Randolph Hearst, had made much of his fortune from Black Hills gold. To his delight, they bought the idea and agreed to offer medals, cash, and college scholarships as prizes.

Usually Borglum announced his inspirations the moment he had them. This time, uncharacteristically, he kept quiet until the Hearst organization had accepted and perfected his idea and was about to release the first publicity on it. Then he told the Mount Rushmore commission about it. He thought he had executed a brilliant coup, and it appeared that he had. Hence, the response of the commissioners must have shocked him. They were upset. Powerfully upset. They were not opposed to the Entablature nor to Rushmore publicity, but they were concerned about the legality of what Borglum was doing. The congressional act under which Rushmore was being funded said the Entablature must "be indited by Calvin Coolidge," and even though Coolidge was dead the act was still law. Unless or until it was changed, if it *could* be changed, no other Entablature wording could be lawfully used. Accordingly, the commission was of the opinion that this effort, too, would backfire. It would place both Rushmore and the Hearst papers in an embarrassing position that Hearst's competitors were sure to exploit to the limit.

Norbeck was at the Mayo Clinic in Rochester, Minnesota, for treatment of his cancer and, as he said, was "in no position to take the initiative." From his hospital room, however, he did write to Boland:

> I am disturbed that [Borglum] seems to have proceeded in violation
> of the law. . . . I want to play fair with Coolidge, who made the
> monument possible. I don't intend to betray him just because he is
> dead. . . . I want to say frankly to you that I am not going to be a
> party to this deal under any circumstances.

At the same time the senator asked his son Harold, who was an attorney, to get an opinion on the matter from the National Park Service lawyers and pass their comments on to John Boland. Soon thereafter, Harold Norbeck reported to Boland that according to the "informal decision" of the Park Service chief attorney, "(a) Coolidge wording must be used; (b) The right to change wording does not rest in Congress, as court probably would consider the matter in the same status as a will."

Upon hearing this, Boland tried to get Borglum to drop the contest, but to no avail. Acting for his father, Harold Norbeck then tried to do the same, but only succeeded, he said, in arousing the sculptor's "resentment and ire."

Next, in a front-page story headed by a four-column cut of men at work on the Washington face, the Hearst papers announced the contest to the nation. This blocked Norbeck, Boland, and the others from continuing their efforts to stop it. By continuing to press the issue, they could only cause embarrassment to the monument work and to the Hearst papers. Instead, they agreed to hold the legal question "in greatest secrecy," and at the same time to refrain from endorsing or even acknowledging the contest. That way, they believed the commission could refuse to have the winning essay carved on the mountain if such carving should indeed prove to be unlawful.

Borglum, on the other hand, was determined to force at least Norbeck to publicly endorse the contest, and urged him "to come out with a statement" supporting it. Norbeck refused. Thereupon, in Norbeck's words: ". . . he promptly appoints a new [contest] committee and makes me chairman of same, and puts out publicity in such a way as to make it appear that [President] Roosevelt named the committee."

As history would prove, Borglum had a good thing going and knew it. Unfazed by the objections of Norbeck and the others, he continued at full tilt to pursue it. Together, he and Hearst executives asked President Roosevelt to head the contest's judging committee. Roosevelt, unaware of the contest's questionable legality, agreed. Next, they asked Eleanor Roosevelt, Interior Secretary Harold L. Ickes, nine senators, and a few other notables to serve on the committee, and all these accepted also. Then Borglum persuaded the Underwood Typewriter Company to advertise the contest and to offer twenty-two new typewriters as prizes. All of which kept Borglum and Rushmore in the national headlines.

It was a year of headlines and stories that gripped the public interest. Outlaws Clyde Barrow, Bonnie Parker, John Dillinger, Baby Face Nelson, and Pretty Boy Floyd all fell before the guns of the law. The nation fell in love with five little girls known as the Dionne Quintuplets born to a French-Canadian family. California physician Francis Townsend was proposing to end the Depression through his Townsend Plan—a plan under which the government would give an income of $200 per month to every citizen over age sixty—and all across the country elderly Americans were forming Townsend Clubs and singing "Onward Townsend Soldiers." A carpenter named Bruno

Hauptmann was arrested and tried for the 1932 kidnap-murder of the infant son of Charles and Anne Lindbergh. And in industry after industry across the nation there were eruptions of bloody violence between strikers and strike-breakers. People heard about these things in radio broadcasts by Hearst columnist Walter Winchell, who talked like a machine gun and began his broadcasts by barking, all in one breath, "Good-evening-Mr.-and-Mrs.-North-America-and-all-the-ships-at-sea—Let's go-to-press!"; and they read about them in the headlines. And—thanks to the efforts of Borglum and the Hearst editors—the Rushmore Entablature story stayed right up there with the others.

In late April, Borglum, too, appeared on radio. Speaking on the Columbia Network, he told the nation about Rushmore and the Entablature, and in so doing won for his contest the support (albeit reluctant) of Peter Norbeck. On first hearing that Borglum was going to speak, Norbeck was disgusted. He was not sure whether this Entablature rumpus was a time bomb or a circus, but either way he was against it. After Borglum's speech, however, Norbeck saw it a little differently. "I heard Borglum over the radio about Rushmore," he wrote, "and I think he got away very good with his stuff."

As it turned out, Borglum did indeed "get away very good with his stuff," not only in his speech but in the whole contest. One hundred and eight thousand manuscripts were submitted according to one account; 800,000 according to another, probably exaggerated, one. The result, as South Dakota's other senator, William J. Bulow, pointed out, was that "a million dollars could not have purchased the advertising thus produced."

It turned out also that the commission need not have worried about Borglum trying unlawfully to carve the winning essay on the face of Rushmore. Senator Bulow, a member of the committee appointed to select a winner from among the five finalists, explained why: "The committee made its choice, and Borglum promptly turned it down. He took a look at the four others and threw them away. He said someone would have to write a better history than had yet been written or he would write one himself."

50. In 1975, Park Service employees installed a bronze plaque bearing William Burkett's prize-winning 1935 Entablature Contest essay.

The grand prize was won by a Nebraska youth named William Burkett, and it enabled him to attend four years of college. More than forty years later, when Burkett had become a prominent California financier and patron of the arts, he told the author that he owed much of his success to the Rushmore Entablature Contest. As a consequence, he said, he held so deep an affection for the monument that he would like to be buried near it.

To his great disappointment, Burkett never saw his words carved on

Rushmore, for, a few years later, the Entablature was dropped from the monument plans. He was, however, guest of honor at a 1975 ceremony in which the National Park Service installed in the Rushmore visitors' center a bronze plate upon which Burkett's essay is inscribed.

Busy as he was with the Rushmore contest that spring, Borglum was just as busy trying to scare up more Federal money for the work. Since the monument was now under the jurisdiction of the Department of the Interior, he began by asking Secretary Ickes for help. Ickes, who for good reason was known nationally as "The Old Curmudgeon," responded with characteristic bluntness. He was against the whole idea of carving mountains, he said. He did not even want to see Rushmore now that Borglum had been whittling on it, he continued, because what the sculptor was doing there was akin to carving initials in the trunk of a beautiful tree. Period.

A little later, Borglum was invited to a dinner at the White House, and there he found better fishing. Given in connection with the Entablature contest, the dinner gave the sculptor an opportunity to expound on Rushmore. Expound he did, and by the time the evening was over he had President Roosevelt more or less convinced that the monument was no mere novelty but a thing of considerable value to the entire nation.

Thus encouraged, Borglum now approached Norbeck, who had returned to Washington, and asked him to introduce in the Senate a bill that would (1) provide $400,000 in new Rushmore funds, and (2) eliminate the requirement for matching each Federal Rushmore dollar with a private one. Still ill and tired, the senator was not sure *anything* more for Rushmore could be gotten out of Congress. He was sure, though, that asking for what Borglum wanted would destroy their chances of getting anything at all. He did agree, however, to introduce a bill for some lesser amount of money, and that also would end the fund-matching requirement. Then, to Norbeck's chagrin, Borglum said he was going to stay in Washington and help the senator get the job done. Or, to quote Norbeck, "He said he was going to stick right here until HE saw it through!"

The reason for Norbeck's chagrin was that Borglum had "helped" him with bills before, and had always managed to create so much confusion that the senator's job had been made harder rather than easier. Once, in fact, Norbeck had been moved to write to Boland, "I cannot even start [on this bill] until he quits." And this time, Norbeck thought, was going to be worse than ever. Busy as a bee in a clover field, Borglum was flitting from one congressman to another but without coordinating his efforts with Norbeck or even letting the senator know whom he had seen or what he had told them.

In mellower times, Norbeck probably would not have minded this so much. But now, when his body felt heavy and his spirits were often low and everything was an effort, he resented what he regarded as Borglum's meddling and made sharp complaints about it.

The records show, however, that Borglum this time actually was doing quite a bit of good. He favorably influenced several congressmen; he had obtained at least some Rushmore support from the president, although it was not yet clear just how much; and, as Norbeck was quick to concede, the Entablature publicity was proving to be very helpful.

The fruit of these efforts was that a bill authorizing $250,000 more of Federal funds for Rushmore and eliminating the matching requirement was passed by Congress in June—but it barely passed. This was a great step forward for Rushmore, and it well may be that without Borglum's lobbying activity it could not have been made.

But even while Borglum's national activities were improving Rushmore's financial position and public image in 1934, his local activities were creating turbulence in the project's internal operations. For that was the year when Gutzon Borglum declared war on John Boland.

21. Borglum and Boland—
Irresistible Force,
Immovable Object

On May 7, 1934, Gutzon Borglum discovered that John Boland had canceled, without first consulting him, an order for Rushmore publicity photographs that Borglum had placed without first consulting Boland—and Borglum blew up. It was one of those hot and muggy Washington, D.C., days when people who are fast-moving and impatient are apt to become sticky and sweaty and short of temper, and Borglum, in Washington to lobby for the new Rushmore funding bill, was fast-moving and impatient. Hence, this may have had something to do with why he began his war on Boland on that particular day. But one way or another the war would have come anyhow. Borglum's correspondence leaves no doubt of that.

Unlike Hamlet, the sculptor saw no possible nobility in bearing with patience the slings and arrows of outrageous fortune. On the contrary, he invariably took arms against his seas of troubles, and the sea facing him at that time was a rough one. He was trying simultaneously to run the Entablature contest, organize the season's carving at Rushmore, and to raise $50,000 for the revival of Stone Mountain. He thought he needed to be in Washington to lobby for the funding bill, he did need to be at Rushmore to try solving the problems caused by the fissures in the new Jefferson site, and he was frustrated at not being able to be in both places at once. He had managed to raise only $72 of the $50,000 he had confidently promised an Atlanta citizens' group he could and would raise for Stone Mountain. He was put out with the commission for neither helping with nor endorsing the Entablature contest, nor even giving him credit for the brilliance of the idea. He was being humiliated by creditors who were trying to garnishee his income, and even more humiliated by a lawsuit filed by Mills Drug Store in Rapid City for fishing equipment he had bought but not paid for. On top of all that, the holders of his ranch mortgage were again moving to foreclose, and he was so far behind in his payments that he had no defense against them.

It all added up to a burden that would have broken an ordinary man, and even though Borglum was far from ordinary it should have broken him. Norbeck feared that it would, and wrote: "You have altogether too much to do. . . . You are breaking under the load. . . . You have not yet come to realize that there is a limit even to your strength. . . . You have got to change your ways." Borglum, however, did not change his ways, and even though he was severely bent by his load at times, neither did he break. Instead, he began an attack on the person he believed to be the main source of his troubles: John Boland.

On the surface of it, Boland seemed a most unlikely target for Borglum's wrath. He had always been one of the sculptor's steadiest supporters and had granted him, probably, more and larger personal favors than all other Rushmore officials together. What is more, Borglum knew this and heretofore had appreciated it. Until about the middle of 1933 he had always affectionately referred to the little businessman as "Johnny," and had never said a hard word against him. Even so, the nature of their association and the difference in their personalities had made unavoidable the conflict that now arose between them.

Once begun, Borglum expanded his war to include almost every facet of his association with Boland, but it would always remain centered on the question of who was supposed to be in control of what on the Rushmore job.

To understand this conflict, which from 1934 to 1938 was to be probably the project's greatest problem, one must first untangle the often confused issue of just who at Rushmore was *supposed* to control what.

The best way to start is by thinking of the project as having been divided into two categories: the *creative* work of designing and carving the monument, and the *supportive* work of providing and managing the facilities and personnel needed to make the creative work possible. Borglum, according to his contract, was to conduct and control the creative part of the job, and the commission was to take care of all the rest of it. Thus, Borglum was supposed to be to Rushmore as a surgeon is to the hospital where his surgery is performed. The surgeon is responsible for the proper performance of his art, and the hospital is responsible for providing the facilities and personnel he requires for that performance. The surgeon has no authority over the hospital and its employees generally, but he does have control of the operating room and its personnel when he is operating. The hospital has no authority over the surgeon in his practice of surgery, but it has complete authority over its own facilities and personnel at all times other than when they have been placed at the surgeon's disposal.

Similarly, Borglum had been engaged to design the monument, "to supervise and direct all operations on the face of the cliff having a direct and immediate bearing on the appearance and artistic qualities of the monument," and to supervise and direct "all workmen engaged upon those operations," and that was all. According to Borglum's contract, everything else was the responsibility of the commission. The commission was supposed to organize the project and manage its business affairs; construct and maintain all buildings and other structures; install and operate such services as electric power and compressed air, the overhead tramway, etc. Also, it was the commission and not Borglum that was to furnish the project's personnel and that had the authority to hire, promote, and discharge employees.

To the extent that sound business practices and the budget would allow, the commission was expected, of course, to provide these services in accordance with Borglum's recommendations. Especially, this was true in the hiring, promoting, and discharging of those employees engaged in carving or other of the creative operations for which Borglum was responsible.

As established by the commission, the project's chain of command was as follows:

(1) The *Commission*. The governor of the entire operation. Commissioners served without pay.

(2) *Executive Committee*. Prepared Rushmore's budgets and drew up its contracts, worked with Borglum in planning the work. Members served without pay.

(3) *Chief Field Officer*. The project's general manager. Responsible for determining the project's needs for equipment, supplies, services, and personnel. Then, as the appointed watchdog of the Rushmore bank account, responsible for balancing those needs against available assets and for furnishing them in order of their priority within the limits of those assets.

This position was filled by John Boland, who also was given the duty of managing Rushmore's purchasing, payroll, accounting, and other business affairs, and who handled these things through the facilities of his Rapid City Implement Company office.

Boland served without pay from mid-1929 until November, 1932, at which time the commission voted to pay him one hundred dollars a month for his services and to pay a portion of his secretary's salary.

(4) *Project Superintendent*. Intended to be in direct command of Rush-

more's on-site facilities and personnel. Responsible for operation and maintenance of all support operations, facilities, and equipment. Accountable to
Borglum when engaged in activities in the sculptor's area of authority (such
as carving). Accountable to the commission, through Boland, for all other
operations. Had authority to hire and fire personnel.

What it all boiled down to was this: Borglum, as an independent contractor, was intended to work "beside" the commission and not "for" it nor from
within it. Originally, this arrangement not only had had Borglum's approval
but had been suggested by him. He said then and repeated many times later
that he did not want to be tied down to any but the sculptural aspects of the
job, and undoubtedly he thought he meant what he said. The trouble was,
however, that Borglum was a compulsive manager who tried to take command of every activity he became involved in. It does not appear that he always wanted to. It was just something he did as instinctively as a meadowlark
sings or a cat leaps at a mouse. Moreover, as Rushmore's designer and creator
he quite understandably felt he ought to have the final say in all matters connected with it, and that his own judgment should always prevail over that of
Boland or the commission.

When it came to questions of job authority and of who was supposed to
control what, the most confusing job at Rushmore by far was that of the superintendent. When engaged in supervising carving or activities directly connected with it, the superintendent was answerable to Borglum. In all his other
work he was answerable to John Boland, and the line between the two was
difficult to draw, at best. It was made even more difficult by the fact that
Borglum expected the superintendent to be his subordinate in all things, or as
the sculptor put it, to be "loyal" to him rather than to Boland or the commission. And this, in turn, was what caused the first three of Rushmore's four
superintendents to resign. Their years of association at Stone Mountain
had caused Borglum to have a great deal of confidence in Tucker, who was
Rushmore's first superintendent. The two men had long been good personal
friends, and at Rushmore their relationship at first was as smooth as anyone
could want. But when, in the spring of 1929, Tucker supported Boland's decision to buy electricity from Keystone Consolidated instead of Borglum's proposal for resurrecting the old power plant donated by Samuel Insull, the
honeymoon was ended. In writing later about that incident, Borglum said,
"Tucker went to pieces . . . he betrayed his trust . . ." and therefore "he had
to go." Five months later, Tucker did "go," and there can be little doubt that
the rift his "disloyalty" had caused between him and Borglum was the major
cause of his going.

Tucker was replaced by his erstwhile assistant on the job, J. C. Denison. Denison was a good rock man, an expert with dynamite, and a good practical engineer. His only mountain-carving experience, however, had been what he had gained at Rushmore. Hence, even though it was Borglum who had recommended Denison for the job, the sculptor now felt compelled (as he wrote later) "to take over direct charge" of the rough carving that the more experienced Tucker had been doing. And that might have worked out all right if Borglum had not also felt compelled to take command of all of Denison's other duties as well—duties that Denison probably was more capable of handling that Borglum. As it happened, however, Denison turned out to be just about as hotheaded and independent as the sculptor, himself, and he vigorously resisted this encroachment on his authority. Also, in disagreements over administrative matters Denison tended to agree with Boland rather than Borglum. The result was, as one old Rushmore hand put it, "Denison and the Old Man, why, they fought like cats and dogs." But not for long. After ten months, Denison quit. "Denison went to the bad," Borglum wrote Norbeck. "I charged him with disloyalty . . . [and he] resigned."

The next superintendent, also appointed because of Borglum's recommendation, was Bill Tallman. Tallman had grown up in Stamford, his parents and the Borglums were family friends, and he had studied sculpture for a time under Borglum in Borglum's Stamford studio. Tallman had come to Rushmore in the spring of 1929 to work as a pointer and he had proved to be a good one. This and his sculptural studies qualified him rather well for superintending work on the mountain itself. He was less qualified, however, to superintend the project's non-carving activities. And this, together with his youth, his family connection with the Borglums, and his former studies under Borglum, made it only natural for him to accept domination by Borglum and to subordinate his superintendency to the sculptor's control. Thus, at the time of Tallman's appointment as superintendent in late summer, 1930, Borglum became superintendent in all but salary and title, and he had already assumed a part of the title. Starting back in Denison's time, he had discontinued signing his Rushmore correspondence, "Gutzon Borglum, Sculptor," and had begun signing it instead, "Gutzon Borglum, Sculptor and Engineer."

During all this time, however, Borglum had not been able to dominate John Boland or to infringe upon his authority even slightly. It appears that at first he never really tried to. But as time passed, and Borglum began more and more to feel that he was being, as he said, "hamstrung" by the decisions of Boland and the commission, he began with increasing vigor to challenge those decisions. Then he discovered that Boland was one of those rare men whom all of Borglum's charm and determination and persuasive power could not influence. As Borglum continued to fail in trying to get Boland to do things his way, frustration and resentment began to build up in the sculptor like the silent building of heat in a volcano. By mid-1933, Borglum's volcano had heated to the point that it had begun to mutter and rumble. By early 1934 it was ready for a full-blown eruption. And when Boland canceled the arrangements Borglum had made for Rushmore publicity photographs, the eruption came.

Earlier in the spring, Borglum, as chairman of the Rushmore publicity committee, had announced his intention to order from Charles D'Emery, his old friend and personal photographer in Connecticut, a large number of prints from pictures D'Emery had taken on two previous visits to the memorial. Borglum wanted them, he said, so as "to cover the country with views of this work the world knows nothing about." Boland had responded by saying he would not honor the bill for such an order, and gave his reasons. First, D'Emery's fee was too high and his pictures were out of date. Second, Rapid City's studios (Bell, Harms, Rise, and Vick) all had large files of current pictures of Rushmore; as far as Boland was concerned their work was as good as D'Emery's; and he had found that they could furnish the prints Borglum wanted for about five hundred dollars less than D'Emery. And finally, five hundred dollars spent on carving Rushmore would produce another five hundred dollars in Federal matching funds (this was before the "matching" arrangement had been eliminated), whereas five hundred dollars spent on pictures of the monument would not. Therefore, the actual extra cost to Rushmore for D'Emery's pictures would not be five hundred dollars but a thousand, and that in exchange for what Boland thought to be an insignificant difference in quality.

Borglum disagreed. D'Emery's pictures, he said, "are the best ones today, the only ones worthwhile," and the work of Rapid City's studios was "the cheapest and most worthless on the market." And finally, he thought that as chairman of the publicity committee he should be able to authorize publicity expenditures without having to secure approval from anyone. Accordingly, without telling Boland, Borglum told D'Emery to go ahead with the order. That was Borglum's mistake. When the pictures were finished and D'Emery submitted his bill, Boland, without telling Borglum, sent it right back with a letter saying that the work had not been authorized and the bill would not be paid—and that was Boland's mistake. Had Boland asked Borglum to handle the matter, the sculptor might have been able to do it in such a way as not to lose face with his old friend D'Emery. As it was, however, Boland's action

placed Borglum in a very embarrassing position, and Borglum was not a man
who suffered embarrassment easily.

So, when Borglum learned from D'Emery what had happened, he sat
down at a desk in Washington's Metropolitan Club and personally typed a
four-page letter in which, in sizzling phrases, he told Boland what was on
his mind:

> I have today received a photostat of your letter to D'Emery dis-
> crediting my order. . . .
> In the Stone Mountain work I felt it necessary to control the
> publicity. . . . I act on the same conditions for the Mount Rushmore
> Commission . . . [which] had resulted in the most efficient publicity
> in art in modern times. . . . Interference with it is incomprehen-
> sible. . . . the question of matching and so securing an extra thou-
> sand does not excuse the impropriety nor wisdom [sic] of your
> interference. . . . The publicity I have secured for South Dakota
> is work [sic] millions—and yet you, as an official of the State and
> Commission, hinder me in these ways! !

With that out of the way, the sculptor then moved on in the letter to other
things that were bothering him, one of which was a developing problem with
Bill Tallman. Now in the fourth year of his superintendency, Tallman had
been growing up and developing confidence. Through consultation with
Boland, he had come to understand in which areas of the work he was to be
governed by Borglum and in which areas he was not, and was becoming independent enough to act accordingly. Borglum was finding this to be a most
distressing state of affairs, and he believed Boland to be directly responsible
for it (which he probably was):

> . . . I demand that my officers or men are not demorailized [sic] nor
> corrupted by telling them they need not obey my orders, or telling
> them anything at all that relates to my work. I am responsible for
> Billy's conduct—I am responsible for his work, I shall dismiss him if
> he disobeys me. He is broken hearted over the dual role you have
> compelled him to play. . . .

And there was the matter of how the work force at the mountain should
be used. Whenever Borglum wanted an errand run, an area cleaned up, or
whatever, he was inclined to assign the task to whatever workmen were
handy, regardless of their job classification. This meant that high-priced men

such as drillers and carvers were often seen to be doing jobs that required only low-priced skills. Boland thought this to be an inefficient use of manpower that added unnecessarily to the cost of the job, and had done his best to get it stopped. He had asked Borglum to quit it and had asked Tallman to do what he could to prevent it. Now, Borglum commented on that:

> . . . the Sculptor alone selects and determines who, when, where, and how, the class of men and service from the men employed. He is in complete charge of design, management, and direction of the work and interference with the men for political or other reasons will no longer be permitted.

It is not clear just how Borglum thought Boland was using Rushmore and its men for political purposes, but it is clear that he thought it. And he thought also that Boland, as a director of the First National Bank in Rapid City, was deliberately restraining Rushmore's spending so as to give the bank the use of the money: ". . . you are prepared to risk everything in order to hold petty political influence over a few votes, and the direction or control of the [Rushmore] deposit in your bank."

The thing that was really bothering Borglum, of course, was money. He had had an excellent income from Rushmore in 1933 and had had income from lectures and other sculptural contracts, as well. Unfortunately, he had seen it all disappear into the pockets of his creditors like water into sand. Boland had been making him personal loans so as to keep him going; Borglum, however, had gotten the idea that Boland was at the same time withholding from him some of his sculpturing fees. Examination of Rushmore's books from that time shows this not to have been the case, but Borglum thought it was and wrote: "[with] you owing me money, with complete power to pay, [that] I am compelled to accept from you or your office petty loans is intolerable."

And so it went, with the sculptor accusing Boland of keeping him from hiring "men who understand granite" and "who have judgment or experience above the local voter"; of buying Rushmore's supplies and equipment only from his friends; of having sold an oil tank that was Borglum's property; of being ignorant of sculptural work and yet interfering with it . . . and so on and on.

Borglum wrote that letter on the seventh. He mailed it on the ninth, after adding a handwritten postscript: "Have just read this over after keeping it two days. There is not an unfriendly thought in it. I simply want more help and less trouble. G. B."

Despite the postscript, Boland thought the letter contained plenty of "unfriendly thoughts." "After reading it," he wrote to Norbeck, "my first thought was to resign and be relieved of all this unnecessary trouble, but I have decided I will remain on the job. . . ."

"I can understand how you feel," Norbeck replied. "I was so depressed myself several times that I came pretty nearly quitting. . . ."

Having learned from Boland the state of mind the sculptor was in, and then having learned that Borglum had ordered Superintendent Tallman to have nothing more to do with Boland, Norbeck decided something had to be done to get the man calmed down. But Norbeck was no longer as effective in settling Borglum down as he once had been. Therefore, he tried tactfully to enlist the aid of Commissioner Lorine Spoonts. He wrote telling her in a general way what had been going on, and then said: "You have knowledge of my admiration for Mr. Borglum . . . but all the fine publicity this year has thrilled him very much, and I am afraid that unless we can exercise firmness, with much patience and wisdom, that we might have something approaching the Stone Mountain blow-up."

Because Mrs. Spoonts was a good personal friend of Borglum's, Norbeck did not want to put her on the spot by asking directly for her help. Instead, he just hinted at it and hoped she would take the hint: "I am not writing to suggest anything to you: I am simply writing in order that you may have a little better picture of the whole problem than you might otherwise have."

If Mrs. Spoonts did say anything to Borglum, it appears to have done little good. Instead of calming down, he now began ordering Rushmore equipment and supplies personally and trying to hire men personally, thus expanding even further his challenge to Boland's authority. Obviously, this could not be allowed to continue, and on June 25, at the Alex Johnson Hotel, the commission's executive committee held a special session devoted to the sculptor problem.

At the suggestion of its chairman, Fred Sargent, the executive committee adopted two resolutions. According to the first, the commission would not honor any "bill or obligation contracted for materials, supplies, labor, or otherwise" that had not "first been requisitioned from and approved by the Executive Committee." The second stipulated that additional employees requested by Borglum would be hired only after he had submitted, and received committee approval of, an operational plan showing need for those employees and how he planned to use them.

Borglum, in his own words, was "shocked and distressed," and the fact that the committee had also voted to put Lincoln Borglum on the payroll at a dollar an hour (then the top of the Rushmore pay scale) did little to pacify him. "Those resolutions," he declared, "will destroy the Mount Rushmore Memorial."

The immediate effect of the resolutions, however, was to cause Borglum to shift his attack. Instead of continuing to challenge Boland and the commission by his actions in the field, he now expanded his letter-writing. He wrote to government officials, Park Service officials, congressmen—to anyone whom he thought might help to lift from him the cross of Boland's "interference." As a result, the Park Service file of Borglum complaints grew so fat that Norbeck found it necessary to write to Borglum: "Your letter file will get us all in trouble. . . . If Congress should decide to investigate, it might conclude that the Commission is made up of a bunch of crooks, or that the artist is a nut—or both."

In reply, Borglum said that Boland was uncultured, illiterate, grasping, and "incapable of keeping his word," and the sculptor blamed Norbeck for the problem arising therefrom. "You brought Boland into this thing. He has hindered me ever since he has been on the job, and he never sleeps. . . ."

Upon reading that letter, Norbeck decided that enough was enough. After first wryly observing, "Now, do not worry about your failure to approve everything I do," he proceeded to lower the boom on the sculptor:

I have never known Mr. Boland to do a dishonorable thing. . . . If [he] is doing the things you say he is, it is a matter of proof. If it is true, the matter should be laid before the Board. . . .

I have lately come to feel that you will do something that will prevent the completion of Rushmore. I would not be surprised any morning to find a statement in the papers that Rushmore has become impossible because of interference from politicians. The public will enjoy such a statement from you. You will enjoy the public's reaction to your statement. You will be sitting pretty for a while . . . even though such a statement is without foundation.

. . . after the climax of this matter comes, I do not know how to pick up the pieces. . . . I told you in the previous letter that if I was not able to bring about harmonious work between the Sculptor and the Commission I would not remain on the Commission.

. . . There is no personal ill will on my part. . . . I accept the explanation that you have been ill, but you are certainly in a disturbed frame of mind which does not bode well for the progress of the work. I have made over seven years of effort in this work. It has been a heavy drain on my strength and purse. It keeps getting worse. Your letter made me sick and I am trying to get well.

Even while Norbeck was writing those lines, back in Rapid City attorneys George Phillip and William Williamson, together with John Boland, were completing a legal maneuver that for the next twelve months would protect Borglum from eviction by the mortgage-holders of his ranch. And it was probably this, reinforced by Norbeck's scolding, that caused the sculptor to tone down his attacks for a time. The lull was only temporary, for his basic attitudes had not changed, but during the next two or three months he was considerably more quiet about them.

Despite all this ferment and turbulence, Borglum meanwhile had been making remarkable progress on the mountain. Considering his emotional state, not to mention all the other activities he was entangled in, it is amazing that he could have done so. But then, Borglum was an amazing man. As a result of his efforts, George Washington's collar appeared on the mountain that summer, and his lapels, and by the time work was discontinued in December his left arm and shoulder had begun to emerge from the imprisoning granite.

Most of the year's effort, however, was expended on Jefferson. When it had progressed to the point where Borglum had become confident of the stone in the new Jefferson location, he ordered the old Jefferson head blasted down—and received a great artistic bonus. Perhaps he had known all along that he would. Some people have even said it was why he so willingly abandoned the old Jefferson. In any case, as the rubble of the old head thundered down the mountain it left in its place an opening that separated the upper part of the Washington head from the mother-rock behind it. As a consequence, the Washington head now stood forth from the cliff in splendid, three-dimensional strength, and in time to come that opening would also cause the afternoon sun to highlight dramatically the features of Jefferson and Lincoln. Thus, what had started out as an expensive failure had become instead a great artistic asset.

While working on the mountain, Borglum had not forgotten Boland. He could not. Having started to blame Boland for his troubles, he was now finding more troubles for which to blame him. As a past-president of the Rapid City Chamber of Commerce, Boland was to blame for the chamber not having raised as much Rushmore money as Borglum thought it should have. As a senator in the South Dakota legislature, Boland was to blame for the legislature never having appropriated a dime for Rushmore. As a director of the

First National Bank, Boland was to blame for the bank having refused, on the grounds of Borglum's poor credit, to refinance the Borglum ranch. Then, of course, there was the Mount Rushmore National Memorial Commission. According to Borglum, its members were "men of crude ability," and were "indifferent and uninformed men that are . . . hindering us in any way they can," and Boland, as its executive officer, was the most powerful member of that commission.

And so, as the year came to a close, Borglum's major objective had become the getting rid of John Boland. To get him stripped of his executive powers, to force him to resign from the commission—whatever it took to get him away from Rushmore. From the hill of history we can see that Boland had become Borglum's scapegoat and that Borglum, like the Israelites of old, thought he could dispose of his troubles by driving his scapegoat out into the wilderness. But that was not going to be easy. Boland was just as stubborn in performing what he saw as his duty as Borglum was in pursuing what he thought was a necessary objective. Thus, Borglum's war on Boland had become, and during the next four years would continue to be, the relentless hammering of an irresistible force against an immovable object.

22. "Two-by-Four Engineer, Brainless Jellybean"

The people responsible for building Rushmore started 1935 just as they had started every other year since 1927: in a dither over money. We know now their problem was not as great as they thought it was, but that is because, with the blessing of hindsight, we are able to know how it all eventually worked out, and to know that Congress was beginning to mellow toward Rushmore and was becoming ever more willing to invest in it. But to Norbeck and others, with their all-too-vivid memories of the money struggles of the past, the problem of the future financing looked about as grim as before.

Although they had only about $3,400 on hand, there was another $55,000 of unappropriated funds in the original Rushmore authorization bill, *if* they could get it. But in this depression Congress, beset by funding requests from every conceivable locality and group, authorizing money was one thing; actually appropriating it was quite another. Moreover, even if they did get it, they still would not have enough for a full season's operation.

Norbeck figured they probably could get the $55,000, but beyond that he was pessimistic. "I really have no hopes of getting any more money for Rushmore this year," he told Boland.

Assisted by the National Park Service, on May 9 he did get the appropriation approved, and got, at the same time, his first inkling that Congress was indeed mellowing toward Rushmore. "Rushmore is becoming an institution instead of a joke," he wrote. "It is no longer in the Stone Mountain class."

Thus encouraged, the senator began laying groundwork for a bill authorizing yet another $200,000, only to discover that Borglum was already promoting a Rushmore bill of his own. Norbeck had heard nothing from the sculptor since the first of the year and had not even known he was in town. It was through perplexed lawmakers, who tried to reconcile what Norbeck was

302

telling them with what Borglum had already told them, that Norbeck learned that Borglum *was* in town and *was* promoting a bill. As Norbeck understood (accurately) what he was being told, Borglum's bill would (1) authorize $350,000 for Rushmore; (2) give the Treasury Department jurisdiction over the monument; (3) give Borglum full authority over the project, itself; and (4) replace Borglum's old contract with one the sculptor had drawn up to give himself more authority and a higher fee. The sculptor was promoting his bill, Norbeck was told, by claiming it to be a necessary cure for inefficiency, mismanagement, and political mischief on the part of the present commission in general and Boland in particular, and for the "injustice" in Borglum's present "crooked contract."

By the time Norbeck learned all this, Borglum had already so muddied the congressional waters with his bill that the senator found himself unable to do very much for his own. Therefore, he wrote to Borglum: "I will not even start until you quit, for you will not harmonize your plans with anyone else."

In response Borglum sent Norbeck a copy of his proposed bill, together with a letter explaining in pungent detail the evils the bill was supposed to correct.

"The more I read his letter," Norbeck observed, " the more I see the impossibility of getting anywhere with him."

Thinking that perhaps a face-to-face conversation might do some good, Norbeck then called Borglum at the Metropolitan Club and asked him to come to his office on June 5 for a visit. Borglum agreed, but when the day came, he failed to show up. Instead he sent a special messenger bearing a copy of a letter he had written to the chairman of the Rushmore commission. In its ten pages the sculptor covered a great deal of ground. The part that Norbeck took note of concerned Borglum's strong intimation that if he did not receive a new administrative setup at Rushmore, a fairer contract for himself, and immediate payment of what he claimed was about $14,000 in overdue fees,* he just might leave Rushmore to take up "new work elsewhere crowding upon me."

Judging by what he then wrote to Boland, Norbeck's reaction was hardly what Borglum would have wanted: "Borglum might do like Tucker—he might 'resign,' which would clarify the situation. . . . We could put a new artist at work. . . . It would make us a new complication, but once we get going we probably would be glad for the change."

---

* Rushmore's books show that, at that time, Borglum had been paid all fees due him.

In promoting his own bill, meanwhile, Norbeck had decided to try to enlist the support of the president himself. But that proved to be easier decided than done. "I have been trying for three days to get an appointment at the White House," he noted. "These Democrats all want Republican help, but they are almost afraid to have a Republican be seen around their place."

Twelve days later Norbeck did meet with the president, and presented his case so effectively that Mr. Roosevelt sent him a letter saying: "Your description of the work . . . and its inspirational value to our people . . . convinces me of the need for legislation to authorize an additional appropriation of $200,000."

Armed with this, Norbeck proceeded to introduce his bill. He was worried, however, by opposition from the influential Senator Alben Barkley of Kentucky. But as Norbeck later told Boland, Borglum took care of Barkley.

> Borglum wanted to see Barkley and I gave him the job. . . . I'm glad
> he took it. . . . The next time I saw Barkley he said, "I should feel
> awfully bad if Borglum is not permitted to finish this undertaking."
>
> . . . "Believe it or not," Borglum has done much to sell the National
> Memorial to Congress. . . . It is not the uphill work that we had
> before to get anywhere.

During the dictation of that letter Norbeck was interrupted by a special messenger bringing him another letter from Borglum. In this one the sculptor made it clear that he, too, was aware of his having some influence in Congress, and because of it he now was flexing his muscles. Specifically, he wanted a new contract ("something in writing right away") allowing him a larger fee for carving Rushmore. If he did not get it, he said, he would recommend to Congress that Norbeck's pending Rushmore bill "be set aside." But this letter, too, did not affect Norbeck in the way Borglum must have intended. For, in now concluding his letter to Boland, Norbeck said: "He takes the joy out of my life by making impossible suggestions. I am not going to draw any contract, nor be a party to same until after this bill becomes law."

And, having said that, the senator then phoned Borglum and invited him to come dine that evening with him and Mrs. Norbeck.

From Norbeck's point of view, at least, it must have been a most successful get-together. In telling Boland about it, he said:

> I have the same experience as you do when I am with him—the
> more I am with him the better I can get along with him. . . . there is

no need of our letting [Rushmore] get out of the Commission's hands a second time. . . . The Commission must manage the undertaking, [but] I think that with more conferences with the sculptor we can do it with less friction.

Even more important, less than a week after the dinner, Borglum left Washington and returned to his carving at Rushmore.

Assisted in the House by Congressman Theodore Werner (who had replaced Williamson), on August 29 Norbeck got his $200,000 funding bill passed, thereby giving the monument project a good chance of having at least two more years of life. Then, in another of those amazing bits of Norbeck legislative sleight of hand, he was able to get $20,000 of the money made immediately available, even though none of it had been appropriated yet.

And, with that crowning touch, the old warrior ended his last real battle, and won his last real triumph for Rushmore. There were still to be some smaller skirmishes for him to fight and win, but this was the last big one. He was weary now and ill. More ill than anyone but he, and perhaps Mrs. Norbeck, knew; and his days were growing short.

With the addition of that $20,000, there was almost $80,000 available for the season's work, and at the mountain they were spending accordingly. About fifty men were on the job—the largest crew so far—and they were making progress.

They developed a surface that summer on which to carve the face of Roosevelt, an operation that turned out to be even more nerve-wracking than locating the new Jefferson had been. Day after day they peeled away fissured stone to Jefferson's left, only to find each new surface as fissured as the one before it. They were excavating back toward the inside of the angle in the boomerang-shaped canyon behind the faces. There, 120 feet back from the cliff's original surface, they finally discovered good stone. And, just in time. Thirty feet more and they would have broken through into the canyon behind. Hence, even though today the face of Roosevelt appears to be carved on the solid mass of Rushmore Mountain, it actually is situated on the front of a thin granite wall.

Borglum also, that summer, developed a place for the Lincoln head. He located it where originally he had intended to carve the Entablature—across from Jefferson, on the north side of the vee formed by the excavation for the Roosevelt location.

Much work was done, also, on developing the features of Jefferson, and here a new problem was encountered—and conquered. In refining the shape of Jefferson's upper lip, the carvers struck a "chink"—the workmen's term for uncarvable flaws in the stone. This particular chink was a pocket of almost pure feldspar, not very big but very serious. If it were not eliminated Jefferson would wind up with a million-year-old cold sore. Borglum put Red Anderson and Joe Bruner (a stonecutter he had brought from Indiana) on the job. The way he had them solve it was this: first, they cut out the diseased stone and squared up the hole where it had been, thus producing a boxlike aperture about two feet long, ten inches wide, and ten inches deep; next, they retrieved from the muck pile a piece of good, solid granite and carefully shaped it into a block of the same dimensions as the hole. They carefully drilled two holes in the bottom of the cavity and two precisely corresponding holes in the back of—but not through—the granite block. Steel pins were placed in the holes in the cavity and anchored there by pouring molten sulphur around them. Molten sulphur was then poured into the holes in the block, and then the block was promptly shoved into the cavity where the pins encased in sulphur held it fast. Sulphur, when cooled, becomes almost as hard as granite. Finally, the crack surrounding the block was filled with molten sulphur. That was it. Jefferson's cold sore was permanently cured and so beautifully done that only a close-up examination reveals the patch. Amazingly enough, in all of the 12,000 or so square feet of fine-finishing on the monument, the only patch, even today, is that little area of less than two square feet on Jefferson's lip.

It was hot on the mountain that summer, and the warm weather lasted late into the fall. But, when it changed, it changed dramatically. With a normal high temperature of about fifty-five degrees and a normal low in the high twenties, the end of October in the Black Hills can be, and often is, a time of golden Indian summer. However, on October 30, 1935, the temperature in Rapid City plunged to eleven degrees, a record low for that date. It fell to six degrees on the 31st, to two degrees on November 3, and to zero on November 4—all were records. After four record low temperatures in five days, Borglum and Boland figured Someone must be trying to tell them something, so they shut the job down for the year. It was just as well, for the bank account was also sliding down toward zero.

Less than a month later, Tallman resigned as superintendent. In a letter to the commission he stated his reasons:

. . . My duties at the mountain are no longer that of Superintendent and I feel it is unfair to the Commission for me to continue . . .
when Mr. Borglum has reduced my work to that of timekeeper and clerk to order supplies according to his demands. . . . As Mr. Borglum

maintains the feeling he has toward the Commission as a whole and toward certain of its individual members, it is very difficult to work with him as an employee of the Commission.

My second year here I was made Superintendent. [when] other business called Mr. Borglum away . . . I was left to carry out the work according to his instructions. . . . Both in letters to me and for publication, Mr. Borglum complimented me on the handling of the men and the direction of the work. . . .

Last year, Mr. Borglum no longer believed I was able to direct the work on the mountain. He accused me of willfully interfering with his orders and hindering the progress of the work. He accused me of being so friendly with Mr. John A. Boland, whom he believed to be working against him, that he could not trust me. From the way he spoke of the Commission, his attitude seemed to be that he had little regard for many of its members and as much as possible would ignore them. . . . finally he posted a notice informing the men that I was no longer in charge of the work on the mountain. . . . I am of the impression he did not notify the Commission [of this]. . . . Perhaps I should have resigned at that time but I needed my salary badly. . . .

As to Mr. Borglum's accusations—my capability is a matter of opinion . . . but I deny that I have ever willfully interfered with his orders or hindered the progress of the work. . . . He has failed to sight [sic] a specific instance and I know of none. I have at all times carried out his orders . . . even though I might have disagreed with his judgment in issuing them. I cannot deny my friendship with Mr. Boland because he has been most helpful and just to me, and has to the best of my knowledge done all in his power to cooperate with Mr. Borglum and further the work on Mt. Rushmore. I prize his friendship because he has the reputation with all whom I know, with the one exception of Mr. Borglum, of being most honest and capable. . . .

I value highly the association I have had with Mr. Borglum and the members of the Commission. . . . I shall be as happy as any one connected with the work on the day of the final unveiling for . . . I am proud of the part I have had in it. . . .

Respectfully yours, William S. Tallman
cc: Gutzon Borglum, John A. Boland

Borglum's view of the matter was, of course, somewhat different. He had brought Tallman to Rushmore as a "straight, honorable boy," he said. But in Dakota, Tallman, like Tucker before him, had been "corrupted" by "evil influences in Rapid City," and consequently had "gone to pieces."

In any case, Tallman's going left a gap to be filled, and Boland and Borglum, independently, each arrived at the idea of having the National Park Service send someone to fill it. Their ideas on the *kind* of "someone," however, were not the same.

Borglum wanted someone who would take charge of timekeeping and other clerical details and who would be willing, he stressed to a Park Service representative, to take orders from him. Or, he wanted someone to replace John Boland. Or both.

Boland, on the other hand, wanted someone strong enough and qualified enough to act as project superintendent in the fullest sense of the word— someone who would, in fact, take control of the work on behalf of the National Park Service. Boland said he just had to get the Park Service to assume some authority in the project, because "I couldn't sleep nights. Borglum was driving me crazy."

In February, Boland went to Washington to see about getting the National Park Service to send such a man to Rushmore, and immediately he ran into hard sledding. Borglum had continued to pepper the Park Service with letters describing his problems with "left over politicians" in the Black Hills: "the clique and cabal in Rapid City that corrupts what it can control and kills what it cannot control," and Senator Norbeck, "who would sell his mother for a vote." After reading that correspondence the N.P.S. Superintendent of Memorials, John Nagle, had decided he would just about as soon drop one of his engineers into a pot of boiling water as to assign him to Rushmore. Accordingly, he turned Boland down. Boland, however, would not be denied. He kept going back until, during their fourth visit, Nagle finally gave in and agreed to send an engineer who would be instructed, he said, "to supervise technical phases of the work, and thereby relieve Borglum of such duties and permit him to devote his time and efforts to the artistic features."

Accompanied by his wife and four rambunctious young sons, National Park Service engineer Julian Spotts came to the Black Hills on June 29, 1936, which was one of the hottest days in the hottest summer the West River country of Dakota had ever recorded. He came driving a brand new Ford V-8 with a house trailer hitched behind it. And he came wondering if he had been out of his mind when, back in March, he had accepted assignment to Mount Rushmore.

At the time it was made, the offer had seemed most appealing. As an engineer he had been intrigued by the challenge of Rushmore, and as an outdoorsman he had been intrigued by what he heard about the Black Hills.

At the moment, however, he was having some second thoughts. The plains he was crossing were treeless and sun-parched and brown. The highway was alternately hard-surfaced and graveled, but with gravel predominating. The graveled stretches were washboarded and rough from heavy use— this being the height of the tourist season—and they were narrow, and each car Spotts met trailed a cloud of choking dust. The boys, restless as caged chipmunks anyhow, had become whiny and fretful from long traveling. A hot prairie wind caused the trailer to sway and slue behind the car. Grasshoppers, riding the wind in arcing flights, spattered on the windshield and lodged in the radiator grill where they caused the engine to overheat.

At Murdo, 150 miles east of the Hills, the Spotts family stopped for gas and water and learned that although it was not yet noon the temperature already had reached 106 in the shade, assuming shade could be found. To top it all off, when they were ready to leave Murdo, the Ford's engine would not turn over. Its overheated pistons had "frozen" in their cylinders, and they had to cool before the engine could be started. "And at that point," Spotts recalled years later, "I was ready to turn around and go back, only the trip back would have been even longer and hotter than the one still ahead."

In mid-afternoon they arrived at last in Rapid City, and parked in the front of the big false-fronted frame building that housed the Rapid City Implement Company. There Julian Spotts and John Boland met for the first time.

Boland liked the reports he had had on the young engineer. In the ten years since his graduation from the University of Missouri, Spotts had successfully carried out several major Park Service assignments, among them that of chief designer and engineer in residence for the construction of Arlington-Memorial Bridge in Washington, D.C. Also, and most important for Rushmore, Spotts had supervised government quarrying work and had come to know granite so well that for a time he had served as inspector of granite purchased for Federal building projects. Now, Boland found, he also liked what he saw. Spotts—tall and lean and prematurely balding—was soft-spoken, unassuming, and quietly genial. But Boland sensed that behind that unassuming geniality there was a spine of steel. And this in his opinion was the most essential of all equipment for a Rushmore superintendent to have.

Because money from the new appropriation could not be used until the start of the government's fiscal year on July 1, Boland told Spotts that work at the mountain had not yet begun. Nor was Borglum yet in the Hills. He had intended to be. He had planned to come directly from a recently completed lecture tour in the Southwest, but instead he had had to return to his home in Connecticut, where vandals had broken in and stolen many valuable art objects and smashed many others. Now, however, Borglum supposedly was somewhere on the road and was expected at any time.

Next, the Spotts family drove to Keystone, where, in a pine-shaded campground, they unhitched their trailer. Leaving his family laughing and splashing in the chilly waters of Grizzly Creek, Spotts then drove up the mountain to look over the Rushmore operation.

He went to Rushmore that day as a tourist. Announcing himself to no one, he simply wandered around asking questions and sizing things up. On the following day he did the same thing. On the third day he went back again, but this time he was being taken by Boland to meet Borglum.

A number of stories have been told about that meeting, and some of them have made it out to have been a pretty spicy encounter. In recalling it two years later, while testifying before a congressional committee, Borglum said: "The first thing I knew was when a Park Service man walked in with the local political leader, and within five minutes he said, 'Now, I understand I am to hire and fire everybody.'" Borglum, so he told the committee, then replied:

> I take it you have carved the sides of mountains, and that you know a carver when you see him; you know, of course, the kind of tools that are needed, and you know the kind of power that is required . . . the wages that should be paid . . . and so forth.
>
> I know perfectly well that you do not know anything about these things; I know that you have never seen this mountain . . . until two minutes ago. . . . I know that you have not the remotest idea of what is going on, and that you have no judgment or experience to bring to bear on anything connected with it.

Spotts's memory of it was somewhat different. "I don't remember saying anything like that," he told this author in 1977. "Of course, it was a long time ago and I might have. But if I did it would have been only as a joke about all this new responsibility I was supposed to be taking on. And, as for Borglum, I remember him as having been very courteous and cooperative at that meeting."

Borglum and Spotts did start out working in harmony, in any case, and for a short time Borglum appeared to be very pleased with the engineer's accomplishments.

Carving began on July 7 and continued through October 30, much of it being performed under working conditions that could only be called vicious. In neither the white man's records nor the Indians' legends was there mention of a summer as hot and dry as that of 1936. Temperatures in July averaged a full ten degrees above normal, and in August and September they averaged five degrees above. But those were twenty-four-hour averages. Midday averages exceeded normal by twice that and sometimes even more. Thermometer readings of 105 were not uncommon in Rapid City that summer, and they reached 110—and 115, at least once—out on the plains. Just what temperatures the men endured on Rushmore cliff, where the sun's heat not only beat down on their backs but also was reflected into their faces from the fresh white stone, heaven only knows. Often as not the stone was too hot for the bare hand to touch, and there were times when the men could work on the cliff only in limited stretches interspersed with relief periods. No matter how much water a man drank on such days, it was never enough; and in the evening he would go home dust-coated and dehydrated and feeling, as an old saying had it, "as dry as a lime-burner's hat."

Nevertheless, they kept plugging away. Suspended in air blue-hazed and pungent from great fires burning in the powder-dry forest to the north and west, they worked so effectively on the hot cliff that Borglum was later to pronounce the 1936 season as having been the most efficient and productive one so far. Fifteen thousand tons of granite were removed from Rushmore that year; enough to pave a four-acre field with blocks one foot thick. The greatest part of it was removed from Washington's chest, from under Jefferson's chin, and from roughing out Lincoln's forehead, eyebrows, and nose. The greatest effort, however, was spent in refining the Jefferson face, which Borglum was hurrying to make ready for a late summer dedication by President Roosevelt.

In 1932, traditionally Republican South Dakota had slipped for the first time into the Democratic column, and in this election year of 1936 the president was coming to try to keep her there. During his visit Mr. Roosevelt had agreed, at Borglum's request, to attend the dedication of the Jefferson head.

The ceremony was to be held on August 30, which was a Sunday, and Borglum had set it for noon because, "any later than that the figure will be in shadow and its features somewhat obscured." Then, on the 29th, Borglum was told that the president would not meet that schedule. Instead, he planned to attend morning services at Emmanuel Episcopal Church in Rapid City, have lunch with local Democratic leaders at the Alex Johnson, and *then* go out to Rushmore. But, when Mr. Roosevelt's special train pulled into Rapid City on the evening of the 29th, his staff discovered that *Borglum* did not intend to meet the *president's* schedule. As the afternoon *Rapid City Journal* explained it:

> Gutzon Borglum . . . notified late today of a change in plans which will delay the President's arrival at the monument until approximately 2:30 PM, said the unveiling of the Jefferson figure will be carried out as scheduled—at noon.

Unbelievable as it seems, there can be no doubt that Borglum really expected the president again to change his plans so as to meet the sculptor's timetable. In their book, *Borglum's Unfinished Dream*, Lincoln Borglum and June Culp Zeitner tell how Borglum, waiting at the mountain on dedication morning, "could scarcely conceal his irritation" when eleven-thirty passed, and then noon, with "still no sign of the President." And William Williamson, a member of a delegation waiting to greet Mr. Roosevelt, said Borglum did not conceal his irritation. In his diary he quoted the sculptor as having declared at one point that he was "going to go ahead with the dedication and let the President go to———!"

Borglum did wait, even so, and the president did show up—exactly when he said he would. Williamson, Republican that he was, had something to say about that, too: "We did our best to stir up a bit of real enthusiasm for him, but the cheering and applauding was very mild and indifferent it seemed to me. It looks as though the popularity of the President in these parts is waning, and the New Deal is slipping." Senator Norbeck was present, viewing for the last time the monument that probably could not have been built without him. His cancer was well advanced now, but he still was trying to go on with his senatorial duties for as long as he possibly could. (Forty years later his example would be followed by another native Dakotan—a young man whose home was only seventy miles from Norbeck's and who was a student at the University of Minnesota—Hubert Humphrey.) Norbeck was mute now; cancer of tongue and jaw had robbed him of the power of speech. To conceal its outward ravages he had grown a beard, and in addition was wearing a towel-like wrapping around his neck. In describing Norbeck on that dedication day, Williamson wrote: "One can hardly recognize the Senator, he is so changed by his illness. . . . He was remarkably cheerful, however, and his eyes twinkled as of yore when he would hand you a brief note calling your attention to something humorous or clever. . . ."

When the president's automobile had been moved into position in front of the reviewing stand, from the stand itself Gutzon's daughter, Mary Ellis,

51. *President Franklin Delano Roosevelt speaking from his car at the unveiling of the Jefferson head, August 30, 1936. Among the dignitaries on the platform is Senator Norbeck (first row, second from the right), bearded and with a scarf to conceal the effects of his cancer.*

waved a flag. Up on the mountain Lincoln Borglum pressed a button, detonating five charges of dynamite. The boom of the pointing machine on the Jefferson head slowly swung to one side, carrying with it the huge flag that had been draped over Jefferson's face.

Then Borglum declared in a ringing voice:

I want you, Mr. President, to dedicate this memorial as a shrine to democracy; to call upon the people of this earth for one hundred thousand years to come, to read the thought and to see what manner of men struggled here to establish self-determining government in the western world.

I would ask this vast audience here, the people everywhere, to join in such a prayer.

Earlier, Mr. Roosevelt had said he would not speak. However, Borglum's appeal was too powerful to be ignored. Accordingly, he responded:

. . . I had seen the photographs, I had seen the drawings, and I had talked with those who are responsible for this great work, and yet I had no conception, until about ten minutes ago, not only of its magnitude, but also of its permanent beauty and importance.

. . . I think that we can perhaps meditate on those Americans of ten thousand years from now . . . meditate and wonder what our descendants—and I think they will still be here—will think about us. Let us hope . . . that they will believe we have honestly striven every day and generation to preserve a decent land to live in and a decent form of government to operate under.

Roosevelt and Borglum could not have known that day just how timely their comments were, for they could not yet have known just how soon and how severely democracy and self-determination and "a decent form of government" were to be challenged by the growing dictatorships of Europe. There were some indications of the coming challenge, however—some straws in the international wind—and upon returning from Rushmore to Rapid City that evening, President Roosevelt saw another of them. It was a message for him that read: "The American destroyer, USS Kane, 38 miles off the Spanish coast, has been bombed by an unidentified plane. The destroyer returned the fire. Neither was hit."

Julian Spotts, meanwhile, after establishing himself in a "six-by-six cubbyhole of an office" in the Rushmore restaurant building, had turned his attention to the power problem that had been bothering Borglum for so long.

Just how much power Rushmore needed was a matter of opinion. Borglum had always argued that it was much more than Keystone Consolidated Mines could furnish. Rushmore should have its own generators, he kept saying. Then they could put more drillers to work and finish the monument much more quickly and efficiently. Boland always countered by saying they had never had enough money to operate full-time even with their present power. Hence, why tie up money in a power plant just to work a larger crew for shorter periods of time? That not only would be silly, it would be unfair to the present employees. Boland and Borglum did agree, however, on the need to correct the irregularity of their present power supply. Most of the time they received enough power to operate well over twenty jackhammers, which was all they could afford to operate. But at times of peak load on the Keystone

52. South Dakota governor Tom Berry, President Roosevelt, and Gutzon Borglum at the dedication of the Jefferson head.

Consolidated system they received power for no more than sixteen hammers, thus putting several drillers temporarily out of business. Boland had suggested they might at least partially solve the problem by "tightening up" on losses in the Rushmore distribution system, but Borglum said that was impossible. ("I've checked everything from Keystone to the drills . . . and losses have been corrected.") Nonetheless, Spotts set out to check the system again, and at the same time to solve the mystery of a large power loss suffered at Rushmore every Monday morning.

He found leaking joints in the line carrying air from the compressors to the mountain, and applied a compound that rusted them shut. He discovered that the blacksmith had tapped the line with a nozzle that cooled him with compressed air while he worked, and Spotts stopped that. These two corrections raised the minimum number of hammers that could be operated simultaneously to nineteen—a gain of nineteen percent. And the Monday morning power loss? "Well, I found that just about every woman in Keystone washed clothes on Monday, and a lot of them had electric washing machines." Not being disposed to try changing the laundry habits of Keystone's ladies, he instead asked the commission to purchase a portable gasoline-driven auxiliary compressor. That increased to twenty-two the minimum number of jackhammers that could be operated. "And after that," Spotts recalled, "we had no more power problems."

Next, he checked the water supply—pumped from a spring in Lafferty Gulch—and found it badly contaminated. Locating a pure water supply in a more distant spring, he ordered Rushmore's water hauled from there.

Then he went to work on the overhead tramway. Borglum, wishing to spare the crew their long climb up the mountain every morning, had been asking for years to have the tramway made safe for carrying men, but so far nothing had been done about it. Now Spotts checked it over and found it to be plenty strong enough. The only danger was that if the cage should break free from the haulage line that controlled it, it would coast down the steep carrier cable and crash against the hoist-house at a speed that would kill or cripple anyone in it. Accordingly, the engineer designed and installed a brake that would engage automatically whenever the cage traveled faster than a certain speed; he added a manual control for use if the automatic feature should fail, and pronounced the tramway safe for passengers.

At the same time Spotts had straightened out and taken over handling all those paperwork details that Borglum had found so maddening. Hence, all things considered, it would seem that Borglum and Spotts would have been getting along famously. As it happened, however, just the opposite was true.

Spotts, Borglum had found, was determined to do exactly what he had been engaged to do. In the conduct of those operations, moreover, Spotts would neither take orders from the sculptor nor be intimidated by him. To Borglum, who during Tallman's superintendency had become accustomed to running things his own way, this was a disgusting turn of events. Accordingly, he again raised his voice to the National Park Service, declaring that it had tied his hands unpardonably, and that he could not do anything without first having to "consult that two-by-four engineer . . . that brainless jellybean."

They clashed over the matter of project planning and reports, and in this they both had justifiable complaints. Governments ever have been prone to demand for their projects elaborately detailed plans together with voluminous reports on how a job is to be done, is being done, and has been done. Spotts, as government's representative, was required to demand these things from Borglum. In the beginning the commission, too, had demanded from Borglum job plans and timetables for use in preparing budgets; then they had merely requested them; and finally they had given up even asking. Borglum did plan his work, it was true, but his were great sweeping plans, spontaneously made, generally stated, and rarely followed. He had to do it that way, he said, because he was an artist and the plans of artists must remain flexible and free-flowing. Thus, he could not give government a precise date for the finishing of Washington's chin nor the beginning of Lincoln's nose. He did not see how government would be benefited by knowing how many man-hours were being spent in carving Jefferson's eye, or by receiving a report on same after it had been done. What it took to do a job was whatever it took, and he could see no reason to keep track of it either during the job or afterward.

Spotts demanded these things, nonetheless, with results that were unsatisfactory to both. Borglum, forced to plan more than he wanted to, complained that Spotts was interfering with his art.

They clashed also over the hiring and firing of personnel. As he was supposed to do, Spotts had insisted upon approving the qualifications of new employees and upon doing the actual hiring. Borglum said this too was interference with his art. He said the engineer was unsuited for hiring the men because he had "never carved a mountain." Consequently, Spotts assured him in a memo that the sculptor would have the final say on hiring men to work on the actual carving: "It is not the policy of the National Park Service to place employees under your supervision who do not meet with your approval." Nonetheless, Borglum continued to protest that he was not being allowed to choose the men who worked under his direction, but because he so obviously was being allowed to choose them he did not protest too loudly. What he did protest loudly was being told he no longer could fire employees. He had never had the authority to do that, of course, because Rushmore's employees did not work for him but for the commission. Even so, he had been doing it anyhow, and getting away with it. But, as Spotts pointed out, Rushmore workers now were covered by Federal employment regulations, and a discharged employee could demand a hearing of his case. If the hearing disclosed his discharge to have been made improperly, he could demand to be reinstated. Obviously, any discharge of a worker by Borglum would be improper because it would be made without authority. Therefore, said Spotts (and Boland), in the future Borglum could recommend the firing of any employee, but that was all. The final disposition of the matter would be up to Spotts. Borglum found this almost too much to bear. He took it as unwarranted meddling in his work, an affront to his judgment, said it was an "unlawful usurpation" of his authority and that it would force him to put up with workers who had been "insubordinate" to him. He stated his case in a letter to the Superintendent of Monuments, John Nagle, and said he was being compelled to suffer "petty bureaucratic entanglements" despite the fact that "I have forgotten more about this than most men can learn." Which caused Nagle to scribble on the letter's margin, "Could he have forgotten *too* much?"

Nor had Borglum forgotten Boland and the commission. He continued to attack both and to insist that they owed him money that they would not pay. This, in turn, led to a National Park Service audit of Boland's books. The audit showed them to be in order, and that Borglum had been paid everything his contract called for. Still, the sculptor persisted, causing Williamson to observe that since the visit of President Roosevelt Borglum's "ego has grown until one wonders that one head can hold it all." Someone ought to "take him in hand," Williamson continued, saying that Norbeck should be the one to do it because, "if any of the rest of us were to do so he would explode."

Unfortunately, Norbeck had taken Borglum in hand for the last time. On December 20, at his home in Redfield, the senator quietly passed away. He had not lived to see Rushmore completed, but he had lived long enough to make its future secure. Without a Norbeck there would not have been a Rushmore. As much as Borglum himself, Senator Peter Norbeck had been Rushmore's indispensable man.

23. Dedication of Lincoln— No Room for Susan B. Anthony

Considering that Borglum's Rushmore activities alone were keeping him busy as a fiddler's elbow, it is hard to see how he ever found time to execute other sculptural assignments as well. He did, though, and one of the pieces thus produced was scheduled to be unveiled in Paris on January 29, 1937.

It was a statue of the inspirational pamphleteer of the American Revolution Thomas Paine, but it was being erected in France because Paine also had been mixed up in the French Revolution. In late 1936, Borglum sent his plaster casts of the Paine work to Paris, where the Rudiers foundry was to cast the final statue in bronze, and then gild it. Borglum followed in January to attend the unveiling, only to discover that he had been led on a transoceanic goose chase. Rudiers had not yet even cast the statue; hence the unveiling could not take place.* What Borglum said to those responsible for this situation seems not to be known, but he would have been justified in saying plenty. It is known, however, that while in Paris he had dinner with Helen Keller, took her to "see" with her fingertips the sculptures of his old mentor Rodin, and was told by her (as he remembered it later), "Meeting you is like a visit from the gods." Then he returned home to see about making a new contract with the Mount Rushmore National Memorial Association.

He had long wanted to secure a new contract, of course, but now it had

---

* At the close of World War II the finished cast of Borglum's *Paine* was discovered in a Rudiers storeroom. On January 29, 1948, it was unveiled in Paris in a park near the American Building at City University.

become imperative that he do so. The reason was a clause in his old contract that read: "The ASSOCIATION agrees to pay the SCULPTOR . . . an honorarium of 25% upon the actual cost of the work . . . but in no case shall such fee or fees exceed [$87,500]." Now Borglum was dangerously close to that ceiling. By the beginning of 1937 he had received Rushmore fees totaling $85,700. Therefore, if he expected to get more than $1,800 from Rushmore in the future he *had* to have a new contract.

Back in 1935, Norbeck and Boland had seen this problem coming and had suggested replacing the sculptor's old contract with a new one that put no ceiling on his fees. At that time, however, Borglum would have none of it. Not, that is, unless the new contract also gave him control of the Rushmore job and increased his honorarium to at least thirty percent. Norbeck and Boland, in turn, would have none of that. Thus deadlocked, the matter had been allowed to sleep, but now it could sleep no longer.

To get the ball rolling, Borglum drafted his own version of what the new contract should be. Under its terms he would be given:

(1) Authority to finish the four presidential figures, carve the Entablature, and hollow out within the mountain a great Hall of Records.

(2) Reimbursement for expenses he had incurred in the past while promoting Rushmore. (His proposed contract did not specify the amount of these expenses, but orally he was saying it came to $14,000 or $30,000 or $16,00 or $80,000, depending on when and to whom he said it.)

(3) Authority over all activities at the mountain and over the purchasing of project equipment and materials, and authority to determine the size and composition of the crew, to hire and fire, and to set salaries.

(4) A sculptor's fee of thirty percent of the cost of the job.

In the early summer the commission produced its own version of a new Borglum contract, and from the sculptor's point of view it was all bad news.

It made no provision for the Entablature and Hall of Records, even though he considered these to be essential elements of the memorial.

It made no provision for reimbursing him for the past out-of-pocket promotional expenses he was claiming.

It gave him no additional conrol over the Rushmore job. On the contrary, it defined the limits of his authority even more rigidly, thereby clipping his wings even further. On top of that, in an effort by the commission and Park Service to force him to make and follow meaningful working plans, they had written into the contract the following: "To the end [of accomplishing] early and orderly completion of all the work . . . the several operations shall be begun and completed in the sequence indicated by a program of operations to be drawn up by the Commission with the advice and counsel of the sculptor, and to be approved by the Secretary of the Interior."

Acceptance of these provisions, all of them contrary to what he had wanted, was a bitter pill for Borglum to swallow. He believed them to be shortsighted and unjust. In his opinion Rushmore without the Entablature and Hall of Records would be but half a monument; if he had not spent all that money on lobbying trips to Washington and other promotional activities the Rushmore project could not have survived; and, unless all project operations were placed under the control of the one man who knew how to carve mountains, the mountain never would be carved.

He did accept the terms, nonetheless. He had no choice. The commission and Park Service held all the aces. Without their approval there would be no new contract. Without a new contract he could receive no more pay from Rushmore. One thing he was determined not to accept, however, was a sculptor's fee of less than thirty percent.

At first it appeared that he would not be asked to accept less. Commission chairman Fred Sargent said Borglum deserved thirty percent and was for letting him have it. William Williamson, frugal though he was, thought so too. Boland, on the other hand, was just as determined to prevent the increase as Borglum was to obtain it. Consequently, the negotiations now became a head-to-head battle between Boland and Borglum.

In organized form, the case Borglum presented was this:

The standard fee for this sort of work was, at a minimum, thirty percent of the cost of the job and more often was thirty-five percent. Borglum had agreed to accept twenty-five percent only because the commission had agreed to have Tucker do all the Rushmore work excepting that which Borglum, alone, could do. Originally, the commission had offered him a higher fee (though he never said how much higher). However, when Tucker insisted upon receiving $10,000 a year instead of $7,500, Borglum had voluntarily reduced his own fee to make up the difference.

When Tucker resigned, he had been replaced successively by Denison, Tallman, and now Spotts—none of whom were competent to do what Tucker had been hired to do. Consequently, Borglum had been forced to take over those extra duties himself, and for eight years had been burdened by them.

Denison had cost the commission $6,000 a year less than Tucker, and Tallman $7,000 less. Spotts was costing the commission nothing; his salary was paid by the Park Service. These enormous savings had been possible only because of the extra burden Borglum had assumed. And yet, the commission had never seen fit to pass a dime of those savings on to him.

Accordingly, said the sculptor, he thought it only right that the commission now pay him something for all that extra work in the past, and he *demanded* to be paid for it in the future. Proper future payment, he said, would be a thirty-five percent fee, but for the good of Rushmore he would accept thirty percent.

It was a strong set of arguments. But as might be expected, Boland met it with a strong set of counterarguments:

Borglum had been talking for years about how he had voluntarily reduced his own fee so that Tucker could be hired, but no one else remembered it that way. In fact, Norbeck once even searched the records for evidence of it, but found none. On the contrary, the record showed that Borglum first had been offered a twenty-percent fee, and when he protested had been offered and had accepted the twenty-five-percent figure. The record showed also that Borglum had signed his twenty-five-percent contract before rather than after Tucker asked for more money, and that it was the commission and not Borglum who had met that demand.

True, said Boland, Tucker's leaving probably had increased Borglum's load. But by how much? Not as much, certainly, as the sculptor claimed. During every carving season he had been absent from the mountain as much as he had been present—much more during the present year—and yet the work had seemed to go forward about as well as when he was there. And might it not be that much of this burden Borglum was complaining about was caused not by necessity but by his compulsion to run the whole job instead of only his own part of it?

Also, Borglum had been complaining for years that because not enough money was being spent at Rushmore, his income had never come up to what he had expected when he took the job. True, it had not. But contrary to what he seemed to think, this was not because of negligence or skulduggery. It was one of the breaks of the game. Few people's incomes these days were up to their earlier expectations. For example, neither had Boland, when he bought the Rapid

City Implement Company, expected his farmer customers to be hit simultaneously by drought, grasshoppers, and the greatest depression in living memory. But it had happened, and Boland's income had suffered accordingly.

Borglum recently had referred to his income from Rushmore as "a pittance," and "the little money" he was getting, and had said that because of it he had, "starved, borrowed . . . been pinched to barely living expenses." But that might be a matter of definition. Since 1930, Borglum's earned "pittance" (and this did not include his receipt of a loan repayment, the balance of his deferred Mount Harney fees, or the interest on both) had averaged $11,500 per year, * and that was more than the salary of a United States senator. During the fiscal year now ending, Rushmore had paid him $15,500, * which was more than the salary of a United States vice-president. Moreover, these incomes were in addition to Borglum's other earnings from sculpture and lectures.

No, the real problem was not what Borglum earned but what he spent. He was taking in enough to place him in the top two percent or so of the country's wage earners, yet he was always broke. Might this be because his definition of "bare living expenses" included a chauffeur-driven Cadillac; almost incessant travel; staying in the finest accommodations; and the constant wining and dining of Very Important People?

Therefore, Boland concluded, it was no fault of the commission that Borglum was always broke. Increasing his honorarium would do no good because he would be broke no matter how much he was paid. Besides, Boland said, he did not want Borglum to continue to be paid on a percentage basis anyhow. "Borglum keeps no records," he said, and therefore "was always of the opinion his fee should be more than computed by this office." This had caused Borglum time and again to accuse him of mismanagement and even of dishonesty, and Boland was tired of it. Accordingly, he said, he would like to see Borglum paid a flat fee of, say, $10,000 per year (the equivalent, adjusted for taxes and inflation, of $84,000 in 1984), or perhaps even paid weekly for the time he actually spent on the job.

---

* After adjusting for inflation and modern tax rates, these were equivalent to 1984 before-tax earnings of about $94,000 and $140,000 respectively.

In making that last suggestion, Boland had gone too far. It infuriated the sculptor, and understandably so. Borglum was an independent artist, and Boland would have him reduced to the status of a hired hand. The commission agreed, and so the suggestion came to nothing. On the other hand, the commission also agreed not to increase the sculptor's honorarium above the present twenty-five percent.

These decisions all were distressing to Borglum, but they had not been arbitrarily made. The Entablature and Hall of Records were dropped because Congress had become increasingly unwilling to fund any work other than on the four presidential figures. The promotional activities for which Borglum was asking expense reimbursement had never been authorized by the commission; they consisted mainly of lobbying trips to Washington and extended stays at the Metropolitan Club there; they had been undertaken entirely on Borglum's own initiative, often in opposition to the commission's wishes and certainly to Norbeck's; also, Borglum had submitted no documented claim for them, and the figures he quoted kept changing from week to week. Borglum's authority at Rushmore had been further limited because the National Park Service as well as the commission believed he had proven as undertalented in business and administration as he was overtalented in art. And his honorarium had been held at twenty-five percent only partly because of Boland; the main reason was the opinion of Park Service officials that Secretary Ickes, who had no great love for either Borglum or Rushmore, would approve nothing higher.

Whatever the reasons, the new contract gave Borglum nothing he had asked for and even took away a little of what the old contract had given him. Nonetheless, he signed it. If he wanted to continue being paid for his work at Rushmore he had to. But he did so feeling cheated, betrayed, and determined to do whatever it took to get rid of Boland, the commission, and this contract they had forced upon him. And because he felt that way, Borglum's 1937 contract was to provide another major turning point in the development of Rushmore.

Meanwhile, in another of those timely coincidences that so often had saved the monument from possible oblivion, a new player had arrived on the Rushmore stage. He was a Black Hills native, former editor of the Hot Springs *Star* and the Custer *Chronicle*, a Rushmore enthusiast, and now a brand-new congressman—his name was Francis Case.

Rushmore had to have the aggressive support in Washington of at least one South Dakota congressman. Otherwise the monument had no more future than two bits in a crap game. Other congressmen might be favorable to the project, but it was not *their* project, and they could not be expected to furnish the dedication and effort required to keep it funded. That could be furnished only by Dakotans, and so far it had been, but only by two of them. Among all Dakota congressmen serving since the beginning of Rushmore, only Norbeck and Williamson had been willing and able to do those things necessary to keep it alive. Now even these two were gone—Williamson out of office and Norbeck dead. Providentially, however, just forty-seven days before Norbeck's death, Case had won a congressional seat.

He had not been expected to. According to the sages of the press, Roosevelt was to have carried the West River country by a wide margin and was to have swept the incumbent West River congressman back into office with him. As it happened, however, Roosevelt had just barely carried West River and with no coattails left for the incumbent to ride upon. Instead, Republican Case won the office, and Rushmore still had in Congress a Dakotan dedicated to its cause.

Borglum knew and liked Case, but had campaigned against him anyhow because, he said, "It would be the height of folly not to support the party that was supporting Rushmore and supporting me." Understandably, however, once Case had been elected, Borglum wanted to win him over to his side of the Rushmore controversies and to gain his support for a new sculptor's contract. Accordingly, he wrote letter after letter explaining to Case the tribulations he was suffering at the hands of Boland, Spotts, the commission, and the National Park Service.

Case, however, had been cast in the mold of Williamson—incorruptible, dryly practical, cautious. He would not buy a horse without first having examined its teeth, and he would not take sides in any Rushmore dispute until he understood that dispute. He took no stock in Borglum's accusations of Boland; he knew Boland too well for that. On the other hand, he liked and admired Borglum, and both for that reason and the good of Rushmore he wanted to keep the sculptor as happy as possible. Hence he responded to Borglum's letters by praising him for his accomplishments and encouraging him in his work, but never supported, refuted, or even commented on the sculptor's various complaints. Also, Case did not allow himself to become entangled in the negotiation of Borglum's new contract.

Instead, Case gained his Rushmore initiation, in cooperation with the National Park Service, in securing a $50,000 appropriation for the monument. Added to the $34,000 Boland had on hand from the past year, this assured ample carving funds for the 1937 season.

At about that same time, Case became unwillingly embroiled in discussions regarding another, most unusual, Rushmore bill. No one connected with Rushmore had had anything to do with the drafting or sponsoring of this bill, or had even been consulted on it. Promoted by the Equal Rights for Women organization and the Susan B. Anthony Forum, and introduced in Congress by Senators Capper of Kansas and Keller of Illinois, the bill called for carving on Rushmore a fifth figure—a portrait of Susan B. Anthony.

The bill brought no joy to Borglum or Case. They were, they quickly assured each other, all in favor of equal rights for women and they had nothing at all against Miss Anthony. However, it already was hard enough to get money out of Congress for carving figures of non-controversial presidents. If the group were expected to include the controversial suffragette, it well might become impossible. Besides, Rushmore was a monument to United States presidents, and Miss Anthony had never been president.

Borglum thought if the proposition were ignored it might go away. "Pay no attention to it," he wrote to Case. "I would brush it aside as I would an annoying fly on a wet day." If instead "it comes to a real fight," he added, "there will be no question of my position." At the same time, however, he hoped this potential hot potato could be handled by Case alone while allowing the sculptor himself to lie low and not take a stand on it.

For a scrapper who never flinched from controversy this was entirely out of character, but Borglum had his reasons. Since dining at the White House during the Entablature contest, and, later, having persuaded President Roosevelt to attend the Jefferson dedication, Borglum had come to believe himself and the Roosevelts to be personal friends. He believed also that he had their unqualified support for his work at Rushmore. Such being the case, he wanted to do nothing that might offend or estrange them . . . and Eleanor Roosevelt was a solid supporter of the Susan B. Anthony bill. Therefore, he told Case: "There is nothing more that I had better say at this time. I mean, I had better not express any opinion. [But] for your own information there isn't the stone on the mountain where the group is for another head. . . ."

As it turned out, they had had no cause for concern anyhow. Congress solved the problem for them. It attached to the current Rushmore appropriation a stipulation that the money could be spent only on figures already begun. Even though no congressman would admit it (half their constituents being women), it was rumored that this restriction was added because of the Susan B. Anthony bill. But, whatever the reason, the Anthony bill was never heard from again.

At the mountain, meanwhile, work was going forward better, perhaps, than ever before. There were several reasons.

One was that the workmen had received an increase in pay. Now, for example, carvers were receiving $1.25 per hour; assistant carvers, $1.00; senior drillers, 75¢; and junior drillers, 65¢. For an era when John L. Lewis was fighting for a wage of 25¢ per hour for mine workers and when the average steel mill worker earned less than $400.00 per year, this was excellent pay indeed, and the crew's morale was correspondingly high.

Another reason was Julian Spotts, whose original competence now had the reinforcement of his Rushmore experience of the past season.

And yet another was the fast-growing sculptural ability of Lincoln Borglum. Gutzon was absent when the 1937 carving began—in fact, throughout the season he would be absent more than present—but Lincoln was there to serve in his place. Lincoln had inherited from his father much sculptural talent, had grown up in the sculptural world, and now had behind him four years of solid Rushmore experience as pointer and then as chief pointer. Accordingly, he had developed in skill to the point where he could function most ably as project sculptor during his father's absences. Furthermore, he seems to have been able to work harmoniously with Spotts, which was something his father could not do.

The weather, too, cooperated with the Rushmore work that year. The winter had been frigid and the spring was unusually dry and cold. But May came softly with gentle warmth and occasional gentle rains. In the canyons aspen unfurled bright new leaves, the valleys grew carpets of wildflowers, and on the mountain the air was fresh with spring. June was gentle too. July was not gentle because July never is; but, this one was the coolest of any in the past five years.

On May 1, when work began, the Lincoln head consisted only of a roughed-out forehead and eye sockets and an irregular granite ridge of nose. Nonetheless, Borglum intended to have the head ready for dedication before summer's end. Considering all that remained to be done on the head, this presented Lincoln, Spotts, and the crew with a tremendous challenge. They met it, however, and met it so well that when Borglum finally returned to the mountain in late July he was moved to write to Case, "About the work, it is proceeding wonderfully well." It had proceeded so well, in fact, that the Lincoln head was ready for Borglum to give it, with his artist's touch, the refinement and character that even the most precise measurements and engineering could not give.

Therefore, Borglum now remained at the mountain to work in his true and undisputed kingdom—the realm of his creative mind and artist's skill. Others might challenge his competence in managing enterprises or handling

money. They might criticize his personality or statements or actions. But they never challenged his competence at carving mountains; nor criticized his ways of doing it. They could not, for in this he stood alone. Undisputed, unchallenged, one-of-a-kind—Borglum.

Constantly sketching in a notebook whose tooled leather covers were worn by time and use, he studied the Lincoln head in the angled light of dawn, the brightness of midday, the shadows of evening. He studied it from viewpoints in the canyon, Mount Doane, and the tramway cage. He viewed it from his studio window and, as ideas and inspirations came to him, he telephoned instructions from there to Lincoln Borglum on the mountain or even directly to carvers on the Lincoln head. Time and again he went to the mountain himself and with paint and brush marked details to be shaped; or, he took up drills and other tools and by his own carving demonstrated to the carvers how he wanted a particular task to be done.

Much of this time and study he devoted to Lincoln's eyes and to the special method by which he was to give them, as well as those of Rushmore's other figures, a lifelike quality rarely seen in sculpture.

Since the time man first began to carve figures in his own image he almost always has been defeated by the eyes. Smooth-carved, as many Greek masters carved them, they are blank and blind as the sides of billiard balls. And those in which the iris is represented by an engraved circle and the pupil by a round pit are dead eyes also, for still they lack the highlights of eyes that live.

At Rushmore Gutzon Borglum met and mastered that challenge. He mastered it with a technique made possible by the size of the figures and the distance from which they were to be viewed; but, that still would have been impossible had he not had the imagination to develop it and the skill to carry it out.

His first step was to carve in the center of the eye a ring, a "pupil," several feet across and deep enough always to be shadowed. Next, the stone center of the ring was carefully reduced and shaped to become a stubby, slightly rectangular, horizontal shaft measuring a foot-and-a-half or so on its vertical sides and slightly less across, and projecting from the back of the round hole outward to a point slightly beyond the surface of the eye, itself.

53. Driller Jack "Palooka" Payne preparing the site for the head of Lincoln.

Those stubby granite shafts are the key to the quality of the Rushmore figures' eyes. From a distance their white tips are not seen as rectangles of stone but as points of light—as highlights in the dark pupils that surround them—and give the eyes, and therefore the heads, the expression and character of life.

This process sounds simple. It was not. Far from it. It took daring to even attempt it, and it took great skill to execute it successfully. Projecting unsupported, the stone "highlight" shafts were vulnerable to breakage in carving, and if broken would have been difficult, if not impossible, to replace. The "pupils" in the eyes of each figure had to be precisely placed and uniformly angled, and the same was true of the "highlight" shafts within them. Any miscalculation, any miscarving, and the figure would wind up cockeyed.

As it happened, the work was done artfully, precisely, and with no breakage. And thus, by his imagination and skill Borglum gave to the eyes of these gigantic figures the expression and sparkle of life.

Borglum set the dedication of the Lincoln head for September 17, which was the 150th anniversary of the signing of the Constitution. He planned the ceremony also to be a commemoration of a "roll of honor" of men who had been important to Rushmore and now were dead. In addition to the more familiar names, his list included Dr. C. C. O'Hara, geologist and former president of the South Dakota School of Mines; Joseph Cullinan and Julius Rosenwald, former Rushmore commissioners; Bruce Yates, former general manager of the Homestake Mine, and Senator Coleman DuPont, both of whom had been responsible for large financial contributions; and Andrew Mellon, former Secretary of the Treasury.

On the eve of the dedication, Borglum gave a banquet for program participants, dignitaries, and various of his friends. One guest was Louella Jones, a willowy beauty, daughter of a South Texas rancher, niece of Commissioner Lorine Spoonts, and soon to become Mrs. Lincoln Borglum. Another was Robert Dean, owner-manager of KOBH, Rapid City's new (and only) radio station. And yet another was Lynn Brandt, a young NBC announcer who had come to do a network broadcast of the dedication.

The inevitable banquet speeches included "some good and some bad,"

54. The Lincoln head nearing completion, probably about 1940.
Notice the technique Borglum used to give highlights to the
eyes and, also, the irregular composition of the stone.

Robert Dean later recalled, "but the only one I remember was Brandt's. It was impressed on my mind forever by what happened the following day." In the part of the speech that Dean found so memorable, Brandt said: "My father is a minister, and he told me always to say a little prayer before a difficult broadcast and everything would turn out all right. I won't need to say a prayer this time. My prayer will be on that mountain tomorrow."

The dedication was held on a weekday rather than on a weekend and started at the early hour of ten in the morning. It was held at the very tailend of the tourist season, and it included no participants of national prominence. Accordingly, it should have been but lightly attended. In fact, however, just the opposite happened. When the ceremony started, the parking lot was full and cars were lined up for almost a mile back down the road.

The affair opened with Lynn Brandt giving the radio audience a description of the monument. Next, there were the customary speeches. Then came the climax.

Borglum stepped to the microphone and gestured for silence. Up on the top of Rushmore and unnoticed by the crowd, Fourth Cavalry bugler Henry Swift moved to the top of the Washington head where, bugle poised, he now stood at attention.

Borglum in a dramatically ringing voice cried out, "I will now call the roll of those whose understanding, sympathy, and instant aid has made this great memorial possible:

CALVIN COOLIDGE!
ANDREW MELLON!
COLEMAN DUPONT!
EDWARD RUSHMORE!
JULIUS ROSENWALD!
J. S. CULLINAN!
BRUCE YATES!
DR. O'HARA!
PETER NORBECK!

55. NBC announcer Lynn Brandt describing the dedication of the Lincoln head on September 17, 1937. He startled the crowd, and his radio listeners, by announcing that the head of Franklin Roosevelt soon would be carved on the mountain.

They are with the gods! We will keep their faith! We will carry on!"

There was a moment of silence. Then, from the top of the Washington head came the faraway sound of the bugler blowing Taps. Plaintive, distance-muted, drifting, it seemed not to break the silence but only to float through it, and the crowd was moved. "There were many tears," said Robert Dean. "Even my wife was sobbing quietly by my side." Borglum, too, was moved, and his voice choked as he went on to say:

Where greatness is promised, history and civilization will never forgive its absence or those responsible for its failure. . . . This monu-

56. The face of Theodore Roosevelt begins to take shape in late 1937.

ment has but a single purpose, to borrow a line from Lincoln's Gettysburg speech: "That these men shall not have lived in vain; that under God the nation they built shall have a new birth of freedom, and that a government of the people, by the people, and for the people shall not perish from the earth!"

From beneath the Lincoln head there came the dust and thunder of a dynamite blast . . . and another . . . and yet another.

The great flag enshrouding the head began to slide to one side, and Episcopal Bishop W. Blair Roberts stepped to the microphone:

Grant, oh Lord, that this monument which we here dedicate may be for all generations to come a reminder of the exalted patriotism and the pure, unselfish service which we owe to our country and to Thee.

The Fourth Cavalry band atop the Lincoln head and the Homestake band on Mount Doane together struck up the *Star Spangled Banner*, and again there was weeping in the crowd.

"A perfect dedication," everyone said later. Everyone, that is, but announcer Brandt, who had gotten his Roosevelts mixed up. "Next to Jefferson," he had announced, "is an aperture which, in a few years, will reveal the face of our present president, Franklin Delano Roosevelt." The crowd, startled, had shouted "No! No!" reported Robert Dean, "and Brandt quickly corrected himself. But the 'Franklin Delano' had gone out over the network, and millions of listeners had heard it."

At a Borglum reception that evening, Brandt was morosely nursing a drink and wondering if he still had a job, when Louella Jones came over to him. "Maybe, Honey-bunny," she said in the soft speech of South Texas, "you shoulda said that li'l 'ol prayer after all!" Unbeknownst to Brandt, however, Borglum already had taken steps to see that the young announcer did still have a job. In a wire to NBC the sculptor said Brandt should be forgiven his slip of the tongue because, after all, "We all make mistakes."

Once the Lincoln dedication was out of the way, Borglum turned his energies to other matters. He was now going to bring about some "constructive readjustments," he wrote to Francis Case. And if Case wondered what the sculptor meant by that, he did not have to wonder very long. For now Borglum began an all-out campaign to get rid of Spotts, Boland, the commission, the Park Service, and his present contract, and to gain for himself the complete control of Rushmore.

24. Borglum and Boland—
Immovable Object Moved

Much as Borglum wanted now to proceed with getting rid of the commission and his new contract, he needed first to see about getting paid for his past summer's work. The last of the fee authorized under his old contract had been paid to him in June, and he could receive no more until his new contract had been formally approved by Secretary Ickes.

Ickes approved it on November 7, but as far as his pay was concerned, Borglum discovered, that was a beginning and not an end. Now he had to submit through the proper channels a claim for his back pay. Prepared by Williamson and signed by Borglum, the claim was submitted to the commissioners in December, was approved by them in January, and was passed on to the National Park Service. By this time Borglum had been seven months without income from Rushmore, was again in trouble with his ranch mortgage, and was threatening to have the whole matter investigated by the United States Senate. To bail him out, in February the Mount Rushmore National Memorial Society (not the commission) advanced him a thousand dollars, and again the ranch was saved.

His claim, meanwhile, was drifting unhurriedly through the channels of bureaucracy—through the Park Service, to Secretary Ickes, to the comptroller general. In late March the claim finally was paid. It came to $10,594, but Borglum received only $7,946. Twenty-five percent ($2,648) went to Washington attorney John Harlan, whom the sculptor had engaged to speed up the settlement. Trying to follow a claim through the maze of government, however, is about like trying to track a rabbit through a rockpile. When it enters it disappears, never to be seen or heard from again until, in its own good time, it chooses to emerge. Hence, even though Harlan's efforts obviously were profitable to Harlan, it is hard to say whether or not they were of any real value to Borglum.

While all this was going on, Borglum also had been preparing his assault on the commission, the Park Service, and his new contract. Although probably not consciously, he had been doing it much as a nation prepares for a war—publicly proclaiming the righteousness of his cause, enlisting allies, and establishing an operating base from which to attack.

He had first begun publicizing his cause at the Lincoln dedication. There, in remarks broadcast by NBC and heard by millions, he had declared that it was his "bounden duty" to make of Rushmore "an immortal work of fine art that ranks with the best of Greece, Egypt, or Rome," but that so far he had "not been aided or permitted such aids as to assure" that result. Still, considering the handicaps he was being forced to work under, he thought he had been doing rather well:

> In its execution—without proper tools, without adequate power, without any trained assistants, it is an accomplishment without parallel in this or the old world. To date, ridiculous as it seems to any informed mind, what has been created here has been accomplished in spite of these aids. . . . We have literally driven a super-clipper into the stratosphere of noblest human aspiration on a crust and a gallon of gas, and that in spite of a resisting and unbelieving world.

In a Lincoln dedication booklet published for national distribution in the spring of 1938, the sculptor developed his case still further. In addition to his dedication-day remarks the booklet contains a separate statement in which Borglum goes on to say that Rushmore "was undertaken by the State [of South Dakota], which, however, failed to provide funds"*; that the work had been "definitely put in hand" only because at the 1927 dedication of the mountain, President Coolidge had authorized Borglum, personally, to go and obtain Federal money from Secretary of the Treasury Andrew Mellon**; that Borglum had found it necessary to take on more duties at Rushmore than he had contracted to perform, but that no compensating adjustment had ever

---

* The work was not undertaken by the state but by the Mount Harney Memorial Association, which was a private organization. Neither did the state ever accept, or imply that it would accept any financial responsibility for it.
** Actually, Borglum's visit with Mellon took place about seven months *before* the 1927 dedication and was not arranged by Coolidge but by Senator Norbeck.

been made in his contract; and, (again) that he was working under the "serious handicap" of having "no trained sculptor's assistants."

In his quest for allies, Borglum sought the support of Congressman Case, but only on condition that "you are ready to help *without political advice from people who are responsible for all our trouble.* . . ."

He sought the support of President Roosevelt, also, and in letter after letter told the president about his problems. "I must have *friendly* representatives of government who are not interfering with *my* part of the work," he told Mr. Roosevelt. And, he wrote to Mr. Case, "I have declined to the President in writing to have anything to do with Nagle and Spoots [sic] or to allow them in any way whatsoever to direct . . . or impose their ignorance on the Memorial. . . ."

Doane Robinson by this time had long been disconnected from Rushmore affairs. Now, age eighty-two, he was retired from his position as state historian and, in his own words, had become "a farmer with the grime of toil on my fists." Nonetheless, he was the father of the Rushmore Memorial, and he still was a prolific author whose words, within the state, were well known and well heeded. Which may explain why Borglum set out to enlist Robinson's support also (or, at least to alienate him from supporting the opposition) and wrote:

> . . . some day you will realize [as] I have long realized that a dammed little two by four racket in Rapid City has been riding your neck the way they have been riding mine. . . . You probably don't like to admit it, but you can't help but know . . . that Norbeck and Boland and one or two lesser lights, if you can call them lights, have always been in the way of your being on the Commission—preserving that empty honor for . . . paying political debts.

As his base of operations Borglum selected the Metropolitan Club in Washington, D.C., and in February went into residence there. "I am going to stay here till [the Rushmore situation] is corrected," he wrote to Robinson. "I tell you I am not going to Rushmore until it is corrected." He made a similar statement to John Boland, who replied by saying there was no provision in Borglum's contract allowing him to refuse to work. Regardless of that, Borglum responded, he was not going to return until Rushmore's problems had been settled to his satisfaction, and inasmuch as he had not been paid for his past season's work, he should not be expected to.

How Borglum, during times when he had no money and no income, was able to maintain himself in places such as the Metropolitan Club—and often for months at a time—is something no Rushmore scholar seems ever to have figured out, and certainly never has explained. Nonetheless, Borglum never failed to manage it whenever he saw the need. And this time, once he was settled in, he commenced his attack.

To Fred Sargent, chairman of the Mount Rushmore Commission, he wrote a letter so abusive that Sargent promptly resigned. Probably this was not the result Borglum had expected. However, he was trying to get rid of the commission, and with this one stroke he had, temporarily at least, decapitated it.

He continued "to keep the President informed," and believed he had won his unqualified support. "The President himself may come on the Commission . . . this all in confidence," he wrote to Robinson. In fact, however, the sculptor by now had told Mr. Roosevelt a good deal more about Rushmore's problems than Mr. Roosevelt had ever wanted to know. Consequently, the president, trying to get out of Borglum's line of fire, in March asked Secretary Ickes for "a solution and some form of reply to Gutzon Borglum."

Ickes, who himself had been receiving pointed correspondence from the sculptor, replied with characteristic testiness that, because Borglum would not hold still for "any type of supervision," he did not think there *was* any solution. Nonetheless, he called on Arlo Cammerer, Director of the National Park Service, to find out if, as Borglum kept insisting, Spotts actually was interfering with the sculptor's art; and, while he was at it, to find out what kind of man this John Boland was that he could keep Borglum so constantly on the warpath. Cammerer, in turn, sent his Superintendent of Memorials, John Nagle, to Rapid City and Rushmore to make a quiet investigation.

As a result of Nagle's detective work, Cammerer reported to Ickes that John Boland was "an excellent man personally, a useful citizen, a successful businessman, and a loyal supporter of Rushmore." Moreover, without Boland the Rushmore work would have been conducted much less effectively than it actually had been. As for Spotts, Nagle could find no evidence of his meddling in Borglum's part of the work. On the contrary, he seemed to have been bending over backwards to avoid even the appearance of it. And Spotts had been performing his own duties so well, said Nagle, that the work now was proceeding far more effectively than under "the emotional, day-to-day policy which had been previously maintained."

Borglum received a copy of the report, and exploded. In a letter to Case he pronounced it a falsification; "a deliberate misstatement intended to deceive and cover up Rapid City's misdeeds."

Meanwhile, the sculptor had gained the unquestioning support of two old friends, Senator Key Pittman of Nevada and Congressman Kent Keller of Illinois, and with their help had drafted still another Rushmore bill. Similar to the one he had prepared in 1935, in addition to completing the presidential figures down to the waist it called for carving the Entablature, excavating for the Hall of Records, and constructing a gigantic stone staircase (Borglum called it "The Grand Stairway") from the sculptor's studio up to the mouth of the little canyon behind the heads, and thus to the entrance to the Hall.

The bill also called, of course, for an authorization of money. Borglum wanted $600,000, for that was what he now claimed would be needed to finish the monument. Pittman and Keller objected. Asking for that much, they said, almost surely would kill the whole bill. Borglum then agreed to $300,000 instead, saying that if Congress would give him that much he would raise the balance "personally and privately."

The most important feature of this bill, however, was its provision for an entirely new Rushmore commission on which Borglum, himself, would serve and that, for all practical purposes, he would control.

Keller introduced the bill in the House on April 28, and got it scheduled for a hearing on May 5 before the Committee on the Library—a committee of which he, personally, happened to be the chairman.

The hearing was a red-letter event for Borglum. Never before had he been invited to appear before *any* congressional committee considering a Rushmore bill, but this time he was to be the star witness and, as such, would have a chance to completely air his complaints and to build his case. He had wanted to appear before earlier hearings, of course, but Norbeck always had managed to get him headed off. Throughout his entire career, Borglum's public statements were studded with sweeping claims impossible to fulfill, spur-of-the-moment statements inconsistent with his previous statements, and with recollections of facts and events not as they actually were but as they would most effectively serve his purpose of the moment. It appears now, and Norbeck suspected then, that Borglum did not do this deliberately. It was just that the unconscious tendency we all have to believe a thing is true just because we have said that it is true, as well as the tendency of our minds to edit our memories to our own advantage, in Borglum was developed to an exceptional degree. Accordingly, he seems to have made even his most startling claims and misstatements in the belief they were cast-iron truths. Nonetheless, this is the sort of thing a critical interrogator can use to make mincemeat of a witness's case. Norbeck, therefore, had taken great pains to see that Borglum was never exposed to interrogation by a congressional committee.

But, now that Norbeck was gone, Borglum did get to appear before a congressional committee, where his testimony did include impossible claims, inconsistent statements, and inaccurate recollections. Contrary to what Norbeck had feared, however, it got neither Borglum nor Rushmore into any trouble at all. On the contrary, from the standpoint of what the sculptor was seeking, the hearing was a smashing success.

Everything worked in Borglum's favor that day. He handled himself very well when testifying; the chairman, Congressman Keller, was one of his staunchest allies and manipulated the hearing accordingly; and, aside from Keller, who was his friend, none of the committee knew enough about the Rushmore project or had read enough of the government's Rushmore file to give him much trouble anyhow.

Hence, for example, when Borglum declared that his fee should have been thirty-five percent of the job's cost instead of twenty-five percent, and therefore, he had been underpaid in the amount of $100,000, no one asked how, on an expenditure to-date of $534,000, he figured a ten-percent difference to be $100,000. When he accused the Park Service and "its man" (Spotts) of creating expense inefficiency in the work, no one pointed out that at the end of Spott's first Rushmore season—1936—Borglum, himself, had said it was the most efficient and economical season so far. When he said that if he were permitted to run the job by himself his "businesslike manner" would allow him to complete it for a half to a third of what it would cost otherwise, no one asked what his "businesslike manner" entailed to make such a claim possible. And, when he declared that another $600,000 was needed for completion of the monument, no one asked him to reconcile that with his assertion in 1935—when $190,000 less had been spent than now—that if Congress would but give him another $335,000 he could finish the job.

In his testimony the sculptor recited his familiar litany of complaints: "incompetent untrained labor"; inadequate power; destructive meddling by the Park Service; disgracefully low pay for himself; obstruction by "local politicians"; and so on and on. However, he gave his testimony calmly and gracefully. He indulged in none of the caustic language to be found in his correspondence of that time, and he never mentioned Boland or Spotts by name.

Perhaps it was because Borglum's observations had been uncharacteristically mild that Chairman Keller set about supplying the fire and acid the sculptor had not brought forth. "What Mr. Borglum has been compelled to hint at here, I will say openly," Keller declared. He then gave the committee to understand that Borglum had long been victimized by "a commission that is practically dead"; by a Park Service that "does not know a thing about carving mountains" and whose representative (Spotts) "ought to be kicked off the place"; and by a "local political leader" whose name was John Boland.

One member, Congressman Treadway of Massachusetts, did attempt to raise some challenging questions. Among other things, he wanted a clearer understanding of just how the proposed authorization was to be spent; he wondered why Borglum wanted to control the whole operation himself; and if Borglum were to control it, Treadway wanted to know what point there was in even having a commission; and he wanted an explanation of just what the sculptor meant when he said he was being hampered by "political interference." In each instance, however, Chairman Keller intervened to steer the conversation in a new direction, and Treadway never did get any solid answers, which was to have disturbing consequences later when the bill came before the House.

A. E. Demaray, present to testify for the National Park Service, of which he was associate director, attempted to refute Keller's charge that the service was interfering in Borglum's art and performing its own Rushmore duties badly as well. When he did, Keller met him head-on. As recorded in the hearing minutes:

> The CHAIRMAN: It is perfectly ridiculous . . . while the work is being done poorly, and your Department does not do anything about it. It is a perfectly rotten situation.
>
> Mr. DEMARAY: I have never said the work is being done poorly. Everyone has the greatest admiration for it.
>
> The CHAIRMAN: So have I.
>
> Mr. DEMARAY: Then why do you say it is being done poorly?
>
> The CHAIRMAN: Because it is being done poorly. . . .

Congressman Keller then went on to say that the Park Service, being entirely incompetent in the matter of carving mountains, should not be involved with Rushmore at all. "You do not know a darned thing about it," he declared, "and we are not going to let you do anything about it."

"I can assure you, Sir," retorted Demaray, "if you will leave the Park Service out of it entirely, and give us no responsibilities, we will be very much delighted."

Congressman Case, who was to be the hearing's final witness, had listened to the proceedings with a mixture of pleasure and dismay. The committee seemed to favor letting Borglum have control of the Rushmore project, and

Case did not think that wise. Like most others involved with the monument, he thought it should be placed firmly under the control of the National Park Service. Nor did he like the idea of authorizing present funds for the Entablature and Hall of Records. He wanted to see the presidential figures completed first. Otherwise, Rushmore might wind up as a monument with no finished parts. He thought Boland, the commission, and the National Park Service had been unjustly castigated in the hearing. And he had noticed that a stranger listening to the proceedings would have come away believing every positive thing done for Rushmore, including the raising of all funds, had been done by Borglum alone, and that all others involved either had done nothing or had actually hindered the sculptor in his efforts.

On the other hand, Rushmore badly needed the $300,000 the bill would authorize, and he was pleased that the committee seemed favorably disposed toward it. Because the committee was, it seemed wise to give the bill his apparent full support now, and perhaps later he could try quietly to get its objectionable features amended out. It seemed wise, also, not to risk offending Keller or Borglum by openly contradicting anything they had said.

Accordingly, when asked to make his statement, Case delivered one that was a politician's masterpiece. He appeared to say much while actually saying little, praised many and criticized none, and at the same time managed to restore some credit to Rushmore people who either had been ignored or stripped of it in the preceding testimony. He praised the committee for its friendship to Rushmore; Keller for his "understanding of the principles of America"; and Borglum for his ability "not only to inspire people with the works of his hands but with his vigorous exposition of American ideals." He then let the committee know that in addition to Borglum and his skills, Rushmore existed because of the "integrity of the idea of Doane Robinson"; "the dogged persistence of the late Senator Norbeck"; the efforts of the commission; "and by no means least, the men who have worked on the mountain, call them rough miners, untutored carvers, or what you will." Interestingly enough, he did not mention John Boland; which may have been because he did not want to risk provoking a sharp response from Keller or Borglum, for it is certain that Case had Boland much on his mind.

Logically, of course, Boland should have been one of the witnesses. He knew more than anyone else about Rushmore's administrative and financial structure, and, as well, he should have had the opportunity to defend himself against the charges certain to be made against him by Borglum. Knowing this, Case had invited Boland to appear, hoping at the same time that he would refuse. Boland did refuse, and for exactly the reason that had been worrying Case. If he were to be quizzed under oath about Borglum's methods of operation, Boland said, his answers might well destroy the entire Rushmore enterprise. Therefore, he would just stay home and keep his mouth shut. Which he did until he read the Associated Press story on the hearing.

The story appeared on May 6, a day that many people in Rapid City no doubt thought had gotten off to a miserable start. Just before daylight the rain of the night before had changed to snow, falling thick and heavy in air that was not quite freezing. John Boland, however, thought it was the very best of mornings. A slight, brisk-stepping figure in gray hat and overcoat and black cloth overshoes, he walked from his West Boulevard home down to his office on Main Street through a hushed torrent of great white flakes that settled into slush on the sidewalks and into a water-heavy blanket on the broad, newly green lawns of the boulevard. Out in the country, he knew, that same blanket was melting softly into the thirsty earth, nourishing the roots of range grass, alfalfa, and winter wheat. That was good for the farmers. What was good for the farmers was good for Rapid City Implement Company. And, yes, it was a very fine morning indeed.

When he arrived at his office, however, the mood of the morning changed. Over at the *Journal* they had received an AP teletype on yesterday's committee hearing on Rushmore, and they thought Boland would like to see it and perhaps make a comment.

Washington. May 6—(AP)—Gutzon Borglum, sculptor, blamed local politics, yesterday, for slowing work on the Mount Rushmore national memorial. . . .

"I have got to have more men and more power," Borglum told the house library committee during the discussions on the Keller bill to create a new Mount Rushmore memorial commission. . . .

"I can't finish the heads with those miners. I have got to have carvers and they block me every time," Borglum protested in charging the engineer for the present . . . commission . . . "interferes with the jobs."

Borglum contended local interests dictated who should be hired to help him. In this he was supported by Representative Keller (D-Ill.), committee chairman, who said, "yes, John Boland of Rapid City runs the whole thing."

As it happened, Boland would do more than make a comment. He prepared a full statement, sending one copy to Congressman Case and another to the *Journal* in time to be quoted along with the AP story that afternoon. It read as follows:

STATEMENT OF JOHN A. BOLAND, SECRETARY OF THE MOUNT
RUSHMORE NATIONAL MEMORIAL COMMISSION, COMMENTING
UPON THE ASSOCIATED PRESS REPORTS OF THE COMMITTEE
HEARING OF MAY 6, 1936.

Since I became a member of the Commission in March, 1929, there has been no political interference Nationally, State or county, either on the part of the Republican or Democratic organizations. On the contrary, both political parties . . . have been most helpful.

The Commission has never been financially able to provide more power. To provide additional power as suggested would mean practically all funds would have to be expended for new equipment and little money would be left to carry on the work.

To my knowledge, no former superintendent, nor the present resident engineer has dictated who should be employed . . . nor have I attempted to control employment of the men. Mr. Borglum has always directed who should be employed . . . through the superintendents and his assistant, his son Lincoln.

I have never interfered with Mr. Borglum in his work. I have endeavored to conduct only the purely business affairs of the Commission . . . in a businesslike manner.

Mr. Borglum is an artist and I am a businessman. Therefore it is only natural that we should at times disagree regarding the business functions of the Commission. Such differences, however, have never been serious and an amicable understanding has always been reached.

My only desire is to have the Mount Rushmore project completed in the best possible manner, and to have Mr. Borglum carry on his great work, with the able assistance of his son, Lincoln, the continued cooperation of the Commission, and the efficient supervision of the National Park Service.

Considering the circumstances, it was a remarkably restrained commentary, and, in a covering letter to Case, Boland explained why:

Enclosed find a clipping from the Rapid City Daily Journal of May 6.

There was a great deal I could have said in answer to Congressman Keller and Sculptor Borglum, but in completing my statement I was as charitable as possible with Mr. Borglum as I wanted to be helpful to Rushmore.

Upon receiving Boland's statement, Case submitted it to the committee, first adding a comment of his own: "It would be unfair to the committee and the Congress, as well as to the persons involved, if these hearings did not include a statement from Mr. Boland . . . who has been the subject of considerable discussion in the hearings. . . ." And, headed by Case's comment, the statement was made a part of the official record of the hearing.

Keller, in reading Boland's statement, thought he saw a way to fulfill Borglum's dream of getting rid of the man. Boland had said his only desire was to have the Mount Rushmore project completed. To be completed, it needed the authorization included in the proposed new bill. Therefore, on May 12, Keller wired Boland:

. . . IT WILL SIMPLIFY AND MAKE MORE CERTAIN THE
AUTHORIZATION IF THE PRESENT COMMISSION VOLUNTARILY
RESIGN EFFECTIVE JUNE 30 . . . . I UNDERSTAND THE REMAINING
COMMISSIONERS HAVE EXPRESSED A WILLINGNESS TO RESIGN AND
I THEREFORE SUGGEST YOU WIRE ME SPECIFICALLY YOUR OWN
WILLINGNESS OR UNWILLINGNESS TO RESIGN AS SUGGESTED SO
THE COMMITTEE MAY ACT ACCORDING[LY]. . . . I HAVE ONLY ONE
OBJECT IN SUGGESTING THIS . . . AND THAT IS TO MAKE CERTAIN
THE COMPLETION OF THE DREAM OF MY BELOVED FRIEND
NORBECK.

When drafting that wire Keller failed to mention one key point. It was true the commissioners, including Boland himself, had said they would like to resign, for they had become increasingly tired of receiving little but accusations in return for their efforts. However, their "expressed willingness" had a string attached to it. Because it did, and because all this maneuvering against him had gotten his back up, Boland sent Keller this reply:

WILLING TO RESIGN ANY TIME . . . *IF* PENDING RUSHMORE BILL
BECOMES LAW. SUCH RESIGNATION NOT BASED ON UNFOUNDED
CHARGES OF SCULPTOR. . . . *COMMISSIONERS WILLINGNESS TO
RESIGN REFERRED TO IN YOUR TELEGRAM WAS WITH THE*

UNDERSTANDING THAT THIS NATIONAL MEMORIAL BE TURNED OVER
TO NATIONAL PARK SERVICE FOR COMPLETION.
(Emphasis added.)

Francis Case received a copy of the wire and promptly responded, "STRICTLY CONFIDENTIAL—AM PROUD OF YOUR STATEMENT AND YOUR TELEGRAM." Keller, having been caught bluffing with a pair of deuces, made no reply at all.

Next, Case began planning an amendment to the bill—now called the Pittman-Keller bill—that would assure control of Rushmore by the Park Service. However, Boland asked him to drop it.

> I do think it would be unwise for you to make any objection either in the Committee or on the Floor, for the important thing is to secure the authorization. . . .
>
> Should the bill pass . . . you should call on the President and request him to . . . [place] the work of the Commission under the administration of the National Park Service, not only to administer the funds, but to supervise the work.
>
> When calling on the President . . . I will be thankful if he is informed as to my character, ability, honesty, etc., for I know the Sculptor has endeavored to convince the President that I am "no good."

And so, unamended and accompanied by a favorable committee report, on June 6, the bill came before the House—the sixth on an agenda of seven memorial authorization bills to be considered.

"It was surely a bad day for anything of that character," wrote Case, "and half a dozen served notice on me they were going to object to the Rushmore bill." By doing some frantic last-minute bargaining Case finally "had all but one of them taken care of," and that one was Congressman Treadway, who was still smarting from the way Keller had brushed aside his questions during the committee hearing. "He told me repeatedly," said Case, "that he simply had to object, [and] I sat down beside him in sheer desperation . . . simply waiting for the execution."

That waiting was even worse than Case had feared. The first memorial bill called was defeated. So was the second. And the third, and fourth, and fifth. In the gallery, Borglum got up from his seat and went back to the Metropolitan Club. He said later, "I just couldn't stay and see Rushmore defeated, too." Hence he missed seeing Case win his spurs as Norbeck's successor.

When the Rushmore bill was called, Treadway attempted to get it held over for later debate, and had he succeeded it almost surely would have been the end of the bill, at least for that congressional session. However, the speaker misunderstood what Treadway had said. By that time Case had gotten the floor, where he announced that Treadway's request "was simply for an explanation." Then, before the flabbergasted Treadway could react, "the Speaker called for passage of the bill and it went through."

Next, as Boland had suggested, Case tried to see President Roosevelt about keeping the monument under the Park Service, but could not get an appointment. The president's free time was being taken up by preparations for the wedding of one of his sons.

Then the congressman attempted to get the Park Service itself to try to retain control of Rushmore, but he got no help there, either. "Demaray . . . takes the position that the Park Service is out under the new legislation." Which, of course, is exactly where the Service wanted to be.

Pittman and Keller, both Democrats with long congressional tenure, did have the president's ear, and the upshot was that Borglum got his handpicked commission. Among the new appointees were Pittman and Keller, Congresswoman Isabella Greenway, and Washington attorneys Herman Oliphant and Russell Arundel, all close friends and loyal supporters of the sculptor. Lorine Spoonts, also his good friend, had been reappointed. And these, together with Borglum himself, constituted a majority of the twelve-member body.

On the other hand, there were only two South Dakotans on the new commission, Senator Bulow and William Williamson, and Williamson was there reluctantly. He had tried to resign along with the rest of the old commission, but President Roosevelt refused to allow it. Without Williamson there would have been no one on the commission but Borglum who really knew very much about the Rushmore project.

And now Borglum's dream had been realized and his promise had become fact. He had vowed to get rid of the old commission and the Park Service and Spotts and Boland—especially Boland—and he had. When the new law became effective on July 1, the United States Treasury Department would take over Rushmore's bookkeeping, and the new commission—*his* commission—would take over all the rest of it. Moreover, aside from the Treasury Department for its expenditures, that commission would be accountable to no one but Congress.

Borglum also had said he would not come back to Rushmore until the situation there had been "corrected," and he kept that promise, too. He returned in early July, which was after Spotts had gone and Boland's resignation had become effective. Actually, Boland was still on the job, having been asked to take care of Rushmore's business affairs until the operation could be reorganized. When Borglum was asked if this was all right with him he said it was and that, in fact, he would be glad to allow Boland "to gasp a little longer, like a trout in the sun."

The important thing was that Boland had been defeated. The irresistible force had overcome the immovable object.

25. Borglum Takes Over the Mountain

orglum was in an expansive mood when he returned to the Hills. Not only had he just won a sweeping victory, he had money in his pocket. In addition to the back pay he had collected in March, he now had received $5,419 for his services so far to Rushmore in 1938. On top of that he had a fat new authorization for the project and no one to interfere with his spending of it, and so his prospects for future income looked better than they had in years.

"Gutzon Borglum was in . . . today, having just come back from his triumphs in Washington," William Williamson wrote in his diary on July 7. Williamson, who was the sculptor's local attorney, then added, "I got $1,000 out of him for Rhodes [the ranch mortgage], $500 for Pennington County Bank [on an overdue note], and $100 for myself. He says, 'I am here to head up activities for the Commission at Rapid City hereafter.' . . . Boland appears to be out. It is unfortunate."

As if the very heavens were celebrating (or protesting) Borglum's triumphant return, on that same afternoon a great, booming thunderstorm rumbled across the southern Hills. At half-past three it fired a lightning bolt into The Hidden City, a tourist attraction operated by Ray Sanders, the ex-cowboy who in 1925 had set up Borglum's temporary camp at the foot of Rushmore. The bolt severely shocked seven people at Hidden City, and rendered one person unconscious. It splintered a flagpole, fused electric wires, shattered light bulbs, tore switches from walls, and sent a surge of electricity racing at the speed of light along the miles of power line to Rushmore.

At Rushmore the afternoon's dynamite charges all had been laid, but they were not due to be fired until four o'clock. Men still were scattered across the face of the cliff, and driller Ernest "Bill" Reynolds, suspended in a sling-seat, was working almost on top of one of the explosive-loaded holes. The power surge sped into the powderman's detonator box and jumped the open switch.

The charges exploded. Driven by the blast, Reynolds was swung on his cable out into space, then he crashed back into the cliff. Scratched and bruised by flying stone, half-stunned and beginning to bleed, he noticed that the heel was missing from one of his shoes and that the other shoe was missing altogether. He still had his feet, however, and the feet worked, and all his other parts seemed to be working, too. As indeed they were. Aside from the scratches and bruises and a temporarily damaged eardrum, he was not injured. Neither were any of the other men. The crew had enjoyed an escape as miraculous, and as narrow, as years before when the A-frame collapsed. And, of course, it was a narrow escape for the project itself. Always on shaky ground as it was, any accident causing death or a number of serious injuries almost surely would cause it to be shut down forever.

On August 4, at Borglum's Rushmore studio, the new commission met to get itself organized and to establish its policies. And if there had been any doubts of Borglum's control of that commission, this meeting disposed of them. In his private diary, Williamson described the proceedings:

> Key Pittman, Arundel, Keller and Oliphant had been here for some days, but the Sculptor had been careful to keep them out of Rapid City and away from Boland and myself.
>
> Before I had been in there ten minutes it was perfectly clear that the cards were stacked. Key Pittman assumed the position of chairman without being chosen. When it came to the selection of officers, Arundel said, turning to Borglum, "Who do you want?" Most any other man would have retired and suggested this was a matter to be determined by the Commission. Not so with the good Sculptor. He proceeded to name them, and they were accordingly nominated and elected.
>
> Next, we came to the executive committee. . . . Again Arundel said, "Let's find out who Borglum wants." Pittman and Keller chimed in . . . Borglum then named the executive committee. Five were named. I was not one of them. Sen. Bulow then said, ". . . Mr. Williamson has been on the Commission from the beginning, and on the executive committee . . . and knows more than any of the rest of us about it. It seems to me he should be a member."
>
> Mr. Borglum threw up his hands and . . . looked a bit flustered and said, "Yes, of course I meant to mention him. Naturally he should be a member." So . . . Pittman, Keller, Williamson, McDonald and Arundel were nominated and elected.

Next, the executive committee met to organize. Again the little special pleader for the Sculptor asked Mr. Borglum who he wanted. He then named the officers and they were promptly appointed.

Borglum had already been made general manager with full power to hire and fire . . . and fix wages and salaries, despite the fact I had called attention of the commissioners to the fact that both the law and the contract placed this duty squarely on the shoulders of the commissioners. The law was ignored and the contract was ordered rewritten. . . .

Then Arundel wanted to make Mr. Borglum a member of the executive committee and an officer of the Commission. I suggested the impropriety [and] illegality of such procedure and [said] that we had contracted with Mr. Borglum to do the work, and I wanted to know if he was to contract with himself as well as to manage everything. For once I was sustained by the chairman and Keller. Arundel looked a bit confused, reddened and said, "Well, I guess that is alright." That same proposal was made by Mr. Borglum in Washington . . . so Arundel, as usual, must have been echoing his wishes.

. . . The sculptor must have a major voice in selecting the personnel, and I had drafted a by-law which provided he should select such personnel as he might find necessary . . . but that such personnel should be paid according to a schedule to be fixed by the Commission or Executive Committee. This, however, was brushed aside. . . . Inasmuch as Borglum's commission is 25% of all monies expended . . . it seemed to me that he should not be permitted to control salaries whose increase would increase his return of 25%, but this was strictly overruled with the statement that only he knew what they should be paid. . . .

No provision whatever was made . . . to keep expenditures within available funds or appropriations, and the sculptor could commit the commission to expenditures in any amounts, even beyond the ability of the commission to meet. This . . . resulted, after some argument by me—somewhat emphatic—in Mr. Oliphant incorporating the language that I desired in the by-law. [This] discussion took place before the executive committee was named, and I think was what induced the sculptor to leave me off. . . . I think he really intended that I should be on, but when he found that I thought the law and the contracts should be given some force he decided to leave me off, and but for Bulow I would have been off.

. . . I venture the prediction now that [this new organization]
will double the overhead of the past under Boland and myself and
the Park Service.

In this same entry (which may have been the longest in his forty-odd years
of diary-keeping) Williamson went on to give a penetrating and probably
quite accurate evaluation of the Borglum-Boland conflict:

I think that Mr. Boland has been too conservative and restrictive
[about] permitting the sculptor to go full speed ahead, but in no
sense to the extent claimed by the sculptor.
The Commission made the mistake of delegating too much authority to Boland. . . .
I made repeated attempts to correct some of the troubles by getting the Commission together, but this was resisted by Mr. Boland
in one form or another. . . .
That Boland had become weary and impatient with Borglum,
and was not always as considerate as he might have been, is doubtless true.
Mr. Boland, however, is a high-class, competent businessman and
has performed very valuable and lasting services . . . and the time
will come when even Mr. Borglum will become able to appreciate
the disinterested services which he has rendered.

Although Borglum had kept his vow not to return to Rushmore himself
until he had been freed of Boland and the Park Service and other such bur-
dens, he had sent Lincoln to carry on in his place. Which explains how before he had even come back to the job he had earned that $5,400 fee for cur-
rent work.

Lincoln, together with Spotts, began operations on May 9, putting a few
men at work on Washington's neck and lapels but concentrating most of his
effort on the head of Roosevelt. At the close of the past season the Roosevelt
face had been little more than a vertical wall that contained a suggestion of
eye sockets and was ridged by a crude slab of a nose. By the time Gutzon
returned, however, Roosevelt's features had begun to emerge recognizably
from the surrounding stone.

In July, following Spott's departure on the first, Lincoln Borglum was officially promoted to project superintendent. He was paid $4,800 a year,
which in those days was a very large salary for a young man of twenty-six, but

he proved to be worth every cent of it. Blessed with an abundance of natural talent, he was rapidly becoming a skilled artist in his own right; he was trusted by Gutzon and liked and respected by the men; he had acquired a wealth of practical Rushmore experience during the past six years; and there was in his nature a quiet steadiness that helped to counterbalance the erratic moods of his father. From now on, consequently, Lincoln's superintendency was to make an enormous contribution to the project's success.

Also in July, Gutzon set drillers at work on the north wall of the slotlike canyon behind the heads, there to begin fulfilling his longtime dream of a great, cavernous Hall of Records excavated from within the living granite.

It was a true Borglum dream—elaborate, gigantic, ambitious. The Hall's entrance was to be a polished stone panel forty feet high, inlaid with gold and lapis lazuli mosaics and surmounted by a bas-relief American eagle with a thirty-nine-foot wingspread. The entrance itself, some twenty feet high by fourteen wide, was to have cast-glass doors opening into a high chamber eighty feet wide and a hundred feet long. And, said Borglum:

> The 360 feet of wall space will be panelled and recessed to a depth of 30 inches. Into these recesses will be built illuminated bronze and glass cabinets into which will be placed the records of the West World accomplishments, the political effect of its philosophy of govern-ment, its adventure in science, art, literature, invention, medicine—typed upon aluminum sheets rolled and protected in tubes.
>
> These cabinets will be sealed and may be opened only by an act of Congress. . . . On the wall above them, extending around the en-tire hall will be a bas-relief showing the adventure of humanity dis-covering and occupying the West World; it will be in bronze, gold plated.

Also, the hall was to contain busts of great American men and women, said Borglum. "Benjamin Franklin's statue shall be among the first," he told President Roosevelt, "and your own, [and] . . . I will give Susan B. Anthony a place with the gods in the great hall. Her friends should be happy."

Such an expansion of his dreams had become possible, of course, because the sculptor now had an ample budget and freedom to spend it as he chose. This, in turn, had expanded his personal income to a very remarkable size. During the last half of 1938 his average monthly fee came to a little over $2,700 (equivalent to perhaps $25,000 in 1984 dollars adjusted for taxes and inflation), which was well above the average *yearly* income of American families. Upon receiving only $2,200 in October, however, Borglum complained that his income had been "very much reduced" from what it had been under the old commission. But he probably was complaining only from force of habit, for when Treasury Department accountant George Storck told him he was being ridiculous and showed him why, Borglum said, "I beg you not to take me too seriously."

The last half of 1938 was a very good time for Gutzon Borglum—a time of triumph, achievement, and hope. He had full control of his mountain, a superintendent he could work with, money for the job, and money in his pocket. The Congress and the president appeared to be growing ever more favorable to the monument and ever more willing to invest money in it. Time

57. Besides indicating the location of the Hall of Records, this photograph shows the narrow canyon behind the heads, and how little rock was left when a carving surface finally was developed for the Roosevelt head.

OF RECORDS

and again, Rushmore had almost been destroyed by financial crises and by the kind of personal conflict that had destroyed Stone Mountain. But now, or so it appeared, these crises and conflicts were past and the road ahead was open and smooth. Hence, these were golden months for Borglum, the best in all his years at the mountain.

Unfortunately, however, the golden months had been numbered even before they began. Although neither Borglum nor anyone else yet realized it, the final and insurmountable threat to the Rushmore work was already gathering and growing, and had been for several years. It was what people were calling, for want of a better term, "the world situation."

Supposedly, the World War had made the world safe for democracy. But it had not. Like boats drifting toward a waterfall, the governments of Europe were drifting at increasing speed toward another war and were trying at the same time to pretend that they were not. German dictator Adolf Hitler was saying that war was an "unlimited madness" and Germany wanted no part of it. He had declared in a recent speech, "We have no territorial demands to make in Europe. Germany will never break the peace!" At the same time, however, he was making territorial demands, and in an attempt to avoid the agony of another great war the Western powers were giving in to them. In the spring of 1938 Hitler had managed, in the words of Winston Churchill, "to liberate Austria from the horrors of self-government." Britain and France had protested that action, but that was all, and when six months later Mr. Hitler announced he now would like to have Czechoslovakia, they did not even do that. Instead, they agreed at a conference in Munich not to interfere in the takeover of Czechoslovakia if Hitler, in turn, would promise to behave himself in the future—which, of course, he did promise. This led British Prime Minister Neville Chamberlain to announce upon his return home that the Munich agreement had produced "peace with honor." "I believe it is peace in our time," he said. "Now go home and get a nice quiet sleep."

Americans followed these developments with interest, but being protected by the vastness of the Atlantic Ocean and being in a pacifist mood as well, they refused to become over-excited by them. The Depression had provided Americans with all the bad news they cared to read, and now they pre-

58. The Hall of Records as it appears today. Note the steel compressed-air pipes on the floor of the tunnel, which still remain there after forty years.

ferred upbeat stories such as that of millionaire-sportsman Howard Hughes, who in July had flown an airplane around the world in only three days and nineteen hours and upon his return was met by a cheering crowd of 20,000. Or offbeat stories like that of the young radio dramatist Orson Welles, who in a Halloween radio play had scared millions of people out of their wits by making them believe Martians had landed in New Jersey.

One American who did recognize the threat to Europe as a threat also to the United States was President Franklin Roosevelt. In January of 1939 he asked Congress for a huge increase in spending for national defense, and thereby set off a barrage of hostile criticism. It was heartless, roared his detractors, to even think of more defense spending while there still were Americans who were hungry, poorly housed, and unemployed. "We can't eat guns!" they thundered, and accused the president of being a lackey of the armament manufacturers.

Happily unaware that the growing threat to democracy itself in Europe was becoming a threat also to the "Shrine of Democracy" in the Black Hills, Borglum continued carving throughout the winter of 1938–39. He had erected a six-level scaffold across the Roosevelt face. There, in canvas-walled spaces more or less heated by coke-burning stoves, workmen molded the features of that zesty, noisy president who had been called The Bull Moose and also had been the inspiration for a cuddly stuffed toy called a Teddy Bear.

Much was done also in the Hall of Records that winter, and from the standpoint of weather it was a good time to do it. The tunnel and the little stone canyon in which it was being dug both provided shelter from the winter wind. That, however, was the only good thing about working there. In the closeness of the tunnel the clattering jackhammers made a racket that at first was annoying, then became maddening, then almost unbearable. And even worse than the noise was the dust. In making a hole, a drill pounded the stone into a flour-fine dust that had to be removed from the hole as it accumulated, for otherwise it would cause the drill to stick. In the olden days of hand-hammered drills this was done by use of a "spoon," a tiny cup-shaped scoop attached to a stiff wire handle. These modern power-drills, however, removed it with blasts of compressed air fired through a hole running lengthwise through the center of the drill. For every foot of hole drilled, about a pint of dust was thus produced and blown out to hang as a floury fog in the air of the tunnel. It was a fog so thick that some men refused to work in it. But because there were others who preferred working in the dusty air of the tunnel to the frigid air on the face of the cliff, the tunneling went on.

All this activity required so much money that in January Borglum found it necessary to return to Washington to seek appropriation of the $250,000 remaining in the previous year's authorization. There, he appeared before the House Subcommittee on Appropriations and found it a less pleasant experience than his previous appearance before a congressional committee had been. Unlike Keller, the chairman of this committee was not inclined to run interference for the sculptor, and, unlike the members of the previous committee, the members of this one had done their homework. They asked searching questions, and whenever Borglum happened to give one of the inaccurate or even impossible answers that Norbeck had always worried about, this committee was able to recognize the inaccuracy.

Noting that Borglum's proposed annual budget for Rushmore included $35,000 in fees for himself—a sum three-and-a-half times greater than the annual pay of a congressman—one committee member wondered if the sculptor might not be using the monument simply as a device for enriching himself. Borglum declared that he was not, which was true. But to prove his point he unfortunately also declared that there never had been a year in which he had received as much as $10,000 for his Rushmore work—which was not true and the committee knew it. His income from Rushmore during the past ten years had averaged $11,594, and in calendar 1938, alone, he had received $20,100.

Various committee members observed that the project had been dragging on for so long that it was beginning to appear endless, and wondered when Borglum thought he could get it wound up. Given the requested appropriation, he replied, he could probably finish it all—the Grand Stairway and Hall of Records included—by mid-1940 and certainly by the end of 1940; a performance which, in fact, would have been impossible under the best of circumstances.

Next, Borglum was asked if he thought the requested $250,000 would be enough for finishing the job. Even though he had told the previous year's committee that $600,000 would be required, and that this statement was now a matter of record, he replied, "I say so." This prompted Mr. Dirksen of Illinois to ask the sculptor if he would agree to a provision making this appropriation the final government contribution to Rushmore. Astonishingly, he said he would. Borglum's erstwhile echo, Russell Arundel, was thunderstruck. Present on behalf of the Rushmore commission, Arundel knew the work could not possibly be finished for $250,000. Such a provision would be "a drastic step," he said, and he tried to get Borglum to withdraw his statement. Borglum, however, stuck to his guns. "I know how much stone each man can take out," he said, "and I think we can do it."

All in all, it was not one of Borglum's better performances, and if the committee had been hostile to him or to the Rushmore work itself, it might have ended Rushmore's Federal funding right then and there. The committee, however, was not hostile. A number of its members knew the sculptor personally and liked him, and realized that one sometimes had to make allowances for his rhetoric. Also, the committee did want to see the Rushmore monument completed if that could be done without creating an endless drain on the Federal treasury. Therefore, after writing in a provision to make this the final Rushmore appropriation, they sent the bill on to the Congress, where, in due course, it was passed. And by this they made possible, among other things, the great Rushmore baseball team of 1939.

26. Government
Takes it Back

Now that he had command of the largest budget in Rushmore's history, Borglum in the spring of 1939 set out to hire the largest crew in its history. And upon hearing of this, the workmen sent a delegation headed by Merle Peterson to call on Lincoln Borglum.

"Hear you're going to hire more men," said Peterson.

"Yep," Lincoln replied, "quite a few of 'em."

"In that case," Merle said, "how about hiring guys who are good ballplayers?"

"So long as they can put out a day's work, it's OK with me," said Lincoln.

Having established that, the members of the Rushmore team began a recruiting campaign. They persuaded Bob McNally, star catcher for the powerful Rapid City Cement Plant team to give up his cement plant job in exchange for one at Rushmore. Orville Worman, manager of Rapid City's Red Owl grocery store and known to be a hot shortstop was similarly persuaded. They recruited Teddy Crawford and Frank "Casey" Jones, ace pitcher and center fielder respectively, from the Civilian Conservation Corps. Then they financed a trip by Casey Jones to the eastern part of the state to recruit his brother Glen, who was said to be—and was—a remarkable second baseman.

The result was a baseball team that old Rushmore hands still refer to with something approaching reverence, a team that functioned as smoothly as a troupe of trained seals, a team that with a little luck would have wound up the year as state champions instead of, as it happened, being tied for third place.

At about the same time that the new appropriation was passed, which was in March, the Black Hills Power and Light Company completed the long-awaited power line to Rushmore. Thus, another of Borglum's troubles was disposed of, for he now had available all the electricity he could use, and then some.

It seemed, however, that at Rushmore good news almost always came accompanied by bad news. The bad news in this case was a statement by President Roosevelt that on July 1 the control of the Rushmore work would be returned to the National Park Service, and Borglum's new hand-picked commission would be stripped of most of its power. This act cast no reflection on Borglum or the commission. It was made simply as a part of a general government reorganization plan. Nonetheless, it made the sculptor furious, and he immediately launched a campaign to get it reversed.

He began with a letter to Senator Pittman in which he declared that Boland and the Park Service already had almost wrecked Rushmore, and that because the Park Service was "most intolerable" he would resign before allowing it again to control his work.

Next, he tried to enlist Congressman Case in his campaign, but Case was a man who always looked before leaping. Borglum was telling him that returning the project to the Park Service would destroy it. Boland (now on the sidelines but still vitally interested) was telling him that because of Borglum's inefficient practices, *not* returning it to the Park Service would destroy it. This led Case to conduct his own investigation. Upon completing it, he wrote to the commission's secretary, Russell Arundel:

> The general impression of the people who came to see me was that considerably more progress was made on the figures themselves during the two years Mr. Spotts was on the work than was accomplished in any other comparable period of time. This in spite of the fact that the last two years have seen a much larger expenditure of funds.

Although Borglum did not win Case's support, he was supported in his campaign by Senator Pittman who, in June, arranged for Borglum and himself to meet with President Roosevelt. In that meeting, Borglum stated his case and Pittman restated it, and in the process they ripped the Park Service up one side and down the other, but it did no good. The president remained firm, and on July 1 the transfer was made.

It was a decision that pleased no one except Boland and Case and perhaps a few others of similar mind. The Park Service, having had enough of Mr. Borglum the first time, did not want to take Rushmore back. Nor did Mr. Ickes, the short-tempered Secretary of the Interior, want it back, and he said:

> When I have anything official to do in connection with Gutzon

Borglum's enterprise at Mount Rushmore I always feel like equipping myself as a man does when he fusses with a beehive. Mr. Borglum has customarily made it so unpleasant . . . that I groaned all night following the day when I learned that the Mount Rushmore National Memorial Commission had been sent here for administration.

Borglum, on his part, snorted: "That order put me right back where I was . . . at the mercy of unsympathetic men who have no idea of how life can be given to blocks of granite!"

As things turned out, however, the new arrangement was far less trying for Borglum and the Park Service than either had expected. Under what it called a program of "minimum participation" the Park Service assumed only those powers and duties it was required to assume. It took control of personnel policies, took on the duty of approving expenditures and budgets, and assumed the right to have a voice in the making of contracts. It did not, however, send another Spotts to Rushmore. Instead, it allowed Borglum to keep Lincoln as his superintendent, and because of that the sculptor was to find the new arrangement only irritating instead of intolerable.

Borglum suffered another great disappointment that summer when he was forced to stop his work on the Hall of Records. To make it even worse, it was his friends on the hand-picked commission who did the forcing. Despite Borglum's easy declaration that with the new appropriation he would be able to complete all phases of Rushmore, the appropriations committee had turned out to be willing to recommend new funds only if assured they would be used first to complete work on the presidential figures. Whereupon Senator Pittman, speaking as chairman of the commission, had given such assurance, and with that as a condition the committee had made the recommendation.

Still, that did not stop Borglum. He was convinced that the Hall was essential to the success of Rushmore. He was equally convinced that congressmen who knew nothing of monuments had no business trying to tell him how to build one. Besides, now that Congress had made the appropriation it would have a hard time taking it back. Accordingly, he went ahead just as if Pittman's promise had never been made. The commission, of course, tried to stop him, but it did it timidly—asking him to stop rather than ordering him to—which did no good at all.

At the same time, however, Congressman Case had been making an on-the-scene investigation of work in the Hall and in July reported to commission secretary Arundel that:

Men were required to work with dry drills in a small space, where fine dust was so thick . . . that it was impossible for one man to see another a few feet away. This practice is not permitted in mining operations and those who spoke to me about it were sure the men were in danger of contracting silicosis and that future damage claims against the government would result.

In view of the pledge to the Appropriations Committee this condition should be easy to correct.

With that the commission found the courage to act, and work on the Hall was suspended. Intended to be only temporary, the suspension turned out to be permanent, and today the Hall looks exactly as it did when the four o'clock whistle blew on that July day more than forty years ago. On the canyon wall a space that has been smoothed off for the Hall's entrance facade is pierced by a tunnel that is about twenty feet high and ten wide at the entrance and that grows progressively lower as it proceeds to its end some seventy-five feet deep in the mountain.

And Borglum suffered yet another disappointment when at last he acquired a highly skilled sculptural assistant and then almost immediately lost him again.

The new assistant was thirty-year-old Korczak Ziolkowski, a great hulk of a man rugged enough to fight bears with a willow switch . . . and win. He had been born in Boston, orphaned at the age of one, and until the age of sixteen, when he ran away from home, had been raised by an Irish prizefighter. Although he was almost entirely self-educated and self-taught, Ziolkowski's training had been good enough and his talent great enough that later in this summer of 1939 his bust of Paderewski would win a gold medal at the New York World's Fair.

Emil Flick, Borglum's ranch manager and moviegoing companion, remembered Ziolkowski's coming to Rushmore:

Mr. Borglum had been in the East on a speaking trip, and when he got back he said, "Emil, I've just met a capable young sculptor in Chicago, and I'm bringing him out here as my assistant. I want you to fix him up with the cabin up the creek [on the ranch] and make him feel at home. Yes sir! I have great plans for Ziolkowski!"

Not long after that Mr. Borglum said, "Korczak and his wife have just come in and are at the cabin. Let's walk up and make 'em feel at home."

Well, the Ziolkowskis dined that night with the Borglums, but they invited Christine and me to come up for supper on the next evening.

It was a crude cabin with no running water, and the supper was just a lap-supper. Just the same, when they greeted us Ziolkowski— a most handsome man—was wearing a beautifully embroidered shirt with great flowing sleeves and he had on a white sash, and Mrs. Ziolkowski was wearing an elegant evening gown.

He said, "Would you like a drink?" And I say, "You bet!" Well! He started mixing up Manhattans, and after about six shakers of 'em we really were getting acquainted!

With that there began a friendship that was to remain firm and warm until Emil's death some thirty-eight years later.

Ziolkowski and Borglum quickly became good friends, also. They were much alike, these two—strong-minded, opinionated men who heard their own drummers and marched to them, each driven by a creativity that told him no matter how much he accomplished it would not be enough. Both being absorbed in the world of sculpture and speaking its special language, they spent a great deal of time together. And, as they did, Korczak was by turns amused, surprised, and impressed by the things he learned about Borglum.

He learned, for example, about Borglum's unusal habit of walking into movie theaters without buying a ticket:

We'd had dinner together at the Alex Johnson, and afterwards our wives went off somewhere to shop, so Borglum said, "Korczak, let's step over to the Elks Theater and see a show."

Well, when we got there I took out my wallet and started up to the window and Borglum stopped me. "Hell! Korczak!" he said, "just walk on in. I never pay to see a movie here."

He learned, too, about the sculptor's puckish sense of humor (which most people did not, for Borglum did not display it nearly as often as he might have):

Riding down the mountain one day in Borglum's limousine with Charlie, his colored chauffeur, driving, Gutzon said, "Korczak, tell me, what do you really think of the Rushmore heads?"

"Mr. Borglum, I think they're magnificent," I said.

"Come now, Korczak," he said, "nothing is perfect. Surely there must be something I could have done to improve them."

"Really," I said, "I can't think of a thing." But he just kept after me, and said, "Korczak, are you *sure?*"

"We-e-ell," I said, "maybe you could have turned the heads a little more to the south."

Well! He just *glared* at me. Then he barked, "Ziolkowski! Why don't you mind your own goddamn business." And then he grinned.

But the experience that impressed Ziolkowski most and that he still recalled movingly four decades later occurred one day when he and Gutzon were standing at a place where all that can be seen of the carvings is the profile of Washington standing splendidly against the sky. "Borglum gazed at the profile for a long time. Then he said in a choked sort of voice, 'Look! Korczak, look! I can't believe I did that!' Then he wept."

Unfortunately, this warm association lasted only two months, but brief as it was it would change Ziolkowski's whole life and ultimately would make him about as well known nationally as Borglum himself.

The breakup came on a hot afternoon in August when Ziolkowski was working in the studio and Lincoln Borglum, accompanied by pointer Jim LaRue, came in to take off measurements from the Roosevelt model for transfer to the mountain. During the ensuing conversation Korczak and Lincoln somehow fell into a disagreement, then a fuss, then a fight. The subject, whatever it was, is unimportant and doubtless was insignificant. The fight was simply a case of two aggressive, husky young bucks locking horns. Lincoln was a big man and a rugged one, and certainly no sissy. But Korczak, a goliath who had to restrain his strength when carving lest he shatter the marble, was even more rugged. As a consequence, Lincoln got the worst of it and had to be taken to Custer for minor repairs.

Gutzon, who had been away on a trip when this happened, realized when he returned that he would have to let Korczak go. Judging by the letter of dismissal he wrote—a letter so tactful and considerate that until his death

59. The view Borglum saw when he said to Ziolkowski, "Look! Korczak! I can't believe I did that!" And then he wept.

43 years later Ziolkowski kept a photo enlargement of it mounted in his studio—Borglum did not do this in anger nor to avenge his son. After all, being well able to look after himself, Lincoln certainly would have resented and been embarrassed by that sort of parental shielding. But Lincoln was project superintendent, and Borglum well knew that no project manager can allow staff members to beat up his superintendent and still expect to maintain discipline in a crew as rough-and-tumble as that which built Rushmore.

Shortly after leaving Rushmore Korczak went to New York to receive the gold medal he had been awarded at the World's Fair. Then he dropped in at the Players Club, of which Gutzon had long been a member and to which Korczak also belonged. There, as Korczak later recounted it, he fell into conversation with the ancient bartender Hans, who once had been valet to Edwin Booth, the great actor who had founded the Players Club:

> He asked me what I had been doing, and I said I'd been out in the Black Hills working with Gutzon Borglum.
>
> "Ahhh, yes! Mr. Borglum!" Hans said, "a most remarkable and talented man.
>
> "I remember when he first became a member here, many years ago. He was kind of a brash young man—confident and a little cocky.
>
> "Now, it so happened that at the same time we had living here a well known old painter, Mr. ___, whose hobby, y' might say, was putting brash young fellows in their places. So . . . one evening when Mr. Borglum was very new around here he came into the bar and ordered a drink, and when he did Mr. ___ came up to the bar too, and said, 'I say, young fellow, what is your name?' (Which, of course, he already knew, but he was leading up to something.)
>
> 'Gutzon Borglum,' says Mr. Borglum.
>
> 'I'm sorry, how was that again?'
>
> 'Gut-zon Bor-glum.'
>
> Then Mr. ___ says, 'I'm sorry and I don't mean to be rude—uh, Hans, would you make me another drink?—but I *still* can't get that name.'
>
> By this time Mr. Borglum is getting pretty irritated, so he says, *very* distinctly, '*Gut-zon Bor-glum!*'
>
> And Mr. ___ says, 'Well, young fella! *Gut-zon Bor-glum* may sound like a name to you, but it sounds like passing wind in a bathtub to me!'

"Mr. Borglum was very quick-witted," said Hans, "and it wasn't very often anybody could get the best of him. But that time he was left totally speechless!"

Following service in World War II, Ziolkowski returned to the Black Hills to stay. He came at the request of a group of Sioux Indians led by Chief Standing Bear, who had asked him to carve on a Black Hills mountain a monument honoring the country's original occupants.

For this purpose, Ziolkowski personally bought, some ten miles southwest of Rushmore, a mountain whose top is a solid granite ridge. There, he began carving a statue of the Sioux war chief Crazy Horse, seated on a pony, and since his death in 1982 the work has been continued by his wife and children. This work is not being done in bas-relief as at Stone Mountain, nor as half-round figures on a cliff-face as at Rushmore. Rather it is the conversion of an entire mountain ridge into a single statue in-the-round. Because of this and its gigantic size it is the most ambitious sculptural enterprise yet undertaken by man.

Even so—perhaps partly because of Borglum's discovery at Rushmore that those who control the money may also try to control the work—the Crazy Horse project is financed, and therefore controlled, entirely by the Ziolkowskis themselves. In the beginning Korczak paid for it with income from a dairy farm he established for that purpose at the mountain's base. Now, it is supported entirely from fees paid by sightseeing visitors.

At Rushmore a modern water system and plumbing were installed in 1939, and modern toilet facilities were constructed to replace the smelly, old-fashioned outhouses that had served the monument's visitors until then.

At the same time, Borglum put in a modern water system at his ranch, and for the first time there, too, the Borglum's and their guests could enjoy the advantages of indoor plumbing.

Also, a huge new studio was under construction for Borglum at Rushmore, and had it not been for delays caused by the transfer of the project back to the National Park Service it would have been finished. Borglum was infuriated with the Park Service over the delay, and he was also quarreling with the service over the studio's design. Nonetheless, he did have the satisfaction of knowing the studio was being built and soon would be available to replace the overcrowded and overpublic one about which he had been complaining for so long.

Meanwhile, Borglum had brought the Roosevelt face to the point where by early summer it was ready for dedication—and in the process had scored another sculptural coup: the carving of Roosevelt's spectacles. They consist only of a carved nosepiece and a small ridge, suggestive of a frame, striped lightly across each of Roosevelt's upper cheeks. All the rest, in Borglum's words, "is imagination." But it is enough. To the monument viewer the spectacles are there, and they are complete.

The dedication, which included a pageant written by Ziolkowski's wife to commemorate the fiftieth anniversary of South Dakota statehood, took place on the evening of July 2. Like so many of Borglum's previous dedications—beginning with the unveiling of Lee at Stone Mountain clear back in 1924—this one, too, was preceded by rain that miraculously cleared away just in time.

Held on a Sunday evening, it was by far the best attended of all the Rushmore dedications—about 3,000 cars and 12,000 people—and unquestionably it was the most colorful. The precipitation in its passing had left a sky that was clear and air that was mountain-cool and smelled of rain-freshened earth and pine and stone. Low in the eastern sky there hung a fat moon just one day past full, and above the night-dark forest the gathering crowd could see the great stone faces looming moon-washed and pale against a field of stars.

William S. Hart, a noted Western actor in silent films who had spent part of his boyhood in Dakota Territory, was there—having been flown from Hollywood by the famous stunt pilot Paul Mantz. Also present from Hollywood was the tenor Richard Dennis. And eighty-three-year-old Doane Robinson was there, too, wearing the same swallow-tailed coat and derby hat he had worn fifty years before at the ceremony in which South Dakota had become a state.

Hart, as his part of the program, made a speech appealing for justice for America's original citizens—the Indians—and it was a dramatic one for he made it partly in English, partly in Lakotah (Sioux), and partly in Indian sign language. Unfortunately, he talked longer than had been allowed for in the schedule of CBS, which was broadcasting the event, and the announcer found it necessary to cut him off and move to the next part of the program. As Robert Dean described it:

> At one moment Hart's voice was echoing out over the mountains through the loudspeakers, the next, he suddenly found himself talking into a dead mike. . . .
> Bill Hart was really mad. He kept shouting . . . trying to make the dead mike bring his words at least to the crowd, but the loudspeakers drowned him out. Then he began simply shouting impreca-

tions—at Borglum, at me, at whoever was responsible for what was
happening to him. . . .

And then, just as the situation was about to become a real crisis,
Louella Jones [Borglum, Lincoln's wife] rushed up to him, threw
here arms about him, and smothered his curses with kisses, saving
the day.

Richard Dennis sang, and that was dramatic, too, for he sang Irving
Berlin's new song, "God Bless America." The crowd was moved by that,
greatly moved, and Borglum was heard to say, "I have done a lot of things I
am proud of, but . . . I would gladly abandon my sense of accomplishment in
all I have done if, by doing it, I could claim authorship of one song, 'God
Bless America.' Only one in thousands can see my art, but every man, woman,
and child with an ounce of American blood may stand with reverently bowed
head and sing that song."

The most dramatic event of all, however, was the unveiling—which in this
case was not an unveiling at all, but an *illuminating*. It began with a spectacular display of set-piece fireworks showing in turn, an Indian and white
man greeting each other, a steamboat, a covered wagon, a locomotive, a map
of the state, and an American flag. Just when the set-pieces had died away
into darkness, a sudden salvo of giant rockets climbed high in the night and
exploded into flares that illuminated the Rushmore faces. Then, as the flares
settled and died their light was replaced by that from twelve huge floodlights
gradually being turned up, and the crowd gasped and murmured with awe.

There were speeches (naturally), and in one of them Judge A. R. Denu of
Rapid City said:

I hope . . . America's Shrine of Democracy will proclaim with mute
eloquence for unnumbered centuries the basic truth that, by the law
of nature and nature's God, the individual and not the state is the
basic unit of society.

And he was followed by Borglum, who declared:

We are at the spearhead of a mighty world movement—an awakened
force in rebellion against the worn and useless thought of yesterday. . . . We are reaching deep into the soul of mankind, and
through democracy building better than has ever been built before.

Even as they spoke, however, that "mighty world movement" was getting ever deeper into trouble, and those world leaders who, unlike Judge Denu, believed that the individual existed only to serve the state were growing steadily more powerful and more dangerous.

In August, Hitler and Stalin concluded a "non-aggression pact" that actually was an agreement for their joint aggression against Poland. At dawn, eight days later, German aircraft, armor, and infantry began pouring over the Polish border, and the world learned a new German word—*Blitzkrieg*, meaning "lightning war."

On September 3, Great Britain finally declared war on Germany, and on the 4th France followed suit. But that was all they did, and Hitler's troops continued to roll over Poland. On the 17th, the Soviet Union attacked Poland from the east. Ten days later, divided between Hitler and Stalin, Poland had vanished from the map.

After Poland, Hitler remained quiet while building up strength for an assault on the West, and the West remained quiet hoping maybe Mr. Hitler would change his mind and settle down. It was a time of false calm called "the phony war" or "the *Sitzkrieg*," and it again encouraged both the European democracies and the United States to think perhaps a holocaust could be avoided after all. In truth, however, the Western democracies had appeased their way into a position where their only choice, now, was the very war they had been trying to escape. The struggle had been irreversibly joined, and never again would the world be the same.

Meanwhile, things were going as well at Rushmore as they were going ill in Europe. Surprisingly, considering that Jefferson and Roosevelt still were completely unshaped below the chin and Lincoln below the beard, Borglum at last was confining himself to performing that work which the commission and the Park Service had been trying to get him to perform—the fine-finishing of all four faces.

At the same time, he was complaining that he could not do the finishing, at least not properly, because he still lacked qualified craftsmen and could find none to hire. To some extent, his concern was understandable. This was delicate work, all-important work. True sculpture was done by "feel," rather than by engineering measurements. It was that subtle shaping that was necessary to make the monument a work of art instead of merely a great stone novelty. Accordingly, it demanded all the skills Borglum could draw from others as well as from within himself.

And yet, while he complained that he could not do it well because he did not have competent craftsmen to help him, he *was* doing it well because he *did* have them. His own men, those "cast-off miners," as he had sometimes described them, whom he had trained, now were proving they had learned better than he knew. They had learned both from him and with him (for on this job Borglum still was learning, too) and in the process had developed a surprising sensitivity to the work.

One example of that sensitivity could be found in their use of the plaster masks. Borglum had long made a practice of keeping in the winch-house, and/or suspended over the mountain, a mask cast from the model of whichever head was being carved at the time. Looking at it a carver could gain a better idea of just how a particular detail he was molding should be shaped and of how it fitted into the composition as a whole. "But," Borglum often told them, "if you *feel* the mask . . . close your eyes or put it behind you, just *feel* it—your fingers will tell you much more about what you are supposed to be doing than your eyes will." This was easy for Borglum to say, for he had spent a lifetime developing sculptural sensitivity. But it could hardly have been expected to work for these men who knew of sculpture only what they had learned on Rushmore's cliff. Nonetheless, it did work for them. "It was absolutely astonishing how much it helped and how much your fingers alone could tell you," said Red Anderson. Which, in turn, showed just how far these "cast-off miners" had come since the day when they had appeared at Rushmore seeking only a job—any kind of job.

In carving the monument the rough-shaping was done by the drillers, who worked down to within about six inches of the finished surface of the heads, and in the process they removed granite by the foot and by the ton. Then the carvers took over. By "honeycombing"—drilling grids of very shallow and closely spaced holes and breaking out the material between—they worked down to very near the finished "skin," and in so doing they removed stone by the inch and the pound.

Then came the fine finishing. This was done by carvers using "bumpers" —light, handheld pneumatic hammers driving short steel shafts tipped with four sharp, stubby fingers that chattered against the granite and removed it by the fraction of an inch and by the ounce.

As a part of the finishing, carvers "bumped" away the polka-dotting of round freckles left by the holes drilled in honeycombing, and they smoothed away the roughness created by breaking away the stone between those holes. That was the easy part. Then, closely supervised by Gutzon or Lincoln, they shaped on the stone faces those subtle nuances—those mounds and hollows and rounded wrinkles—that give living faces age and character and personality. And that was the hard part. Much of it was free-form sculpturing of

details that were not found on the models but were newly designed by
Borglum as he studied the faces in the light of morning and afternoon and
evening from the studio, canyon, and tramway cage. Slow, tedious, expensive,
it was the final test of Borglum's genius and the craftsmanship of his men. If
successful, they would leave for posterity magnificent stone portraits. If they
failed they would leave only gigantic stone cartoons.

Through hot September, rainy October, unseasonably sunny November
and December, the finishing work continued. Then it was 1940, and with
the coming of the new year there appeared indisputable evidence that both
Rushmore and Borglum had become national institutions. In the case of
Rushmore, the evidence was the February 24 issue of the *Saturday Evening
Post*. Spread on its cover was a Lincoln Borglum color photograph of the
Washington carving in profile, and inside was a Rushmore story illustrated by
Lincoln Borglum photographs. And in Borglum's case the evidence was that
at last he had been invited to join that illustrious company of sports figures,
film stars, and the like who are hired to say nice things about the products
of various manufacturers. Hence, readers of national magazines now saw
a photo (taken circa 1927) of a young-looking Borglum working on his Rushmore models, and below the photo they read:

THE HANDS OF
GUTZON BORGLUM
SCULPTOR

Born in the rugged splendor of
Idaho, his accomplishments are
those of the pioneer: audacious,
imaginative, purposeful . . .
The world honors him as a
great sculptor.

GUTZON BORGLUM'S WATCH IS A LONGINES CHRONOGRAPH

THE WORLD'S MOST HONORED
HANDS WEAR THE WORLD'S
MOST HONORED WATCH

And in another ad, above a picture of Borglum suspended in a sling-seat
on the side of Lincoln's nose, they read:

60. *One of the masks taken up onto the mountain, for Borglum and the carvers to refer to.*

SCULPTOR GUTZON BORGLUM
tells of years of work . . .
nervous strain . . . headaches

Below, you see him inspecting the
70-foot head of Lincoln. Incessant
drilling, many problems, meant
headaches. He says:
"I always take Bromo-Seltzer for
headaches . . . it relieves nervous
strain, stomach upsets too."

The timing of the latter was more appropriate than the agency preparing it could have known, because for Borglum 1940 was indeed a time of problems and headaches and nervous strain, and of irascible temper as well. A major reason, undoubtedly, was his health. In February and again in September he was hospitalized in Colorado Springs. The February confinement, Mary wired Case, was "for slight surgical attention and to get toned up," but it may have been more serious than that, for upon his return he was attended for a time by a trained nurse.

He was hearing himself criticized for spending too much money on the current carving with too little visible result and was much upset by it. There always was some basis for that sort of criticism. Efficiency simply was not one of his long suits. In this case, however, when he was involved in fine-finishing, whose results were more essential than obvious, the criticism was largely unjustified. And regardless of whether it was or not, Borglum found it to be infuriating.

He was furious, too, with the Park Service for insisting that he confine his present efforts to the faces alone. "I know it was their work that stopped all work on the mountain except the heads," he wrote to Arundel, and added that the Service was engaged in "troublesome sabotage."

Also, the Park Service still was insisting he prepare and submit some sort of organized plans and realistic cost estimates for his work, and he lashed back saying this was an absurd attempt "to apply road-builder practices . . . or sophomoric engineering to the carving of a great portrait."

On top of all that, the service now had taken over responsibility for all landscaping in the Rushmore park area. This was what the service was supposed to do. Borglum had been engaged only to design and create the monument itself. Nevertheless, Borglum did not see it that way, and wrote to Case: "The Commission has urged upon me the control of the landscaping, not by a special resolution, but by desire of the members, and it is part of my job anyway."

The Park Service also had been talking about bringing in crews from the Civilian Conservation Corps to do the actual labor of landscaping, and Borglum did not like that either:

> I think the park service . . . will go down in history without a
> laurel wreath. Their CCC camps are filled with no-good men . . .
> [who] are not worth anything. They clutter our roads, run into
> people, do not know how to drive a truck, and the few hours they
> work a day amounts to nothing.

Done through the commission and by Rushmore men, Borglum would receive twenty-five percent of the landscaping cost as his fee. Done by the Park Service and CCC, he would receive nothing. Hence, it is likely this had much to do with his objection, for he needed the fee. True, he now was receiving an average of over $2,500 a month from Rushmore, and in addition was receiving fees from product endorsements, lectures, and other sculptural contracts. The problem was that he was almost $200,000 in debt (well over a million in 1984 dollars), and interest alone was costing him around a thousand dollars a month. Consequently, to manage his debts and still maintain his standard of living he required an enormous amount of income

Astonishingly, despite his economic headaches and his health and irritation with the Park Service, Borglum now had become reconciled with his old adversary John Boland. Partly this was because Borglum found it almost impossible to hold a grudge after its immediate cause had been removed. Partly it was because he had discovered that Boland had not really been responsible for many of his previous problems after all. But the reconciliation appears to have been effected mainly by Mary and Ethel. Perhaps it was because both had been teachers that these tiny, down-to-earth women seem to have regarded their husbands' feuding as a ridiculous scrap between two grown-up little boys in a schoolyard, and to the extent they could prevent it they simply were not going to put up with it. Accordingly, invitations again were being passed between them and, as had been the case so long ago, the Borglums again were occasional dinner guests at the Bolands, and the Bolands were enjoying dinners, picnics, and fishing at the Borglum ranch. Once again Borglum was throwing his arm across Boland's shoulders and calling him "Johnny," and was saying (just as Williamson had predicted he would) that Johnny Boland had been one of Rushmore's indispensable men. For his part, Boland was a little more reserved about it. Not long ago this chummy sculptor had been calling him illiterate, uncultured, corrupting, grasping, and a political opportunist, and that was hard to forget. But Boland tried, and to a substantial extent he succeeded. Hence, even though their reconciliation was not as perfect as it might have been it was far better than anyone could have expected, and it was a warming thing to see.

27. Last Days of Gutzon Borglum

Even before Borglum went to the hospital in February it had become apparent that with the money on hand he was not going to be able to finish even the faces of the four presidents, let alone their figures or anything else. Which in turn meant he and the commission again must take their money buckets to Washington and hope a benevolent Congress would refill them.

The prospect was not encouraging. To most of those involved, it was becoming increasingly clear that the Rushmore clock was approaching midnight. But not to Borglum. That was an idea he simply would not and could not accept, and he wrote to Case: "There is no question in my mind but that the Nation will respond to any sums necessary to perfect this work which was conceived without funds and carried forward on a shoestring!"

The nation's financial watchdogs, however, were not feeling all that responsive. Borglum and Park Service officials together had figured out they needed another $318,000, and to make it a good round figure the Department of the Interior then submitted to the Bureau of the Budget a request for approval of $350,000. The Bureau came back with the stunning statement that it would approve $86,000 and no more.

In July and again in August the matter came before the House Appropriations Committee, where it fared no better.

Then, as had become his habit, Borglum appealed to President Roosevelt —and got no help there either.

According to Case, the reason for all this was that the bureau, the committee, and the president, "have been told before that this appropriation or that appropriation would definitely wind up the work," and they were getting tired of having it always turn out otherwise.

Unquestionably, however, the real reason was another and much larger one. Rushmore by now had become something of a national institution and an article of national pride. Accordingly, however much it might grumble about Borglum's astonishingly inaccurate cost estimates, Congress in other times undoubtedly would have continued to fund its construction. But not in these times. Not when Congress and the nation were bewildered and not a little frightened by the speed at which Europe and possibly the world were falling apart.

The "*Sitzkrieg*" had ended in the spring—had ended with a German offensive that had conquered Denmark in three hours, Norway in six weeks, Holland in three days, Belgium in eighteen days, and France in thirty days. All of which moved columnist Walter Lippman to write, "Before the snow flies again, we may stand as the last great democracy on earth."

In October the Rushmore appropriation bill came before Congress, and by then it had begun to appear that Lippman had been right. Britain was being bombed and London was burning, and, in nightly broadcasts by Edward R. Murrow, Americans were hearing it burn. Moreover, Hitler was massing a fleet for the invasion of England, and there was little reason to believe the invasion would fail.

The members of Congress were confused and divided. Those called "America Firsters" argued that the United States should remain snugly behind its oceans and let Europe fend for itself. One of these was Borglum's friend Senator Pittman, who declared to the Senate that Great Britain should just retreat to Canada and let Hitler have the British Isles. Others—and more of them every day—agreed with Winston Churchill, who had said: "Upon this battle depends the survival of Christian civilization. . . . If we fail, then the whole world, including the United States, will sink into the abyss of a new Dark Age." Americans, generally, seemed to feel that way also, and a Gallup poll showed seventy-one percent of them in favor of giving Britain some sort of support.

There was a growing feeling, too, that the United States had better get prepared to defend itself, and defense was expensive. Accordingly, it was hard to see how Congress now could be expected to give any support, however small, to something as relatively insignificant as the carving of a mountaintop out in Dakota. It did give the support, nonetheless, and the $86,000 bill was passed. This bill, however, included the proviso suggested by Senator Dirksen for the previous one—a proviso making this the government's *final* investment in the Rushmore carving.

Because of Gutzon's health problems and his activities elsewhere, much of the 1940 carving was performed by Lincoln. When he was there, Gutzon

studied the faces from all angles and in all lights and designed the subtle details necessary to making them true works of sculpture. Most of the time,
however, he then passed these designs on to Lincoln for execution.

With the work thus laid out and with Lincoln to supervise it and an experienced crew to perform it, things at the mountain went smoothly through
the summer. With one notable exception—the tramway accident.

The tramway cage was a wooden structure—"a sort of Chic Sale outhouse
without a top," one workman described it—capable of carrying five or six
persons at a time. It was suspended from large pulleys running on a seven-
eighths-inch cable stretched from the hoist house on Mount Doane to the
A-frame on top of the Roosevelt head some thirteen hundred feet distant and
four hundred feet higher. The cage was propelled by a three-eighths-inch
cable driven by a large drivewheel at the hoist house. The drivewheel was supposed to be fixed on its axle by a steel key, and both wheel-hub and axle contained key-seats for that purpose. Actually, however, the wheel had been fastened by a set-screw driven through the hub and into the key-seat of the axle.
Now, undetected by anyone, the set-screw was working itself loose.

There already had been one tramway accident. It had occurred some
years earlier, and had it been timed just a little differently it might have cost
Rushmore the life of its sculptor. As hoist operator Edwald Hayes recalled it:

> The Old Man showed up wanting to ride to the top, but I had a load
> of water cans on the way up already, so he had to wait. Just before
> the load got to the top, the hoist drive-shaft broke. That set the cage
> free and it came back down just whizzing. It crashed into the loading
> platform and smashed all to pieces and scattered water cans all over
> the place. If the Old Man had showed up about three minutes earlier
> it would have been him in the cage instead of those cans.

For a while, that incident had put a damper on men riding in the cage, but
now it was time-dimmed and half forgotten. Besides, in 1936 Spotts had put
an emergency brake on the cage just in case such a thing were to happen

61. Borglum in the tramway cage. The chain above his
head is attached to the brake arm, which broke on the day
the cage ran away and crashed.

again. So . . . when Gus Schramm, Adolph Valdez, Howdy Peterson, Alfred Johnson, and Norman "Happy" Anderson boarded the cage early on the morning of June 2, they were jostling and joking and unconcerned.

They were probably within about two hundred feet of the top of the mountain when the loosening set-screw finally let go.

Instantly the cage began racing back toward the hoist house, eleven hundred feet behind and almost four hundred feet below.

"Hit the brake!" yelled Peterson.

Someone pulled the chain controlling the brake handle. The cage slowed, then stopped.

Next, they released the brake slightly, and the cage began easing slowly downward. Then the brake started smoking. Its metal shoes grasped the cable

62. Some of the structures on the clifftop. At left center is the A-frame and platform that were wiped away on the day the A-frame collapsed.

with a pinching action, and the resulting friction was causing them to over-heat. Kept engaged enough to make the cage move slowly and safely, the brake shoes would become red hot and soft and would fail. The only alternative seemed to be to apply the brake intermittently and try thus to come down in a series of spurts and jerks. With mechanic Howdy Peterson watching the brake and calling instructions they did just that, and traveled nervously but safely . . . for about eight hundred feet. As Peterson recounted it later:

> We'd go along and I'd say, "Hit it again!" and they'd hit it and stop the cage and we'd let the brake cool. Then we'd do it again, and we were coming down all right. Then Schramm—a *big* fella, weighed about two-twenty-five—he pulled the chain so hard the brake-arm broke. And, Boy! Rrrooommm! Down we went!

Foreman Matt Riley happened to be at the hoist house at the time, and with great presence of mind he levered a piece of two-by-four against the spinning cable drum and slowed it somewhat. Otherwise the accident probably would have been fatal.

As it was, the cage struck, smashed, and flung its passengers willy-nilly onto the loading platform.

Valdez seemed to be unhurt. Schramm was temporarily unconscious. Peterson was bruised and lacerated and so was Johnson. Happy Anderson was missing, at least for the moment. Then he was found lying in the door of the blacksmith shop according to some, and in the weeds beside the compressor house according to others. No one seems to be quite sure how he got there. Some say that just before the crash he jumped, hoping to land on the roof of the compressor house. Others say he was thrown out of the cage when it struck. But even though the event may have been confused, its result was not. Anderson had a fractured arm and several broken ribs.

All who had been in the accident were sent by Lincoln to Rapid City, where they were hospitalized for observation. Five were sent, but through a mix-up six were hospitalized. Glen Jones, who had helped take the men to town, explained (or has been quoted as having explained), "By God! Those nurses took one look at me and threw me in a room and put me to bed, and I wasn't even *in* the damn thing when it wrecked!" But, as Howdy Peterson commented later, "Ol' Glen was quite a card. He was a real cutup." Hence, it is quite possible the mix-up was engineered by Jones, himself.

As it finally turned out, all injuries but Anderson's were minor, and his

healed completely and with no lasting damage. And so ended the most serious accident in all fourteen years of Rushmore's construction.

The days of summer flowed past and then it was fall, and with fall came
money from the new appropriation, making it possible again to continue
carving throughout the winter.

It was a presidential election year, and Franklin Roosevelt, winning fifty-
five percent of the popular vote, was returned to office. Much to Borglum's
dismay, however, South Dakota returned to her traditional loyalties and gave
fifty-eight percent of her vote to Roosevelt's opponent, Wendell Willkie.

There was war talk in the air that fall, and the talk was growing.

A Selective Service act was passed, and in November young men began
receiving letters in which President Roosevelt extended his greetings and directed them to report to their local draft boards for classification.

On December 29, the president proposed yet another response to the
growing threat—a program of massive aid to embattled Great Britain. He
called the program "lend-lease" and said it was intended to make the United
States "the great Arsenal of Democracy."

In grand disregard of this shift in national emphasis, the mood of Congress, and the clause in the last Rushmore appropriation bill making it the
final one, Borglum, early in 1941, again set out to get Congress to bestow
another financial blessing upon his monument. The way things were, he
should have seen this as a proposition too hopeless even to attempt, but
"hopeless" simply was not in the man's vocabulary. Now more than ever his
determination was a mighty river fed by at least three streams.

One stream was financial. He never said so, but it had to have been. Even
with his income from Rushmore he was in financial hot water. Without it he
faced financial disaster.

Another was patriotic. Gutzon Borglum believed with all his heart in the
"American Dream," and he believed he was creating at Rushmore a symbol of
that dream so significant and everlasting that no congressman in his right
mind would dare vote against its funding.

But the most powerful of Borglum's motivational streams seems to have
flowed from his hunger for creative fulfillment and recognition. And Mount
Rushmore, his supreme creative achievement, had become his obsession, reason for living, ticket to immortality.

These always had been Borglum's Rushmore motivations, and had they
not always been strong there would have been no Rushmore Memorial. But
despite his seventy-four years and tiring body, they were now at their fullest
flood. They had enabled him to convince himself, the Rushmore Commis-

63. *The interior of Borglum's new studio, showing
his view of the mountain, about 1941.*

sion, and a remarkable number of Park Service and Department of the Interior officials that Congress even now could be persuaded to give Rushmore another appropriation.

Accordingly, the sculptor and Park Service officials together worked up a budget calling for an appropriation of $278,000 and submitted it to the Department of the Interior. The Department, in turn, included it in its own current funding request to the Bureau of Budget.

Next, Borglum wrote to President Roosevelt, asking his support of the Rushmore funding request.

Then, in what had become an annual event as predictable as the return of the swallows to Capistrano, he set off for Washington to fight personally for the requested funds.

Mary went with him this time, and on the way they stopped in Chicago, where Borglum was to deliver a speech. While there, he consulted a doctor friend about some prostate trouble he had been having.

The doctor recommended surgery.

The surgery was performed on February 17. Three days later, while on her way to the hospital, Mary slipped on a patch of ice and broke her wrist. Nonetheless, arm in a cast, she continued to stay beside Gutzon at the hospital, where both he and the doctor thought he was recovering nicely. Actually, however, he was not. Surgery in the pelvic area is especially likely to produce blood clots, and in Borglum's case it had. Now, undetected and dangerous, the clots were wandering about in his system.

He still appeared to be doing very well on the last day of February, when Russell Arundel dropped in with a crushing piece of news. President Roosevelt had announced he was cutting non-defense spending to the bone, Arundel said, and would approve no more money for such projects as Rushmore. The Shrine of Democracy must now give way to the Arsenal of Democracy.

Two days later one of the blood clots lodged, and Borglum suffered, but survived, a pulmonary embolism.

Mary sent for Lincoln at Rushmore and Mary Ellis in Nevada, both of whom arrived within forty-eight hours.

Early on the morning of March 6 another blood clot lodged and produced an embolism that even the indomitable Borglum could not withstand. A few minutes later, a week to the day after he had learned he would receive no more money for Rushmore, Gutzon Borglum was gone.

On the following Sunday, at just before eleven o'clock in the morning, the men of Rushmore assembled outside Keystone's white-steepled Congregational church at the foot of Mount Aetna. In Sunday-best suits usually a little too tight in the shoulders, hair slicked down and smelling of Brilliantine, faces sun-browned and weathered above white shirt collars, moving with sober restraint and therefore with the self-conscious awkwardness of men whose usual movements are sweeping and unrestrained, they formed into a column. Then, preceded by an honor guard of Keystone Boy Scouts and with Alton "Hoot" Leech standing inside the door and calling their names from a roll, they marched into the church to pay their final homage to Gutzon Borglum.

Borglum's body was not there. It had been temporarily interred in Chicago from where, three years later, it would be moved to Forest Lawn in Glendale, California. Hence this was not a funeral but a memorial service. A service held by and for that Rushmore "family" with whose lives the life of Borglum had been so long and intimately intertwined. Even the minister, the

Reverend Carl Loocke, was one of the "family" and had been with Borglum on that long-ago day in August when the sculptor had climbed for the very first time to the top of Mount Rushmore.

Outside, the clouds were low and it was cold, and occasionally the church windows were brushed by snow. But inside, the church was warm, a little too warm if anything, and it smelled solemnly of hot stove and hymnals and old pine pews and of roses that banked the altar.

While hymns were being sung by the Keystone Choir, the men who together with Gutzon Borglum had built Rushmore sat gravely and somewhat uncomfortably in the crowded, hard-bottomed pews, and remembered. . .

. . . The Chief hadn't been easy to work for. Demanding, impatient, quick-tempered, sometimes harshly unforgiving. But then, maybe it took a guy like that to handle this hard-nosed bunch. A soft, easygoing man couldn't have done it, that was for sure. But the Chief had been able to, and had managed to win their loyalty while he was at it. . . .

. . . He was a fighter. Man, was he ever. Not afraid of anybody or anything. He'd have tackled hell with a garden hose if he'd had a reason to, and you just had to respect somebody like that. . . .

. . . And a talker—he could have talked a dog off a meat wagon. Ziolkowski had said one time, "That man could sell you the Brooklyn Bridge and then make you glad you'd bought it." If he hadn't been able to do that—to talk all kinds of people into all kinds of things—the Rushmore job probably would have died a long time ago. . . .

. . . He was a moody cuss. When he was up you couldn't do anything wrong, and when he was down you couldn't do anything right, and you never knew which way it was going to be. . . .

. . . But the big thing was, down under all that impatience and temper and moodiness Borglum was as big-hearted and generous as anybody you'd want to meet. New men didn't see that at first and were likely to think he was a real sonavabitch. But the longer they were here the more they realized he was just the opposite. . . .

. . . He had cared about the crew, that was the thing. Really cared. He never was chummy with 'em. He was stand-offish and kept his place like an officer in the army. But he looked out for his men. . . . He was a nut about their safety. For instance, he was always running his hands over the sling-seat cables, feeling for a barb that meant a broken strand. One barb and out that cable went. Said he wasn't going to have one of his men hurt if he could help it, and except for Happy Anderson in that freak cage accident, in all the Rushmore years none had been. . . .

. . . He'd bawl you out until you just wanted to stomp him, then if he thought you needed it he'd give you the shirt off his back. . . . Lots of times if one of the guys was broke and really up against it, the Chief would dip into his own pocket and give him some money, and unless the guy told it himself nobody would ever know about it. . . .

. . . Borglum was a crackerjack of a sculptor, all you had to do was to look at Rushmore to know that. . . . But more important, he was a crackerjack of a *man*. Like the old-timers used to say, he was somebody you could ride the river with. . . .

The choir had finished, and now Badger Clark, nationally recognized poet and poet laureate of South Dakota, was giving the eulogy:

. . . he did not die, this artist, engineer and dreamer. He will live longer than the monument he created. Coming generations five thousand years hence will not ask who the characters on the mountain are, but who carved them.

The Reverend W. E. Hartung pronounced a benediction, and then it was over.

Meanwhile, the nation, too, was remembering Gutzon Borglum and was discussing and evaluating both him and his work.

When a private figure dies it is customary to say only nice things about him, and his funeral is one occasion when members of the clergy not only are permitted but expected, if it be necessary, to indulge in perjury. The public figure, however, is not so considerately treated. Editors, colleagues, competitors, friends, enemies, and the general public all join in a merciless winnowing of his deeds and misdeeds and virtues and vices, and in passing judgment on what his place in history should be, if any. And so it was with Borglum.

Dynamic, aggressive, verbal, multitalented, he had made a national impact. There was no doubt about that. Nor had he ever been tainted by even a hint of public or private scandal. However, he had died with his Rushmore memorial far from finished as he had planned it. And he had died as he had lived—embroiled in all sorts of altercations and controversies. So the question was: Would his Rushmore monument now be regarded as only an interesting but unfinished novelty? And would its sculptor be remembered only as an interesting and controversial eccentric? Or would history give one or both of them a more exalted place?

The answers were quick in coming. Critics of the traditionalist sort, such as those who admired the works of Norman Rockwell, declared the Rushmore carving to be a great work of art. Those who admired the three-eyed ladies of Picasso insisted that it was not. However, fine art or not, almost all were agreed that the Rushmore carving indeed had been a magnificent accomplishment.

In recalling Borglum, some editors and commentators mentioned only his virtues and his genius. Others spoke also of his flamboyance, contentiousness, and bristly temper. But again almost all were agreed that there was in Borglum a greatness that dwarfed into insignificance whatever shortcomings he might have had.

Soon there remained no doubt that even though it was unfinished, Mount Rushmore would go down through the ages with all the meaning and majesty Borglum had intended it to have. And there remained no doubt that Gutzon Borglum, himself, would be remembered as an American giant.

The boy from the Nebraska plains at last had captured his moon.

28. Shrine of Democracy— The Dream Fulfilled

G utzon Borglum was gone and that could not be changed, so now it
was time to try to pick up the pieces and figure out what to do next.
The opinion of most editors and commentators and of the general
public was that the pieces could not be picked up, and that the Rushmore
work should be shut down now and forever. Rushmore's workmen disagreed,
and immediately following their memorial service for Borglum they all signed
a petition that read:

> We, the men who have worked under Gutzon Borglum on
> Mount Rushmore in past years do hereby and hereon unanimously
> petition the Mount Rushmore Memorial Commission to permit
> Lincoln Borglum, his son, to take full charge and complete the work
> as to his father's wishes.

Mary Borglum disagreed also, and wrote to Congressman Case, "Of
course the thing dearest to [Gutzon's] heart was Rushmore and the wish that
Lincoln should carry on. . . ."

And William Williamson disagreed, and told the press: "To accomplish
such a project requires a man of exceptional qualifications. . . . I am of the
opinion that Lincoln Borglum is better qualified to complete the project than
any other man."

The Rushmore Commission, as it turned out, was of the same opinion.
Meeting in Washington, D.C., on March 17, it instructed Williamson to prepare a sculptor's contract for Lincoln. Williamson complied so promptly that
he had the contract drafted before the day was over, and on the following
morning it was approved and signed.

At the same time the commission submitted to the Park Service a new budget calling for an appropriation of $250,000, but this was just wishful thinking and a waste of time. Even before Borglum's death there would have been no chance of getting such a thing approved, and now there was absolutely none. In fact, the Department of the Interior did not even pass it on to the Bureau of the Budget. Instead, the department asked for, and in due time the Park Service received, only enough money to maintain the monument for viewing by the public. Consequently, what the commission now had to work with, and all it would ever have, was about $50,000 remaining from the appropriation of the previous year. How could it best be used? That was up to Lincoln, and ten days later, as a guest on the CBS radio program, "We the People," he announced his plans: "The sculpture work on the faces was completed before Father's death, and the features of the four presidents will not be touched. We've got to finish the hair on Jefferson, Roosevelt, and Lincoln and do some work on Lincoln's collar and on his head. That's the immediate program."

Actually, Lincoln had somewhat understated his task. The features of Roosevelt did require additional finishing, and there remained, as well, some necessary work on Washington's collar and lapels.

That was what he had to do, and he had only $50,000 to do it with. He was but twenty-nine years old and not yet known as a sculptor—only as a sculptor's son. Now, as the new head of the Rushmore work he would be in the national spotlight, and any evidence of immaturity or ineptitude would be promptly noted and publicized. It was a sobering challenge, and he must have found it a frightening one as well.

That summer of 1941 was a restless, fermentive season, both on the mountain and off. A strange season of growing prosperity accompanied by equally growing uneasiness.

ON FOLLOWING PAGES:

64. The status of the carving in the summer of 1941, after Gutzon Borglum's death and as Lincoln Borglum undertakes the finishing of the monument. Note that work is being done on the hair of Jefferson and Roosevelt, on the collars of Washington and Jefferson, and on the beard of Lincoln. On Washington's head the dismantling of one of the buildings has begun.

Drawn in a large part by Rushmore, tourists were swarming to the Hills as never before, and the businesses catering to them were busy and prospering.

After a solid decade of drought, the rains at last had returned to the West River country and grass grew deep on the ranges and crops grew lush on the farmland. Moreover, war was raging in Europe, and because wars are great consumers of food, prices for cattle and crops were steadily rising. Wars also being great consumers of metal and minerals, closed mines in the Black Hills were being reopened and open mines were being expanded.

Across the nation, defense plants by the hundreds were being established to make tanks and ships and airplanes and guns and clothing. They were hiring people by the tens of thousands, but because the armed forces now were inducting men also by the tens of thousands there were far fewer people to be hired than before.

What it all came down to was this: the country had moved with bewildering speed from a time of too many people for its available jobs to one of too many jobs for its available people, and the Great Depression was ended.

People knew this, and yet they did not know it. It was something hard to realize and even harder to trust. Anyone willing to work could have economic security now . . . and, yet, it did not feel like security. It was a melody played off-key. The prosperity had a false feeling about it and carried the odor of gunpowder and blood. Increasingly, also, there was a feeling that before long the war would demand American gunpowder and American blood. Thus, even while enjoying the beginning of this new prosperity people were disquieted and restless, as birds are restless before a gathering storm.

On the mountain the job was going very well indeed. Lincoln Borglum was performing superbly—doing with skill all that had been expected of him, and more. The men, too, were performing superbly but their mood was different now. On the mountain, as in the nation, there was an underlying restlessness. They could see handwriting on the wall and they needed no Daniel to tell them its meaning. It said the days of the job were numbered and soon

65. The finishing work on the Roosevelt head, after Gutzon Borglum's death. Note the subtle ripples and wrinkles that Borglum had carved into the "skin" of the face to give it age and character, the polka-dot pattern left by "honeycombing" that was then removed, and the way Borglum created the illusion of Roosevelt's spectacles.

layoffs would begin, and the crew would dwindle and then be gone. And this was the sobering thing—a dark knowledge from which grew a mixed crop of emotions and long silent thoughts.

Fourteen years this job had been going on—almost a third of a working lifetime. During those years the men of Rushmore and their families had shared each other's triumphs and tragedies and everyday living. They had watched each other's children growing up, and among those children there had been a considerable amount of intermarriage. They had worked together, played together, looked out for each other, squabbled with each other, and in the process had become a family bound by ties almost as strong as those of blood. Now that family was about to become torn up and scattered, and this was a hard thing to think about.

Hard, too, was the thought of leaving the job unfinished as Borglum had planned it. For, gradually and probably without realizing it themselves, these crewmen had become caught up in Borglum's Rushmore dream and had come to feel about the job much as Borglum had felt. They had come to believe they were creating a thing so unique and magnificent and everlasting that it would come to be known as one of the wonders of the world, and a thing that was certainly too important to be left uncompleted. Lincoln Borglum was saying that with their faces fully finished the portraits of the presidents would be as effective and majestic as if they had been carved to the waist as originally planned. Perhaps Lincoln was right. Perhaps they might be even more effective because this way all attention was focused on the faces, and that was where all the character and expression was. But the Hall of Records—*that* ought to be finished, and now that Rushmore had a water system it could be done by wet-drilling and thus without all that killing dust. Located almost exactly halfway between the nation's coasts, carved in the heart of a bombproof mountain where earthquakes were unknown, and in a dry climate as well, the Hall would be, as Borglum had said, a perfect storage place for records and artifacts of American history and for the preservation of such national treasurers as the Constitution and Declaration of Independence. Yes, both in spite of the war and because of it, the Hall ought to be finished. But it would not be finished, and that was disturbing.

One good thing about the job coming to an end now, and about the only good one, was that other jobs would be easy to find. A year ago it would have been difficult, and before that it would have been next to impossible. But no more. In the Black Hills, and in nearby Wyoming and Montana and Colorado, mines were looking for hardrock men—drillers, machine operators, powdermen, and others—and were paying top wages. Further from home, defense plants also were looking for men and paying top wages. Moreover, at Rushmore, where pay always had been good, there had been almost no layoff time during the past two-and-a-half years, and many among the crew had built up a cushion of savings. As a consequence, the future did not look disturbing financially, but in other ways it did.

The trouble with those other jobs was that they were just jobs. There was nothing special about them, and the men of Rushmore had become accustomed to feeling special. Sculpting with drills and dynamite, they had been doing work no one else in the world had done. They had been building something no one else in the world had built. There was pride in that. And prestige. A feeling of being kings of the mountain. When they left Rushmore they would have to leave that feeling behind, and it would not be easy to do.

Still . . . the memory of what they had accomplished during their Rushmore days would go with them, and with passing years they were to find ever greater satisfaction in that memory and to take ever greater pride in that accomplishment. Just before his death thirty-six years later, Red Anderson would say, "I think now that Rushmore has been ninety percent of my life." Nor was he alone in that feeling. For when the men of Rushmore had passed from youth to age they would come to know, as only the elderly can really know, how fleeting are the accomplishments most men leave behind them. They are ripples from a stone cast into a pond, shimmering for an instant and then gone and forgotten. And they would be warmed by knowing their achievement at Rushmore had been no mere ripple in a pond. It would endure beyond the time of their grandchildren's grandchildren—perhaps even beyond the time of mankind itself. It was from their toil and sweat and perseverance that the monument had been molded, and so long as it should live a part of each of them would live also. In building Rushmore the men of the crew, like Borglum, had bought themselves a piece of immortality.

Not until years later, when they had aged and mellowed, would Rushmore's men give voice to these thoughts about the breaking up of the crew, the job left unfinished, and the special feeling they had gained from being Rushmore's builders. Now they kept these things to themselves, because in this kind of crew the expression of deep or sentimental feelings was a thing too embarrassing even to contemplate.

And so, on its surface that final season at Rushmore seemed no different from all the seasons before. Hard work and horseplay and Saturday night dances and Saturday night fights. Meanwhile, the days were slipping by and the remaining tasks were being finished—Roosevelt's face, Lincoln's head, Washington's lapels, and the rest.

Then summer was gone and it was October, and the aspens turned yellow in the canyons and the nights grew cold, and Rushmore's rooftops glistened with morning frost. Most of the remaining jobs had been done and most of the remaining money had been spent, and layoffs were begun and the crew commenced melting away.

On October 31, the mountain for the last time echoed the chatter of bumpers and the clamor of drills. Then, at four o'clock on that day it was returned to the timeless silence from which Gutzon Borglum so many years before had roused it. And at that moment the great faces carved upon it appeared just as they do today, and as they will appear to generations yet unborn.

At almost the exact hour that the carving of Rushmore was ended, the war that had ended it drew its first American blood. For, on the night of October 31, 1941, out in the North Atlantic a German submarine torpedoed the American destroyer *Reuben James*, and the *James* went down still carrying two-thirds of her 145-man crew. Five weeks later the war again was to claim American blood, and far more of it—at Pearl Harbor.

Thus, the time of creating a Shrine of Democracy was brought to an end, and the time of fighting to preserve democracy was begun.

How long our present American democracy may yet endure, or even if it can endure, no one can say. But however long it does endure, the mountain-carved monument to its beginnings will endure also . . .

Mount Rushmore.

APPENDIX

"History of the United States of America"
by William Andrew Burkett
Winning essay,
Entablature Contest, 1935

Bibliography

Index

"History of the United States of America"

Almighty God, from this pulpit of stone the American people render thanksgiving and praise for the new era of civilization brought forth upon this continent. Centuries of tyrannical oppression sent to these shores, God-fearing men to seek in freedom the guidance of the benevolent hand in the progress toward wisdom, goodness toward men, and piety toward God.

1776   Consequently, on July 4, 1776, our forefathers promulgated a principle never before successfully asserted, that life, liberty, equality, and pursuit of happiness were the birthrights of all mankind. In this declaration of independence beat a heart for all humanity. It declared this country free from British rule and announced the inalienable sovereignty of the people. Freedom's soldiers victoriously consecrated this land with their life's blood to be free forever more.

1787   Then, in 1787, for the first time a government was formed that derived its just powers from the consent of the governed. General Washington and representatives from the 13 states formed this sacred Constitution, which embodies our faith in God and in mankind by giving equal participation in government to all citizens, distributing the powers of governing, threefold securing freedom of speech and of the press, establishing the right to worship the Infinite according to conscience, and assuring this nation's general welfare against an embattled world. This chart of national guidance has for more than 150 years weathered the ravages of time. Its supreme trial came under the pressure of civil war, 1861–65. The deadly doctrines of secession and slavery were then purged away in blood. The seal of the Union's finality set by President Lincoln, was accomplished like all our triumphs of law and humanity, through the wisdom and the power of an honest, Christian heart.

Far-sighted American statesmanship acquired by treaties, vast wilderness territories, where progressive, adventurous Americans spread civilization and Christianity.

1803   In 1803, Louisiana was purchased from France. This acquisition extended from the Mississippi river, across the fertile prairie to the Rocky mountains, and paved the way for America's pre-eminence among the nations.

1819   In 1819, the picturesque Florida peninsula was ceded as payment of Spanish obligations due to Americans.

1845   In 1845, Texas, having patterned American democracy during the 10 years of freedom from Mexican rule, accepted the invitation to join the sisterhood of states. In 1846, the Oregon country was peacefully apportioned by the 49th parallel as the compromised international boundary of the two English-speaking nations.

1848   In 1848, California and territory likewise rich in natural resources was acquired as the consequence of an inevitable conflict with Mexico. In spirit of mutual concession, the United States granted additional indemnities for the adjustment of the international boundary, extending from the Rio Grande to the Gulf of California.

1850   In 1850, Texas willingly ceded the disputed Rio Grande region, thus ending the dramatic acquisition of the west.

1867   In 1867, Alaska was purchased from Russia.

1904   In 1904, the Panama Canal Zone was acquired for our people to build a navigable highway enabling the world's people to share the fruits of the earth and of human industry.

Now, these eras are welded into a nation possessing unity, liberty, power, integrity and faith in God, with responsible development of character and devoted to the performance of humanitarian duty.

Holding no fear of the economic and political, chaotic clouds hovering over the earth, the consecrated Americans dedicate this nation before God, to exalt righteousness and to maintain mankind's constituted liberties so long as the earth shall endure.

—WILLIAM ANDREW BURKETT

BIBLIOGRAPHY

BOOKS

Athearn, Robert G., *American Heritage Illustrated History of the United States*. New York: Fawcett Publications, Inc., 1971.

Casey, Robert J., *The Black Hills*. New York: Bobbs-Merrill Company, Inc., 1949.

_____, and Mary Borglum, *Give the Man Room*. New York: Bobbs-Merrill Company, Inc., 1952.

Davies, A. Mervyn, *Solon H. Borglum—A Man Who Stands Alone*. Chester, Conn.: Pequot Press, 1974.

Dean, Robert J., *Living Granite (The Story of Borglum and the Mount Rushmore Memorial)*. New York: Viking Press, 1949.

Fite, Gilbert C., *Mount Rushmore*. Norman, Okla.: University of Oklahoma Press, 1952.

Hoover, Herbert, *The Memoirs of Herbert Hoover*. New York: The Macmillan Company, 1952.

Leedy, Carl H., *Golden Days in the Black Hills*. Rapid City, S.D.: Privately printed, 1961.

Manchester, William, *The Glory and the Dream*. Boston: Little, Brown & Company, 1974.

Morison, Samuel Eliot, *The Oxford History of the American People*. New York: Oxford University Press, 1965.

Nevin, Charles Merrick, *Principles of Structural Geology*. New York: John Wiley & Sons, 1942.

Parker, Watson, *Gold in the Black Hills*. Norman, Okla.: University of Oklahoma Press, 1966.

_____, and Hugh Lambert, *Black Hills Ghost Towns*. Chicago: The Swallow Press, Inc., 1974.

Pirsson, Louis V., and Charles Schuchert, *Introductory Geology*. New York: John Wiley & Sons, 1924.

Price, Willadene, *Gutzon Borglum, Artist and Patriot*. New York: Rand McNally & Company, 1961.

Reader's Digest Editors, *The Story of America*. Pleasantville, New York: Reader's Digest General Books, 1975.

Reeves, George S., *A Man from South Dakota*. New York: E. P. Dutton & Company, Inc., 1950.

Shirer, William L., *Rise and Fall of the Third Reich*. New York: Simon & Schuster, 1960.

Sugrue, Thomas, and Col. E. W. Starling, *Starling of the White House*, New York: Simon & Schuster, 1946.

Watkins, T. H., *Gold and Silver in the West*. New York: Bonanza Books, 1971.

Williamson, William, *William Williamson—An Autobiography*. Rapid City, S.D.: Privately printed, 1964.

Zeitner, June Culp, and Lincoln Borglum, *Borglum's Unfinished Dream*. Aberdeen, S.D.: North Plains Press, 1976.

PERIODICALS AND ARTICLES

Adelstein, Stanford M., "The Man Who Made Mount Rushmore—Why?" *Frontier Airlines Magazine*, Spring, 1973.

Black Hills Engineer Editors, "Chronicle Of President Coolidge's Summer In The Black Hills," *The Black Hills Engineer*, Vol. 15, No. 4 (Rapid City: South Dakota School of Mines, November, 1927).

Borglum, Gutzon, "The Political Importance And Character Of The National Memorial At Mount Rushmore"; "What Is Beauty In Sculpture?"; "Engineering Problems To Be Met In Mountain Sculpture," *The Black Hills Engineer*, Vol. 18, No. 4 (Rapid City: South Dakota School of Mines, November, 1930).

———, "Art That Is Real And American," *World's Work*, June, 1914.

———, "The Confederate Memorial," *World's Work*, August, 1917.

Bulow, William J., "When Cal Coolidge Came To Visit Us," *Saturday Evening Post*, January 4, 1947.

———, "My Days With Gutzon Borglum," *Saturday Evening Post*, January 11, 1947.

Case, Leland, "Where B.C. Means Before Custer," *The Black Hills* (book), edited by Roderick Peattie. New York: Vanguard Press, 1952.

Clark, Badger, "The Black Hills"; "The Tourists Came"; "The Mountain That Had Its Face Lifted," *The Black Hills* (book), edited by Roderick Peattie. New York: Vanguard Press, 1952.

Connolly, Joseph P., "The Geology Of Mount Rushmore And Vicinity," *The Black Hills Engineer*, Vol. 18, No. 4 (Rapid City: South Dakota School of Mines, November, 1930).

D'Emery, Charles, "Carving The Largest Monument In The World," *The Mentor*, February, 1928.

Friggins, Paul, "Don't Fence Me In!," *The Black Hills* (book), edited by Roderick Peattie. New York: Vanguard Press, 1952.

Hunkins, R. V., "The Black Hills, A Storehouse Of Mineral Treasure," *The Black Hills* (book), edited by Roderick Peattie. New York: Vanguard Press, 1952.

Lincoln, Francis Church, "Engineering Practices At The Mount Rushmore National Memorial," *The Black Hills Engineer*, Volume 18, No. 4 (Rapid City: South Dakota School of Mines, November, 1930).

O'Hara, C. C., "President Coolidge In The Black Hills," *The Black Hills Engineer*, Vol. 15, No. 4 (Rapid City: South Dakota School of Mines, November, 1927).

_____, "The Black Hills, Birthplace of the Americas," *The Black Hills Engineer*, Vol. 18, No. 4 (Rapid City: South Dakota School of Mines, November 1930).

Robinson, Doane, "Inception and Development of the Rushmore Idea," *The Black Hills Engineer*, Vol. 18, No. 4 (Rapid City: South Dakota School Of Mines, November, 1930).

Stanley, John A., "Preparing the Presidential Home in Custer State Park," *The Black Hills Engineer*, Vol. 15, No. 4 (Rapid City: South Dakota School Of Mines, November, 1927).

SPECIAL PUBLICATIONS, UNPUBLISHED MANUSCRIPT MATERIAL, DOCUMENTS, AND MISCELLANEOUS

Bellamy, Paul, "Peter Norbeck—A Biography," unpublished ms., Richardson Archives, University of South Dakota, Vermillion, S.D.

Paul Bellamy Papers, Richardson Archives, University of South Dakota, Vermillion, S.D.

Francis Case Papers, Layne Library, Dakota Wesleyan University, Mitchell, S.D.

City Council of Atlanta, Georgia, resolution condemning Gutzon Borglum for his conduct at Stone Mountain. Issued March 2, 1925.

Richard F. Hughes Papers, South Dakota Historical Resource Center, Pierre, S.D.

Mount Harney Memorial Association contract with Gutzon Borglum.

Mount Rushmore National Memorial Commission, annual reports 1929 through 1939.

_____, minutes of meetings 1930 through 1933.

Mount Rushmore National Memorial Society, records and papers, E. Y. Berry Archives, Black Hills State College, Spearfish, S.D.

_____, *Mount Rushmore National Memorial*, published prior to unveiling of Washington head, June 1930.

_____, *Mount Rushmore National Memorial, Shrine of Democracy*, April 1938. Published following unveiling of Lincoln head.

_____, *Program, Golden Jubilee of Statehood, 1889–1939* (unveiling of Roosevelt head), July 2, 1939.

Mount Rushmore scrapbook, compiler unidentified, E. Y. Berry Archives, Black Hills State College, Spearfish, S.D.

Peter Norbeck Papers, Richardson Archives, University of South Dakota, Vermillion, S.D.

Merle Peterson's scrapbook, presently in the possession of his widow.

Doane Robinson Papers, South Dakota Historical Resource Center, Pierre, S.D.

Rushmore photograph collection, National Park Service Visitors' Center, Mount Rushmore National Memorial, Keystone, S.D.

Mabel Smith's private diaries, kept by the author's mother.

Stone Mountain Confederate Monumental Association, a resolution canceling the Association's contract with Gutzon Borglum. Issued February 24, 1925.

———, statement describing the Association's dealings with Gutzon Borglum. Published as a broadside, March 15, 1925.

William Williamson Papers, Richardson Archives, University of South Dakota, Vermillion, S.D.

William Williamson's private diaries, Richardson Archives, University of South Dakota, Vermillion, S.D.

NEWSPAPERS

Rapid City Journal
Sioux Falls *Argus-Leader*
Chicago Tribune
New York Times

PERSONS INTERVIEWED BY AUTHOR

Otto "Red" Anderson: From 1929 through 1941 worked at Rushmore as a driller, then as a carver.

Ethel Boland: Widow of John Boland.

Monica Borglum Davies: Daughter of Gutzon Borglum's sculptor brother Solon. Widow of A. Mervyn Davies, who wrote and published an exhaustively researched history of the Borglum family.

William Burkett: National winner of the Entablature contest conducted by Gutzon Borglum in 1934–35.

Margaret Champion McClure: Daughter of James Champion, carpenter at Mount Rushmore. Sister of James Champion, Jr., who worked at Rushmore first as a call boy, then as a driller, then as a carver.

Dr. Leland Case: Black Hills native and onetime Black Hills newspaperman, author, and historian. Brother of Congressman/Senator Francis Case.

Ed Coad: Keystone native. Call boy at Rushmore during summer of 1930.

Herb Conn: Under a contract with the National Park Service, Conn annually inspected the Rushmore carvings for signs of weathering and sealed cracks to prevent chipping of the granite by freezing water.

Jarvis Davenport: Prior to his death in 1979, Davenport served on the Executive Board of the Mount Rushmore National Memorial Society. During Rushmore construction days he served with John Boland on the board of directors of the First National Bank of the Black Hills.

Hoadley Dean: Former president of the Mount Rushmore National Memorial Society.

Francis A. "Bud" Duhamel: Rapid City business leader and friend of Gutzon Borglum. Active in Rapid City Chamber of Commerce during Rushmore fund-raising and construction days.

Emil and Christine Flick: Personal employees of the Borglums from mid-1930 through early 1941. Emil looked after Borglum's ranch and sometimes acted as his driver. Christine prepared the Borglums' meals, ran the kitchen, and looked after their house.

Edwald Hayes: Native of Keystone. Rushmore hoist operator from 1934 through 1941.

Robert "Bob" Himebaugh: Native of Keystone area. Worked as a powderman and as a driller at Rushmore.

C.C. Jacobson: Active in Rapid City Chamber of Commerce during Rushmore construction days.

Martha Linde: Keystone native. Black Hills historian and author. Compiler of a history of Keystone and surrounding areas.

Ida Lyndoe Townsend: Daughter of Keystone storekeeper Art Lyndoe, who bought what was left of John Boland's store after the big fire of 1917. Has made an effort to keep track of Rushmore crew members and their families since Rushmore construction days.

Nell Norbeck Hood: Daughter of Senator Peter Norbeck.

Howard "Howdy" Peterson: Keystone native. From 1929 through 1941 worked at Rushmore as mechanic, maintenance man, and steel nipper.

Dr. Jack Redden: Professor of geology at the South Dakota State School of Mining and Technology; a recognized authority on the geology of the Black Hills.

Lester Ripple: Retired operator of fish hatcheries in the Black Hills. Has records showing how many and what kind of fish were planted in Squaw Creek for President Coolidge to catch.

Willard L. Roberts: Senior Curator of Mineralogy at South Dakota State School of Mining & Technology and an internationally recognized authority in the field of mineralogy.

Bill Robinson: Grandson of Doane Robinson.

Ray Sanders: Game Lodge horse wrangler who established and maintained Gutzon Borglum's first camp at the foot of Mount Rushmore.

Julian Spotts: National Park Service engineer. Engineer on Rushmore project in the summers of 1936 and 1937.

Korczak Ziolkowski: Award-winning sculptor who worked briefly on Mount Rushmore. He later began carving, on a mountaintop only a few miles from Rushmore, a gigantic statue of the Sioux chief Crazy Horse. Since Ziolkowski's death in 1982 this work has been carried on by his wife and children.

INDEX

PHOTO CREDITS

The author wishes to acknowledge with deep gratitude the courtesy of the following individuals and institutions in supplying illustrations for this book.

Edwald Hayes: 47; Robert Himebaugh: 25, 62; Mount Rushmore Memorial Society: 38, 48; National Park Service: 2, 3, 4, 5 *(Rev. Carl Loocke)*, 6, 20, 24, 26, 27, 30, 32, 34, 40, 42, 43, 49, 51, 52, 55 *(Bell Studios)*, 56; Rapid City Journal: 1 *(South Dakota Dept. of Highways)*, 7, 18, 23, 31, 39, 41, 44, 45, 46 *(Bell Studios)*, 50, 53, 54, 57 *(South Dakota Dept. of Parks and Tourism)*, 58 *(South Dakota Dept. of Parks and Tourism)*, 59, 61, 63, 64, 65; South Dakota School of Mining and Technology: 9 *(Carl Rise)*, 10 *(Flynn's Studio)*, 11 *(Carl Rise)*, 12 *(Carl Rise)*, 13, 14, 15, 16, 17, 29, 33, 35, 36 *(Carl Rise)*, 37; William Williamson Papers: 8, 19, 21, 22, 28, 60 *(all probably by Charles D'Emery)*.